AFRICAN AMERICAN STATE VOLUNTEERS IN THE NEW SOUTH

AFRICAN AMERICAN
STATE VOLUNTEERS
IN THE
NEW SOUTH

Race, Masculinity, and the Militia in
Georgia, Texas, and Virginia,
1871–1906

JOHN PATRICK BLAIR

TEXAS A&M UNIVERSITY PRESS
College Station

First edition

(∞) This paper meets the requirements of
ANSI/NISO Z39.48-1992 (Permanence of Paper).
Binding materials have been chosen for durability.
Manufactured in the United States of America

Library of Congress Cataloging-in-Publication Data

Names: Blair, John Patrick, 1960– author.
Title: African American state volunteers in the New South : race,
    masculinity, and the militia in Georgia, Texas, and Virginia, 1871–1906
    / John Patrick Blair.
Other titles: Prairie View A & M University series.
Description: First edition. | College Station : Texas A&M University Press,
    [2022] | Series: Prairie View A & M University series | Includes
    bibliographical references and index.
Identifiers: LCCN 2022015961 | ISBN 9781648430732 (cloth) | ISBN
    9781648430749 (ebook)
Subjects: LCSH: Reconstruction (U.S. history, 1865–1877)—African American
    troops. | African American soldiers—Georgia—History. | African
    American soldiers—Texas—History. | African American
    soldiers—Virginia—History. | United States—Militia—African
    Americans—History. | Southern States—Race relations.
Classification: LCC E185.63 .B57 2022 | DDC 305.800975—dc23/eng/20220506
LC record available at https://lccn.loc.gov/2022015961

To my wife, Jacqueline; my mother, Barbara;
and all the African American citizen-soldiers
who served during these years.

CONTENTS

LIST OF ILLUSTRATIONS AND TABLES

Figures

Tables

FOREWORD

I have always considered myself privileged to have worn the military uniform of the US, like my father and grandfather before me. Beyond my paternal lineage, military service connected me with the generations of black men that defended this democracy, even at times when that democracy did not always recognize their citizenship as legitimate.

Nonetheless, American history contains many stories of black servicemen like the Buffalo Soldiers and the Tuskegee Airmen. Those stories are ones of sacrifice, pride, and service. But, they are more than mere stories of black men in uniform. They are now interwoven into the fabric of this Republic.

In the decades following emancipation, military service for men of color was tenuous. Regardless of race, the commonality among all servicemen was the camaraderie that developed because of the hardships of military service. Camaraderie aside, the growing racial animosities of the burgeoning Jim Crow era led to two societies, one white and one black. Sadly, those animosities were also evident in the military. A segregated military was commonplace and our history illustrates that black servicemen were often brutalized while wearing the uniform.

Thankfully, John Blair adds a new story to our history. *African American State Volunteers in the New South* highlights the experiences and challenges of those black servicemen in the state militias of Georgia, Texas, and Virginia in the last quarter of the nineteenth century. This was a time when overt racism unapologetically permeated nearly every aspect of society. Nonetheless, these men served with unwavering patriotism even though full citizenship was often an elusive concept. Blair's engaging narrative weaves a story of experiences against the backdrop of a society becoming increasingly influenced by racial constraints. For example, Blair discusses the challenges faced by black service-men who were praised for their role overseas, then, once the conflict ceased, found themselves despised by white society.

African American State Volunteers in the New South supports the primary intent of the Prairie View A&M University book series of illustrating the experiences of the black community and the ways in which those experiences contributed to the betterment of American society. I feel a personal connection to these men. The camaraderie among black men in uniform extends beyond our concept of time. Even though stories of black servicemen exist in American history, there are many, many more to be told. This is one step towards telling those missing stories.

—Ronald E. Goodwin, *Series Editor*
Prairie View A&M University

ACKNOWLEDGMENTS

First, I would like to recognize the local historians who, through their volunteer activities, collect and preserve the history of their communities. Among them are Travis Holloway, who quietly spends his time researching the contributions of African Americans in Augusta, Georgia, and has shared so freely of his findings. Another is Reverend Charles L. Hoskins, who graciously drove across the city of Savannah to meet me and welcomed me into his home, where we spent an afternoon in his office discussing his published works, surrounded by over thirty years of his research on Savannah's African American community. And I must especially thank Mary Lauderdale of the Black History Museum and Cultural Center of Virginia at Richmond, who kindly opened her door to me even though the museum was in the process of moving into its new building, the Leigh Street Armory. Her kindness and willingness to share resulted in numerous other contacts and information that I would have undoubtedly missed.

Next, I want to acknowledge those librarians and archivists who on a daily basis keep the records of our nation's history safe and secure, people who are excited to share glimpses of that history with researchers such as myself. I would like to specifically recognize Steve Engerrand and his staff at the Georgia Archives, who responded quickly to my requests. I want to include a special thank you to Amanda Mros, who assisted greatly in keeping me organized by coordinating between the older and newer versions of finding aids that I was using and by maximizing my time at the state archives by efficiently providing the next round of research materials. Linda Pickering greeted me every single morning with a pleasant smile that set the tone for the day and contributed to an overall pleasurable research experience in Morrow, Georgia.

A very special thanks goes to Francine Archer of Virginia State University's archives. Even though the only archivist on staff, Francine provided a very high level of customer service not only during my brief visit but also afterward by cheerfully responding to my photograph request. Her dedication, shared knowledge, and enjoyable demeanor created a positive and successful research experience that should be a standard across the research community. I sincerely appreciate all of her assistance.

Thanks also goes to my fellow graduate student Jared Donnelly, who, during a long drive from a student conference in Lincoln, Nebraska, to Bryan, Texas, politely listened and provided solid suggestions during my discussion about expanding the earlier research that I had conducted on African American citizen-soldiers. He promoted a renewed level of energy toward initiating and completing this project.

I also want to express my sincerest appreciation to all the members of my graduate committee and to the History Department at Texas A&M University. My committee members—R. J. Q. Adams, Charles Brooks, Carlos Blanton, and James Burk—listened patiently, allowed me to explore new ideas, and provided positive reinforcement and steady guidance over the course of this research.

The department graciously provided valuable research funding for travel to Georgia and Virginia on multiple occasions, allowing not only a detailed examination of primary source documents but also the opportunity to make contacts in the local African American community. The ability to build relationships in person remains an important aspect of historical research that is often overlooked, and it was these relationships with likeminded historians that provided sources and materials often undervalued and underappreciated beyond the confines of that area.

Most importantly, I cannot say enough about my graduate-committee chairman, J. G. Dawson III. His breadth and depth of knowledge of US and military history strongly contributed to the success of the dissertation from which this book developed as well as his ability to gently identify shortcomings that required further research or clarification. He served as an ever-eager mentor who rewarded good work with positive, constructive comments, and the early morning calls on Saturday congratulating me on the argument presented in a chapter here or there served to only enhance my confidence toward completing this project. I believe his leadership and skill as a professor set the highest of standards. Every action, small and large, performed by him throughout this process is greatly appreciated. I only hope that one day I might be worthy of such efforts.

Finally, I must include a word about those to whom this book is dedicated. My wife, Jacqueline, has been a constant source of encouragement and enthusiasm throughout this research, many times sitting patiently and reading my lengthy chapters. My mother, Barbara, is gone, but her memory continues to remind me of the importance of education in one's life. Lastly, the African American citizen-soldiers named and unnamed in this volume, despite insurmountable odds, worked to overcome the obstacles they faced to improve their lives—may their example continue to inspire future generations with their work ethic, positive attitude, perseverance, and appreciation of the value of education.

AFRICAN AMERICAN STATE VOLUNTEERS IN THE NEW SOUTH

1

Introduction

The Forgotten Few

THE CONTINUED PRESENCE OF armed, uniformed black militia companies throughout the southern United States from the 1870s to the early 1900s illustrates one of the highest achievements of African Americans in those decades. They remain one of the most understudied and misunderstood segments of not only black history but also the shared history of the South and the United States.

While acknowledging the prevalence of racial violence and discrimination that characterizes southern US history of the late nineteenth and early twentieth century, this study contends that the experiences and actions of African American men serving in the state volunteer military organizations of Georgia, Texas, and Virginia constitutes one of their unappreciated achievements. By serving in the state militia, black men sought, through their service, to validate their rights as citizens and to improve their social status during a period of racial segregation. Furthermore, the presence of such units strongly suggests that race relations were flexible enough in the former Confederate states during those years to allow armed, uniformed black men to participate in official martial activities and that the states of Georgia, Texas, and Virginia

1

considered them valid military organizations. Thus, when the political leaders of those states dissolved the black militia, it signaled the end of that flexibility and acceptance.

This book compares and contrasts the experiences and activities of black militiamen in three former Confederate states—Georgia, Texas, and Virginia. This comparative structure, using the militia to view aspects of the complexity of racial relationships that existed up to 1906, clearly illustrates the existence of racial flexibility in these three states that continued past what has been generally accepted as the end of the Reconstruction period. Granted, there were limits to this flexibility, and the various military organizations remained segregated, yet state and military officials not only recognized and accepted black militia participation but also provided them with arms, ammunition, and equipment. Some states authorized and funded training exercises and officially approved several instances of using the black militia in quelling unrest or by publicly assembling, armed and prepared in the event of lawlessness. Some white local-government officials also supported the black militia units. All of these examples clearly confirm that these African Americans composed a military component of state armed forces that functioned as more than social groups authorized for ceremonial events. And yet, several state or local studies dedicated to the African American experience are mostly devoid of any discussion of militia activities or do not address their recognized value within the black community.[1]

Racial conditions from the 1870s to 1906 were complicated and reflected the ways government and military officials viewed these African American military organizations. The existence and activities of those very organizations within the public military sphere demonstrated the ability, loyalty, discipline, and, more importantly, manliness of the nation's newest citizens. The African American leaders of these military organizations in all three states often overlapped as political, educational, and religious leaders. Their desire and efforts to uplift members of their communities continued as a constant theme of their service, and they endorsed the work of both Booker T. Washington and W. E. B. Du Bois, who remained allies during these years.[2]

Another important component of southern and American social life in the late nineteenth century involved the complicated issue of "colorism." "Colorism" related to the level of privilege or discrimination based upon the shade of one's skin in an effort to determine if the perceived amount of "whiteness" contributed to the acceptance of the African American militia by the larger, surrounding white society. It remains an open question if African American men gravitated toward the leadership of lighter-skinned members of their community. Some even wondered if this dynamic played an important role in the obvious flexibility of the racial relationships in Georgia, Texas, and Virginia.

The bulk of the historical research concerning the African American military experience from the 1870s to 1906 centers on either the regular US Army "buffalo soldiers" who fought the Plains Indians or the black volunteers and regular black troops who engaged the Spanish in Cuba and the Philippines. The experiences of state militia volunteers, with a few minor exceptions, remain neglected.[3] Those studies that do concentrate on state volunteers or active militiamen have, for the most part, been contained in a few scattered journal articles, with additional scholarship lacking. Since 2007 few new studies have been introduced. One, *Brothers to the Buffalo Soldiers: Perspectives on the African American Militia and Volunteers, 1865–1917* (2011), edited by Bruce A. Glasrud, republishes five previously available articles on black militia organizations, including one published in 1955.[4]

Roger D. Cunningham, one of Glasrud's contributors, highlights the activities of the black militia in Virginia, contributing to the historical record of southern African American state militia volunteers. He divulges that Virginia governor Fitzhugh Lee became the only southern governor to activate a black militia company but neglects to pursue this fascinating occurrence further.[5]

Cunningham did seek to rectify this scholarly void with a comprehensive military history of black volunteers outside the South in *The Black Citizen-Soldiers of Kansas, 1864–1901* (2008). He observes the lack of scholarship on black state volunteers and argues that "over the past forty years, much has been written about the men of the U.S.C.T. [US Colored Troops] and the buffalo soldiers," but as for the "experiences of hundreds of [post–Civil War] black militiamen, their contributions and history has been ignored and lost."[6] But again, he places most of his effort during the Civil War, the hostilities against the Plains Indians, or the actions of Kansas Volunteers during the war with Spain. Cunningham also leaves unexplored many of the socioeconomic and political activities of the various units and seems to struggle with whether or not Kansas officials genuinely considered these African American men as part of actual military organizations.

Most of the historians who have examined black state volunteers seem either unable or unwilling to grasp how the African American militiamen saw themselves during 1870–1906. Frances Smith's "Black Militia in Savannah, Georgia, 1872–1906" (1981) contributes little information on any of the socioeconomic dynamics of the men who either led or served in the militia from that southern city.[7] Smith relies on good contemporary news articles but fails to expand on their meaning and does not draw upon the multitude of primary-source documents available at the state archives. Her tendency to focus on the view of the society that surrounded the black militia and not on the accomplishments of the men or the accommodations by state officials results in only a partial history. On the other hand, Charles Johnson's research in *African American Soldiers in the National Guard* (1992) contributes a positive view of black military service during this period. Although the states rarely utilized these men, Johnson contends that their "experience in the National Guard afforded former soldiers and recruits the opportunity to participate in militia activities" and allowed them to be "available for militia duties during any civil disturbance, major disaster, or declaration of war."[8] Both of these investigations into African American militia service are in need of an update and expansion.

One updated study of black militiamen in the South is historian Gregory Mixon's *Show Thyself a Man: Georgia State Troops, Colored, 1865–1905* (2016). Combining "race, gender, and social and political change in the late nineteenth-century United States," he seeks to frame the role of Georgia's militia in the context of a "changing American context of imperial expansion, race and racism, and definitions of citizenship, manhood, and inclusion."[9] Even though *Show Thyself a Man* reveals his exhaustive research, over one-half of the book is dedicated to the time period prior to the creation of the Georgia State Troops, Colored. And while his contribution remains significant, Mixon fails to note the level of racial flexibility that continued throughout this period, evident in the actions of Georgia's legislature and its governor as well as the examples of cooperation between white and black militiamen. He links military membership and manhood for African Americans but fails to link the involvement of the Prince Hall Masons, and their common objective of making better men, at the highest levels of Georgia's black militia. By omitting these important aspects, one cannot grasp a complete understanding of this period in Georgia history.

The study of manliness, masculinity, or manhood relates directly to the lives of African American men who served in the militia. Others, including Michael Kimmel, argue that, at the turn of the century, the traditional foundations of these concepts had eroded due to rapid industrialization, the closing of the frontier, and most of all the increase in immigrant and black migrant populations in urban areas. Kimmel, in *The History of Men: Essays in the History of*

American and British Masculinities (2005), contends that, while manhood expressed one's inner character, the concept of masculinity had to be constantly validated, or proven; for many African American men, militia service offered this opportunity.[10] But according to Earnestine Jenkins and Darlene Clark Hine, the focus of men's studies has too long remained a discussion of "public accomplishments of great men" and thus has "marginalized certain groups" and "negated the importance of certain groups," mainly African Americans.[11] The process of constructing a black masculinity diverges within the scholarship, with Marlene Connor arguing that the aspects of white-defined manhood were "confusing and ill-defined" for the black male who had to develop "a new culture that protected and empowered him within his environment, his own neighborhood."[12] Conversely, literary scholar Simone Drake has determined through the use of a 1907 memoir by African American Nat Love that "black masculinity, like much human identity, is produced in ownerships of property, community and self," thus formulating that both black and white men shared similar definitions of masculinity construction.[13]

Gail Bederman also investigates the concept of masculinity at the turn of the century in *Manliness and Civilization: A Cultural History of Gender and Race in the US, 1880–1917* (1995).[14] In her initial chapter, "Remaking Manhood through Race and Civilization," Bederman maintains that black men's lack of manhood—as defined by society—led to their social segregation and political disenfranchisement. With 180,000 Black men serving in the Union army, and despite their unequal treatment, she points out, "they understood that enlisting was their most potent tool to claim that they were men and should have the same rights and privileges as all American men."[15] She also identifies how the discourse of civilization and the influence of Theodore Roosevelt produced consequences for definition of manliness in the Gilded Age and the Progressive Era. Roosevelt's exploits during the war with Spain symbolized the very nature of manhood—courage, bravery, aggressiveness, and so on. Unfortunately, this discussion of civilization further enflamed the perceived racial stereotypes of African American men, even though they demonstrated that same strength of character on Cuban soil.

Therefore, the obvious connection between military service and militia membership, citizenship, and masculinity should create, in the words of Mike O'Brien, "fertile ground for the study of gender identities and ideologies," yet "remarkably little has emerged in the way of serious historical work on this question."[16] In his study of early twentieth century militia in Ontario, Canada, O'Brien examines how the cultural concept of masculinity changes at different times and, with it, the convergence of its definition with the concept of class. He also contends that his research offers insight into the study of labor, gender, and military history while stating that "quantitative work, for instance, on the demographic makeup of the Militia with respect to class, occupation, ethnicity and other factors is badly needed."[17] Ehren Foley contributes to the scholarship that O'Brien advocates. With "'To Make Him Feel His Manhood'" (2012), Foley explores "black male identity" through the lens of the African American militia of South Carolina from the end of the Civil War to only 1870, declining to pursue the struggle into the later decades of the century.[18]

To place African American militia membership in another context, it is important to review examples of studies regarding the effect of colorism within the black community and its perceived or actual benefits from outside that community. According to Duke University law professor Trinia Jones, "people often confuse skin color and race because skin color is used to assign people to racial categories."[19] But the two concepts are interpreted differently. Like racism, which assigns status by racial group, colorism is based upon a person's skin color, and society determines their social status based upon the lighter or darker the hue. Therefore, while there is potential for interracial conflict, skin-color preferences may lead to intraracial discord as well.

Historian Willard Gatewood researches an example of these disputes. In *Aristocrats of Color* (1990), Gatewood argues that whites supposedly perceived the "mulatto" class as "intellectually superior to blacks," who were "agitators for social equality and civil rights." Some in the black community agreed that the mixed-race leaders were troublemakers who became obstacles to "unity and solidarity," posing "as leaders of blacks in order to win recognition and support from whites and in the process monopolizing the choicest positions open to blacks."[20]

Organizations, such as Tennessee's Nashville Blue Vein Society, based membership on the ability to see a person's veins through their light skin. Others, like the Brown Fellowship Society of Charleston, South Carolina, highlight the concept of colorism within the antebellum black community by demonstrating the exclusiveness of not only lighter-skinned African Americans but darker blacks as well. Established by several mixed-race members of Charleston's St. Phillips Episcopal Church, the Brown Fellowship Society only admitted "free lighter skinned African Americans . . . , but sometimes darker-skinned individuals with naturally straight hair were permitted as well." According to Sarah Bartlett's research, this group intended "to provide respectable funerals for Society members, support widows, and educate surviving children."[21] Gatewood assesses the Brown Fellowship Society more harshly by asserting that its members "exploited the labor of slaves and discriminated against all Negroes of darker complexion."[22] Historians Elijah Horace Fitchett and James Browning support this view. They argue that the lighter-skinned African Americans' exclusiveness drove the darker blacks to form their own society, the Humane Brotherhood. Yet historian Robert L. Harris Jr. disagrees with these conclusions. He contends that the society members who did own slaves did so "for benevolent purposes," and while there were differences among free African Americans in Charleston, "socio-economic status seemed to be a more significant variable . . . than complexion."[23]

Historian John Dittmer agrees that "skin color, however, was not as important as political allegiance and ideology in separating black Republicans."[24] But there were several instances in Georgia that clearly exemplified discrimination within the post–Civil War black community based upon skin color. Dittmer points to a political clash between the "light-skinned elite" against a "black" faction over the control of the district nominating committee in Savannah and a similar rivalry in Augusta. Other incidents included activities at St. Stephen's Episcopal Church of Savannah, where in 1872, the "near-white vestrymen" sought to exclude "all of the black Negroes," and in the state capital, where Atlanta University's exclusive fraternity chose its members based "'on color and financial status.'"[25] Twenty years after the episode at St. Stephen's, black newspaper editor Solomon Johnson decried the "preference for light skin or high yellows among some blacks in Savannah" and advocated, "'we are all of one race; therefore, such foolishness should be discarded.'"[26]

Any study of skin color is wrought with contention and difficulty, especially during the latter half of the nineteenth century, in the United States. Federal census enumerators in 1850 were instructed to either enter a "B" or "M" for "black" or "mulatto" when counting persons of color, leaving the space blank for white persons, but there were no clearly defined specifications as to what constituted each of those terms. The next census had neither standards nor instructions to the enumerators for classifying individuals by color. In fact, the US Bureau of the Census did not attempt to clarify racial categories until 1890, and even then the level of subjectivity only resulted in a wide swath of confusing interpretations. For example, any person with dark skin that had ten-sixteenths "Negro" blood should be recorded as black; less than ten-six-teenths, but not more than six-sixteenths, would be considered mulatto. There was also a category of "quadroon" for persons having between three- and six-sixteenths, while anyone with less than three-sixteenths should be documented as an "octoroon." The emphasis on these categories centered on the study by "race scientists" of the effects of racial mixing and whether this had a detrimental influence upon society.[27]

To complement the confusing census returns and more useful registers, the annual company muster rolls of the various African American commands of the Texas Volunteer Guard offer insights into the study of color. State laws required officers to complete the yearly return, and each company's secretary or commanding officer entered such descriptive information on the roll that could be used to identify any of the unit's members. These traits included a militiaman's eye and hair color, his age, and his complexion, which was also mandated for the state's white troops. Again, there was simply no guide to determine any of these physical categories, and the interpretation varied widely by company and by the individual making those entries. To compound this confusion further, often the person who completed this information within a company changed. The results were a continually changing view over the years of how to determine a militiaman's skin color. Recognizing these challenges, this book will illuminate, especially based on the muster rolls, how African American militiamen *classified themselves* in terms of "light" or "dark" skin hue. And, since the militia organizations elected their own officers, the potential influence of that categorization can contribute to our understanding of colorism within the ranks of the "colored" volunteer militia.[28]

In a turbulent period of US history fraught with violence, struggle, and uncertainty, a forgotten few African Americans banded together as men to assert their rights as citizens through state military service. Their experiences across geographical space were similar but not the same. Still, they sought to define themselves and to improve their lives through militia service and connect their social, political, and legal status with that military service in these three southern states. This book illustrates that those militiamen made contributions in the early days of the civil rights struggle that reveal how the hardening of racial relationships and the construction of black manhood over time led to the demise of their extraordinary military organizations.

2

─◊◊◊─

"To Have the Most Worthy"

Legislating the Black State Volunteers

THE PROMULGATION OF discriminatory state laws and practices coupled with the simultaneous acquiescence of African American military involvement exposes an increasingly complex social structure within southern society. This structure was challenged by an evolving, intertwining, and active black community. For example, the laws for the public defense enacted by the Georgia General Assembly over the course of thirty-five years, from the end of Reconstruction to the demise of the Georgia Volunteers, Colored, illustrated the practice of ever-increasing racial exclusionary restrictions upon the state's military organization. While subjecting only white male citizens to military duty, these restrictions continued to allow black men to serve as citizen-soldiers in the state volunteers. Such laws support the contention that racial attitudes, or relationships, remained just flexible enough for African Americans to remain active militarily within a public sphere that intersected with the existing, traditionally all-white military establishment.

A thorough examination of the *Code of the State of Georgia* from 1870 to 1905 discloses opportunities that enabled leaders in the African American military community to successfully negotiate the interpretation of the law to their advantage or, at times, completely avoid some potentially restrictive practices. In other cases, these leaders even utilized the legal code and precedence to claim equal treatment under the law. While many measures arguably sought only to improve the efficiency of the state's military force, in reality, their enactment over time adversely affected African American military participation.[1]

The laws enacted in Georgia can be compared to those occurring simultaneously in Texas and Virginia. This comparative examination not only illuminates the challenging and complex social relationships within each of these states' military organizations but also demonstrates a level of racial flexibility that evaporated over time, broadening our understanding of these practices across the South. In Georgia, racial relationships evolved through legal restrictions in state laws governing the numerical troop strength of African Americans in the state's military as well as the process of examining and commissioning officers to command the various military groups comprising soldiers of color.

To Provide for the Public Defense

The volunteers, or active militia; the reserve militia; and the Georgia Military Institute composed Georgia's military organization in 1870. Title XI of the *Code of the State of Georgia* in 1868 clearly affirmed that "all able-bodied free *white* male citizens between the ages of twenty-one and forty-five years, residents of this State, and not exempted by this Code, are subject to military duty." Section 1077, Chapter I of the *Code* directed that "free men of color" also were subject to call by any volunteer company, provided they did not serve as part of a city's fire department, for service "in the capacity of musician, pioneer, mechanic, or servant." But with the new legal circumstances of African Americans, this section contained an annotation declaring this "would seem to be contrary to the Constitution, and laws changing the status of free persons of color." By 1873, this section of Georgia's *Code* changed to read that this requirement of free men of color had been "superseded by 14th amendment to [the] Constitution of United States," thus addressing the comment earlier posed by the annotation. Still, the law called into to question whether African Americans were "subject to military duty." Georgia did not specifically deny military service to them; it only refrained from subjecting them to it. Yet, more than ever before in the United States, military service and citizenship remained connected. The door remained open to form volunteer companies, and African American men soon petitioned the state to do so following the inauguration on January 12, 1872, of a leading former Confederate officer, Democratic governor James Milton Smith.[2]

The legal statutes guiding the military structures of Texas and Virginia were virtually identical to those of Georgia, with a few exceptions. All three states divided their militia organizations between an "active" component, composed of volunteer groups, and a "reserve" militia that included all able-bodied male citizens in the state between the ages of eighteen and forty-five not exempt by any laws of the United States. Virginia allowed those with religious objections to opt out of military service with a payment to the state, while Texas maintained, in addition to its militia force, six companies of rangers organized into the Frontier Battalion.[3]

Governors and legislators had options in guiding and developing military operations within each state. While Georgia lawmakers struggled with the matter of compulsory military service for their African American citizens, Virginians authorized their reserve-militia administrators to record all persons in each company district "liable to military duty, listing white and colored militiamen separately."[4] This statement appears to be the only legal statute guiding military affairs in Virginia to specifically segregate African Americans. Texas failed to designate any separation of the races in its militia law of 1870 or in its amended version in 1873. This lack of language may simply reflect that the legislators of neither state felt the need to address this issue; after all, segregation remained the traditional order of the day in the South. Virginia's governor appointed the general and field-grade officers (major, lieutenant colonel, and colonel) of the reserve militia as well as company commanders, but the latter only when the company was activated and only on a temporary basis. It was also up to the governor to accept or reject the petitions of companies requesting recognition. Likewise, the militia law of Texas gave the governor the right "to appoint and commission all general, field, company, and staff officers," and he too then decided whether to accept or reject a militia company for state service.[5] In Georgia, the governor assumed these same responsibilities. Thus, it was clear that the chief executive in each state occupied a crucial role in the operations of the reserve militia. The actions of each governor remained influential and operated within the framework of legal statutes and military regulations governing the uniformed, armed militia and its volunteers. Their actions best illustrate early racial restrictions and accommodation toward African American military participation.

The Georgia Volunteers

In 1878, Sidney Herbert, the editor of the Military Department column of the *Savannah Weekly News*, published a pamphlet entitled *A Complete Roster of the Volunteer Military Organizations of the State of Georgia*. Even though Herbert acknowledged that it was not an official publication, he explained that it was "carefully made up from official sources," and the assistance he received in its compilation made "it officially accurate in all its most important details." This post-Reconstruction publication, to be used by the governor's newly appointed State Military Board to revise the military laws of the state, potentially revealed the dismal condition of Georgia's volunteers.[6]

Herbert confirmed the custom of segregation. The African American military organizations, described as "Colored Companies," were listed separately from the other military units, while the ethnic Irish and German infantry companies in Augusta and Savannah remained with the "white" commands. Of the total 172 white infantry companies, Herbert only listed fifty-three that were active, referring to them as "live," while he identified seven of them as disbanded, or "dead." The condition of the white cavalry component was even worse, with only eight active commands out of a total of sixty-nine, and of those "live," Herbert could not learn of the location of three of them. Surprisingly, the African American component of the state volunteers included forty-two companies—forty infantry, one artillery, and one cavalry. Of these commands, both the artillery and cavalry organizations were active, along with twenty-five of the infantry companies. Therefore, as published, only 37 percent of Georgia's white and 62 percent of its African American infantry component could be counted on in time of a crisis.[7]

Questions linger as to whether Herbert's information reflected exactly how deficient the condition of the volunteers was as of 1878 or if it uncovered something else, such as a simple lack of recordkeeping or correspondence with the state. Herbert admitted that he compiled this listing over a short sixty-day period to allow the State Military Board to utilize his work during its deliberations. Did rushing its completion to make a publishing deadline contribute to the amount of unknown or incomplete information? The fact that the governor created a military board may support the conclusion that there were problems in Georgia's military that he wanted to address. Even considering these points, Herbert's compilation clearly showed that the traditional white military companies still enjoyed a two-to-one numerical advantage over African Americans in the state volunteers. For some Georgians, the very presence of black military companies might have created alarm no matter the numerical superiority of the existing white commands.

Some evidence supports the assertion that Georgia sought to improve its military forces at this time with changes in state law. The reorganization of 1878 did not include any numerical restrictions on African American participation despite the level of racial antagonism that still existed. If the activities and numbers of soldiers of color, uniformed, armed, and equipped, had severely alarmed Georgia society, then arguably the law should have included provisions to circumscribe African American volunteer militia companies.

In fact, the first action to legally constrain the numerical strength of black troops did not occur until 1885, when the Georgia General Assembly mandated that "the volunteer forces of the State shall be the active militia of the State, . . . of which the white commands shall be known and designated as the Georgia Volunteers, and the colored commands as the Georgia Volunteers, colored." The law that officially created the "Georgia Volunteers, colored" also limited their organization to a total of only "twenty companies of infantry, one of cavalry, [and] one of artillery." The volunteers, comprising the white commands, surpassed their earlier two-to-one advantage, as the state allowed them to not exceed "fifty companies of infantry, seven companies of cavalry and three companies of artillery." Even as this law mandated the return of all state-owned military property by those commands not recognized as part of these organizations, a provision in the act allowed "any command which existed prior to the 16th day of October, 1880, which may elect to maintain itself, if not made part of said force, . . . shall remain intact." Lawmakers, as will be seen, could have easily made this date much earlier than 1880, such as 1861 or even 1870, but they did not. Granted, this date may have been more important to white commands, yet with the greater advantage in numerical strength, one would have to question if this proviso served a different purpose. Members of the assembly who passed this section of the law knew full well that all the African American companies that had existed in the 1878 *Complete Roster* had an opportunity to maintain their organization.[8]

Furthermore, with this new restriction on the companies comprising the Georgia Volunteers, Colored, evidence reveals that lawmakers may even have initially considered fewer than twenty. Writing one month prior to this new requirement being signed into law, Capt. William H. Clark, an African American commanding the Augusta Cadets, expressed his level of frustration to Georgia's adjutant general, John A. Stephens, by writing: "The bill has been amended so often since it was first offered until I doan't know what this bill is in full. . . . I see however that thare is to be only 17 colored companys allowed in the State."[9] Clark went further by conveying his desire that Stephens, a former Confederate officer, should have the honor of selecting those black companies, and "I hope you will not forget my command," reminding him that the Augusta Cadets formed "one of the oldest company in the city our commission date back to July 31st, 1876."[10]

Conversely, seeking to ensure his independence, Capt. Thornton Turner of the Atlanta Washington Guards wrote directly to Gov. Henry Dickerson McDaniel, also a former Confederate officer.[11] The captain, with his lieutenants, petitioned the governor "to have their company placed upon the roll of independent companies of this State as we have elected to maintain ourselves under the act of 13th Oct 1885." Turner demonstrated his knowledge of the law and even reminded McDaniel that this company of African American militiamen had existed since 1877, therefore qualifying under the provision for independent companies.[12]

Both Clark and Turner sought different paths under this new law, which attempted for the first time to limit African American military participation in Georgia. Clark in his letter may have referenced only infantry companies, of which his command was a part, or may have believed the entire African American military component allowed in Georgia would only consist of seventeen companies. His correspondence demonstrates that he was discussing a number lower than what the assembly agreed upon one month later. And, while it demonstrated his understanding of the statute, Turner's application to Governor McDaniel also divulged African American support for the provision that increased the maximum number of units allowed. Therefore, Clark's proposal clearly makes known that even in 1885, when there was agreement to limit the number of African American military companies, a level of flexibility still remained that allowed continual participation by existing black military organizations. Both the Atlanta Washington Guards and the Augusta Cadets served in the years ahead, at least until drastic changes occurred in the spring of 1899.

Throughout the period 1885 to 1896, the Georgia Volunteers, Colored, built their military structure centered on three battalions of infantry located in Atlanta, Augusta, and Savannah, with cavalry and artillery at Savannah and several independent companies at Macon, Albany, and Rome. Following what must have been a lackluster performance during the 1895 annual inspection, the commanding officers of several Savannah companies of the 1st Battalion were summoned to the meeting of the Military Advisory Board in February

1896. Accompanied by their battalion commander, Lt. Col. John H. Deveaux, five captains presented their case as to why their unit should not be disbanded. After the meeting, Deveaux expressed "confidence in the board and the governor in the full belief that no injustice will be done any of the colored troops, but that full opportunity will be given to them to demonstrate their efficiency." He further explained why he believed that "there are many reasons why the standard of the colored troops should not be expected to be as high as that of the white troops," citing no aid or encouragement by withholding uniforms, a lack of armories, and the men not having "the benefit of the encampments that the white troops have had."[13] The lieutenant colonel and his captains evidently made a strong and reasoned argument since none of the commands were disbanded; in fact, only four companies of *white* troops were disbanded in 1896.[14]

Incidents surrounding the mustering out of African American US Volunteers in 1899 throughout Georgia after the cessation of hostilities with Spain prompted a substantial backlash against the state's soldiers of color.

The shift from headlines like "Patriotic Negroes" who "want to whip the brutal Spaniards" in the *Macon Telegraph* on March 31, 1898, to the *Baltimore Sun*'s "Negroes Must Go" one year later demonstrated the precarious position that undoubtedly all black militiamen occupied in their respective state's military organizations—guilt by association. The *Sun* reported that Georgia's governor, Allen Daniel Candler, had become incensed over "the riotous and disgraceful conduct of the volunteer negro immune regiments which were stationed at Chickamauga and Macon, and which shot their way through this and other States on their way home after being mustered out recently."[15] He vowed "not to retain one of the colored companies in the State service" and immediately issued the order discharging the entire 2nd Battalion, Georgia Volunteers, Colored, stationed at Atlanta. The newspaper left no doubt that all of the companies would be dissolved when it quoted the governor and adjutant general as being convinced that "negro [*sic*] troops are a 'menace to the peace and order of the State.'"[16] Remarkably, even with this serious threat to eliminate African American military participation in Georgia, their complete dissolution did not occur.

Governor Candler did disband the majority of the black military companies, but enough of a relationship must have persisted, whether political, economic, or other, to prevent most African American militia organizations from suffering the same fate. Not only did the state retain the battalion at Savannah and its artillery battery, but it also kept the black company at Macon, despite the city being in the area where most of the violence occurred. Eventually, one of the disbanded companies in Atlanta was allowed to reassemble, and the governor permitted a new company, the Maceo Guards, to organize at Augusta in 1900. Perhaps these events depict a compromise between the governor and certain members of the General Assembly who still relied on the support of the African American community within their districts. When the legislature approved another act to reorganize the state's military forces on December 18, 1900, it determined that it would not exceed sixty companies of white infantry and seven companies of black infantry, officially termed "colored." Gone was the African American cavalry, the Savannah Hussars, but the artillery battery endured. This short-lived victory in 1899 averted the complete destruction of Georgia's African American militia organizations.[17]

On January 21, 1903, Congress passed the National Militia Law, commonly referred to as the Dick Act after its sponsor, Republican senator Charles Dick of Ohio, and Pres. Theodore Roosevelt signed it into law. While the law initially received popular support for its provisions to adequately train, uniform, and arm the National Guard of each state, others viewed it with skepticism due to its higher standards that could adversely affect the participation of some citizens. Still others feared that the act would possess an equalizing affect between the races and might even "degrade a Southern Soldier by putting over him a negro officer."[18] Passing the "act to promote the efficiency of the militia" put forth the race question in the minds of many southerners, who at this time could not bring themselves to even maintain a segregated military organization. The fear of social equality within the military materialized again later that year during maneuvers at Fort Riley, Kansas. Field training pitted a skirmish between white militiamen from Texas and regular US Army black cavalrymen. The *Dallas Morning News* detailed how three Texas privates "were badly handled" and that the state's "officers will not allow their men to leave their tents at night," signaling the possibility of racial violence.[19] In the end, Georgia's leaders at this time could not envision any situation where black troops could be of any service. This attitude, coupled with the potential social issues lurking from the provisions of the Dick Act, led state lawmakers to dissolve the black volunteers. On August 19, 1905, the General Assembly approved "An Act to Abolish the Colored Troops of the State of Georgia from the Militia of this State," thereby ending all African American involvement in the militia.[20]

Such actions can be compared to events and legislative actions in Virginia and Texas. These two states also gradually, and legally, reduced the numerical strength of their African American volunteers.

The Texas Volunteer Guard and the Virginia Volunteers

In 1878, when Herbert accumulated his information on the entire force of Georgia Volunteers, Texas only authorized four black militia organizations, one each stationed at San Antonio, Galveston, Austin, and Waco. From 1878 to 1906, when African Americans served as members of the Texas Volunteer Guard, this number remained relatively unchanged except during a brief period. Growing into an infantry regiment of nine companies—it should have been ten, but the Davis Rifles of Houston failed to qualify—commanded by Col. Andrew M. Gregory, the black militia of Texas reached its zenith in 1880. Gregory, after controversies surrounding his role in attempting to establish an African American militia company at Marshall, lost his commission in 1883. When several of its units failed to muster for annual inspection, the regiment was reduced to a battalion in 1885.[21] The 1st Battalion, Colored Infantry consisted of five to six infantry companies until the last African American company was dissolved in Texas in 1906. The state also failed to recognize, much less accept, the petitions of two new African American infantry companies in 1895—one from Richmond and the other from Fort Worth. This denial came after the regular US Army officer inspecting the battalion at its annual training recommended that "one more Company be *added* to this Battalion, making a total of six, for the sake of symmetry, convenience in drill, etc."[22]

In the East, the adjutant general's annual report of 1879 to the governor of Virginia denoted that the state's active militia in 1878 comprised thirty-four infantry companies, four artillery batteries, and one cavalry troop. Surprisingly, of this total, fourteen of the infantry companies were African American. But by the time the adjutant general compiled his report for that year, the white infantry companies had grown by six, the black companies by two, and the state had added an additional cavalry troop and artillery battery.[23] These numbers are quite similar to the information published by Herbert at the same time in Georgia. Yet unlike their neighbors to the south, when they finally limited the size of their state's volunteer force in 1884 to sixty companies of infantry, ten cavalry troops, and eight artillery batteries, Virginia legislators failed to limit African American participation within this structure. By 1885, the white volunteers consisted of twenty-one infantry companies, three cavalry troops, and six artillery batteries, while Virginia's soldiers of color composed nineteen infantry companies. While the numerical peak of the state's African American citizen-soldiers occurred in 1882 with twenty infantry companies, the economic burdens of maintaining uniforms and equipment slowly eroded that force to only eight companies by 1898. Whereas the 1903 Dick Act contributed to the demise of both the Georgia and Texas black militias, the controversy that enveloped the 6th Virginia Volunteers when many of its troops refused to serve under white officers during the war with Spain further hastened the end of African American militia inclusion in Virginia.

Clearly, these three southern states initially allowed considerable African American involvement in their military forces in the 1870s. During that decade, however, each state also sought through different means to curb their membership. Georgia circumscribed the African American component of its volunteer force through legislative action, though neither Virginia nor Texas chose to do the same. Still, the last two states accomplished numerical limitations through the decisions of their adjutant generals. Even though taking different paths, each state slowly tightened its grip on African American involvement by limiting the number of companies by 1885. But even then, Georgia still allowed some groups to function as independent companies beyond the legal restriction. Similar events occurred in Texas and Virginia at about this time, with legislation passed to improve the condition of each state's forces. Inspections exposed companies that failed to comply with standards, prompting the state to disband those units, thus limiting the number of organizations and allowing the state's to concentrate its limited military resources to fully equipping a much smaller force. Racial violence and the staunch refusal of African American officers and men to comply with legal, although arguably unjust, orders further contributed to numerical reductions in Georgia, the elimination of Virginia's African American militia volunteers, and possibly stymied any potential growth in Texas. Yet again, Georgia, the state that had circumscribed its black militia force, granted recognition to new units even after such turmoil had occurred within its own borders.

Into the new century, the passage of the Dick Act, with its lack of mandated equal protection, sought to improve the condition of the nation's state military organizations. In doing so, southern states simply eliminated their African American volunteers rather than face potentially difficult, and unacceptable, racial social conditions as well as the loss of local control over their forces. Therefore, through the prism of numerical troop strength over a period of time, the levels of African American participation in militia companies in

Georgia, Texas, and Virginia reveal an unexpected fluidity of racial accommodation immediately following Reconstruction, especially in light of the involvement of the former Confederate officers who replaced Republicans in government. These ex-rebels permitted African American militia units to exist much longer than expected, but this tolerance slowly eroded over time and led to the eventual elimination of black units in the South by 1906.

Another example of this slowly evaporating racial accommodation can be further illustrated through the process of how these three states tested African Americans officers as to their qualifications to command and serve in the state volunteer forces.

Georgia's Board of Examinations

Based upon the recommendations of the State Military Board, the Georgia General Assembly approved "an Act to provide for the better organization, government and discipline of the volunteer troops of the State" on October 16, 1879. This new law codified a wide range of administrative issues that had plagued Georgia's volunteer military force, distinguishing it from the (reserve) militia by declaring, "no laws relating to the militia shall be held to apply to the volunteers unless so expressly provided." Yet it did specifically subject the volunteers to the "legislation and *control* of the State." With this act, Georgia recognized for the first time that men of color, capable and "not under 16 years of age," could enroll as volunteers. Previous legislation did not specifically prohibit them from joining military groups, but this act acknowledged their right to form companies. Nevertheless, it did restrict them to segregated companies and battalions, organized and identified along the same US Army standards as Georgia's white units. There were no restrictions on men of color who could serve as officers. Although they obviously commanded African American enlisted citizen-soldiers, there were no distinctions regarding testing requirements between them and white officers.[24]

Perhaps addressing a previous concern or deficiency, Georgia sought, also for the first time, to set out in great detail the election and appointment of officers. These instructions directed that the election of officers could occur only after five days' notice had been provided to the company's members, and the polls would remain open for no longer than two hours. The law specified that only members of the unit could cast a vote, that the individual with the plurality of the votes won, and that the election had to be supervised by a properly qualified individual, usually a justice of the peace. It also bestowed upon the battalion commanding officer the ability to assemble his own staff;

company commanders could do the same by appointing their noncommissioned officers. Each organization, whether battalion or company, could adopt its own governing rules so long as such regulations did not conflict with Georgia law. Interestingly enough, the measure also provided that a battalion, no matter the number of companies it contained, would be commanded by a lieutenant colonel and that to "every major now commanding a battalion a lieutenant-colonel's commission shall be immediately issued."[25] This provision would seem to indicate an immediate promotion from major to lieutenant colonel to every African American officer commanding a battalion. But the law also specified that no company or field-grade officer elected to command would receive his commission "until he shall have satisfactorily passed an examination touching his competency for the office by such persons and in such manner as the Governor shall prescribe."[26] These conflicting sections of the law seemed to indicate a method that could be employed to restrict or even prevent African Americans from obtaining this rank, despite a battalion of "colored" troops then existing at Savannah. The governor could alter "the manner" in which men of color would be examined and, more importantly, was within his legal authority as commander in chief to employ, if he so chose, only white officers to examine African Americans. Records disclose that white officers did test black officers, but that often black officers tested other African Americans. Thus, a more fluid racial relationship existed within Georgia's military volunteer organization than previously known.

Col. Clifford Wallace Anderson was president of the State Military Board, which revised the military laws governing the state volunteers. An 1869 graduate of the Virginia Military Institute, Anderson served as the commanding officer of the 1st Volunteer Regiment of Savannah at the time of his appointment. In a letter to Adjutant General Stephens in 1884, he noted that, during the deliberations of the board, its members discussed the state's recognition of its African American military organizations. He asserted, "I was then & am now in favor of the State doing so under *proper* restrictions; as by commissioning them & giving them recognition, we could better control them & use our influence to have the most worthy of their number elected as their officers."[27] This letter illuminates Anderson's acceptance of African Americans in the state's militia. Still, he remained wary of who would lead these troops. His correspondence reflected both a distrust of the African American rank and file and a confidence in his ability, and others, to influence those same soldiers to elect military officers acceptable to the dominant white society. It is important that Anderson set his focus on the election of officers and not on the examining process as the means to control. The outcome of these elections divulge that this distrust was either unfounded, as some of the most talented individuals in the black community assumed this level of military responsibility, or that Anderson, and others, did in fact exert the proper level of influence to ensure their election.

Initially, the requirement to examine elected officers to determine if they were qualified to command remained a somewhat informal affair set in motion by an order from the Office of the Adjutant General. The process consisted of an oral examination held in front of an appointed board of officers. In most instances, these boards consisted of all white officers, but not in all cases. The results of the examinations also varied; at the highest level of command for African Americans—lieutenant colonel—William A. Pledger was the only African American ever denied a commission.[28]

Black battalion commanders did not assume the stereotype of "Uncle Tom," and neither did the examination simply become a "rubber stamp" process. Each of these men actively fostered relationships that bridged the racial divide in their community prior to and during their military service and were active in a wide variety of racial uplift organizations, from education to business, fraternal groups to the Republican Party. Each individual represented what one would refer to as a "race man," as defined by the words of the editor of Savannah's African American newspaper, the *Savannah Tribune*—"no white man of any principles whatever has any respect for any man who has not self respect enough to love his race and do his part to advance its interests."[29]

In 1880, with the election and examination of William H. Woodhouse as lieutenant colonel of the 1st Battalion, Georgia Volunteers, Colored of Savannah, African Americans achieved a historic milestone. Woodhouse, described by the *Augusta Chronicle* (as published in the *Atlanta Constitution*) as "an intelligent colored man," endured a four-hour-long examination given by the state's adjutant general, John Benjamin Baird, and the commanding officer of the Augusta Battalion of Georgia Volunteers, Lt. Col. Wilberforce Daniel.[30] The examining officers questioned Woodhouse on his "knowledge of military tactics and such other branches of military science . . . necessary and important to the proper discharge of his duties." They concurred that he was "well and studiously versed . . . and . . . fully competent to command said battalion."[31] Six years later, Deveaux, the editor of the *Savannah Tribune* and a leading state Republican official who worked as the customs collector for the Port of Savannah, won the election as lieutenant colonel of the battalion. He successfully completed his examination in the presence of Colonel An-

derson and two former Confederates, Lt. Col. William Garrard and Maj. John
Flannery.[32] Anderson respectfully submitted his report to the state adjutant
general, finding Deveaux "fit, competent & skilled," and recommending him
for his commission.[33]

The examinations of four other African American lieutenant colonels highlighted still further the objective promotions of those "most worthy." In 1884,
William A. Pledger, the editor of the *Athens Blade* and former captain of the
Athens Blues, completed his examination to command the 2nd Battalion, but
problems arose. Writing to Governor McDaniel, Pledger decried that during
his examination, he "was not dealt with fairly and respectfully ask[ed] that
[McDaniel] look into the matter." The issue remained, he concluded, not one
of an examination that prevented his assumption of command, but one that
was not strenuous enough. Characterizing his experience as a "farce of an
examination," with only two of the three officers assigned to the examining
board in attendance, Pledger wrote that of those two men, only one held an
active militia position, and that beneath the rank for which he (Pledger) had
been elected. The other one, he explained, was the lieutenant colonel of the
Atlanta Battalion, a command that had "been for a long time defunct."[34] When
Pledger did not receive his commission, the sometimes volatile Republican
must have realized that there was a distinct possibility that, no matter what
he had scored, the inattentive examination demonstrated feigned interest in
his promotion.

Another black officer had better fortune. Augustus Roberson Johnson, the
principal of the First Ward School of Augusta, received notification of his election as lieutenant colonel of the 3rd Battalion, Georgia Volunteers, Colored on
July 14, 1885. The state's adjutant general also communicated to him the need
for a competency examination as prescribed by Section 1103(r) of the Georgia
Code as well and the names of officers to administer his examination—Lieutenant Colonel Daniel, Capt. John J. Cohen, and Capt. I. Clarence Levy—all
white men from Augusta. While the adjutant general did not provide details
as to the manner of the examination, Johnson successfully completed his
evaluation and eventually received his commission from the governor.[35]

Lastly, merchant John Thomas Grant revitalized the 2nd Battalion, now located at Atlanta, with his election as lieutenant colonel in 1890. Grant completed his competency requirements in front of an examining board composed,
as usual, of three white officers—Lt. W. L. Calhoun, Capt. A. C. Sneed, and
Capt. M. B. Spencer—all from the 4th Battalion, Georgia Volunteers. Another
businessman, Floyd Henry Crumbly, who as a lieutenant served as Grant's

adjutant, would succeed him as the battalion's commander on November 21, 1892. The presiding officer, and quite possibly the entire examining board, remained the same from two years earlier. In addition to operating their own businesses in the city of Atlanta, both Grant and Crumbly actively participated in a variety of political and civic organizations.

Colonel Anderson accomplished what he sought to do in commissioning only those men he considered "most worthy" to command the state's African American military organizations. Both Grant and Crumbly had already been recognized as leaders in Atlanta's black community and were acceptable to Anderson. Pledger's contrived examination seems to illustrate the impossibility of him ever receiving a commission issued by the governor. Nonetheless, the adjutant general never specifically ordered "whites-only" examination boards.

Lieutenant Colonel Johnson of Augusta responded to the adjutant and inspector general, Col. John McIntosh Kell, who ordered the examination of three lieutenants from one of Johnson's companies, the Douglass Infantry, named for Frederick Douglass, by two white captains on March 31, 1890.[36] Johnson did not question the competency or trustworthiness of these two officers, noting, "I have not the slightest objection to them." He did question their assignment to the examining board, however, as Kell's order specifically stated, Johnson pointed out, "'If the officer elected is a member of a company attached to a battalion, etc. then the inspecting officer to be appointed by the Adjutant and Inspector General shall be *one of the officers* of such *battalion, etc.*'" Since neither captain served in his battalion, Johnson wanted to call "attention to the *letter,* and as I understand it, the *spirit* of the law as layed [*sic*] down."[37] The lieutenant colonel also stated to the adjutant general, "I indulge the hope, Sir, that you doubt not the competency of the officers in this battalion to conduct this examination . . . confiding in your honor and ability to enlighten me in reference to this matter." Within four months, Kell enclosed the order for Capt. John Lark of the Augusta Light Infantry to examine three lieutenants in the Douglass Infantry in a letter to Johnson. Relying upon *Upton's Infantry Tactics,* it directed Lark to examine the officers' knowledge of company and squad drill, the school of the soldier, and the school of the company.[38] Two weeks later, the lieutenants' commissions were forwarded to Johnson.

For company-grade officers, the use of African Americans to examine their fellow elected officers occurred frequently in the early years of the 1890s. Still, the practice of these evaluations apparently did not proceed in a standardized manner. In most instances, the captain of a company would usually examine his own lieutenants. Yet there was at least one instance where both Lieutenant Colonel Grant and his battalion adjutant, Lieutenant Crumbly, received orders to examine the first and second lieutenants–elect of the Atlanta Washington Guards per the governor's instructions. And on other occasions, as occurred in August 1890 and again in July 1891, orders were issued to a captain of a different company to test another's junior officers. Capt. Joseph H. Hammond, commanding the Union Lincoln Guards, evaluated lieutenant-elect Joseph L. Mirault of the Forest City Light Infantry, and Capt. William H. Royall of the Savannah Light Infantry tested the newly elected lieutenants of the Forest City Light Infantry. Almost a year later, Capt. Lymus A. Washington conducted an examination for the lieutenants-elect of Hammond's company. Since this pattern of testing only occurred in Savannah, this might have simply been the local practice. But with these orders coming from the adjutant general for those companies only, it may have signaled his acquiesce to a request from Lieutenant Colonel Deveaux.[39]

Similar inconsistencies arose with the examination of captains elected to command the various companies. Usually, the lieutenant colonel of the battalion tested his company commanders, but on some occasions a captain from a different company would examine the captain-elect, akin to the practice of examining lieutenants assigned with the 1st Battalion in Savannah. During the winter of 1890, Hammond tested his fellow captain-elect Henry Walton of the Savannah Light Infantry, while Capt. James H. Carter of the Colquitt Blues received orders to examine Nelson Law, captain-elect of the Chatham Light Infantry. Almost a year later in Macon, Capt. Lewis Mosely of the Bibb County Blues was dispatched to investigate the competency of captain-elect Sandy A. Lockhart of the Lincoln Guards. While it was not uncommon for African American officers to test the abilities of their fellow company-grade officers during this period, there was at least one occasion when an African American lieutenant colonel participated in the examination of a field-grade officer.

On October 2, 1890, Lieutenant Colonel Deveaux, commanding the 1st Battalion, Georgia Volunteers, Colored, of Savannah, received orders informing him that the election returns from his battalion had resulted in William H. Royall being selected for major. They further instructed him to obtain the services of two captains, Hammond and Carter, to comprise Royall's examining board. In the end, Royall received his commission from the adjutant general through Deveaux on December 11 of that same year.

According to Georgia's law, once these African American officers obtained their commission from the governor, it "shall continue until death, resignation, promotion or dismissal."[40] While newly elected officers had to undergo competency examinations as required by law, it remains unclear if individuals already serving had to complete an exam to retain their commission. What is clear is that two of Georgia's adjutant generals, Stephens and Kell, issued orders to African American battalion and company commanders to administer examinations of fellow officers using *Upton's Infantry Tactics*, a common practice throughout the early 1890s, but one that ended soon thereafter.

With the passage of "an act to provide for the examination of persons elected to or nominated for any commissioned officer in the volunteer forces of this State," the General Assembly in 1892 required that all "examinations shall, in all cases, be written."[41] The annual reports of Georgia's adjutant general prior to this date did not even mention the examination process, but in his report the following year, he called this legislative statute "an epoch in the military system of the State."[42] This law became the first step in not only standardizing the examination process but also improving the level of professionalism of the officer ranks within the state forces. There appears to be no negative consequences for African American militia participation from this new requirement. First, most of the officers listed in the adjutant general's annual report for 1894 obtained their commissions prior to the act's approval on December 23, 1892. Granted, there were some vacancies identified in the annual report. It also uncovered a roster of the "Georgia Volunteers—(Colored)," comprising three battalions of infantry, a cavalry troop, and an artillery battery, with at least four officers who had completed the written exam and had successfully obtained their commission (the governor could waive the exam for chaplains).[43]

The 1892 legislation allowed Georgia's governor "to establish one or more boards for the examination of all persons applying for commissions."[44] Yet when Lt. Col. Isaiah N. Blocker formally requested an examining board comprising officers of the 3rd Battalion in 1896, he received a rebuttal from the assistant adjutant general informing him, "as there is at present an examining board at Augusta it is not deemed necessary to order another at present; your request will be considered in the future."[45]

Concurrently with this period of transition away from African American officers testing their fellow elected officers, state officials sought to increase the officers' knowledge to include administrative functions and Georgia's military laws. Unfortunately, the adjutant general could not obtain the necessary funds to publish these regulations. The first problems with black officers successfully completing a competency examination seem to have occurred about this same time. Julius Maxwell of Savannah, who would later serve as a lieutenant in the Savannah Light Infantry, failed his evaluation on March 3, 1894.[46] Per the 1892 law, he was ineligible to stand for election for twelve months and thus had to wait for another chance at a commission.

In other cases, white officers serving on an examination board sought to circumvent this stipulation by requesting a concurrent second chance. In October 1897, 2nd Lt. William L. Grayson, secretary of one examining board, communicated to the adjutant general that second lieutenant–elect John H. Jenkins of the Union Lincoln Guards had failed to obtain a majority ruling in favor for his commission. Grayson, with a recommendation from Capt. U. H. McLaws and the support of his company's senior officers for another opportunity, requested guidance from the state.[47] Maj. William S. Rockwell, the president of Jenkins's board, after a careful review decided, in order to "to prevent any injustice being done the candidate, . . . respectfully [to] suggest that he be again ordered before the Examining Board."[48] It does not appear that Jenkins ever obtained his commission. In May 1898, he declared, "to the present date I haven't heard a thing of my examnation as to weather I will be commishion or not and what to dough I daunt know."[49] Jenkins also asked whether he "would be given another tryal," signaling that the adjutant general most likely disapproved of Rockwell's suggestion.[50] Whatever the ultimate decision, this same letter contained the notation "failed to pass" written at the top of the first page.

Some officers sidestepped any recommendation requesting second-chance testing in violation of the law by simply asking for a postponement of the examination, as occurred with 1st Lt. Alexander N. Thomas and Capt. John C. Simmons of Savannah as well as with 2nd Lt. Benjamin N. Davis of Macon. In Thomas and Simmons's case, it was also in the best interest of the examining board to postpone testing because the two men were among a group that included *white* officers of Savannah companies who did not possess the appropriate study materials.[51] With Lieutenant Davis, Capt. John P. Ross, president of his examining board, ascertained at the outset that Davis had never seen a set of regulations or laws governing the Georgia Volunteers, concluding "that it would be an injustice to him to require him to stand the examination without having been furnished with the laws."[52] Ross simply deferred the examination for thirty days. Davis later successfully passed and gained his commission on March 8, 1899.[53]

Lastly, the adjutant general's annual report for 1900 listed a much smaller African American component—one battalion of six infantry companies and an artillery battery—of Georgia's volunteers due to issues arising in 1899. It also documented the date of rank or commission for the twenty-six officers of the battalion. Of those men, twenty-one received their commission from the governor after the legislature passed the law requiring written examination. There were a multitude of issues that adversely affected African American militia participation. Apparently, the laws and practices surrounding the examination of officer candidates prior to issuing a commission were not among them, at least not in Georgia. From 1872 to 1884, the state's governors, all of whom were former Confederates, issued over 150 commissions to African American officers serving in volunteer organizations.[54]

After reviewing Georgia's instances of evaluating its black militia officers, it is now only natural to ask if the legal requirements to obtain a militia officer's commission affected African Americans in Texas and Virginia. Both of these states enacted laws or military guidelines to evaluate the qualifications for its uniformed militia-officer ranks. There is no indication that any of these men suggested that the regulations prevented African Americans from obtaining a commission.

Competency Exams in Texas and Virginia

The military code for Texas neglected to even mention examinations for officers until 1889. Even then, it became the responsibility of the state's adjutant general and judge advocate general to prepare "a code of regulations, not inconsistent with law, for the government and regulation of the volunteer guard ... [that also] shall provide for the examination of certain military officers."[55] Adopted on July 1, 1889, and revised on July 1, 1895, the *Rules and Regulations for the Government and Discipline of the Texas Volunteer Guard* contained two rules that address the examination of officers. "Rule No. 6—The Election of Company Officers" asserted that the governor, at his discretion, would "appoint boards to examine into the competency and fitness of all officers appointed or elected."[56] Yet "Rule No. 7—The Election of Field Officers" specifically required newly elected officers to prepare themselves to appear before an examining board within sixty days of their election. The rule continued by stating that if the candidate passed, then the commission was to be issued; if not, then a new election was ordered. Additionally, an unsuccessful candidate could stand for another election, but if he failed the exam twice, then he had to wait for two years before attempting again.[57] Therefore, Texas officials illustrated more concern for the competency of field officers versus company officers, where African Americans would obviously be more prevalent. Even so, three African Americans obtained the rank of major to command the 1st Battalion, Colored Infantry—Eugene O. Bowles, Jacob Lyons, and James P. Bratton—after the legislature enacted these regulations.[58]

The legislators of Virginia, on the other hand, quickly established a professional standard for all their officers in its law, which called for reorganizing the state's military forces as early as 1871. This statute prompted the governor to appoint a three-person examining board in each county to test the military knowledge of newly elected officers of its volunteer companies. Each candidate only had thirty days following his election to apply to this board for an examination. If successful, he obtained a certificate from the board to be turned in to the governor. As state's commander in chief, the governor would then present a commission to the officer. The law further compelled newly organized militia companies to uniform each of its members and secure a full complement of officers in three months or face the possibility of dissolution.[59]

Unlike Georgia, where written examinations were required beginning in 1893, it seems that Virginia's militia officers, both field and company grade, continued to be "examined orally by a board of officers convened by the Adjutant General."[60] This board utilized questions regarding "drill regulations, United States Army Regulations, State Regulations, and Military Law, and organization" to evaluate officers.[61] The initial legislation called for an examination board in each county, but this requirement was soon modified to conduct the competency tests either at Richmond or have the adjutant general or his representative, the inspector general, travel to various sites in the state to either conduct these exams or to form boards of examination.[62] Virginia reimbursed all officers, including African Americans, for their travel to the capital, provided they successfully passed the examination.[63] For example, "Expenditures from the Military Fund," part of the adjutant general's annual report, noted that on February 9, 1887, Capt. William H. Johnson of the Petersburg Blues received payment for "mileage for self and two Lieutenants attending before Board of Examiners."[64] This annual report also included the "Report of the Assistant Inspector-General," written by Lt. Col. Joseph Lane Stern.[65] Stern reported that there was a "very perceptible improvement made by the volunteers since the last inspection," attributing this enhancement to both the acquisition of the regulation uniform and "of the examination and passing of a large number of officers by the boards of examiners."[66] Specifically mentioning the "colored troops," Stern expressed that their companies have not increased their membership and asserted, "in their case this is doubtless largely due to the fact that they are not fully officered in quite a number of companies, many of those having applied for examination failing to pass; but on the other hand, several of the colored officers have passed the examinations very creditably, and make very efficient officers."[67]

Virginia, similar to Georgia, also created its own Military Board, composed of the governor, adjutant general, the senior officer of volunteers, the assistant inspector general, and the secretary of the commonwealth. The board's duties included controlling expenditures, directing reimbursements, and enacting resolutions binding upon the state's militia. Taking another positive step toward professionalism, it also created a monetary fund available to all military organizations in Virginia. At its meeting on March 18, 1887, the board resolved that each infantry company would receive $3.50 for every officer and enlisted man present at the annual inspection, while cavalry and artillery commands would be granted $5.00 for the same. The militia organization could, with the approval of the majority of board members, requisition up to the balance of their account for whatever "is suited to promote the efficiency of a military organization."[68]

There were, nevertheless, several requirements placed upon the organizations before they could obtain this much-needed funding. Each company had to possess the minimum number of members required by law and "shall have the full quota of officers duly examined, passed and commissioned, and these officers uniformed and equipped in accordance with General Orders No. 1, 1886."[69] This all had to be accomplished by July 1, 1887, based upon the company's performance in the 1886 annual inspection. A review of the listing of the "Colored Infantry" officers and companies in the 1887 adjutant general's report shows that, out of the sixteen infantry companies, fourteen possessed their full complement of officers and five requisitioned for uniforms during the year, denoting their successful compliance with the requirements to receive funding. In his attached report, Lieutenant Colonel Stern conveyed that, during his tours of inspection for that year, "sixteen officers were examined, eight of whom passed and eight failed."[70] Unfortunately, it remains impossible to determine the ethnic breakdown of these men directly, but by referring to the listing of "Colored Infantry," it appears that only one, or at most two, of the officers who failed might have been African American. Capt. A. A. Miller of the Hannibal Guard of Norfolk remained listed as the commanding officer of the company, but his name did not include a date of rank. Nor was there a listing for a second lieutenant in the Attucks Guard of Richmond. Of course, these omissions could simply demonstrate that Miller was successful in his election as captain but had not yet had an opportunity for examination, while the Richmond company had not yet elected a new lieutenant. Either way, the worst-case scenario in 1887 remains that out of eight officers who failed their examination, perhaps only two of them were African Americans.

One can hardly contend that the process of examination hampered black participation in the militia. In fact, Stern noted in his report that since the resolution of March 18, 1887, twelve to fifteen white companies had been disbanded, but the state had dropped only three colored companies. Virginia's inspector general saw that the obstacles to African American participation "in many cases are the inefficiency of the officers and the poverty of the men," adding that "experience has shown that competent colored officers can be found, as there are some six or eight colored companies in the service officered by men who give entire satisfaction." Stern remained sympathetic to the plight of the African American militiaman. He emphasized his "great concern to know what to recommend" when he saw poverty as the underlining cause for why a company could not come up to standard, "yet they hold on without officer and without proper uniforms and are anxious to 'soldier.'" His report eventually recommended that sixty days be allowed the officers of the Hill City Guard and the Virginia Guard, both of Lynchburg, as well as the Libby Guard of Hampton to report for examination and, if they were successful, to further allow their commands an equal amount of time to uniform themselves, thus relaxing the standard of completion of July 1—at least in this instance.[71]

By 1894, Stern, in his capacity as Virginia's inspector general, reported to the adjutant general, Brig. Gen. Charles J. Anderson, a former Confederate, that across the state, "there are several officers in the service who have not complied with the law and appeared for examination within the time prescribed. This kind of negligence on their part is very damaging to discipline, and the service suffers very much thereby. The law should be enforced in every case."[72]

Still, Stern previously had not been able to recommend the dissolution of the Flipper Guard at Fredericksburg because of "the willingness of the men to do duty" before finally admitting that "willingness alone does not constitute a service organization"; if called into service, "the company would not be found efficient."[73] He therefore recommended the disbandment of the company. But the men's "willingness" to prolong their service was demonstrated in the pages of the 1896 annual report. It recorded a disbursement to the company's commanding officer, Capt. Lucius G. Gilmer, as well as the Maj. J. B. Johnson, commanding the 1st Battalion Infantry, "for cash paid for making uniforms."[74]

Also in that report, the "Disbursements from the Military Fund since Last Report, for Year ending October 20, 1896," confirmed the success of other African American militia companies within the state's system of examination of officers. Both black battalions, as well as eight of their respective infantry companies, received funding under the resolution of March 18, 1887. In addition, 1st Lt. J. A. C. Bannister received his reimbursement for travel after successfully passing his exam for quartermaster of the 2nd Battalion.

Although struggling, these African American militia companies demonstrated their determination to remain a part of Virginia's military forces.

Conclusion

The governors and legislatures of Georgia, Texas, and Virginia, dominated by Democrats following Reconstruction, did not immediately eliminate military participation by African Americans through legal statute. In all three states, the leading government officials, with only a few exceptions, were former Confederates who one might have expected to act expeditiously to eliminate the black militia as soon as possible. Instead, Governor Smith of Georgia approved numerous petitions from African American citizens across his state requesting to form military companies beginning in 1872. In Virginia, former Confederates likewise allowed black men to fully participate in their state's militia when that force reorganized in 1871, well before the traditional accepted end of Reconstruction in 1877. And in Texas, other former Confederates approved African American military organizations, even though black militia had been seen in that state as an instrument of Republican Party repression. When Georgia's legislators sought to first limit participation through the number of military organizations, they also provided for opportunities for existing companies to continue to serve. Neither Texas nor Virginia limited black military participation by law.

Slowly over time, white leaders in these states took what began as a loosely formed and virtually unregulated citizens militia of segregated companies and attempted to organize, discipline, and supply those organizations. Although continuing to maintain segregation, some legal statutes in Georgia, such as the law for the election of officers or the payment of armory rent, contained no discriminatory restrictions. And when both Virginia and Georgia sought to strengthen the competency of their volunteer officers through examinations, Georgia laws left some negotiable space in the wording that allowed the African American military leadership an opportunity to push for more control within their organizations, often examining those elected within their respective commands. Moreover, in Virginia, when this testing process remained in the hands of white officers, the historical record fails to reveal that examinations were used to exclude African Americans from becoming officers at either the company or battalion level.

Racial relationships possessed a remarkable and astonishing level of flexibility throughout this period. It was not until 1898 that serious reservations arose concerning the actions of black federal soldiers and black US Volunteers during the war with Spain, which led to the elimination of Virginia's African American militia component and almost did the same in Georgia. Even so, Georgia recognized new black military companies after 1898, while state troops in Texas continued their activities into the new century. Arguably, by 1905, the state of race relations had deteriorated to the point that fear of possible racial equality in state military units brought on by the passage of the federal law aimed at improving the efficiency of the entire US militia system, coupled with increasing fear from state leaders to utilize black militiamen, all contributed to the demise of the African American militia. White political leaders in the South, specifically in Georgia, Texas, and Virginia, could no longer accept black men as state soldiers.

Nevertheless, their activities as citizen-soldiers and their military organizations in these states illustrate just what African Americans were able to accomplish for more than thirty years after the traditional end of Reconstruction. Colonel Anderson of Georgia favored African American military participation, segregated as it was, but sought only the best of the black community to serve as officers. One can assert that it was not through his efforts the "most worthy" were chosen, but rather from choices within the ranks. Through a form of military service, those very men sought to demonstrate their US citizenship and manly status. In the public sphere, black militia officers and soldiers unmistakably illustrated the complexity of racial relationships and social conditions in these three southern states.

3

———

"Composed of Men of the
Same Race and Color"

Organizing the Black State Volunteers

ONE OF THE MAIN motivations for African American men to enlist in a state military establishment in the 1870s to the early 1900s centered on how they recognized and expressed some of their rights as citizens. Throughout the South, black militia organizations, under the auspices of Democratic governors, legislatures, and military officials—often seen as hostile to the ambitions of African American citizens—continued once the question of citizenship had been resolved by the provisions of the Fifteenth Amendment to the US Constitution. Granted citizenship, black men now had the legal right to join the ranks of state military forces.

The existence of Georgia's African American militia units from 1872 to 1906 demonstrates the significant exercise of rights and involvement of blacks in southern society during that time. African American leaders somehow negotiated the formation of these local militia companies, and conditions across the state, especially in several cities and towns, allowed and even supported the growth of such organizations. Many African American men grasped the opportunity to participate in the state's volunteer forces, reinforcing the drastic change in their social and political status. The size and scope of their units varied, however, affected by shifting political forces and susceptible to the legislature's ever-changing legal statutes enacted to curb their activities and growth.

The treatment of the Georgia Volunteers, Colored, can be contrasted with their fellow African American citizen-soldiers in Texas and Virginia. Such a comparative analysis discloses that racial relationships in certain areas remained pliable enough for African Americans to establish and maintain armed, uniformed military groups in the post-Reconstruction South for several decades. It divulges some of the similarities in the communities that formed these volunteer companies, including possible motivations to serve that went beyond citizenship. But it also shows that often the ability to create a local militia company did not necessarily foster the longevity of that unit. Ultimately, the altering and hardening of race relations over time and geographical area during this thirty-three-year period illustrates the fragile status of those black state militias.

"Duties as Citizens of This State": Georgia

The legal statutes governing the formation of volunteer military organizations initially required a minimum of fifty-three members to form a company, having "the same rights, privileges, and . . . subject to the same duties as such organizations in cities."[1] Following their enrollment as a member of the company, each citizen-soldier would attempt to uniform himself. Around the same time, a petition would be sent to the governor to request an election of officers. When granted and once completed, the newly elected commanding officer could apply for arms and accoutrements from the state. This same law specifically directed that "arms and accouterments shall be supplied to the volunteer corps, whether uniformed or not, by requisition on the Governor, in such manner and upon such terms as he may direct."[2] Obviously, this granted full discretionary powers to the governor to determine which militia commands, black or white, would receive arms from the state. This clearly could lead to a governor not arming those military companies comprising one's political rivals, while conversely, he could reward those who provided political support by issuing them state-procured firearms.

Prior to Georgia's readmission to the Union on July 15, 1870, federal law had forbidden the reorganization of its militia forces in order to eliminate any conflict with US troops then present in the state. On July 13, one African American state senator, Tunis G. Campbell, put forth "a resolution calling for the arming and equipping of volunteer militia by the Governor."[3] Campbell realized the potential of what might occur with the withdrawal of federal troops, yet the Republican governor, Rufus Bullock, failed to act. Surrounded by controversy and facing almost imminent impeachment, Bullock fled the state in 1871. In a special election held in December of that year, voters chose Democrat and former Confederate colonel James Milton Smith to replace Bullock as governor. Within three months of his inauguration, Smith received his first petition from African American men requesting recognition of their militia company and the required gubernatorial order to officially elect officers.

Organized on March 30, 1872, Savannah's Union Lincoln Guards became the first state-approved African American volunteer company in Georgia. The membership elected Richard D. Goodman as captain, who thereafter wrote Governor Smith on April 10, 1872, asking for commissions for the elected officers as well as arms and accoutrements for the company. Goodman's letter acknowledged his new status, and that of the other sixty-two men listed, by setting forth this "petition of the undersigned citizens" who wish "to acquire a knowledge of the military art & to perfect ourselves in the Drill & Discipline of the citizen soldier." He also referred to the *Code of Georgia* with the general statement, "according to the laws of the State of Georgia," thus, demonstrating not only his own knowledge of his legal standing but asserting them as well. Furthermore, Goodman revealed that at least some members of his company were veterans, writing, "we the undersigned Ex. Soldiers of the US Army & volunteer company of Sav[annah]. Ga."[4] This letter clearly illustrated Goodman's understanding of the connection between citizenship and the citizen-soldier. In addition, it demonstrated that this group of African Americans, at least, who had volunteered to fight for their freedom during the Civil War, now sought to take their lawful place as militiamen in order to affirm their rights as citizens and to continue that struggle for freedom, if needed, within their home state.

Within the month, three additional petitions arrived in Governor Smith's office, from the Forest City Light Infantry, the Savannah Chatham Light Infantry, and the Savannah Colored Volunteers. Each of these letters shared similarities with Goodman's request, specifically reminders of the men's citizenship, reference to existing laws allowing them to organize, and even their knowledge of the law requiring the governor to order an election of officers following their organization. Yet the correspondence also differed from the content of Goodman's petition. For the first time, a white attorney, Amherst Willoughby Stone, submitted a petition for the organization of an African American militia—the Forest City Light Infantry. Stone, a native of Vermont, had arrived in Georgia before the Civil War. A staunch Unionist, he fled to avoid conscription but later returned to Atlanta to serve as a judge on the circuit court. The request listed no officers, as Goodman had, since none had been legally elected, but the accompanying muster roll noted a membership of fifty-three privates and noncommissioned officers, as well as, for the first time, six honorary members. Stone's letter did not request any other assistance from the state.[5]

The Savannah Chatham Light Infantry's petition, written by company secretary James B. Lewis and dated April 22, not only asked for the election of officers but also requested the election be held at either the office of King Solomon Thomas, the African American justice of the peace of Savannah's Fourth District, or "such other place as your Excellency shall think proper and under such superintendance as shall ensure justice." Lewis further explained that the petitioners wished "to inform themselves of the duties of soldiers and the general military tactics of the country, that if needed as such they would be able to respond," giving evidence that the sixty-seven enrolled men and six musicians had a serious sense of purpose in the formation of their organization. He also asked the governor "at the proper time to furnish the necessary arms and accoutrements" and to "please address the answer to or in care of Geo. Washington Wilson, atty. at law." Following the example of the Forest City Light Infantry, this company had legal representation. Wilson, unlike Stone, was born in Georgia and served as a clerk on the Chatham County Superior Court before entering private practice.[6]

Three days later, a "Committee to Petition," consisting of three of the Savannah Colored Company's sixty-two members, submitted its request asking for the governor to issue the order for the election of officers. The Savannah Chatham Light Infantry and the Savannah Colored Volunteers would later change their names to the Chatham Light Infantry and the Savannah Light Infantry, respectively. These companies also shared similar history in that both previously had served as axe companies "doing excellent service for the city in fighting fire."[7] Whereas, the Union Lincoln Guards provided an example of the relationship between previous African American wartime military service and the militia, the Chatham and Savannah Light Infantry companies revealed a connection between militia membership and community service.[8]

It is not clear when the state's only African American cavalry troop, the Savannah Hussars, was formed, but the men hosted their "Fourth Grand Anniversary Pic-Nic" on August 7, 1876, at Woodlawn Park, leaving one to deduce that they organized in 1872. It is also unclear as to when the Union

Delmonico Guards formed in the city. In a letter responding to Governor Smith's denial of their petition on October 2, 1873, Capt. William Yates wrote that he did not believe it unfair to deny recognition based on the unavailability of arms, asserting that he and the men would be willing "to wait for one (1) or 2 (two) years."[9] Yates informed the governor that the company was already uniformed and armed, "under the strictest discipline of senior Capt. R. D. Goodman," and closed the letter with, "we remain Firm and Freed Patriots."[10] Using the same location as the Hussars, the Guards celebrated their first anniversary at Woodlawn in August 1875, signaling that the governor eventually relented and officially recognized the company. Possibly, the unit may have continued as an independent command, participating in the celebration of the thirteenth anniversary of the Emancipation Proclamation in Savannah on January 1, 1876. Whatever the case, these men eventually received the authorization order from Gov. Alfred Holt Colquitt and elected officers on November 6, 1877; the following year, Sidney Herbert identified the Union Delmonico Guards as a "live" company.[11]

Savannah witnessed continued growth in its African American militia companies throughout the 1870s and into the 1880s. But such expansion was not without controversy. The extreme racial violence, voter fraud, and voter intimidation that surrounded the 1868 elections was still fresh in the minds of Georgia's citizenry four years later. Regions throughout the state had erupted in considerable violence between the Ku Klux Klan and members of the Union League, each supporting opposing political parties. Civil unrest occurred in the city when two African Americans and one white policeman were killed after workers from the Georgia Central Railroad attempted to cast their votes. Believing they could quickly complete the balloting process and return to their jobs, the white workers attempted to force their way through a group of African Americans who had arrived earlier, leading to an outbreak of gunfire and resulting in the deaths. At the center of much of Savannah's political intrigue lay one of the most controversial African American figures in Georgia's Reconstruction period, Aaron Alpeoria Bradley. Described as "an incendiary leader from the Savannah District," Bradley "was an obstreperous member" of the State Constitutional Assembly, "tackling with venomous impartiality, first the democrats and then the republicans." One of the few African Americans admitted to the bar in Massachusetts prior to the Civil War, he later won election as the state senator from Georgia's First District but resigned "to avoid expulsion as a seducer, for which crime he had been convicted and sentenced in a northern state." Even though Bradley fought fearlessly for African American civil and political rights, his abrasive style only complicated racial relationships in Savannah. So, as the early black militia volunteers organized and elected officers in conjunction with the governor's approval in the spring of 1872, residual fears from 1868 surfaced as well as new anxieties concerning the upcoming election.[12]

On July 11, 1872, Savannah lawyer, city councilman, and lieutenant colonel of the Savannah Volunteer Guards William Starr Basinger wrote Governor Smith a lengthy letter, conveying information he recently had received from "a man employed in a gunsmith's shop." He described the potentially dangerous situation: "The gun dealer, who employs this man as his principal assistant, has received orders for about 700 muskets from negroes who are forming volunteer companies here, with bayonets, cartridge boxes, etc., to correspond. And orders for about 500 more, say 1200 in all, are promised. The negroes are negotiating with him also for a large supply of ball cartridges; the percussion caps are already ordered by another party." Basinger continued by declaring his informant had overheard the expression "'we will have things our way this time,' or words to that effect," and relayed that "the 'captains' (who seem to be negroes who were once in the US Army) 'talk very stiff.'" While expressing the opinion that he had yet "to understand to what in particular they refer," Basinger obviously understood enough to write to the governor his concerns. Interestingly enough, he also included the statement, "the negroes ordering these arms expect to get the money to pay for them from white men who remain in the dark," seemingly indicating some of Savannah's white citizens provided financial support for the African American volunteers.[13]

Later that year, in September, the mayor's office wrote to the governor and enclosed a "certain affidavit charging Aaron Alpeoria Bradley, a prominent negro leader in this City, with threats against the public peace at the elections which will take place this autumn." Mayor John Screven feared that Bradley would lead a contingent of approximately 1,500 men, including the armed black militia in the city and "a large number of negroes from South Carolina and the neighboring country in Georgia," to surround the polls at the courthouse to prevent whites from voting. His solution to this potential problem was not to call for additional white military assistance from the state, but to obtain from the governor an order to "place the companies (white) under the direction of the Mayor and add to them any company or companies of negroes whose officers have been elected under Executive orders." Screven believed that issuing such an order would "surprise and flatter them (especially if extended in common as it should be to the white companies also)" and would therefore give the black militiamen "a legitimate duty, which if they refused would at once lay their hidden intentions bare and make them subject to the deserved consequence of their refusal." His plan called for using these troops for riot duty and to prevent any armed individuals from entering the city. The "negroes themselves," placed at the entrances to Savannah, he argued, "would have the duty of arresting and disarming those of their own color," while "the Police and the remaining troops would be retained in proper position to protect the peace and good order within the city." This singular piece of correspondence provides invaluable insight into the complexities of the racial relationships within Savannah. The mayor, expressing fear and distrust on one hand, proposed to use those same African American troops that troubled him to prevent violence by other African Americans.[14]

The governor did issue the order for Screven to direct the activities of Savannah's militia, but he only activated seven companies of white militia and placed them under arms at their armories, where they remained. With no violence occurring in the city during the fall election, municipal leaders believed that having these volunteer companies prepared to meet any threat prevented violence, rather than realizing that their fears might have been unfounded from the beginning. Despite the overly anxious city councilmen, mayor, and undoubtedly others, the growth of African American volunteer companies in Savannah continued.[15]

Two additional organizations of black militia established themselves in Savannah by 1875. The Lone Star Cadets banded together on April 13, 1875, and by October, the Georgia Artillery was hosting "'a grand ball' . . . at McIntire's Hall."[16] Serving as the only African American artillery battery in the United States, this unique unit purchased two 10-pounder rifled Parrott cannons and requested assistance from the governor for "two carriages, harness and all the equipment that belong to the cannons," which seemed to signify that it may have bought them from the state.[17] Governor Colquitt did not provide the gun carriages, but the men of the battery marched forward, ordered and received uniforms from Philadelphia, had carriages built by Savannah wheelwright Daniel O'Connor, and in 1878 requested and obtained an inspection of their equipment by Maj. George P. Andrews of the US Army and Capt. John F. Wheaton, the commanding officer of the city's white militia battery, the Chatham Artillery.[18]

The year of that inspection witnessed the creation of the Colquitt Blues, named for the sitting governor and former Confederate colonel, and the Georgia Infantry. William H. D'Lyon forwarded the request for elections of officers for the Colquitt Blues on July 10, 1878, with the names of fifty-three men on an enclosed muster roll. This would be the second company in the state that D'Lyon had organized. Gone were the references to citizenship in this petition, instead citing only the "provisions of Sect. 1078 and 1079 of the Code of Georgia." The election was ordered on July 13.[19]

Sidney Herbert listed John Stiles as the captain of one of the "Georgia Infantry" "colored" companies—the other company by the same name was located at Augusta. According to the *Savannah Morning News,* Stiles's unit, sometimes referred to as the Georgia Light Infantry, received an order for the election of officers from Governor Colquitt on August 19, 1878.[20] Lt. Col. William Garrard, commanding the 3rd Battalion, Georgia Volunteers (white) of Savannah confirmed this election date later in an 1886 letter. Writing to the adjutant general concerning Stiles's command, Garrard stated, "it appears to me as his company was organized in 1878."[21] Stiles had expressed concern about the status of his command to Garrard following the passage of the act that formally set the size of the "Georgia Volunteers, Colored" to not more than twenty infantry companies.[22] The battalion commander knew full well that providing a date prior to October 16, 1880, to the adjutant general would guarantee the survival of this company as an independent command in compliance with the new law. He also shared that Stiles "has been through the War, with 9th Ga. Regt and has always born the best character & his command appears to be a fine one in every respect" and that he took "pleasure in writing this[,] as the Captain of this Company is a member of the Band of my command & we all like him very much."[23] This recommendation by Garrard indicated that Stiles had served, probably as a musician, with a *Confederate* infantry regiment. More importantly, with the captain's current participation in the battalion band, the lieutenant colonel officially violated the act "to provide for the better organization, government and discipline, of the volunteer troops of this State," which in 1879 legally segregated the volunteers into "companies composed of men of same race and color."[24]

Seeking to improve the structure of their organization, perpetrate their active status, and advance the progress of the African American community in Savannah, most of the black companies met over the course of several days in July 1880, resolving to form a battalion of colored infantry in the city.[25] This had not been their first attempt. In 1877, seven captains from Savannah's African American volunteer companies asked Colquitt for the order to conduct "an election for a commander of said battalion."[26] The governor asked the adjutant general to hold this petition, but the men attempted again three years later. William H. Woodhouse, who had signed the initial 1877 request, and Louis B. Toomer were selected as the committee to petition again for orders from the governor sanctioning the election of field officers.[27] Once achieved, Woodhouse won the election, successfully stood his examination, and became the first African American lieutenant colonel to command the first African American infantry battalion in Georgia state history. The battalion would celebrate its twentieth anniversary with a parade and picnic at Lincoln Park on August 14, 1900.[28]

Remarkably, Savannah even appears to have possessed a military academy for African Americans. The *Weekly Echo* reported on December 2, 1883, that "the Georgia Cadets of the Colored Military Academy, received their new guns on Thanksgiving Day, from New York, and paraded through the principle streets of the city."[29] This article also mentioned the winner of a drill prize as Sgt. J. Small of Company B, signifying that the academy enrolled more than one company of young men. Later newspaper accounts mentioned the Savannah Zouaves and the Chatham Zouaves, which might have been the "two juvenile Zouave companies in line" during the Emancipation Day parade in 1894.[30]

There may have been several other volunteer companies of African Americans in Savannah that did not receive the authorization to elect officers in order to complete their organization under the law. The Lincoln Light Infantry attempted to gain official status throughout 1872 and into 1873 without success, even selecting Magistrate Thomas as drillmaster and who later interceded on their behalf to Georgia's secretary of state. Likewise, the Grant Guards made their first effort in 1873, followed by another in 1874, but were denied the opportunity to officially serve. The *Savannah Morning News* reported on the activities of the Hunter Rifles and the nonuniformed East Savannah Guard but noted that "neither of these companies are recognized as military companies, the Governor not having authorized an election of officers."[31] Much of the history of these organizations and the men who composed them are unknown, but what is absolutely clear is that there existed a substantial number of African American militia companies in Savannah during the decades after the Civil War.[32]

Historian Frances Smith argued that, "had Savannah's white citizens felt threatened, they would have pressured state authorities for tight controls on black companies," but it is obvious that some did fear the capabilities of the city's African American contingent.[33] And historian Robert Perdue, writing about race relations in Savannah prior to the twentieth century, asserted, "although there was often racial violence in the political arena and discrimi-

nation against blacks in the courts and in some jobs, there were also areas of
racial cooperation and harmony." Perdue does not advance an interpretation
that a harmonious environment existed in the city at this time. In fact, this
period seemed to be characterized by fear and anxiety for all groups of Savannah's citizens. Still, despite this uneasiness, African American military service
not only existed in the city during Reconstruction but also grew across the
state well into the 1880s.[34]

Henry McNeal Turner, an African American chaplain in the Union army
during the Civil War who later served briefly in the Georgia legislature, tes-
tified before a joint select committee of Congress in 1871 concerning his observations of the 1868 election. His comments supported not only Perdue's
contention concerning the level of violence and discrimination but also his
assessment of this initial racial cooperation and accommodation. Turner affirmed that "Macon is a city of very good order" with "a great number of very
high-toned and dignified citizens there, men of wealth, who are opposed to
this wholesale excitement and disturbance."[35] He further revealed that after
his life had been threatened during his tenure in the state legislature, which
resulted in his home being guarded for several nights by "a large number of
colored men, probably a hundred and fifty, . . . with guns, pistols, etc.," that a
"harmonial meeting" took place in the city hall, during which "several speeches were made by white and colored men."[36] The assembled biracial audience
then passed resolutions denouncing disorder and guaranteeing protection to
African Americans. Turner, in answering questions regarding the regions of
Georgia where the most violence occurred, replied, "they have been most numerous between Macon and Augusta." He further elaborated by identifying
the counties of Putnam, Wilkinson, Baldwin, Hancock, Washington, Monroe,
Sumter, Lowndes, Wilkes, and Columbia "as among the most prominent."[37]
Additionally, Turner's comment that "colored people run to the cities as an
asylum" was corroborated by a fellow former African American state legislator, Thomas Allen, who argued that there was "no safety for colored people
except in the large cities."[38]

These statements under oath helped illustrate regional conditions within a
wide swath of Georgia and served to provide further understanding concerning the rise of both official and unofficial African American military activities.
First, from the late 1860s to the early 1870s, many rural African Americans
relocated to Georgia's urban centers to avoid violence. Collectively, these
individuals sought better employment opportunities, a better life beyond the
limitations of agriculture, and communal safety for them and their families.

Second, black men could, and did, publicly arm themselves to protect their leaders and their community. Asserting their constitutional rights not only embraced military activities but also included political and civil rights. Third, these actions prompted city officials, at least in Macon but possibly in other cities as well, to negotiate with their African American residents to avoid violence and to work together for a reasonable and peaceful, albeit temporary, solution to the political and social disturbances, which may have contributed to the "very good order." Lastly, in addition to their understanding and expression of their rights as citizens under state and federal law, their desire for self-protection must also be recognized as one of the root origins of African American military participation in the 1870s.

The first petition to the governor from a black volunteer company outside the city of Savannah arrived in the spring of 1872, almost simultaneously with those from the Forest City Light Infantry. Four "temporary officers" representing the Lincoln Guards of Macon requested an order for their election on April 18, 1872. When a prompt reply failed to materialize, Nat D. Sneed sent a letter to Colonel Alexander that referenced a conversation he had with Governor Smith, who had promised the order would be forthcoming. Within days, Sneed and the other three men received their commissions. By the end of that month, the Grant Guard Infantry at Augusta applied for an order for elections, but it appears that this request failed. But the officers of another company, the Colored Home Guards at Madison, succeeded in getting their organization approved, obtaining their commissions on June 29, 1872. More black militia units formed the following year, and neither Macon nor Augusta had long to wait for others to follow their lead.[39]

Sometime in the summer of 1873, William D'Lyon went in person to present an application to Governor Smith for the Central City Blues of Macon. In a letter following this meeting, D'Lyon, who had heard of elections in Savannah and Augusta, reminded the governor of his promise of providing an answer in "two or three weeks" and that he was "one of your supporters." Smith responded to D'Lyon, resulting in further correspondence in which he explained to the governor, "what we most desire is the recognition of the corps by the state government." D'Lyon added, the "company are prepared to furnish our own armes our uniforms are nearly all finished and paid for."[40]

The choice of the name for this unit caused a stir in Macon, since it had previously been used by a local company raised for Confederate service in 1862. Learning of commissions now being issued to African American officers, the Confederate veterans who had served in the original Central City

Blues, an organization that bore "such a part in the war for Southern rights, and having so proud a record," sought redress from the governor to force a change in the new unit's name.[41] Arguing that they wished to reorganize their command for state service, these former Confederates felt entitled to its old name. Eventually, the African American volunteers adopted the designation Central City Light Infantry. D'Lyon, commissioned captain of the company, resigned on June 4, 1878; moved to Savannah; and later organized the Colquitt Blues there in July 1878.[42]

The Douglass Infantry of Augusta, the Grant Guards of Sandersville, and Atlanta's first African American volunteer company all petitioned the governor in 1873, with only the volunteers in Augusta and Atlanta achieving recognition. Receiving word that the Guards had been denied their petition, Capt. Wesley Simmons reassured Governor Smith that, even though they had already armed and equipped themselves, the company was "under strict discipline."[43] "An attempt to incite insurrection" in 1875 at Sandersville and the corresponding trial afterward provide some evidence as to the state of racial tensions in that Washington County community. Acting on information from other African Americans, city and state officials arrested a group of black men who reportedly had been seen "in various parts of the county at night organizing and drilling (all done secretly) and wearing badges of different colors." White citizens thought that these men intended to "murder the inhabitants, burn and pillage" the neighboring city of Wrightsville.[44] The trial, held in Sandersville under heavy guard, resulted in an acquittal for all defendants. Still, the *Atlanta Constitution,* upon reporting the results of the legal proceedings, printed that a mass meeting of "the negroes of Washington County" was to meet at Sandersville to select two men "to go to some other state to select some suitable place to emigrate to."[45] While it is not possible to learn if the men who drilled at night in the woods were the Grant Guards and had decided to continue their organization, this incident did confirm an atmosphere of fear and distrust in a community whose African American population sought to escape from rather than to remain in Washington County.

Unlike Sandersville's company, the Douglass Infantry of Augusta received their commissions six days after forwarding their request to the governor. Their petition, like many others, not only reflected the names of all its members but also indicated that they had already "uniformed themselves in accordance with the law, and regulations of similar organizations, of the State" and had already purchased Enfield rifles.[46] Writing in 1878, Lieutenant Colonel Daniel of the Independent Volunteer Battalion conveyed to the governor that the Douglass Infantry "comprise the very best portion of our colored people."[47] The officers of the Atlanta Light Infantry obtained their commissions only three days previous to the Douglass Infantry's request. The capital city would add a second black company, the Fulton Guards, in the summer of 1874.[48]

The next few years showed more success by African Americans in organizing military volunteers throughout the state, including some cities that for the first time could take pride in their unit. Black men at Augusta established the Georgia Infantry and the Richmond Guards in March 1874, then the Augusta Light Infantry in June 1875. African Americans in Macon formed the Bibb County Blues in September 1874.[49] The unit's captain, Spencer Moseley, was known as "a quiet, good and peaceable citizen" whose company, according to the mayor, was composed of "law abiding men, . . . well liked, well drilled, . . . [with] good uniforms, and . . . a safe foundation."[50]

Several communities boasted their first African American militia companies. These included Brunswick (Glynn County Colored Militia Guards), Quitman (Butler Light Infantry), Valdosta (Lincoln Guards), Griffin (Griffin Light Infantry), and Americus (City Blues). Columbus inaugurated its first company, the Columbus Volunteers, with the commissioning of its captain, William Albright, and other officers on June 1, 1874. African American residents of Thomasville, too, created that town's first company, the Union Blues, the same month as the founding of the Volunteers. Men from Bainbridge originally petitioned the governor in May 1872, but like some of their fellow volunteers they had to wait, achieving recognition two years later. Finally, despite "great apprehensions among all good citizens both white and black that a riot is in contemplation" and "reports of nightly drillings and knowledge of extensive purchases of cartridges and other ammunition," as communicated by the town's mayor to Governor Smith in 1874, the first African American military company, the Grant Guards, was raised in La Grange. The mayor, in this same letter, opined "that the most intelligent colored people are opposed to the actions of a majority of their race," which seemed to indicate that he did not view the city's African American population as one group.[51]

Colquitt's administration authorized additional African American volunteers in the late 1870s. Both Columbus and Thomasville augmented their first companies with the arrival of the Columbus Light Infantry in 1877 and the Thomasville Independents in 1878. The last was under the command of Joseph Simeon Flipper, the brother of Henry Ossian Flipper, the first African American who graduated from the US Military Academy at West Point, New

York. Augusta raised two more companies in 1878—the Colquitt Zouaves, named in the governor's honor, and the Augusta Cadets. The city of Atlanta experienced the most growth during this period, with four new companies—the Atlanta Washington Guards (1877), the Capitol Guards (1878),the Georgia Cadets (1879), and the Governor's Volunteers (1879). Smaller communities in the state also contributed new companies, including Eatonton (Putnam Blues), Milledgeville (Middle Georgia Volunteers), Rome (Rome Star Guards), Midway (Harrisburg Blues), Compton (Newton Guard), and Riceboro (Georgia Lincoln Guard). While Sidney Herbert also recorded the Athens Blues, named for its hometown, and the Home Guards, based at Irwinton, it is unknown when those companies were established; he did at least confirm their presence in 1878. The Fulton Blues were also included in Herbert's compilation, but this probably was in error, as this was also the name of one of Atlanta's white companies. Easley Smith, listed by Herbert as the captain of the Blues, had replaced Capt. James Williams of the Fulton Guards in November 1874, serving until 1883. Smith's name gives evidence that his unit was an African American company, so Herbert probably should have registered it as the Fulton Guards instead. Regardless, Colquitt received more petitions from African American commands during the rest of his administration, some of which he denied, but the majority of which obtained recognition from the governor.[52]

F. Marion Sheppard of Talbotton, for example, petitioned the governor on behalf of the Talbotton Light Guards on May 3, 1880.[53] No further records of this company appear to exist, nor are any commissions recorded. Moreover, the Marietta Light Infantry, a company whose captain was a future delegate to the National Guard Union meeting held in Kansas City in 1884, was not listed in Herbert's publication but appears to have been created sometime between 1880 and 1883.[54] Georgia's adjutant general later recorded that this company could "not exist under the act of 1885," meaning it had not formed prior to October 16, 1880.[55] The more successful and active units included Albany's Colquitt Guards and the Darien Volunteer Guards, both formed in 1881.[56] The number of militia companies in nineteen counties indicated the high level of participation in the black militia after the traditional end of Reconstruction.

It is important to emphasize that the Georgia General Assembly legally segregated the volunteers by "race and color" as part of legislation set forth to improve the organization of the militia. Section IV of the authorizing act dictated that "every company of infantry, or cavalry must be attached to a battalion of the same arm" unless, of course, there were not at least three compa-

Georgia Counties with African American Militia Companies, 1878. Adapted from *Georgia County Outline Map*, Carl Vinson School of Government, University of Georgia.

nies located in close proximity of one another.[57] In compliance with this legal requirement and immediately following Savannah's successful organization of the 1st Battalion in July 1880, Atlanta pursued the same course and created the 2nd Battalion with the city's five infantry companies. Since this law mandated a minimum of three companies per battalion, it appears that Augusta might have lost several of its African American volunteer companies by this time. Within a few years, the city had recovered to warrant the formation of the 3rd Battalion, Georgia Volunteers, Colored.[58]

With endorsements from the city's white mayor, Patrick Walsh, and the highest-ranking white militia officer in Augusta, Wilberforce Daniel, Augustus Roberson Johnson, writing to the state adjutant general, requested the addition of the Attucks Infantry to his battalion in 1886. Johnson noted that the two companies he had designated to join his battalion, the Colquitt Guards and the Tolbert Light Infantry, were "not in existence" and that "neither of them [had] ever been armed nor uniformed from organization."[59] His endorsements, coupled with the comments of John Neibling, a justice of the peace in Augusta who characterized the Tolbert Light Infantry as being "composed of as good and respectable (col'd.) citizens as we have in Richmond County," signaled the existence of some racial cooperation in the city during the mid-1880s.[60] While the Light Infantry had been established with the Attucks Infantry in 1884, two years later only the Attucks company remained.

Nearly twenty years after the Civil War, the year 1884 became the high-water mark of Georgia's African American military participation. A year later, the general assembly limited their presence in the state militia to "not more than twenty companies of infantry, one of cavalry, [and] one of artillery." This legislation did allow those units that had formed prior to October 16, 1880, to remain as independent commands, and the astonishing growth of such units came to an end. Others would attempt to join the state volunteers, such as the Gordon Cadets of Augusta, comprising "young colored men," in 1888 and a cavalry company, the Colored Liberty Volunteers of Fleming, in 1892. Neither received state approval due to the limitations on the number of organizations allowed by law.[61]

Finally, in a surprising turn of events, one new company, the Maceo Guards of Augusta, was accepted into state service on November 16, 1900, and a "reorganization" of three organizations that had been disbanded—the Fulton Guards, Union Lincoln Guards, and the Georgia Artillery—came back into service.[62] The state's adjutant general, Phill G. Byrd, just the year before had recommended that *all* the African American volunteer units should be disbanded. At the beginning of the twentieth century, he failed "to see where the Georgia State Troops, Colored, are or can be of any service to the State, from a military standpoint."[63] By that time, that contingent had shrunk to only one artillery battery and a battalion of seven companies—four in Savannah and one each in Atlanta, Augusta, and Macon—all headquartered in Savannah. The size of the African American volunteer force remained in this drastically curtailed condition until the state legislature dissolved all black companies in 1905, leaving Georgia with an all-white militia.

Georgia Counties with African American Militia Companies, 1900. Adapted from *Georgia County Outline Map*, Carl Vinson School of Government, University of Georgia.

"Will Make Good Soldiers, Peaceful Citizens": Virginia and Texas

Elected with the support of conservative whites and moderate Republicans, Gilbert Carlton Walker became the thirty-sixth governor of Virginia in July 1869. The election also resulted in twenty-nine African Americans winning seats in the state's general assembly. Walker's inauguration and the legislature's approval of the Fourteenth and Fifteenth Amendments to the US Constitution set in motion the actions that resulted in Pres. Ulysses S. Grant signing the bill readmitting Virginia to the Union six months later. Many African

Americans who had supported Walker's Republican opponent, Henry Wells, feared the unraveling of their civil and political rights. Still, they continued to enjoy the right to vote and to hold office, and black farmhands and artisans could and did seek employment elsewhere.[64]

Richmond's African American population had grown by over 60 percent by this time, and the state's port cities, Norfolk and Portsmouth, had seen their black residents increase 20–50 percent from their pre–Civil War numbers. Black men successfully won elections for local offices. Twenty-five African Americans served on either Richmond's Board of Alderman or its city council from 1865 to 1895, where, according to historian Virginius Dabney, "relations between blacks and whites . . . were said to be better than those between the races in the state legislature."[65] These African American city leaders gained substantial benefits for their constituents. It was within this environment that Richmond became the first city in Virginia to raise a black militia company.[66]

On the night of April 17, 1871, at two different hotels in downtown Richmond, over one hundred African American men, "composed of the best material" and known to "have been soldiers," met to form the state's first black militia companies—the Attucks Guard and the Richmond Zouaves.[67] Just the month previous, the General Assembly of the Commonwealth of Virginia had approved legislation reestablishing the state's military forces.[68] April in Richmond not only witnessed the formation of these two African American militia companies but also five white companies composed of "many men who had served in the Confederate Army."[69]

The Richmond Zouaves may have never enrolled the minimum of sixty men as required by law, and it appears that their captain, Richard H. Johnson, in 1873 became the commanding officer of the Carney Guard of Richmond. Per the legal requisite, the officers of the Attucks Guard, who "will make good soldiers, peaceful citizens," successfully completed their examinations but, despite being touted as "composed of the most highly respected colored men in Richmond," failed to obtain their commissions from the governor.[70] Apparently, one of the examining-board members had objections to them for reasons unclear other than "Democratic prejudice." Yet other citizens wondered, "when will such nonsense cease?"[71] Warwick Reid, who had reportedly been elected the captain of the Guard, never obtained his commission with this company. Nevertheless, despite the difficulties, the unit soon achieved state recognition. Robert Hobson received a commission as its captain. Soon thereafter, state military representatives inspected the company at its armory in March 1872. With the establishment of the Attucks Guard, Richmond's African American community had garnered enough support to overcome this initial obstacle to one of the most visible signs of their citizenship. And, soon, other companies followed.[72]

As in Georgia, African American volunteer militia companies flourished in Virginia during the 1870s. William H. Richardson, Virginia's adjutant general, reported to the governor in 1873 that the state had four "companies of men of color, . . . uniformed and armed." Following the formation of the Attucks Guard the year previous, the state now recognized the Carney Guard, also of Richmond; the Union Guard of nearby Manchester; and the Petersburg Guard of that city. Richardson communicated to the governor that "these companies have deported themselves with soldier-like propriety."[73]

"The mayoralty and the other city offices" at Petersburg, according to the observations of Edward King in 1873, "remained in the hands of white Radicals, and the negroes had made no special struggle to secure them, although they are to the whites in the city as eleven to nine." The local conditions there provide a glimpse into the success of its African American volunteers. Instead of an adversarial relationship prompting self-protection, the numerically superior black population combined with sympathetic Republican Party city officials supported the founding of the Petersburg Guard. Even when James Lawson Kemper, a lawyer, Democrat, and former Confederate general, won the gubernatorial race in the year of his travels, King wrote that Kemper "has thus far done everything that he could to develop good-will and confidence between the races," even having vetoed a bill whose purpose was "to invade the liberties of the city of Petersburg and to take from it its self-government because the majority of the voters there were negroes."[74]

Kemper's election initiated a shift in Virginia politics but did little to dampen the martial spirit in Richmond. With companies there, now augmented with the Virginia Grays, and at Manchester, African American Virginians successfully formed the 1st Battalion of Colored Infantry in the summer of 1876, a full year before their fellow volunteers in Savannah applied to their governor and four years before actually accomplishing that feat in Georgia. A fourth company, the Lincoln Guard, initially named the Attucks Jr. Guard, was also raised at Richmond.[75]

Beyond the confines of the capital and its surrounding area, the African American communities of the port cities at Hampton Roads brought forth the next group of volunteers for new companies. Norfolk established the Langston Guard in 1873, but it appears that the company had not been officially accepted into state service at the time of the adjutant general's yearly report. King observed from his travels to this area, "there is a large negro population in Norfolk, and the white citizens make great struggles at each election to keep the municipal power in their own hands," indicating a different racial situation there than in Petersburg.[76]

Portsmouth, just across the Elizabeth River from Norfolk, created a company two years later. The Virginia Guard, raised in 1875, was followed the next year by the Seaboard Elliott Grays, under the command of Capt. G. A. Corprew, who was commissioned on January 1, 1876.[77] Lastly, the Libby Guard, of Elizabeth City, to the north of Norfolk and Portsmouth, had been "inspected and commissioned" but was, according to the adjutant general, "not yet quite ready to be armed."[78]

Many other cities bolstered Virginia's contingent of African American volunteers. In the fall of 1877, Lynchburg's Hill City Guard entered state service, followed in February 1878 by a company known as the Virginia Guard. Not to be confused with the company of the same name at Portsmouth, this company would be referred to as the Lynchburg Virginia Guard. Returning to the state's cradle of postwar African American military service, an independent command known as the State Guard formed in Richmond in May 1878. The capital's neighbor to the south increased its force by two additional companies, the Petersburg Blues and the Flipper Guard, that same year.[79]

By 1880, there were a total of nineteen companies of African American volunteers in Virginia's active militia. Norfolk had created its second company the year before—the National Guard—and added a third in 1880—the Hannibal Guard. And, the black militiamen of Richmond recruited another company, the L'Ouverture Guard, that summer. The total number of companies, especially those in the vicinity of Hampton Roads, now necessitated the need to create an additional infantry battalion. Established on May 31, 1881, the 2nd Battalion of Colored Infantry incorporated Norfolk's three companies— Langston Guard, National Guard, and Hannibal Guard—with Portsmouth's two companies—Virginia Guard and Seaboard Elliott Grays—to form the state's largest African American infantry command.[80]

One year later, the last two volunteer companies of African Americans were raised in the state. Named for the departed Republican president, the Garfield Light Infantry organized in Fredericksburg, while Staunton produced the Staunton Light Guard.[81] With only nine companies in the state's two battalions, there remained an additional ten independent companies, several of which, specifically the one in Richmond and the three in Petersburg, could have created a third battalion had either the men or the state so desired. This did occur ten years later, but by that time, Norfolk had lost the Hannibal Guard and all those previously existing in Portsmouth had been disbanded. By 1891, the state placed all militia companies within battalion-size commands.

Virginia Cities with African American Militia Companies, 1881. Adapted from
Virginia Counties and Independent Cities Map, Wikimedia Commons.

For Virginia's African Americans, one battalion had its headquarters at Richmond and the other at Petersburg. Therefore, the companies had successfully maintained their strength in two infantry battalions within the state's military structure, but overall the black militia had lost half its numbers from ten years earlier.[82]

Virginia, unlike Georgia, failed to recognize any additional African American volunteers after 1882, but the state did seek to build on the military's desire for an improved and more efficient force by organizing the remaining black infantry companies into battalion-size commands in 1891. At the same time, Georgia continued to authorize three battalions of African American infantry. Both states had initially recognized active militia volunteers comprising African Americans in 1872, and they shared other similarities. Perhaps the most common characteristic involved the size of the African American population within their urban areas. These large communities provided the militia companies with both manpower and financial support. Several cities, including Richmond, Petersburg, and Savannah, had African Americans serving in local government. Beyond this, many always seemed to possess the requisite number of prominent men who could operate within both the black and the white spheres of society. The presence of an antebellum free-black population in both Georgia and Virginia may have contributed to the initial rise of African American volunteer companies in Savannah and Richmond. Free blacks had also lived in Fredericksburg and Augusta. African Americans overwhelmingly worked in agriculture during this period, but substantial labor needs became necessary beyond the rural areas. The port of Savannah had similar labor characteristics to Virginia's Norfolk, Hampton, and Portsmouth. Other locales required labor for railroad yards, manufacturing centers, and the handling of agricultural products. More than this, the presence of a politically active and strong local Republican Party drew African Americans to each state's political center at Richmond and Atlanta, even expanding beyond those two cities as party patrons obtained federal employment in return for their support, especially at the post offices or customs houses. With only minor exceptions, the state of Texas also shared many of these characteristics.

In Texas, just one year after Democratic governor Richard Coke won the election in 1874, the state continued to maintain at least four black volunteer companies: the Coke Rifles in San Antonio, the Capital Guards and Austin City Rifles of the capital, and the Island City Rifles at Galveston. This seems contrary to the expectation that once the Democratic Party had taken control of the office of governor and of the legislature within a former Confederate state, the forming or retention of local African American military organizations would end.

Constitutional amendments and subsequent federal legislation enacted gave black citizens of the Lone Star State the prospect of exercising the same rights as those granted to African Americans in Georgia and Virginia. These included, of course, the rights to vote, to serve on juries, to hold office, and to federal protection of those and other rights enjoyed by fellow citizens of the United States.

Centers of commerce with employment opportunities, such as Houston, Galveston, and San Antonio, experienced explosive population increases. Galveston's railroad terminus complimented its port, the most important in Texas, which mirrored the significance of the shipping and rail networks at Savannah. Between 1860 and 1880, the island city's population grew over 200 percent, as did the cities of Houston and Austin. San Antonio, like Atlanta, hosted a US Army post and served as an important railroad center, experiencing an increase in its citizenry of over 100 percent. The movement of African Americans into these cities contributed to these expansive population growth. By 1876, while Galveston had enrolled the Lincoln Guards, both the Coke Rifles and the Capitol Guards were listed as "companies disbanded during the year" in the adjutant general's annual report.[83]

Areas with a majority of black voters, identified as the "Black Belt" of Texas—according to historian Lawrence Rice, "those counties lying generally east of a line from Corpus Christi to Austin, through Waco, Dallas, and on to Denison"—elected African Americans to the state legislature consistently from 1871 to 1883. Many of the local communities within these counties chose black officeholders, among them Galveston's Norris Wright Cuney, who stepped into the leadership of the state Republican Party upon the death of former governor Edmund J. Davis in 1883, and Houston's state legislator Richard Allen. This geographical area of Texas became the initial center of the state's black militia activities.[84]

The Texas Militia Act of 1879, which coincides with Georgia's act "to provide for the better organization, government and discipline" of its volunteer troops that same year, gave African Americans the legal right to establish militia companies. Article 3347 of the Texas law set forth certain qualifications before a company could be accepted into the state's Volunteer Guard. Within a single year after this legislation, Texas boasted one complete regiment of African Americans, containing ten infantry companies. Joining the existing organizations located at Austin, Galveston, and San Antonio, black

Texas Counties with African American Militia Companies, 1880.
Adapted from *Texas—County Outline Map,* Perry-Castañeda Library
Map Collection, University of Texas at Austin.

men banded together at Bryan, Brenham, Corpus Christi, Waco, and Calvert. Houston's Davis Rifles, while officially designated as Company H, did not qualify under the requirements of the 1879 law until 1881. Difficulties arose in some of these communities, such as Bryan and Calvert, which led to the loss of their organizations. The Coke Rifles in San Antonio disbanded but later reorganized themselves as the Excelsior Guard in 1882, the same year the city of Dallas raised the Cochran Greys, who later changed their name to the Cochran Blues.[85]

Texas maintained a black regiment for another two years, but from 1883 to 1885, several events prompted white politicians and military officials to review the state's African American volunteers. First, the commanding officer of the regiment, Col. Andrew M. Gregory, traveled to Marshall, Texas, to assist the black community there in forming militia companies. Alarm swept through the city's white society, and within days, the state adjutant general arrived and relieved Gregory of his duties, citing his unauthorized involvement in this recruiting as well as alleged payment for his services. In 1884, the regiment's colonelcy still remained vacant, and over the course of the following year, five of the regiment's companies fell victim to dissolution—the Austin City Rifles, Brenham Blues, Grant Rifles, Davis Rifles, and the Cochran Blues.[86] During that same year, the state disbanded ten white companies, but the white militia also gained eighteen new organizations. In 1886, the white component lost five companies, yet these were replaced by twenty-one new units, while only one African American volunteer command was established—the Valley City Guard at Columbus. All of these changes to the state's military forces occurred at virtually the same time as Georgia was choosing to limit by law its number of African American volunteers.[87]

With the reduction of the number of companies, the adjutant general created the "Colored Infantry Battalion," to be commanded by Maj. George W. Wilson of Galveston in 1886. This organization remained in place until Texas eliminated the state's last black volunteer company in 1906. Unlike Virginia, Texas continued to organize African American companies from 1886 to 1900 in an effort to fulfill the strength requirement of this battalion as set forth by the policy of Adj. Gen. W. H. Mabry, who in 1886, argued, "if the militia is not to fall to pieces it must have help, and if it is ever to be thoroughly efficient and useful for the real purposes of its organization, existence and support by the public, it can only be made so by learning to act in concert and solidly in larger bodies than single companies."[88] Including the state's black troops in this policy even won support from US Army captain Richard I. Eskridge, who had been detailed to inspect the "colored" battalion.[89]

The battalion both lost and gained commands over the next few years. The city of Bryan organized a new company, the Brazos Light Guard, in the summer of 1887, and by year's end, the Ireland Rifles had established themselves at Seguin. But the next year, the African American community of Corpus Christi lost their company. In 1890, Austin resurrected the Capital Guards, but the men at Columbus could no longer participate; therefore, the now designated 1st Battalion of Colored Infantry contained only five companies—the Excelsior Guard of San Antonio, the Brazos Light Guard of Bryan, the Lincoln Guards of Galveston, the Ireland Rifles of Seguin and the Capital Guards of Austin.[90]

Musicians, too, took part in the Texas militia volunteers, as they did in Georgia. Throughout all this ebb and flow of membership, some African

American men started a musical group for the regiment known as the 1st Colored Regiment Band; they refused to change their name once the regiment was reduced to a battalion. The adjutant general, in his annual report for 1892, recorded that these men "wished to be assigned at once" and recommended that "their request be granted."[91]

This year also witnessed the formation of the Sheridan Guards at Houston. It became the sixth company in the battalion, but in the years that followed, this company split into two sections, known as Company F, Section A and Company F, Section B. It is unclear the reason for these designations, but they might have stemmed from internal difficulties that occurred in 1896.[92] Whatever the case, the Sheridan Guards eventually had their dual-section organization dissolved and served united as Company F until replaced by the Cocke Rifles in 1899. The Rifles, named for the white commanding officer of the 2nd Brigade of Texas Volunteers, Brig. Gen. Richard Cocke, appear to be the last company of African American volunteers to be accepted in Texas.[93]

Another black company was also named in honor of a white man. The officers of Galveston's Lincoln Guards, all veterans of the war with Spain, voted to change the company's name to the Hawley Guards in 1900. Named for the city's US representative, Benjamin Hawley, the command chose to honor the Republican congressman, who was instrumental in obtaining support for African Americans to serve in the US Volunteers during the Spanish war.[94]

Another important similarity that Texas shared with both Georgia and Virginia was having its governors deny several applications from African Americans. Even though the city of Marshall failed to support the enrollment of a black militia company in 1883, the majority of these requests took place much later, illustrating that race relations had deteriorated to a condition that could not allow further expansion of the state's black military. One company, the Ellis Rifles, organized forty men in Houston in 1890. Peter Williams, who submitted the petition to create this company, later became the first commanding officer of the Sheridan Guards in 1892, but it remains unclear if the Guards had some of the same men as the earlier group.[95] The Queen City Rifles of Fort Worth, represented by A. O. George, attempted twice to obtain recognition as part of the Texas Volunteer Guard—first in 1893 and again two years later. Neither effort was successful.[96] Tony Smith, writing from Richmond, Texas, on May 28, 1895, requested "a charter" for his company, the Richmond Regulars, from the adjutant general.[97] Smith kept up a string of correspondence throughout the year and into the next. In his last attempt, on May 12, 1896, he included a petition signed by forty-six individuals from Richmond "asking

Texas Counties with African American Militia Companies, 1900.
Adapted from *Texas—County Outline Map*, Perry-Castañeda Library
Map Collection, University of Texas at Austin.

that you furnish the Richmond Regulars with all necessary arms and equipments."[98] The company did not receive the approval to serve, but Smith later served his country during the war with Spain and afterward commanded the Hawley Guards of Galveston.[99] Lastly, Lee A. Leonard, writing as the captain of the Cooke Rifle Company of Palestine, forwarded a petition for recognition of his company on June 1896. After repeated attempts, the company failed to gain a position with the Texas Volunteer Guard.[100] Even though the state accepted several black companies during the 1890s, their numbers remained low and barely enough to keep the battalion at strength.

As the new century dawned, and with only a few companies still in service in the state, the opportunity for a large number of African American men to participate in the Texas Volunteer Guards had vanished.

Conclusion

Empowered by constitutional amendments, federal legislation granting citizenship, and the legal right from their respective state governments, some black men sought to continue their military service after the Civil War and to establish new military organizations even following the end of Reconstruction in the South. Located mostly in urban areas—both large and small communities—with sizeable African American populations, many of these companies obtained official recognition from state governors who had all previously served in the Confederate army.

The success of these black men in establishing military organizations within an environment marred by racial and political violence, social upheaval, and distrust signified a remarkable accomplishment. It also pointed to an unappreciated level of accommodation or negotiation that existed initially in these communities and these states.

There were similarities between the cities where black volunteer militia companies formed, such as substantial labor needs, a desire to maintain stable business and economic environment, the presence of US military installations, and even financial support from both racial segments of society. But the most important requirements for establishing a company of black volunteers, arguably, hinged on leadership in the black community and the flexibility of racial relationships. Other factors included leadership provided specifically by African American veterans of the Civil War, prominent businessmen of both races, and influential religious figures. All of these men sought to embody the guarantees of the US Constitution through military and black political activities and through who could successfully negotiate with the existing power structure.

When the states sought to improve the efficiency of their military forces, those efforts, coupled with the economic disadvantages faced by African Americans and the loss of cooperation or the deterioration of racial relationships, adversely affected the membership of black militia companies. Measures taken by Georgia, Texas, and Virginia illustrated that the efforts to improve their military forces took place almost simultaneously. The worsening of racial relationships occurred differently in each of them. A vital similarity among these three states was that each had governors and adjutant generals, most of whom were former Confederates, who sought to arm and supply these black militias. These unusual actions provide evidence that the African American volunteers served in proper military organizations, not merely symbolic ceremonial groups.

4

"With Said Arms No Discrimination Shall Be Made"

Arming and Equipping the Black State Volunteers

DESPITE THE TUMULTUOUS social, economic, and racial strife that characterized the post-Reconstruction South, the Democratic governors of Georgia, Texas, and Virginia still granted approval to African American men to form volunteer militia companies, issued officer commissions, and accepted these organizations into the state's military establishment. Almost immediately, these units began to forward requests for rifles, ammunition, accoutrements, and other military equipment. The governors and their adjutant generals, many of whom were former Confederate officers, faced difficult political and social decisions in allocating sparse state resources.

Each state struggled to supply the demands for arms and equipment, and competition for military provisions highlights one of the largest sources of friction between the governments and their African American citizen-soldiers. Social etiquette always dictated preference to the senior and more experienced organizations—the white volunteer militia companies—and this pattern never changed between 1870 and 1906. Still, these conditions did not prevent African American militia officers, and some civilian leaders, from asserting and successfully claiming their rights within the state's military establishment. The response of each state not only revealed areas of discrimination but also illuminated what these African American volunteers *could and did* accomplish, given their circumstances. The open and very public demonstration of training and participation by black militia companies for more than three decades indicated several important factors about Georgia, Texas, and Virginia. First, it strongly supports the assertion that the governments of these three southern states approved and even accepted the existence of African American volunteer militia companies as military units, segregated as they were. Second, the military officials in each state attempted, within the bounds of social protocol, to equip and supply these companies, exposing again the considerably complex racial relationships existing during these decades. And lastly, contrary to the rise of legal restrictions suppressing further growth of African American volunteer companies, it appears that Texas and Virginia may have improved their responsiveness to the arming and equipping of these military organizations.

An Act to Distribute Arms in Georgia

The military organization of Georgia in 1868 consisted of the Georgia Military Institute, the volunteers, and the militia. For clarification, the "volunteers," or active militia, were companies composed of men who had received legal recognition from the state and whose officers had obtained their commissions from the governor in his role as commander in chief. The "militia," on the other hand, simply encompassed those men of appropriate age who could be called upon to defend the state—in other words, an untrained reserve force. Title XI of the *Code of the State of Georgia* for 1868 clearly stated, "arms and accouterments shall be supplied to the volunteer corps, whether uniformed or not, by requisition on the Governor, in such manner and upon such terms as he may direct."[1] This law, as mentioned earlier, existed during Reconstruction governor Rufus Bullock's administration and possessed the potential for the governor not only to arm his political supporters, which would include the state's African American military companies, but also, obviously, to exclude arming any organization that voiced opposition to his programs.

With the accession of James Milton Smith to the office of the governor in 1872, , the legislature, now controlled by a Democratic majority, acted quickly to modify this law. Approving "an act to regulate the distribution of arms to the volunteer companies of this State" on August 24, 1872, this new legislation specifically required the governor to supply, "first, to such companies as were organized and existing prior to the first day of January, 1861, as have already, or may within the next three months after the passage of this act, reorganize." Furthermore, for those "companies organized since the first day of January, 1872, . . . it shall be within the power of Governor to furnish arms, or not, according to his discretion."[2] In clear language, this act not only gave the priority of supplying weapons to those companies that had existed in the state during the era of slavery but also allowed the governor to completely ignore all African American volunteer companies if he so chose. Nevertheless, on February 22, 1873, the general assembly amended this act by eliminating the requirement that clearly favored the former military companies, which had served the Confederacy. Instead, the legislators agreed upon a less politically charged statement that allowed the governor to "make such distribution of arms . . . as, in his judgment, may be most conducive to the public interest."[3] The reason for this change became clear within the next few days.

On March 3, 1873, Congress passed an act reinstating the provisions of the US militia law of 1808 that authorized and directed the secretary of war "to distribute to such States as did not, from the year eighteen hundred and sixty-two to the year eighteen hundred and sixty-nine, receive the same, their proper quota of arms and military equipments [sic] for each year."[4] This 1808 legislation and the amendatory acts that followed authorized the expenditure of $200,000 per year for such military supplies to be provided to the states based upon their level of representation in the House of Representatives. Obviously, Congress had suspended this law following the secession of the southern states; still remarkably, it had determined to "reimburse" those states by providing the equipment previously withheld during this seven-year pe- riod. The significance of this law was in its last few sentences, which stated that these arms and military stores will be supplied "provided, that in the organization and equipment of military companies and organizations with said arms[,] no discrimination shall be made between companies and orga- nizations on account of race, color, or former condition of servitude."[5] While the specter of the return of federal authority may have been present, Georgia's government and military officials realized the boon of military equipment that would have been lost if they had chosen not to amend the state's exist- ing law.

This federal legislation served to supply the diminished stocks of arms, ammunition, and military equipment for the southern states. With the current representation in the House, Georgia sought to gain approximately $47,264 toward the purchase of military stores, while Texas and Virginia would net $27,008 and $54,016, respectively.[6] It remains unclear how much of this money was actually paid to the states. What is clear, however, is that an appropriation made sixty-five years earlier, which had remained unchanged, fell woefully short of its intended purpose. In 1874, Capt. R. M. Hill of the US arsenal at Augusta, Georgia, expressed his frustration to Col. S. C. Williams, the secretary of Georgia's Executive Department: "By Act of Congress, dated April 23rd, 1808—$200000 yearly is allotted to the States according to their quotas, for the arming and equipping of the Militia, the Ordnance Department has done all in its power to have this amount increased, proportionately to the increase and growth of the states but so far without effect."[7] To further understand the inadequacy of this annual appropriation, if Georgia used this funding for muskets only, which cost approximately $15 apiece, the governor could not even provide arms for ten full infantry companies averaging forty men each.[8] This problematic federal funding often resulted in companies within battalions, or even men within single organizations, possessing weapons of different calibers and/or multiple types of firearms. Furthermore, the unavailability of arms prevented many of the earliest African American commands from gaining recognition.[9]

The first issue of arms and ammunition to an African American volunteer company in Georgia occurred on September 29, 1873, when the Atlanta Light Infantry, commanded by Capt. Jefferson Wyly, a US Army veteran who had risen to the rank of sergeant during his three-year enlistment in the 28th and 24th US Infantry Regiments, obtained fifty Springfield rifled muskets with accoutrements and two thousand rounds of ball cartridges.[10] The following month, on October 23, the Forest City Light Infantry of Savannah received the same type and amount of equipment and ammunition. At the time, this company was also commanded by a veteran, Capt. William H. Woodhouse, a free-born African American who had served as a musician in the bands of the 25th and [47]th Georgia Infantry Regiments of the Confederate army.[11] Lastly, on November 28, Macon's Lincoln Guards, commanded by Capt. George Fraction, also received the same type and amount of arms, accoutrements, and ammunition as the Atlanta and Savannah companies.[12]

These three infantry units represented only a small number of the total force of Georgia's African American military organizations, but the importance of their supply hinges on the fact that they received the same number and type of Springfield rifled muskets that the white volunteers did. And, while ten of the fourteen white infantry companies received one thousand more ball cartridges in 1873, that still meant that four white commands received the *exact same type and quantity* of arms, accoutrements, and ammunition as their "colored" counterparts. Not only does this support the contention that the African American volunteers were indeed military organizations rather than mere social or ceremonial "clubs," but it also firmly demonstrates their recognition and acceptance, albeit segregated, within the state's military establishment.[13]

Of course, the issue of arms and equipment did not occur without controversy and frustration. In September 1873, Capt. Nat D. Sneed of Macon's Lincoln Guards requested arms to be supplied to his company. The governor responded by inquiring if any weapons in possession of its members had previously "been furnished by the state or general government." The captain replied that the arms were the private property of the individuals and were "old and mostly unserviceable."[14] Sneed, in a third letter, again requested arms for his command. Receiving what must have been an unacceptable reply, the African American officer strongly conveyed his frustration to Georgia's chief executive, whose behavior he characterized as evasive, deceptive, and "unworthy of yourself and the state, you misrepresent."[15] Sneed's strong protest, bordering on insubordination toward the state's commander in chief, was followed by the statement, *we will purchase arms*," and a warning that the governor's "conduct will have the effect of inducing colored men to organize all over the state into military companies independent of and not subject" to his jurisdiction.[16] After this month-long series of correspondence, 1st Lt. Frank Disroon of the Guards apologized to the governor, stating, "we, the company don't believe that you will or would punish us for Sneed's private actions" since the command did not "wish to make any strife between the State and company."[17] While this apology calmed the situation, the resignation of Captain Sneed on October 24, 1873, probably did more to alleviate the friction, remarkably resulting in the Lincoln Guards becoming the third African American volunteer organization to receive fifty rifled muskets, accoutrements, and two thousand ball cartridges when other companies may have been deemed more worthy.

The concern about lack of arms forthcoming to African American volunteer companies as prescribed by the federal law also prompted a meeting of black military leaders in Savannah on February 26, 1874. Unfortunately, it is not evident who attended this convention, which former Georgia congressman Henry McNeal Turner presided over. This meeting produced a list of grievances bound for the attention of Congress that included the same accusation Sneed had made toward Governor Smith. Charging discrimination in favor of white companies in the distribution of arms, the African American militia officers also agreed that the governor had failed to organize colored military companies and that those that were activated received the old muzzleloaders, while white commands obtained newer breech-loading rifles. Their petition supplemented these charges with an objection to the wearing of Confederate gray uniforms by the state's white militiamen as well as their failure to carry the national colors. Finally, these officers requested that Congress relieve the governor of his military duties and that the national government provide for the organization and discipline of the state's militia forces.[18]

John H. Estill, the editor of the *Savannah Morning News* and acting military aide-de-camp to the governor, dismissed this indictment of Smith and the charges leveled against the state's white militia volunteers. Citing tradition, Estill argued that Georgia's white militiamen not only wore gray but also donned blue or even green uniforms and that each organization previous to the war had carried only its own flag, a practice simply continued upon postwar reorganization. Estill described the accusation that units did not march with the national flag as "absurd." Furthermore, he commended the governor's actions in recognizing numerous African American volunteer companies and reminded Turner that the approval of those organizations was met "with little delay." Estill asserted, in response to the most serious charge that Smith disregarded federal law, that many white companies still carried muzzleloaders or had no firearms at all. But he failed to respond to the charge of favoritism in issuing breechloaders versus muzzleloaders, mentioning instead that those who had applied first to the governor received preference. Perhaps in the thinking of Estill and others, federal law did not specifically prevent the state from issuing arms to those military organizations that took precedence because of seniority. In other words, any company could reestablish its organization even if originally formed, for example, during the days of the American Revolution, and by taking its former name also take its history, thus becoming more senior than those brand-new units (without predecessors) formed at the same time. Nevertheless, the adjutant general records, for the most part, support Estill's argument for the governor's actions recognizing African American volunteer companies. And while there were multiple uniform colors, Turner's petition took exception to the gray being worn, not that it was worn by members of all-white militia units. Still, the discriminatory charge toward the distribution of arms merits further examination.[19]

The Annual Return in Georgia

The first annual reporting for Georgia's African American volunteers began sporadically in 1875. Of the nine reports available, only two companies specified their possession of arms, both of them original organizations that acquired weapons in 1873. Captain Woodhouse, who submitted a return, failed to note whether his company was armed, but it probably was. These reports disclosed that the state provided arms to only 33 percent of the African American volunteer militia; yet if all of the approximately twenty-four companies that existed at the time had submitted a report, and still only three had received arms from the state, then this representation drops to a mere 12 percent. If so, Estill could not have argued successfully against the claims presented by Turner and the officers who attended the colored military convention in 1874.

The next few years exhibited little progress. In 1876, fourteen companies forwarded their annual return to the adjutant general. Of those, only two recorded both the quantity and types of arms in the company, two others only listed the quantity or the type, and the remaining ten stated that they had either received no arms from the state or failed to respond to the question at all. The following year, seven of the eleven African American volunteer infantry companies with an annual return on file did not report having any firearms on hand; of those seven, four noted that the weapons they did use belonged to the men of the company.

Georgia's continued struggle to arm its militia can be further illustrated in a three-page report, recorded on January 10, 1880, entitled "Applications for Arms—not granted—1877, 1878, 1879, 1880." The document detailed the name of the organization, its location, and its branch of service plus the date of the unit's original request for state-provided firearms.[20] Provided to the governor by the state's adjutant general, this report listed thirty-eight volunteer militia organizations, seventeen of which consisted of African Americans. The report portrayed that as late as 1880, Georgia continued to struggle to provide weapons to all its volunteers. This inability to adequately arm its militiamen was not lost on the state legislature, which eventually sanctioned the self-arming of all volunteers. This seems to illustrate the legislators' level of dissatisfaction in the governor's ability, or that of the federal government, to arm the state's troops.

Approved on October 16, 1879, Section XXI of the legislative act to improve Georgia's military forces allowed "any company, of either arm, to which the Governor may be unable to furnish arms and accoutrements, may find its own," if those acquired complied with current US Army regulations and "all companies of the same battalion are armed and accoutred alike."[21] The passage of this law clearly demonstrated the unavailability of appropriate arms for the entire volunteer force. Surprisingly, a further provision of this law mandated ten rounds of ball and six of blank ammunition for every infantry company, regardless of composition—meaning whether white or "colored." Understood as quantities for each man in the company, the act also legislated similar amounts of ammunition supplies for cavalry and artillery commands as well as how much must be maintained if called to the service of the state. While not immediately understood, this "ammunition clause" became clearer in the future.

Within a year, Georgia's adjutant general distributed to various African American militia volunteer companies Springfield breech-loading rifles, often accompanied with full sets of accoutrements, consisting of bayonets, scabbards, cartridge and cap boxes, and rifle slings. Significantly, the adjutant general's ledger also recorded relatively large sums of ball ammunition being shipped to these organizations.

Moreover, this ledger documented other valuable information as well as what many would consider surprising conduct by the state's governor and adjutant general. The Fulton Guards from Atlanta received .45-caliber ammunition in 1885. While the ledger confirmed the issue of seven newer-model Springfield rifles to the Guards, this company must have previously possessed this style of firearm, thus pointing to the use of a model of firearm more common in Georgia's white commands by at least one African American unit. The .45-caliber Springfield breech-loading rifle would later be supplied only briefly to African American infantry companies in 1898.

The ledger not only registered the shipment of arms, accoutrements, and ammunition but also the receipt of the same, providing evidence that Georgia's adjutant general replaced unserviceable equipment for African American military organizations. For example, the Governor's Volunteers, organized in 1879 at Atlanta and under the command of Capt. Jackson McHenry, recorded receiving thirty Springfield .50-caliber breech-loading rifles in 1880, of which they soon returned sixteen to the state.[22] The following year, the company received an additional ten rifles of the same type and caliber. In 1886, the Volunteers received five in exchange for seven unserviceable rifles, and by 1887, it reported forty .50-caliber breech-loading rifles on their annual return to the adjutant general. Others such as the Georgia Cadets, also from Atlanta, were not so fortunate. The Cadets initially received seven .50-caliber Springfield rifles in 1881. Two years later the company returned twenty-one muskets, which they must have previously possessed, but instead of additional Springfield rifles to complement the original seven, the company received twenty-one Enfield .57-caliber muskets. There is no receipt of .45-caliber rifles, but in 1882 and again in 1888, Capt. Moses Henry Bentley received blank cartridges for

TABLE 1. Ammunition issued to Georgia's African American Volunteers, 1880–1889

Year	Company/Battalion	Quantity and Type
1880	Atlanta Washington Guards	200 .58-cal. ball
	Governor's Volunteers	200 .50-cal. ball
1881	Governor's Volunteers	200 .50-cal. ball
	Georgia Cadets	100 .50-cal. ball
	Atlanta Washington Guards	240 .50-cal. ball
	Chatham Light Infantry	400 .50-cal. ball
1883	Rome Star Guards	250 .58-cal. ball
	Governor's Volunteers	100 .50-cal. ball
1884	Governor's Volunteers	200 .50-cal. ball
1885	Augusta Light Infantry	300 .50-cal. ball
	Douglass Infantry	350 .50-cal. ball
	Augusta Cadets	260 .50-cal. ball
	Fulton Guards	200 .45-cal. ball
1886	Governor's Volunteers	360 .50-cal. ball
	Fulton Guards	300 .50-cal. ball
1887	Augusta Cadets	50 .50-cal. ball
	Georgia Infantry	350 .50-cal. ball
	Douglass Infantry	300 .50-cal. ball
	Fulton Guards	100 pistol ball
	Fulton Guards	400 .45-cal. ball
	Governors Volunteers	280 .50-cal. ball
1888	1st Battalion, Savannah	2,260 .50-cal. ball
	Lincoln Guards	400 .58-cal. ball
	Rome Star Guards	300 .58-cal. ball
1889	Lincoln Guards	400 .50-cal. ball
	Georgia Infantry	500 .50-cal. ball
	Fulton Guards	340 .45-cal. Ball

Source: Distribution ledger, VOL1-1701, RG 22, Georgia Archives, Morrow.

this caliber. His annual return of 1887 reflected a mix of breechloaders—possibly both .45- and .50-caliber weapons—but by 1890, while continuing to possess a mixture of rifle types, the Cadets now possessed at least thirty-two breech-loading rifles to only four muzzleloaders.[23]

The lack of arms for the entire state militia prompted the adjutant general to move obsolescent weapons to other companies rather than condemning them. Several instances of this occurred within the African American volunteers. The Douglass Infantry of Augusta reported no arms on hand in 1876 but indicated the use of personal Remington rifles, with no quantity listed, in 1877.[24] On June 25, 1883, 1st Lt. D. Johnston of the Augusta Light Infantry communicated to the adjutant general that his company had received thirty muzzleloaders with accoutrements from the Douglass Infantry.[25] Both the ledger entry from March 29, 1881, and correspondence from Douglass's Capt. Ansel F. Golphin, dated June 9, 1885, requesting ball and blank ammunition recorded that the state had provided the company with thirty-five Springfield breech-loading rifles.[26] Another incident, also occurring at Augusta, involved the Attucks Infantry, but its transfer was very different. Lieutenant Colonel Johnson, commanding the 3rd Battalion, Georgia Volunteers, Colored, appealed for arms since the current weapons in the Attucks Infantry's armory had originally belonged to the Irish Volunteers of that city, a white militia organization. He feared that once reestablishing themselves, the Volunteers would "at any moment . . . call for their arms."[27] This transfer remarkably involved the transfer of arms from a black company to a white one. Granted, the weapons had belonged to the Volunteers previously, but to receive them from a black company signifies the quality of those arms and an accommodation by the Irish to reuse them.

For the year ending May 1, 1887, the number of annual reports from African American military commands surged to twenty. Eliminating the cavalry troop and artillery battery, the majority of the remaining eighteen infantry companies now demonstrated that they had acquired arms from the state, while only four still held their own weapons. These arms are listed as "breech-loaders," ".50 cal. breech-loaders," "muzzle-loaders," "Springfield breech-loading," or simply just ".50 cal." Due to no standardized terminology, the annual reports remain difficult to interpret, but it seems that the majority of these companies continued to drill with .50-caliber Springfield breech-loading rifles, with only two units recording their use of muzzle-loading rifles. The condition of the Union Lincoln Guards of Savannah deserves special attention. Initially failing to acquire arms from the state, this group described their arms in "bad condition" in 1876 and again in 1877, when its return described "the hold [*sic*] of the guns are coundem" and listed them as a mixture of Springfield and Enfield rifles. By 1887, Capt. Morris Joship Cummings noted the company had forty Springfield .50-caliber rifles issued from the state, with 600 rounds of ball and 140 rounds of blank ammunition on hand. The company used all of those blank cartridges and 100 rounds of its ball ammunition prior to June 11, 1888. It remains unclear exactly when the Union Lincoln Guards took delivery of the state-issued arms, but Cummings's report definitively showed that the Georgia government eventually provided weapons to his company.[28]

The records of Georgia's adjutant general from 1890 contain nineteen annual reports out of twenty-two African American military organizations that existed at the time. These appear to be the last such detailed documents that survive.[29] Gone is the private property of the various infantry companies. Those companies were armed uniformly with the .50-caliber Springfield breech-loading rifle, with the exception of the Augusta Light Infantry and the Georgia Cadets, which were equipped with either muzzle-loading rifles or a mixture of breechloaders and muzzleloaders, and the Fulton Guards, which possessed the .45-caliber Springfield rifle. In the years ahead, the quantity and types of arms for each company changed little, other than one unit that still drilled with muzzle-loading rifles in 1897. Georgia officials had progressed from supplying arms to only three African American volunteer infantry companies in 1873 to twenty in 1897. If the state had never intended to use these organizations, then it would have made no sense to have had "about 9,000 rounds of .50-caliber ammunition stored in the basement of the capitol."[30] But the adjutant general soon attempted to provide the 1st Battalion at Savannah and other units with the newer .45-caliber Springfield rifle.

The first attempt by Georgia to supply modern weapons apparently occurred in December 1897, when the acting adjutant general, Oscar J. Brown, informed Lt. Col. John H. Deveaux that he would "turn over . . . 50 Springfield Rifles cal. 45 for Company 'C' . . . also 10 for company 'D' the remaining 35 for company 'D' will be shipped from this office."[31] Two months after the explosion of the USS *Maine* in Havana harbor on February 18, 1898, Brown supplied the African American militiamen with an additional "182 Springfield rifles cal. 45."[32] Immediately upon receipt, Deveaux quickly requisitioned 5,000 rounds of ball and 1,000 rounds of blank ammunition in preparation to defend the city of Savannah or for possible deployment to Cuba.

This "great and very energetic preparation being made for the national defense" also caused Lt. Col. Isaiah Blocker to volunteer his command "in the struggle for the common defense and for the upholding of the honor of the government."[33] While Blocker patriotically offered the services of the 3rd Battalion, Colored, he quickly outlined the immense difficulties its members faced regarding the lack of arms, ammunition, accoutrements, training, and uniforms. He closed his letter asking for requisition forms, so "that I might make requisitions for our needs."[34] Brown politely responded to Blocker's frustrations by stating, "it is well known at this office that little has been done for the Georgia Volunteers, colored, and not much more for the white organizations of the State, owing to the limited means at hand," but the acting adjutant general did commit to ship serviceable .45-caliber rifles and "a certain amount of forty-five caliber ammunition." He asked the lieutenant colonel to complete the enclosed requisitions for other items needed so "articles as can be supplied will be sent."[35] Two days later, Blocker replied that Brown had forgotten to enclose any requisition forms, but that he could "give the necessary information in this communication." Providing specific details for the need for 154 .45-caliber rifles to replace the battalion's current firearms, Blocker also noted that his command consisted of 183 men, with more applying for admission. In no uncertain terms, he forcefully reminded Brown that, "in the event of a conflict with a foreign power, and we are expected to go to the front we shall expect and ask for the latest and best equipment furnished to any volunteer force in any of the states of the union."[36]

The new armament would not be utilized for long. In a twist similar to what befell the Attucks Infantry in 1888, Deveaux received orders in December 1900 to transfer the newer-model Springfield rifles to a white unit, the 1st Regiment, Georgia Volunteers, while receiving back the old-model .50-caliber rifles. Reportedly, the reason for this involved legislative action that removed the Savannah Volunteer Guards from the regiment, converting them into the 1st Battalion of Heavy Artillery, Georgia State Troops.[37] The prevailing Anglo racial thinking of the day, coupled with the legal requirement for companies in the same battalion or regiment to carry the same arms, forced the African American troops to return the arms they had received only two years earlier. Deveaux fired off a telegram to the inspector general asking for a suspension of the order until he had an opportunity to speak with the governor and the adjutant general, all to no avail. Perhaps the only victory Deveaux could claim centered on not having to ship the newer-model rifles until he had received the older models at Savannah.[38]

Georgia government and military officials continued to discriminate against the African American militia volunteers throughout their service. For years, many units went without any support from the state. In what appears as an effort to appease federal authorities, three African American infantry companies received state-issued firearms in 1873, a small fraction of the total known to have existed in Georgia at the time. Obtaining legal authorization to purchase their own arms, which many had already done, the men struggled with the legal mandate to procure the same weapons used by the US Army. Even with the state adjutant general's poor recordkeeping, the surviving documents divulge that most African Americans failed to receive arms from the state during the 1870s. Starting slowly at first, the next decade experienced marked improvement, with all commands bearing arms either issued by the governor or obtained personally. By 1890, all commands finally possessed state-issued firearms. Granted, one company still marched with Civil War–era muzzle-loading rifles, but the majority of units had the older-model .50-caliber Springfield breech-loading rifle; only the Fulton Guards paraded with the same model rifle as the white commands. Even though the state ordered the return of the newer-model Springfield it had supplied to the 1st Battalion only two years earlier, Georgia's inspector general opined that it was his "intention to make this issue of fifty caliber rifles to the colored troops only temporary and to replace them with forty-fives as soon as it could be done."[39]

Georgia's record of providing arms for its African American troops leads to several conclusions. First, the supply of any type of firearms by the state, coupled with ball ammunition, strongly supports the contention that the governor and military officials considered the African American volunteer militia organizations as military units. Second, even though the distribution of arms and equipment to these men was painfully slow throughout the 1870s and 1880s, by 1890, their condition had surprisingly improved. And, while some might argue that no change occurred since the white commands continued to receive preferential treatment, overall the African American infantry, reduced as they were, became better armed toward the end of the century. Lastly, with supplies of ball-ammunition cartridges issued to the various African American infantry companies during the 1880s and 1890s, one must conclude that racial relationships had to have been more complicated than previously thought during those years. After all, in the hands of a properly trained citizen-soldier, a person can be killed as easily with a .50-caliber rifle as they can with one of a smaller caliber. Conversely, events occurring after 1900 illustrate the end of those relationships.

Through the provisions of the Dick Act of 1903, which called for the federal supervision of and better arms, equipment, and training for the National Guard, or organized militia, the US Army detailed inspecting officers to survey the efficiency of each state's military forces. Writing to the adjutant general of Georgia in 1904, the military secretary of the War Department observed that the number of officers and men present at "the recent inspection of the organized militia of the State of Georgia" was "not at all a creditable showing." He further documented that the condition of arms in the black companies ranged from "obsolete, worn-out" to "obsolete, worn-out, worthless," demonstrating an end to the flexibility of relationships between state government officials and African American militia volunteers in Georgia.[40]

"Number of Guns or Carbines the Company Is Responsible For"—Texas

The Texas Volunteer Guard also suffered from poor and incomplete recordkeeping. The annual muster rolls present a range of inconsistencies that failed to reveal the true details of how the state of Texas supplied its African Americans military companies. There appears to have been a standard form provided by the state adjutant general's office as early as 1880, but some companies failed to record anything other than the names of the men enrolled; some simply did not use the form and submitted their rolls on a common piece of paper. More damaging was the exclusion of a company's inventory of military equipment, specifying the type, caliber, and quantity of firearms and ammunition. The Brenham Blues omitted these details from 1881 to 1884, as did San Antonio's Excelsior Guard from 1882 to 1884 and the Gregory Rifles of Bryan in 1880.[41]

Some African American commands, following the receipt of their initial issue of arms, simply did not exist long enough to leave a record trail or had difficulties with administration or leadership, thus, preventing any opportunity to determine the level of state support over any length of time. An example of this can be seen based on the annual reports from the Bryan Light Infantry.

Established in 1887, the company signaled its receipt of thirty-five weapons in 1888 from "Captain McQueen." Capt. D. A. Jefferson recorded the condition of these arms as "very good." The following year, however, the Bryan Light Infantry's new commanding officer, Louis Vanhook, declared that the company had only thirty .45-caliber rifles, which he described as "not good." In 1890, the unit still possessed the same type and quantity of rifles, but Vanhook's annual report noted that these had been received from "Captain Rowler of Jefferson, Texas," and were in "good" condition. Elected captain in 1891, Louis Johnson submitted his first annual muster roll that year in which he stated that the thirty .45-caliber Springfield rifles the company had received from Adj. Gen. Wilburn H. King were "bad." These reports seem to show that at first the Bryan Light Infantry obtained serviceable arms from the Bryan Rifles, the city's white company, but subsequently, Vanhook indicated that he only had thirty rifles when he took command. This situation remains unclear, as the arms issued to Captain Jefferson may have been returned, with Vanhook having received a different set of rifles, or it might reflect that perhaps the company could have simply obtained a better set of weapons from another unit. Based on Vanhook's changing description of their condition, it is quite possible that the white militia company at Jefferson provided the weapons. Later, Captain Johnson, instead of reporting that he had received the company's weapons from Captain Vanhook, which one would expect, described that he had received the arms from the adjutant general—and, of course, the condition of those weapons had changed again. With three different captains and possibly as many different sets of criteria in which to judge the company's arms, such inconsistent reports, at least for this company, make it problematic to determine if the state of Texas responded to their requests or not.[42]

The annual reporting of the Austin City Rifles illustrated a different problem. Led by Capt. Hector Johnson for five years, this company appeared to have fared much better than many of its counterparts. Johnson's command had been issued forty rifles in 1880 by Adj. Gen. John B. Jones that were reported to be in "good condition."[43] Yet Johnson's inability to read or write, coupled with the same *exact* wording describing his company's arms and equipment on all five annual reports, even though from different years, produces some skepticism as to their accuracy.[44]

Some consistency in the responses of the annual muster roll eventually occurred by the late 1880s, but while the questions were standardized, each commanding officer chose to answer the questions in his own way, often omitting physical descriptions of the men and of their nativity, date of enlistment, or even enlisted rank. The muster roll form changed again around 1887, calling for responses to additional questions. These questions included the amount of individual uniform items, such as trousers, helmets, and even chevrons; rifle repair tools; regulation books; and most importantly, the amount of cartridges the company had on hand and the quantity expended during the year. Yet this lackadaisical reporting sometimes continued, as illustrated by the Jim Blaine Rifles of Dallas in 1889, a unit that failed to list anything other than its members' names.[45] Still, even with the problems that arose with such recordkeeping, the years from approximately 1887 through 1898 provided the best glimpse into the provisioning of African American volunteer militia companies by the adjutant general of Texas.

While some companies reported obtaining acceptable arms, others received the oldest rifles in the state inventory and in a condition that often provoked the disgust of the unit's commanding officer. The Hubbard Rifles, located at Waco and commanded by Henry Kelly, reported in 1883 that it had "three guns short of ramrods, one broken," indicating that the company's sixty Remington rifles were most likely Civil War–era muzzleloaders.[46] In Galveston, Capt. Mitt Brantley, commanding the Lincoln Guards, relayed to Adjutant General King in 1886 that his company's "guns are so old and becoming out of order so fast that I would [be] afraid to advance upon an enemy."[47] This same complaint was echoed by Capt. John Sessums of Houston's Davis Rifles and Capt. William Brown of the Cochran Blues of Dallas. Sessums, who later commanded one section of the Sheridan Guards in the city, not only served as the drummer for the Houston Light Guard, a white company in the city, but also worked in its armory as a janitor. He described the Davis Rifles' sixteen weapons—thirty-six men were on the unit's roll—as "very poor" in 1881. Brown characterized his "guns" as "not fit for service" in 1884.[48]

Brantley, again expressed his frustration in 1887, when he stated, "if the company were called on by special civil service it would be unnecessary to go depending upon the guns for they would be of little service."[49] But two years later, the acting inspector general of the Texas Volunteer Guard, Capt. Lamartine P. Sieker, who had been ordered to inspect individual militia companies, both white and black, reported to Adjutant General King that Brantley's Lincoln Guards "have 35 guns in good, clean serviceable condition."[50] The 1886 and 1887 muster rolls disclosed that Brantley had received forty-one "old guns" from the Washington Guards, one of Galveston's white volunteer militia companies, and had listed them as .58-caliber weapons—possible Civil War–era muzzleloaders. After his consecutive complaints, Brantley, on his rolls for 1888, then stated that the company had thirty-seven .50-caliber rifles sent from the "Governor of the State, L. S. Ross."[51] One year later, the Lincoln Guards possessed thirty-five .45-caliber rifles, which Brantley recorded as received from the "State Govt[.]" and in "good order," as supported by Sieker's inspection findings. Unfortunately for the Guards, these rifles may have been the last issued to the company. Beginning in 1893, Capt. Louis Taylor, then commanding the unit, continually documented the condition of the arms as "old and broken."[52] Even Capt. Tony A. Smith of Galveston's newly christened Hawley Guards in 1904 stated, "this command is sadly in need of uniforms and new ordnance as this has been condemned repeatedly and is old and obsolete."[53]

The commanding officers of the Lincoln Guards chose to submit ordnance reports versus annotating the inventory and use of ammunition on their annual muster. The first to do so, Captain Brantley, reported the use of 250 rifle ball cartridges for target practice between October 1, 1888, and September 30, 1889. A year later, Capt. George W. Wilson reported 300 cartridges expended for drill and target practice, recording 580 cartridges still on hand in 1890. When Taylor took charge of the company, he noted on his annual muster in 1891 that the guardsmen had used 35 rounds during the year, with an additional 800 cartridges on hand.[54] With Taylor's inventory of 800 cartridges on hand measured against Wilson's 580 the year before, the adjutant general of Texas was clearly replenishing ammunition for the use of this African American volunteer militia company.

While uncertainty may surround the lack of detailed accounting of the Bryan Light Infantry and the Austin City Rifles, there can be no doubt that after Captain Brantley formally protested the improper condition of his company's arms, he received—not once, but *twice*—better weapons from the state. Whether this set of rifles remained with the Galveston companies or not, by the 1890s, the state seems to have no longer responded to requests for serviceable weapons. Those arms existing in the hands of Galveston's black citizen-soldiers, once initially maintained, had deteriorated by that time.[55]

After the dissolution of the City Rifles, Austin's black community organized a new company, the Capital Guards in 1890. Militiamen elected James P. Bratton as its first commanding officer. Bratton obtained thirty Springfield .45-caliber rifles for his company and communicated that twenty were in "good condition," but the other ten remained in "poor order." He also recorded that his unit possessed 1,000 rounds of ball ammunition. By the end of 1892, the company had expended 300 rounds of that ammunition, and an inspection in September by Lt. Col. John Dowell, the acting inspector general for the Texas Volunteer Guard, indicated that the company's .45-caliber Springfield rifles were a mixed set of 1873, 1878, and 1884 models.[56] The unit gained an additional ten rifles in 1893, but Bratton stated that eight of these were not in good condition. The Guards' complement had decreased to thirty once again in 1894, when Joseph James took command, but its ammunition supply had been increased to 900 rounds of ball cartridges. Serving only a year, James was succeeded by Julius A. Parker. During Parker's five years in command, the Guards maintained between thirty and thirty-five firearms in good condition and kept 500 rounds of ammunition on hand, receiving additional cartridges sometime in 1897–98; the company used 205, leaving 595 on hand. The last rolls for the Capital Guards, led next by Capt. Charles Watrous, declared that the company had thirty-three "good" rifles out of thirty-eight, the other five classified as "condemned."[57]

The Capital Guards, organized much later than many of the other African American volunteer militia companies, received serviceable firearms from the state. For the most part, the commanding officers reported some minor issues with missing parts or a broken stock, but did not continually request new rifles, which was not the case of the Lincoln Guards at Galveston. Perhaps the most significant revelation from the annual reports of these two companies was the amount of ammunition supplied, replenished and used by the companies in these cities.

Like other companies, the Excelsior Guard of San Antonio experienced erratic provisioning of arms and ammunition. The most detailed and useful reporting began in 1886, when Capt. Simon Turner confirmed that the company's thirty-six .45-caliber rifles were "passing but nothing to praise" and further documented "the guns are useable but are very old."[58] Turner was well qualified to judge the condition of the weapons since he had served ten years in the 10th US Cavalry Regiment and saw action against the Plains Indians in 1874–75.[59] The following year, he reported the company had received thirty rifles from "Captain Bitters" of Orange, Texas, although he must not have been too happy with the shipment, characterizing the weapons as "fair."[60] When Captain Sieker traveled to San Antonio to inspect the Excelsior Guard that same year, the acting inspector general "found the arms of this company in fair condition considering the age of their guns." After reading the report, Adjutant General King responded with a handwritten note ordering Sieker to "call in old guns and send 25 to 30 second hand cal. 45. & accoutrements."[61] Accompanying the "good" set of rifles, King also sent 600 rounds of ammunition, which the company promptly put to use.

Like their fellow militia organizations in Galveston and Austin, the Excelsior Guard expended their ammunition. With a total of 600 rounds on hand in 1888, the Guards fired 300 ball cartridges between October 1, 1889,

Excelsior Guard, circa 1900. From Berg-Sobré, *San Antonio on Parade,, 58.*

and September 30, 1890, for drills, funerals, and salutes.[62] The San Antonio company actually may have used more since their 1889 annual report to the state adjutant general documented a balance of 240 cartridges on hand, which if accurate would mean that the company received additional ammunition by the following year, since it afterward recorded a balance of 350 cartridges on hand. Reduced to only 100 by 1894, the following year the Guards now possessed 500 ball and 200 blank cartridges; by 1897 the unit could register only a total of 50 rounds available for its use.[63] Capt. Robert George Ellis pleaded with Adj. Gen. Woodford H. Mabry for more ammunition, requesting 1,000 rounds on October 5, 1897, and again on November 13, 1897. Ellis informed Mabry that he hoped "such an emergency might not arise, yet if the unforeseen should happen, and my Company be called out, I would not be in condition to serve the state, except with empty guns." Mabry responded four days later that he had "no ammunition on hand."[64] After the company expended its last 50 rounds in 1898, no further records exist as to the amount of ammunition in its armory.[65]

During the annual encampment of African American troops in 1891, Texas Volunteer Guard inspector general Col. R. H. Bruce stated he could not comment positively on the condition of arms and equipment but remarked, "never in my life have I seen a better and more thoroughly policed camp in every detail."[66] He asserted that the weapons deficiencies had been "caused of course by the lack of attention by the men to their arms, some guns we would inspect would be full of dust and dirt."[67] Bruce failed to mention that US Army captain Richard I. Eskridge, assigned as inspecting officer for the encampment, observed and wrote that the arms were "badly out of repair" and that "no provision made by the State for repairs."[68] The inspection reports from this encampment also indicated that the Excelsior Guard drilled with .45-caliber Springfield Model 1878 rifles. The other companies present at the camp of instruction handled the Model 1873, the Capital Guards, as mentioned previously, marching with both models as well as the Model 1884. It appears, though, that the Excelsior Guard might have eventually received some newer Model 1884s. In 1896, the company's captain at the time, Eugene Ogden Bowles, along with the unit's former commanding officer John F. Van Duzor and two other black citizens of San Antonio, retired US Army sergeant John H. Martin and Prof. Ed Thomas, petitioned Mabry to exchange twelve of their Model 1878s for the Model 1884 "as *two different patterns* of arms in one command makes a marked contrast." This confirms that sometime between 1893 and 1896, the guardsmen must have obtained some of the newer models.[69] As late as 1899, Captain Ellis specified that the Excelsior Guard's thirty-three rifles were in good condition.[70]

While not suggesting that any of these African American companies ever acquired equipment equal in condition to what their white counterparts used, these accounts illustrated that the Texas governor or adjutant general responded and at least attempted to equip some of the black militia companies with serviceable weapons. These steps strongly support the contention that the state viewed these African American volunteers as military units.

The Annual Reports of the Virginia Adjutant General

Virginia's adjutant generals inspected the state's military organizations in order to submit an annual report to the governor. These provided detailed information on the number of active volunteers, their locations, the types and quantity of arms each possessed, and any service these organizations had rendered to the state. The published reports also displayed to the public and to members of the legislature how Virginia equipped its African American volunteer militia companies, allowing comparisons with the experiences of such organizations in other states.

When Virginia adjutant general Joseph Lane Stern compiled and published his roster of the state's commissioned volunteer officers, he included a discussion of the availability of ordnance to the state "under an old ante-war statute that was fortunately held not to have been suspended by the war"—the provisions of the US Militia Law of 1808. The ordnance stores, Stern wrote, "were obsolete, the rifles being of an old pattern, of about sixty caliber or more; the cannon, Napoleons, six-pounder brass guns, and three-inch rifles, all muzzle-loaders."[71] With these antiquated arms, Virginia set about to rebuild its state military organizations, with each company, or individual member, bearing all other expenses, including uniforms and the purchase or rental of an appropriate facility to house the unit's equipment and arms. For cavalry and artillery units, these expenses became quite a burden. Of course, old equipment and limited finances were not the only hindrance that the state's fledgling military endured. Stern further communicated that Virginia did not require these early military organizations to report their manpower, equipment, and so on to the state, a situation that lasted for thirteen years. After the reorganization of Virginia's military forces in 1871, the first annual report, submitted by Adjutant General Richardson, occurred two years later and registered the existence of four military organizations "composed of men of color, also uniformed and armed."[72] While Richardson failed to document any specific information regarding the type of arms in the possession of these African American companies, the adjutant general declared that by the governor's "order the Springfield rifle muskets, which had been issued to the volunteers prior to this present year, have been nearly all called in and replaced by the breech-loading muskets."[73]

Adj. Gen. James McDonald's 1876 report delineated many more details about the state's growing African American military contingent. Even though he failed to make known how three of the nine companies were equipped, McDonald recorded that the state issued 220 breechloaders for the 231 men of the 1st Battalion of Colored Infantry; 60 breechloaders for the 67 men of Capt. J. H. Hill's company at Petersburg; and 50 muskets for the 80 men of the Langston Guard at Norfolk. Thus, most of Virginia's black militiamen carried weapons issued by the state, an important indication of their official status.[74]

The federal government continued to supply the states, including Virginia, with "arms, ordnance stores and munitions of war" in the years that followed, providing additional specifications as to the types of rifles available for issue. In September 1877, the adjutant general received "125 Springfield breech-loading rifle muskets, model 1868, caliber .50," and by July 1879, McDonald may have obtained Virginia's first set of .45-caliber model "non-cadet rifles." From September 1876 to November 1879, eight African American volunteer infantry companies, while not given the newer-model Springfields, took delivery of both breech-loading rifles and older muzzle-loading models. Of the seventeen white militia companies that accepted arms during this same period, only the Richmond Light Infantry Blues obtained the Springfield breech-loading .45-caliber rifle. Surprisingly, two white military organizations were actually issued muzzle-loading muskets, the Lynchburg Guard and the Norfolk Light Artillery Blues, whose men carried them for infantry drills.[75]

On September 17, 1880, one of Richmond's African American militia units, the State Guard, under the command of Capt. Robert Austin Paul, exchanged their muzzle-loading muskets for breech-loading rifles. Paul, who had used his influence as the messenger of the Virginia State House to organize his company, most likely utilized his relationships in obtaining these newer rifles.[76] His success remained a small consolation for the state's African American volunteers, who only reported nine out of a total nineteen volunteer militia organizations under arms with the Springfield breechloader. The disparity between the white and black commands had grown exceedingly wide by 1880. Issued to twelve companies of white troops, the newer .45-caliber Springfield became the standard shoulder weapon of the majority of these commands, but they, too, still had eleven organizations carrying the .50-caliber breech-loading rifle. Like their African American counterparts who still had two companies without arms, the white contingent of the Virginia Volunteers had two also in the same condition.[77]

Virginia's annual reports not only included the issue of arms to individual volunteer companies but also clearly revealed the discrepancy in the types of firearms issued to the commonwealth's white and "colored" troops. Still, while this illustrates the discrimination of the day, it further illuminates some painfully slow progress made by African American militia companies as well.

By 1884, the inspector general's report of the readiness of the volunteers for war became a part of the annual review by the state's adjutant general. That year also witnessed the first legislative act to provide some financial support to Virginia's volunteers. Enacted on March 17, 1884, this new law dedicated 0.5 percent of all state income, exempting the school fund, to provide "for the relief and behoof of the soldiers of the State." The military fund doled out monies to all volunteer militia organizations based upon the number of men and officers of each company present at the annual inspection, regardless of skin color.[78]

The adjutant general's report for 1885, which also covered 1884, unfortunately reflected that African American volunteers remained the only state troops still drilling and marching with muzzle-loading arms. The condition of these muskets in 1884 ranged from "not well taken care of" by the Hannibal Guard of Norfolk to the glowing comments of "have been most carefully preserved, and are in beautiful condition, reflecting great credit upon officers and men" of Norfolk's other African American company, the National Guard.[79] This was indeed extraordinary praise from Lieutenant Colonel Stern, then assistant inspector general, who stated in this same report, "the muzzle loaders are practically worthless." Taking steps to eliminate the militia's supply of muzzleloaders, Stern called in all such arms, had them replaced with the .50-caliber Springfield, and declared afterward, "the infantry is sufficiently armed for all practical purposes." As a result, by 1886, no African American volunteer militia company retained the old Civil War–era muzzle-loading muskets. And with two of these organizations marching with .45-caliber Springfield rifles, the black militia of Virginia was now better armed than at any time previously in their history.[80]

The Military Advisory Board enacted accountability measures in 1886. These included the elimination of funding for companies found in noncompliance of regulations, defined as the failure to maintain the minimum number of enlisted and officers as required by law, or if the officers had not successfully completed their examination and obtained their commission, or if said officers did not uniform themselves appropriately under the guidelines set by the Adjutant General's Office. Additionally, fines could be administered if a company's books, papers, or state property had been deemed in less than good order. Some might contend these new accountability regulations were meant to deter African Americans from serving in the state volunteers. Over the years, however, the trend fails to support such an argument. The companies regularly turning out between 53.1 and 71.3 percent of their numerical strength when the regulation was first enacted, those present at inspection quickly increased to 84.6 percent in 1894 and 90.5 percent in 1896. African American volunteers eagerly took advantage of the available funding to improve their organizations.[81]

When contrasted with the actions of Georgia and Texas military officials, one glaring omission remains quite obvious within the pages of Virginia's adjutant general reports—the distribution of ammunition. While sporadically

recorded through the years, the supply of ball or blank cartridges to Virginia's
military organizations appeared to have hinged on some perceived emergency. The Petersburg Guard received 300 blank cartridges in 1887, but the
first recorded issue of ball cartridges to African American militia companies
occurred the following year, when Norfolk's National Guard and Langston
Guard received 600 and 300 rounds, respectively. Later that year, Richmond's
Carney Guard took delivery of 1,000 ball cartridges, and the Attucks Guard
finally obtained .45-caliber Springfield rifles along with 1,000 ball and 100
blank cartridges.[82]

The Carney Guard eventually received .45-caliber Springfield rifles in 1894,
the same year Stern suggested that since it was "not desirable to purchase new
rifles at this time, all those not fit for service should be sent to the Government
Arsenal and remilled." He recommended calling in the thirty-three rifles of the
Flipper Guard and twenty of the State Guard as well as those in the possession
of the *white* companies located at "Harrisonburg, Salem, Culpeper, a part at
Alexandria, a part at Charlottesville, [and] all in company 'B,' Third Battalion,
Portsmouth."[83]

The annual report from Virginia's adjutant general in 1896 chronicled only
eight African American infantry companies still in existence, consisting of
thirty-eight officers and 468 men. This small contingent's attendance at inspections exceeded their white counterparts by seven percentage points, demonstrating these citizen-soldiers' continued commitment to their military duty.
The 1896 accounting also contained a report by US Army quartermaster Capt.
John T. Knight, on temporary assignment to inspect volunteers in the state.
Knight's comments, "Statement of the Condition of Virginia Volunteers in
1896," disclosed thirty-eight categories of information concerning the Virginia
Volunteers as requested by the secretary of war. Especially important were
the categories of "armament," "ammunition," and "number, organization and
stations of the brigades, regiments, battalions and separate companies." Even
though at reduced strength, the African American contingent still maintained
two battalions, the 1st, located at Richmond with three companies, and the
2nd, headquartered at Petersburg, with three local companies and two housed
at Norfolk. These battalions remained well equipped with ammunition, with
the 1st possessing 600 ball cartridges per company, while the 2nd held 1,000
per company. At this time, Virginia maintained almost equal amounts of .45-
and .50-caliber ammunition in its arsenals. Another substantive feature of
the report divulged that while some progress had been made, only 36 percent

of the enlisted African American men carried the newer .45-caliber rifle, a marked contrast to their white counterparts.[84]

One year prior to the commencement of hostilities with Spain in 1898, the adjutant general of the United States recorded that the "national appropriations [for the state of Virginia] are used primarily for quartermaster stores, since the Virginia Volunteers are already armed with the Springfield .45 caliber rifle." This statement confirmed that after the initial formation of African American volunteer militia companies twenty-six years earlier, the state had finally armed all of its citizen-soldiers with the same service rifle. As the crisis over Cuba intensified during 1897, Virginia's black militiamen trained for war with this weapon. But within two years, they would not shoulder firearms again as guardsmen for over fifty years.[85]

Conclusion

For many years after the Civil War, the state governments of Georgia, Texas, and Virginia surprisingly furnished their African American volunteer military organizations with arms and equipment during a period of racial, economic, and political strife. Granted, all three of these states continued to struggle to provide adequate ordnance stores for all of their active militia commands regardless of skin color, but they did in fact provide weapons and ammunition for most of their African American volunteers. Segregated first by custom and then by law, these men often received their arms after months of repeated requests. The quality and quantity of those weapons were never quite enough, and seldom did the type and condition of the equipment match what the states provided to their white counterparts.

Georgia appeared to have supplied similar arms to its black militiamen only briefly and to have done so only with the impending threat of war in 1898. Virginia arguably served its African American troops better than either Georgia or Texas since the commonwealth eventually armed its entire military force with, at a minimum, the same-caliber rifle; still, the evidence fails to document the exact model issued to its black troops. And the treatment of African American volunteers in Texas looks to have fallen somewhere in between that of Georgia and Virginia since it, too, gradually provided the newer rifle over time.

From the 1870s to the 1900s (or 1899 in Virginia), African American citizen-soldiers successfully demonstrated their ability to conduct military-type activities within the various cities and communities across these states. Not only did the men appear in public wearing a military uniform and under arms, but they also fired their weapons in salutes, during prize drill competitions, and at target practice. Repeatedly, state officials replaced unserviceable rifles and not only responded to but also filled multiple requests to replenish both blank and ball ammunition.

Even within the discriminatory atmosphere that prevailed in the late nineteenth and early twentieth century South, all of these actions support several conclusions. First, the African American volunteer militia companies were clearly recognized and functioned as official military units in each state's military organization. Second, their participation within the military sphere of society, segregated as it was, remained generally accepted by members of the surrounding community, including elite state and city leaders, and more specifically governors, adjutant generals, mayors, prominent businessmen, and state legislators, who voted to fund the black volunteer militia organizations. Lastly, the actions of state government and military officials in providing military arms, ammunition, and equipment represented a level of accommodation that seemed to have existed throughout the last three decades of the nineteenth century, even as each state sought to reduce its total number of African American militia companies. Nevertheless, the volunteers themselves and each state's leaders considered these organizations as military units, based on their methods of preparation and their participation in activities related to the defense of their states.

5

"An Efficient and Reliable Defender"

Utilizing and Training the Black State Volunteers

WITH THE REORGANIZATION of the active militia in the southern states beginning in the early 1870s, their traditional role as defenders of "home and hearth" soon expanded to encompass constabulary duties, including the guarding of prisoners and the suppression of labor disputes or social unrest. These new responsibilities often pitted the predominately white militia troops against an ethnically diverse group of laborers, rioters, or prisoners, many of whom were African Americans. Surprisingly, other African Americans, as members of the state's volunteer militia force, at times also participated in these policing duties.

These black militiamen had received arms, ammunition, equipment, and in some instances uniforms from the state governments of Georgia, Texas, and Virginia. Following the successful examination of their qualifications, their officers received a commission from their respective governor. And, while the standard of training for these early state military volunteers was uneven, recommendations emphasizing the importance of annual inspections and field training soon echoed through the reports of the respective state military boards, which adopted some, but not all, of these improvements. The positive changes implemented did affect, at times, the African American militia companies.

The experiences and treatment of African American volunteer militia units participating in military- or constabulary-type activities in Georgia, Texas, and Virginia support the argument that they were not mere social clubs but bona fide military organizations. These activities incorporated uses of uniformed militia in the traditional roles of law enforcement, such as guarding prisoners; providing manpower for emergency situations; and quelling labor disturbances. When circumstances led governors or lesser state officials to activate African American citizen-soldiers for civic duties, their reported performance generated publicity. Additionally, by the 1890s, black militia groups commenced state field-training exercises. Government officials responded to the needs of the African American volunteers under their command beyond the confines of regular company drills or a prize competition.

Various unappreciated examples clearly illustrated that government and military officials from these three southern states considered the black militia as military organizations due to how they utilized and trained them. While views of the African American militia changed and were not consistent across geographical boundaries, both within each state and beyond the three, the treatment of black volunteers from the 1870s to 1906 exposed the complexity, geographical differences, and uncertainty of defining racial attitudes or levels of accommodation over time. Lastly, the actions of the African American military leadership illustrated that these men not only understood their duties as members of the uniformed militia but also were determined to participate in the activities of the state's military forces and broaden their place in local and national society.

"To Enforce the Law and Preserve the Peace": Georgia

Savannah's mayor, John Screven, had initially proposed to use the local black militia in 1872 by placing them at the entrances of the city for "the duty of arresting and disarming those of their own color" whom he thought intended to violently disrupt the election process.[1] While some might argue that his decision appeared to have had more to do with attempting to learn the identities of African American militiamen who refused to remain loyal to local and state authorities, Screven's comments signaled his willingness to deploy such forces for riot duty.

Later, the administration of Savannah mayor John Wheaton utilized African American militia volunteers for crowd control and as a military escort for former president Ulysses S. Grant during his visit to the city in January 1880. The 1st Battalion, Colored Infantry, parading in honor of the anniversary of the Emancipation Proclamation, marched to the train depot following their festivities in anticipation of providing an escort for Grant. Alderman Louis H. Montmollin requested a detail from the companies "to keep the platform clear, as there was a great rush of excited colored people *and some whites* as the train rolled into the yard."[2]

As the militia troops quickly formed, Wheaton and Grant boarded a waiting carriage. Led by the city's black cavalrymen, the Savannah Hussars, the "handsome equipage" containing the two dignitaries proceeded to Grant's accommodations at the Screven House. Upon their arrival, the Hussars formed in line at the front of the hotel, while the African American infantry commands gathered in formation on St. Julian Street. Grant, alighting from the carriage, received a loud cheer from the Hussars and from some in the large crowd that had gathered to see the former president.[3]

During this period, it would be highly unlikely or virtually impossible to comprehend that these forces would be employed against anyone *except* other African Americans. Even this scenario, however, seemed to divulge some level of expectation that these black troops would do their duty against any of their fellow citizens. This set up the prospect of sending black militia against riotous African American residents in Savannah.

Around noon on September 19, 1881, while loading the steamship *Gate City,* African American stevedores struck for higher wages. An hour later, those who had been working on the *Dessong* joined the strike. According to the account published in the *Atlanta Constitution,* these laborers had gathered along River Street and, by blocking the bridge over the Ogeechee Canal, successfully halted all business leading to the wharf of the Ocean Steamship Company. When a mounted white policeman arrived, he was met by the crowd and, in his efforts to disperse them, was shot and killed. Mayor Wheaton immediately telegraphed Governor Colquitt with the message, "labor riot imminent here." Referring to the "turbulent negroes," he requested permission to call up the city's militia if the civil authorities could not put "down this riot, which should be crushed out in its inception." Colquitt, apparently seeking a peaceful solution, directed the mayor to "exhaust all civil powers" and to keep him informed of the situation.[4]

The following day, the leaders of the longshoremen, during an interview with a newspaper correspondent, stated that the earlier violence was "brought on by the police." Since their demands for higher wages, driven by the increased costs of provisions, had been ignored, the dockworkers had seen no other alternative to the strike. At the time, about fifty men were involved in the initial walkout, but additional workers, white men from the Georgia Central Railroad's cotton yards and warehouses, soon joined their effort. This action prompted business leaders to send for replacement workers from Macon and other areas across Georgia, which, in turn, prompted laborers from the Savannah, Florida, and Western Railroad to walk off the job. Governor Colquitt, fearing the potential of further violence with this much-larger group of strikers, telegraphed Captain Screven, Savannah's former mayor and commander of the Savannah Volunteer Guards, "to assemble his battalion in their armory."[5]

In anticipation of the replacement workers arriving on September 22, the governor issued Special Order No. 85. Addressed to Lt. Col. John Holcombe Estill, his aide-de-camp, it informed him of Colquitt's orders to Screven and reminded him of the governor's limited power: "I have no authority or purpose to call out [the] military unless due enforcement of process of the courts is resisted and civil authority is powerless to execute the law or in case of insurrection when the General Assembly cannot act promptly."[6] Ten minutes following this telegraph, Colquitt issued Special Order No. 86. Again addressed to Estill, it now prompted the lieutenant colonel to "immediately communicate . . . to Lt. Col. Woodhouse," commanding the 1st Battalion, Colored, the situation and the extent of Colquitt's authority as the state's chief executive. While he hoped the necessity of calling the militia would not arise, the governor, through Estill, reinforced with Woodhouse, "if it should [occur] I shall confidently expect your command to respond to my orders designed to enforce the law and preserve the peace."[7] The *Atlanta Constitution* reported the receipt of this order, noting, "Colonel Woodhouse, colored, has placed his military companies at the command of the mayor."[8]

Occurring almost simultaneously with the arrival of the telegrams, the strikers again blocked the canal bridge and prevented drays from crossing. Savannah police and reserve officers, some mounted on horses, arrived and ordered the workers to disperse. They refused. Thus, when the mounted police attempted to force the men to open the bridge, they met a hailstorm of stones and brickbats. This escalation prompted the police to fire upon the crowd with pistols and muskets, resulting in casualties estimated from one to eight killed, with others wounded and fleeing. Once armed conflict had occurred, the Georgia General Assembly authorized the governor to send military force, if necessary, to quell the violence. Colquitt issued Special Order No. 87, which, while fully recognizing the right of men to refuse to work, also stated that "men willing to work should be protected from any violent interference." The governor, exhibiting the same coolness from the outset of the crisis, again reminded area commanders that "only where the peace of the community is threatened and individual safety endangered and the civil authority is powerless to check disorder, restore quiet, and save life, is the military to be used."[9]

Three men stepped forward to calm the crisis—Lieutenant Colonel Woodhouse, Maj. John H. Deveaux, and Capt. Louis M. Toomer—averting the need to call out the militia. These "three intelligent colored citizens who are well known and respected throughout the state" met with the longshoremen, advising them to return to work and to form a committee to present their demands through mediation.[10] Three commissioned officers of the city's African American militia volunteers had extinguished the crisis. Although Woodhouse did not order his troops into the streets, the governor of Georgia had clearly demonstrated his acceptance of them as a military organization by indicating his willingness to deploy the 1st Battalion, Georgia Volunteers, Colored, if needed.[11]

Just months before the crisis in Savannah, events had transpired in Augusta involving the murder of a white man by an African American. Anderson Jones, a black laborer working as a wood sawyer for the Georgia Central Railroad, received his second guilty verdict in Richmond County Superior Court for the December 15, 1879, murder of John G. Harralson at McBean, Georgia. According to Jones, he did not initially intend to kill Harralson, but newspaper accounts vary. One story involved him in a robbery and murder. Another implied that Jones had challenged the storekeeper for what he believed was an excessive charge. Jones paid the debt only after Harralson had set his dog upon him, resulting in Jones striking him in the head repeatedly with an axe. The news of Jones's execution echoed across the country, reaching north to Minnesota, west to Kansas and Texas, and to the east, even becoming front-page news for Baltimore's German-language *Der Deutsche Correspondent*. What all of these papers and others beyond Augusta missed was the storyline about the joint deployment of white and African American militiamen in a southern city to stand guard at the condemned black man's execution.[12]

On the morning of January 20, 1882, Richmond County sheriff Wilberforce Daniel requisitioned four enlisted men and one noncommissioned officer from the city's volunteer military companies, including the African American units. While some of these "colored" companies asked to be excused, this was not due to any feelings of wrongdoing, perceived or justified, in the sentencing of Anderson Jones to death. Their concern centered on their inability to properly equip themselves for the duty required of them. According to the *Augusta Chronicle,* "the requisition upon the colored companies was made at the suggestion of Judge Snead."[13]

As the clock struck the noon hour, parties of five militia volunteers from each of Augusta's three white companies—the Richmond Hussars, the Clinch Rifles, and the Clarke Light Infantry—together with those from the black companies—the Douglass Infantry, the Colquitt Zouaves, and the Georgia Infantry—reported for duty at the jail. The sheriff assigned these thirty men to positions surrounding the gallows located in the jail yard, while policemen occupied the streets outside. Approximately thirty minutes later, about one hundred members of the community, having received invitations to the execution from the sheriff and including ministers and one of Jones's attorneys, filed past the militiamen into the yard. Jones was brought out and promptly hanged at one o'clock.

Unfortunately, contemporary reports failed to identify the fifteen African American volunteers who stood at attention around the gallows in Augusta. There are no photographs or descriptions of where these men stood in relation to the equal number of white volunteers present. Nor did Snead or Daniel, both former Confederate officers, provide any insight into the motivations of their actions to request these men. The judge and sheriff clearly avoided any social controversy that may have arisen by having an African American commissioned officer present, which would have required the white enlisted men to recognize his authority, yet they did not invite any officers from the white commands. It is highly unlikely this decision was made haphazardly, as the requisition was for equal numbers of men of equal rank, apart from the noncommissioned officer who commanded each section. Snead and Daniel may have wished to have the city's and county's black citizens show support for the execution by inviting them, wanted to gain some sort of influence in that section of the community, or perhaps sought something more sinister, such as using these black volunteers to carry a message highlighting the repercussions of murdering a white man in the city or county. This was not only an obvious attempt to maintain the social order of the day but also plainly illustrates the complexity of race relations at the time. One can only speculate on the reason, or reasons, for utilizing the African American militia for this duty, but arguably most of the above-stated motivations could have been accomplished simply through an invitation to the leaders of Augusta's black community. And it is possible that these local leaders were indeed in attendance among the one hundred witnesses assembled in the jail yard that day. Whatever the background story surrounding the African American militiamen's presence, the fact remains that the invitation was extended to them as recognized members of a military organization and accepted. Snead's actions, through Daniel's implementation, placed these men on apparently equal footing as soldiers with their white counterparts.

Requisitioning troops for duty usually occurred through written orders delivered by hand to the commanding officer. Even if the governor issued such an order, usually arriving by telegraph, it would have to be hand delivered. This painfully slow process to activate the uniformed militia during an emergency became clearly evident at Savannah on April 7, 1889. Suffering its worst fire since 1820 on that day, only the city's wide streets and several parks kept the damage from exceeding the $1.5 million estimate. With this epic loss of property, Mayor John Schwarz decided to sound eleven strokes of the fire alarm, a bell known locally as "Big Duke," as the signal for all military companies to report to their armories for duty. The legal authority for his decision had been sanctioned in the general assembly's act of 1885 seeking "to provide for the better organization, government and discipline of the volunteer troops of this state." The law allowed any civil authority, identified in the statute and under certain conditions, to call out the militia "to enforce the laws and preserve the peace."[14]

Obviously centered on military or constabulary duties, Mayor Schwarz viewed the law as also giving him the legal authority to utilize the militia during "any disastrous conflagration" to "do duty guarding property, and facilitating the work of the firemen." His decision, communicated to the white companies and possibly made in consultation with them, also was relayed to the commanding officers of the city's African American volunteers—Major Deveaux, commanding the 1st Battalion; Capt. John Simmons of the Georgia Artillery; and Capt. Franklin Jones of the Savannah Hussars—one week later. At this meeting, the mayor explained that he did not wish to take the police "from their legitimate duty, leaving a large part of the city unprotected." He

"desired the full co-operation of the colored military in the matter, and requested that when the signal is given, . . . they will assemble promptly at their
armories ready for duty and await orders."[15]

Mayor Schwarz, motivated by the poor response to a destructive fire
months previous, simply may have wanted to utilize the black militiamen as
firemen if such a calamity struck again; after all, two of their units had previously served as axe companies for the city's fire department. But if this was his
intent, then he could have simply ordered the African American militiamen
to respond to all fire alarms, not just the military alarm, which he could have
reserved for only the white commands. Perhaps Schwarz thought that he
could assign the African American companies for emergencies in the black
community, knowing the role Deveaux and others had played in arbitrating
the earlier labor strikes. Whatever the circumstances, the black militia of Savannah were requested to respond to the military signal activating all the city's
volunteers, again demonstrating that, at least by the end of the 1880s, they
were considered military organizations. Despite all the disappointments and
difficulties in maintaining their companies over the years, these men would
still answer the call to duty—it eventually came years later.

In the late evening hours of February 26, 1895, eleven strokes of Big Duke
sent Savannah's entire active militia force scrambling to their respective armories. A crowd, numbering by some estimates between two thousand and
three thousand people, had gathered around the Masonic Temple on the
corner of Liberty and Whitaker Streets to hear a former Roman Catholic
priest, Joseph Slattery, and his wife, a former nun, present a lecture "understood to be very abusive of the Roman Catholic Clergy and the institutions
of that church."[16] A citizens group attempted, through the mayor's office, to
prevent the lecture from occurring, but the city's legal counsel, citing the right
of free speech, advised against any municipal action. As Slattery presented his
lecture, a small crowd began to form outside the temple. Growing restless and
abusive, some listeners hurled bricks and stones toward the building's win-
dows, breaking glass and injuring some of the estimated one hundred people
assembled inside. Threats from the mob to enter the temple impelled the
police to form a human barrier at the entrance. When these officers, too, began
to suffer from the projectiles thrown by the mob, the chief of police reported
his inability to control the situation to the mayor. With their armories just
blocks away, four companies of the 1st Regiment and one troop of the Georgia
Hussars responded and were the first to arrive on the scene. Under the overall
command of William W. Gordon, colonel of the 5th Regiment (Cavalry), and

with the mayor present, the militia volunteers cleared the surrounding streets, maintained a vigil until the lecture was completed, and provided security for Slattery and his wife to exit the building. Col. George A. Mercer, commanding the 1st Regiment, had been in a theater across the city and chose to arrive on the scene in his civilian clothes rather than traveling home to change into his uniform, a process that he claimed would have taken at least an hour.[17]

As expected, the companies of the 1st Battalion, hearing the alarm, mustered in their respective armories. Major Deveaux reported his command for duty to the mayor at 10:00 p.m. He also recorded the presence of every company's commanding officer, five lieutenants, fourteen sergeants, fifteen corporals, and 141 men ready to render service to the city of Savannah. These men remained under arms as a reserve until 11:30 p.m., when they were dismissed by Deveaux.[18]

For some, there was no surprise that the African American militiamen remained in their armories. In addition, the twenty-five-man Gatling gun crew of the Chatham Artillery was held in reserve at their armory just blocks away from the temple. While the armory locations of the various companies of the 1st Battalion are unknown as of 1895, later such structures were positioned in or near black residential or business areas, thus making it quite probable that they were similarly located at this time. If so, the armories were most likely in the northeastern and southwestern fringes of Savannah, thus contributing to the forty-five-minute response time. The armories of the white troops, due to the longevity of their organizations as well as to their members' financial support, had been built near the city center. Their locations provided a distinct advantage by enabling them to answer the alarm in only eight to fifteen minutes. While there are no ethnic descriptions of the crowd, the *Savannah Tribune* characterized them as "hoodlums of the town" and listed the names of eleven rioters as well as their jail sentences.[19]

Both Colonel Mercer and Adj. Gen. John Kell, in their reports, remarked favorably on the service of the black troops, even though they were not engaged. Mercer considered "this prompt assemblage on the ground ready for duty of 341 Officers and men, with 196 additional in their Armories as a reserve, very creditable to the Military of Savannah, and a very cogent argument in favor of the maintainance of a strong and efficient Military force in the State."[20] Kell stated, "it is worthy of notice that one battalion was on the ground in fifteen minutes from sounding of the alarm, and all under arms within thirty to forty-five minutes, including the colored troops."[21] While neither are strong endorsements of the performance of the African American uniformed militia at Savannah, their inclusion in each officer's report suggests at the very minimum they were still considered military organizations.

The social question regarding racial division, or "superiority," would continue to plague Georgia's military forces beyond such emergency duties. Col. Clifford Wallace Anderson, who as a member of the State Military Board, had favored African American participation in Georgia's militia in 1884. But he had also expressed his concerns about racial incidents that year at Sandersville and Dawson as well as the dock strike at Savannah three years previously. Not only was he concerned about potential military issues, such as the location of Savannah's ammunition storage, which had been inadvertently blocked by the longshoremen during that crisis, but Anderson also noted, "in the event of my absence from the city, Lt. Col. Wm. H. Woodhouse is the senior officer & under the law were the troops called out to suppress [a] riot has clearly the right to command the troops." His proposed solution to this dilemma involved his own promotion to brevet brigadier general and to brevet his staff officers to the rank of lieutenant colonel in the event of his absence from the city to ensure that no black officer would command white troops. Eventually, this racial attitude would lead Georgia to establish a segregated "rank list," one for whites and another for the African American commands. This prevailing attitude would affect the future of field training for all the state's volunteer militia organizations.[22]

Efforts to Obtain Field Training: Georgia

Traditionally, Americans possessed an aversion to a large standing army, considering such a force a threat to liberty and a burden upon taxpaying citizens. Therefore, the regular US Army continued to remain an extremely small force relegated mostly to coastal and border defense—responsibilities still too great for its meager numbers. The individual states would maintain local militia forces that would, when needed, answer the call to defend the state or the nation. While the state government supplied arms, it usually did not make provisions for the maintenance or security of those weapons—or much else for that matter. Social gatherings, often seen by some historians as the major function of many militia units, actually became a valuable source of fundraising to defray the expenses forced upon the individual members of each organization. Local companies uniformed themselves, some in the latest military fashions, while others, like the Republican Blues of Savannah, maintained what appeared to be Napoleonic-era attire through the end of the nineteenth century. Without financial support from the state for equipment, maintenance, security and storage of arms and accoutrements, uniforms, horses, artillery carriages, or cannon, it would be impractical during this period to expect either the state or federal government to supply any annual funding for field exercises. If desired, the local military organization, for the time being, would have to conduct—and fund—its own training.

One of earliest mentions of the state of Georgia sponsoring training occurred in 1886. Writing to Gov. Henry McDaniel, that the Military Advisory Board was "not prepared to recommend any radical or sweeping changes in existing laws," Lt. Col. Charles H. Olmstead, the panel's president, emphasized that "in one direction the Board considers legislation important, nay *essential*," which was for "the establishment of a regular camp at some convenient and healthy locality, to which all the troops in the State should be summoned by order of the Governor for at least one week's service each year." Olmstead made a passionate plea to the governor, explaining the aspects of military life that could only be taught and learned in the field. He further lamented to McDaniel, "after the war the ranks were filled by men whose long experiences in the Armies of the Confederacy rendered further instruction unnecessary, but as time has rolled away, one by one, their place have become vacant." Olmsted estimated that "more than nine tenths of the troops of Georgia are men utterly without any experience in military life save that derived from the ordinary drills and parades."[23]

Members of the Military Advisory Board continued to express this sentiment over the next few years. The minutes of the board in 1887 presented the governor both with the recommended language for the legislative assembly "to provide by law how the military shall be trained as well as organized, armed and equipped" and a request for an annual appropriation of $24,000—half of this would be for an annual encampment and the remainder "for the maintenance and support of the military organization of the state." One year later, Adjutant General Kell employed a different tactic in his justification for funding. Calling for "wisdom, economy as well as the justice to our citizen soldiery," he noted, "the great increase shown by statistics for the past nine months, in mining, milling, quarrying, foundaries, factories and all the different appliances of developing and utilizing the resources of this grand commonwealth, must bring to [the] mind of the rational thinker, the necessity of a State Guard or voluntary organization for the protection of commerce and the security of investments."[24]

The Military Advisory Board continued its efforts in 1889 and even expanded its funding request to include "pay and rations, when the force is in active service by the authority of the state," which would include times of war, suppressing riots or insurrections, attending inspection, taking part in a parade, or learning at an annual camp of instruction. The ten-member board elaborated in great detail throughout a fifteen-page report to the governor his constitutional duties as well as that of Georgia General Assembly towards the militia, even taking two paragraphs to define the word "equipment" and the meaning of "to equip."[25] Perhaps the officers, led by Kell as the board's leader and as adjutant general, had expressed their level of frustration, believing that after the legislature had authorized a state militia, it was their responsibility to fund it as well. During that same year, only six companies of white troops, totaling 173 men, attended any type of field training, compared to an aggregate of 4,643 volunteers available for duty in Georgia's active, uniformed militia. Even though these half-dozen companies obtained tents from the state, the men had to finance their shipment to the camps located at Tybee and St. Simon's Islands and the purchase of their own ammunition and subsistence, and many even had to sacrifice their annual vacation to attend the camp of instruction that summer.

For black troops, such opportunities were limited by the same hardships as the white troops faced, and there is no evidence that any field exercises were conducted prior to 1897. Beginning in the late 1870s, the most common practice for the state's black volunteers centered on small, one-or-two-company, in-state, close-order drill competitions. Most of these events usually coincided with an organization's anniversary or in recognition of Emancipation Day or the passage of the Fifteenth Amendment. There is, however, evidence of some black troops traveling to participate in such events across state lines. But none of these so-called encampments were conducted along strict military discipline, supervised by formally trained or regular US Army personnel, and severely lacked the rigors of camp life.

This is not to say that these activities did not have merit. Georgia's African American volunteers boosted their morale through these competitions, built camaraderie and solidarity among themselves, and did hone some military skills such as marksmanship. In 1883, Atlanta hosted the Third Biennial Convention of the National Colored Military, a remarkable event including an infantry contest with companies from Georgia, Colorado, Missouri, and South Carolina. One of the capital city's companies, the Georgia Cadets, had even traveled to Cincinnati and Columbus, Ohio, as well as to Memphis, Nashville, and Chattanooga, Tennessee, to compete against other African American troops. And, months prior to Olmstead's request for state funding toward annual training, Atlanta had already witnessed its second large military drill, conducted with African American volunteer companies from Georgia, Tennessee, and Alabama. Throughout the 1880s, the Georgia Volunteers, Colored, consistently sent at least one company to compete at Charleston, South Carolina.[26] Beaufort and Hamburg, also in South Carolina, served as common destinations, as did Montgomery and Selma, Alabama, and Jacksonville, Florida. Since all of this travel and the competitions were self-funded, when word that the general assembly had authorized an annual expenditure of $6,500 for a camp of instruction in November 1889, naturally, all military commands across the state celebrated.[27]

By February 1890, Capt. Nathan T. Humphry, commanding the African American company in Columbus, inquired as to whether the state would fund the expenses of his men for the upcoming encampment. Humphry had seen information about the encampment in the *Columbus Enquirer* and had received Circular No. 9, issued by the office of the state adjutant general. This circular letter, authorized for issue at the Military Advisory Board's meeting on January 28, 1890, required that "the various commands" will report to the adjutant general by April 7 "whether or not they will be able to take part in the June encampment, and how many officers and men they will probably be able to bring." Furthermore, failure to reply would be considered a negative response; thus, attendance was not a requirement. By April 2, ten African American volunteer companies had reported affirmatively, with a collective attendance estimated at 291–297 officers and enlisted. Accepting the invitation to attend demonstrated that these men understood their role as citizen-soldiers, but their prospective attendance soon became an issue, as one might expect.[28]

The minutes of neither the April 7 nor May 14 meeting of the Military Advisory Board included any discussion regarding whether to allow any "colored troops" to attend the encampment scheduled for June at Augusta's Exposition Grounds. Still, correspondence to Adjutant General Kell from Olmstead, now serving as the state's quartermaster general, mentioned, "the alteration you propose in the Special Order to distinguish white from colored troops is just right and so also is your suggestion that the Board advise the issuance of an order explaining to the latter why they will not be received into camp at this time." Olmstead, writing two days later, informed Kell, "but for the liberality of the citizens of Augusta," the encampment could not have been held since "the appropriations made by the State is much too small to admit of placing the entire force there." This lack of financial resources to adequately support the training of one thousand men justified in his mind "that an encampment for the Georgia Volunteers Colored be postponed until another occasion." Whether Olmstead's calculations of the expenses truly justified this decision, and even if the advisory board intended to conduct training for the African American contingent of the Georgia Volunteers later, the decision for them not to attend seems to have been made days earlier, making this explanation inaccurate at the time.[29]

The next year, Georgia held two encampments, one for the infantry at the National Military Park at Chickamauga, and another for cavalry and artillery command just outside Savannah. Again, authorities stated, "the colored troops will not participate in the encampment this time, but will be provided for next year."[30] Still, the following year arrived, and the state journals only reported an encampment for white troops. Noting this news, the 3rd Battalion's lieutenant colonel, Augustus Johnson, wrote to ask Kell: "Will you please inform what arrangements, if any, will be made in reference to the colored force? Of course, Col. something will be done for us and we will not be left out altogether."[31] The adjutant general's response echoed the same past excuse—"the appropriation made by the General Assembly for a permanent encampment is not sufficient to place in camp the entire volunteer force, this year"—and again he promised—"the Georgia Volunteers, Colored, . . . will be provided for in future encampments."[32] The organized commands of the African American volunteers of Georgia never attended a camp of instruction funded by the state. Ironically, other African Americans were present at the annual field training, although illegal at the time, as musicians or cooks for the white companies.[33]

Eventually, the three African American battalion commanding officers, Lieutenant Colonels Deveaux, Crumbly, and Blocker, determined to improve their organizations rather than concern themselves with field training for the time being. On April 2, 1895, these officers appeared before the Military Advisory Board to urge steps be taken to improve the condition of Georgia's black militias, insisting "they needed equipment and assistance in other ways more than camp duty."[34] But two years later, Deveaux, Crumbly, and Blocker traveled once again to Atlanta to petition the board in February 1897 to "provide such encampment for our troops as the exigencies of the service and the limit of your annual appropriation will admit of at this time." The three officers also requested that their troops receive the "improved regulation arms and equipments as the major part of those now in use are worne and unserviceable."[35] The petition for an encampment of all of Georgia's African

American volunteers failed. Apart from the minor concession of providing twenty tents to the Georgia Artillery—although the black artillerymen had to pay for shipping—and approving $800 combined for all three of the African American battalions, the board continued to ignore the field training of its black troops. If they had made some provisions, they would have witnessed a level of professionalism and commitment to duty as evidenced in the report from Capt. John C. Simmons.[36]

Obtaining permission for an encampment of his battery, Simmons, with one other officer, twenty-seven men, and the command's "two bronze 6 pounder field pieces, carriages and limbers and 2 baggage wagons," departed their armory in Savannah at 3:00 a.m. on August 9, 1897. Traveling along the Ogeechee Road, the battery reached its campsite in little over two hours at a place known as Flowersville, a flag station on the Savannah, Florida, and Western Railroad, six and one-half miles southwest of the city. Simmons recognized his organization's need to "look beyond the instruction gained by mere drill at the armory and upon the streets." Explaining that "much would be gained by the more practical experience in camp," the captain then proceeded to define this "practical experience" in a list of fourteen skills obtained only through camp life and field training.[37]

Moreover, Simmons wrote summaries of each aspect of the camp, including such details as obtaining fresh fish, meat, and ice from Savannah on a daily basis and from the number of pairs of underwear each man would pack to the amount of straw each would receive for his "comfortable bed 16 inches from the ground." The captain also provided a daily report that listed the day's drill activities and orders issued, which included a guard mount. By these details, Simmons demonstrated a thorough level of military knowledge, also recording each piece of camp equipment under guard, the guard posts, and the names and number of each relief as well as the countersigns. He even included a map in his report to the adjutant general that clearly illustrated the locations of each tent, including the hospital and kitchen, as well as where the two cannons with carriages were parked. The encampment, designated Camp Kell in honor of the state's adjutant general, was attended daily by the battalion's surgeon, Dr. Thomas J. Davis, who reported only three minor illnesses during the eight-day exercise. Educated at English College in the West Indies, Davis, a native of Jamaica, had received his medical training at the University of Vermont and had served as the battalion's surgeon since 1888. He was not the only visitor to the campsite. Several dignitaries from Savannah's African American community visited during the week-long exercise, and on

Rev. Jacob Javan Durham. From Bacote, *Who's Who
among Colored Baptists of the United States*, 114.

Sunday, the last day of the encampment, Rev. Jacob J. Durham of the Second
Baptist Church offered a military sermon. The battery then held a dress parade
with members of the 1st Battalion and the Savannah Hussars. Confirming
the military benefits of field training, Captain Simmons proclaimed that "his
command is in first-class condition and is ready for inspection at any time."[38]

The "Colored Encampments" in Texas

The Militia Law of 1879 in Texas actually mandated annual training "at such
time and place as the commander-in-chief may direct" but did not immediately finance this legal requirement. Nevertheless, some state funding for annual
encampments occurred briefly between 1890 and 1893. Unlike its counterpart
in Georgia, the government of Texas did provide training, albeit segregated,
for its African American volunteers, with their training camp conducted at
a different time of the year but often using the same location as the state's
white troops. With success hinging on free transportation from the various
railroads and equipment supplied by the US Army, these camps of instruction

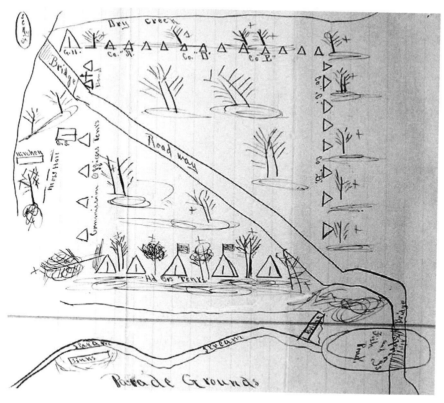

Camp Attucks. Adapted from General Order No. 2, September 24, 1890,
Archives and Information Division, Texas State Library and Archives.

were conducted on strict military guidelines and featured training under the
guidance of various US military officers.

General Order No. 69, issued from the Texas Adjutant General's Office,
authorized the encampment of the Battalion of Colored Infantry near San
Antonio September 24–27, 1890. Maj. Jacob Lyons, commanding the battalion, requested and received the authority to conduct the encampment;
thus, this order resulted from the efforts of one man who sought the same
opportunity for his men that the white companies had received only two
months previously. The men of the battalion traveled for free; were "armed,
equipped, and uniformed under the law"; and received "subsistence without
charge" during the camp as well as, for some companies, during their travel
to and from San Antonio.[39]

The encampment opened with a municipal parade on the morning of September 24. Marching through the streets and various plazas of San Antonio,

this contingent of black troops, comprising five militia companies and two bands, totaled approximately two hundred men.[40] During the parade, the *San Antonio Daily Light* reported that "crowds of both white and black spectators lined the curbstones on the line of parade, and on reaching Alamo Plaza about fifteen minutes were consumed in putting the soldiers through military evolutions for the edification of the public."[41] Upon their arrival at San Pedro Springs, Major Lyons issued his first general order, announcing his assumption of command of the event and designating the military gathering as Camp Attucks. By dedicating this camp of instruction to the memory of Crispus Attucks, Lyons recognized the early patriot's efforts as a citizen-soldier, honored his sacrifice in the name of freedom, and employed him as an example of higher ideals to those in attendance.[42]

Lyons soon after detailed the "daily exercises for the government of troops in camp."[43] This order consisted of the specific times for each scheduled event of the encampment. It dictated the time to sleep, to wake up, to respond for meals, to submit reports to the camp adjutant, and to see the camp surgeon if ill, but more importantly, it listed the times for guard mount, drill, and officers' instruction, each of which consisted of military training. Capt. Richard I. Eskridge of the 23rd US Infantry Regiment, assigned to inspect the troops' encampment, mentioned in his report, "the men show an earnest desire to discharge their duties" but "a want of knowledge of detail."[44]

The last day of the encampment closed with a grand parade on the grounds. The *San Antonio Daily Express* observed two of the companies. The Excelsior Guard appeared "very soldierly in their neat, ornamental uniforms and white helmets, with plumes of blue and white feathers," and "the Galveston company was particularly noticeable for its easy swing and correct company movement."[45]

A year later, Texas Adjutant General Woodford H. Mabry issued General Order No. 12 on August 15, 1891, again directing the battalion to San Antonio to participate in an annual camp of instruction. This order dictated mandatory attendance and stated that those companies "failing to attend Encampment, will be promptly disbanded."[46] Therefore, in contrast to Georgia, rather than consistently postponing a black training camp, Texas confirmed that commands not participating would be removed from service. The encampment, held at Riverside Park from August 19 to August 23, featured guard mount, battalion and company skirmish drill, and, for the first time, a cash prize to the company with the highest score in grounds' and quarters' cleanliness, significant attributes meant to reduce incidents of disease among troops.

This camp memorialized the service of Capt. André Cailloux, another African American military hero, who had been killed in the fight for freedom during the American Civil War. Again Major Lyons, who commanded the encampment, appeared to have wanted to intentionally inspire the battalion's citizen-soldiers with an example of African American heroism.[47]

Once more, the railroads furnished free transportation and the US Army detailed Captain Eskridge as the inspecting officer. Eskridge, accompanied by Lt. Hunter Liggett of the 5th US Infantry Regiment and "three well instructed Sergeants of the Twenty-third Infantry as instructors," recommended in his report that "one more Company be added to this Battalion, making a total of six, for the sake of symmetry, convenience in drill, etc."[48] Of the 188 men enrolled at that time in the Battalion of Colored Infantry, 137 attended the encampment. Mabry favorably reported, "the negro soldier possesses many of the elements necessary for the maintenance of a good volunteer organization, and with proper officers to command him, he becomes efficient in the drill and other duties of camp and field."[49]

In 1892, the railroads discontinued the free transportation of citizen-soldiers, both black and white, to their annual encampments. For the Colored Battalion, this decision resulted in the mandatory attendance of only those companies near Austin. The activities of this camp of instruction mirrored those of the previous two years with one important and meaningful exception. The staff and officers of the battalion, led by Lyons and Capt. John Francis Van Duzor, forwarded to the Democratic governor, James Stephen Hogg, a petition stating:

> the negroes of Texas, of whom we form a part, have a just pride in all that contributes in any way to the upbuilding and greatness of their state and for whose dignity their patriotism would impel them to a willing sacrifice of their lives when called upon to sustain it, and believing that these commendable objects would be, in no little degree, brought about by a liberal encouragement of an increase in the number of companies (there being now only five in the state) from hundreds of good and trusty men, who stand ready and willing to comply with every requirement of the law.[50]

The request failed to accomplish any increase in the number of African American militia companies. But its submission to the governor demonstrated a high level of assertiveness by this small group of black citizen-soldiers. Unfortunately, the day following this petition to the governor, Major Lyons resigned his commission, not in the militia, but as the commanding officer of the battalion. George W. Wilson of Galveston later secured the election to succeed him in command.

The following year, 1893, the legislature again failed to appropriate any funds for transportation to the legally mandated annual encampments. Since the militiamen had to pay their own travel expenses, Mabry gave them "the privilege of selecting the point at which to hold the encampment."[51] Accordingly, on September 4, the adjutant general issued General Order No. 75, calling for the Battalion of Colored Infantry to assemble for a camp of instruction in San Antonio but recognizing that since "said attendance is to be without expense to the State for transportation, this order is not compulsory."[52] The military activities of this encampment, named Camp Wilson after Major Wilson, included guard mount, battalion and company drills, and officer instruction.

Following this brief period, the legislature, due to budget deficits, withheld funding for the Texas Volunteer Guard. Mabry, in his report for 1895–96, recorded "that the Texas Volunteer Guard has been reduced, for lack of proper encouragement, from 64 companies with 3,000 officers and enlisted men, on December 31, 1894, to 48 companies, with an aggregate of 215 officers and 2,246 enlisted men, at this date."[53] Despite this reduction, the Battalion of Colored Infantry remained at its normal strength—five companies. Instead of disbanding through "lack of encouragement," these African American citizen-soldiers resumed the practice of citizen-sponsored events. Major Wilson organized an encampment in Galveston in June 1895 by negotiating reduced fares from the railroad. The Board of Directors of the Afro-American State Fair Association chose Houston to host its event in August 1896. Mabry maintained a headquarters tent on the grounds during the fair, and a board of inspectors composed of high-ranking volunteer guardsmen tended to training needs and to camp and drill evaluations.

"Since we have gone so very far in the matter we would be pleased to have it go out, but we want on the other hand an opportunity to sustain our honest citizenship," wrote W. H. Browning, secretary of the Committee for Arrangements for the African American encampment scheduled for September 1897 at Brenham. Reporting an important economic observation, Capt. Louis Taylor, citing that his "men are all employed in cotton presses and long shore work," requested to be excused from the event since they were "liable to lose their jobs should they attend."[54] After transportation difficulties, the Excelsior Guard finally arrived in Brenham only to receive orders to go home. The reason for this was dire, according to a telegram from the town's mayor to

Adjutant General Mabry on September 22: "yellow fever at Beaumont and the people here are much excited—strict quarantine declared—stop all troops on the way here."[55] The *San Antonio Light* published an article that same day reporting the death of a small boy from the disease in Beaumont and detailed, "many are led to think that the mail service is bringing fever into the state and the governor will be asked to cut out all train service of any kind between Louisiana and Texas."[56] No encampment occurred for the black troops in 1897.

Rendering Service in the Lone Star State

Writing in the late 1970s, historian Lawrence Rice discussed the insignificance of the state's African American militia and argued that "no record of their use for other than parade purposes was found."[57] This assertion shows he obviously had not uncovered the two instances when civil authorities utilized the services of black militia troops in the state.

The earliest known use of an African American company of the Texas Volunteer Guard occurred at Calvert on the afternoon of April 16, 1880. Sentenced to be hanged, William "Bill" Walker was executed in front of "five thousand persons of all ages, color and sexes" who had assembled at the gallows "erected just inside the corporate limits of the city." Walker, an African American whose real name was Richard Knight, had been convicted of murdering James Munroe, an elderly white man, on the morning of August 20, 1876. With only three deputies, Sheriff William Q. Wyser grew alarmed by the large crowd and decided to activate both companies of Calvert's militia "to preserve the peace." The Calvert Guards, the city's white company, and the Salter Rifles, its African American company, "rendered great service in keeping the crowd back from the gallows." The Rifles were named in honor of Charles P. Salter, a prominent local white businessman and former Confederate officer who, as a Republican, had represented Robertson County's citizens in the state legislature. Although none of the newspaper correspondents observing the execution mentioned the number of black militiamen present, at least two confirmed the attendance of Rev. Andrew M. Gregory. Commanding Waco's Hubbard Rifles at the time, Gregory served as Walker's spiritual guide, reading scripture and singing hymns as the condemned man approached his impending death. The next month, the minister would not only become the first African American colonel in the state of Texas but also assume command of the 1st Regiment Colored Infantry, Texas Volunteer Guard.[58]

Nine years later, in August 1889, another activation of black troops took place. While newspaper accounts vary as to the method of murder and even

Sheriff George Monroe Autry. From *Confederate
Veteran* 16, no. 3 (March 1908), 357.

the culprit's last name, there were some similarities in the description of
Christian Munck's killing. A prominent planter near the town of Schumanns-
ville in Guadalupe County, Munck hired some farm laborers, among them a
man named Jesús Gonzalez (or Herrera), to pick that year's cotton yield. In
an apparent argument over wages, Jesús either stabbed Munck in the chest or
bludgeoned him with a weight from the cotton scales. The assailant escaped
to San Antonio, where he was later found and arrested by Guadalupe County
sheriff George Monroe Autry, who promptly took him to the county jail at
Seguin. When the *San Antonio Express* reported that a group of citizens from
neighboring Comal County planned to lynch the prisoner, Autry called out
the town's militia, both the white company and the African American company—the Ireland Rifles.

Under the command of Capt. Jacob Ray, the Ireland Rifles mustered twenty-eight officers and men and reported to Autry at 7:30 p.m. on August 25,

1889. The sheriff deployed the white militiamen of the Seguin Guards around the jail and sent several members of the Rifles to serve "as sentries on the several roads leading into town, the remainder of the black company remaining in their armory subject to call."[59] The *Neu Braunfelser Zeitung* reported that "naturally, they saw no one," but these men remained on duty with their white counterparts through the evening before being dismissed at 3:00 a.m. the following morning.[60]

The *Seguin Record* reported, "Sheriff Autry is enthusiastic in his praises of the military companies." While he did compliment both organizations, Autry characterized the white company as having "splendid discipline" but stated that Ray had "fine control" of his men.[61] Days later, the newspaper registered a complaint by Ray, who took exception to the term "'not called into direct action.'"[62] The captain seemed to have wanted to ensure that everyone knew about the service his men had provided to the community. Perhaps he believed that the sheriff's statement would create the perception that his company was unable or incapable of performing its duty as a military force. Whatever Ray's mindset and cause for concern, Autry had employed the company to protect his prisoner.

These two events, perhaps anomalies in the history of Texas, both involved *white* sheriffs calling for the militia companies from their local community, *both black and white,* to preserve law and order. At Calvert, the companies of militia troops surrounded the gallows in public view of thousands of spectators. Years later at Seguin, the African American company did not occupy the same space as the white troopers, instead performing picket duty along the roads leading into town. Both sheriffs, Autry and Wyser, former Confederate soldiers, clearly recognized these African American companies as military forces that they could utilize—and did—to maintain public order.

Virginia's Public Service

In his annual report to the governor, Virginia's adjutant general, William H. Richardson, reported that the state's militia companies had "deported themselves with soldier-like propriety, and upon the occasion of riotous proceedings at the city of Petersburg, . . . one of them commanded by Captain J. H. Hill, promptly volunteered its services, and aided in preserving the peace of the city." John Henry Hill, commanding the Petersburg Guard, placed his company under arms along with Capt. Samuel D. Davies's Petersburg Grays, the city's white company, not once, but twice during the gubernatorial election riots that occurred in their city during the fall of 1873.[63]

John Henry Hill. Courtesy of James Hugo Johnston
Memorial Library, Virginia State University.

Confusion reigned as to what initiated the hostilities that occurred during a political demonstration in Petersburg on the evening of October 23, 1873. "Eleven or more passenger cars," filled with citizens from Richmond taking part in a "conservative excursion," were reportedly "stoned at the Manchester crossing and in Petersburg." One newspaper alleged that this act may have provided some provocation for the events that followed; even so, the paper described the resulting violence as "a disgrace to civilization." Reports stated that the "whiskey shops were patronized early and often," after which a large group of "roughs and boys" shouted "the most indecent and profane language

possible, insulting ladies, and throwing rocks and bricks at the colored people"; an African American policeman was also beaten. There is no evidence
that this violence prompted any calling out of the militia. But when new trou-
bles arose days later, the troops were called upon to respond.[64]

On November 4, the *Daily State Journal* reported that the Richmond correspondent to the *Petersburg Index and Appeal* had indicated "that the Radicals
have deliberately concocted a plan to get up a riot in this city to-morrow, in
the hope of having an excuse for an appeal to the President to install [Robert
W.] Hughes in case of a closely contested [gubernatorial] election."[65] And
after the key to the state armory was stolen, the level of fear and excitement
caused the mayor of Petersburg to notify the governor and the militia, both
the white and the black companies, to make ready to meet any potential threat.
While historian Roger Cunningham has argued that Captain Davies ordered
the Petersburg Guard to prepare itself, stating, "it is unclear just what the
militiamen actually accomplished," the state adjutant general's report clearly
commended Captain Hill for volunteering his company and for aiding "in
preserving the peace of the city."[66]

It remains unclear how this preservation of the peace was obtained. Did
the Petersburg Guard simply respond to the alarm by gathering at the armory
where they remained under arms? Or, did Hill's company, by taking positions in the streets of Petersburg, actually induce the crowd to disperse? How
the men contributed to putting an end to the "riotous proceedings" remains
unclear. But this event supports not only the contention that the African
American volunteers of Petersburg were seen as military organizations but
also that they were assigned to a constabulary role *together with* their white
militia counterparts.[67]

Thirteen years later, African Americans responded to a local emergency
that took place at Richmond. On the evening of August 31, 1886, an earthquake
shook parts of the United States, extending as far north as Pennsylvania, west
to Ohio and Indiana, and south to Florida. At Virginia's capital, the superintendent at the penitentiary sounded the alarm when he was confronted by
ten to twelve inmates at the inner gate of the prison yard. Hammering on the
rusted iron of the old jail and taking advantage of the structural damage from
the quake and its aftershocks, the prisoners knocked out the transoms above
their cells and escaped. One newspaper reported that "the negroes seemed
most alarmed, but whites and blacks equally indulged in efforts to liberate
themselves." Hearing the shouts from the prison, many of Richmond's citizens
believed that one or more of the buildings at the penitentiary was on fire,

triggering a response by the police, the fire department, and the militia, who arrived "in such numbers as to render an outbreak impracticable."[68]

The Carney Guard, under the command of Capt. Charles B. Nicholas, had assembled at the armory for drill that evening. Hearing the alarm from the penitentiary, Nicholas quickly marched his entire company there and "were received with great cheers by the thousands of people assembled about the prison." They arrived before any of the city's white companies, who had taken the time to issue ammunition in their armories before deploying. Due to their lack of ammunition, however, the *Richmond Dispatch* reported that "their services were not made use of when the detail was made to remain at the penitentiary during the night." In his annual record of his company to the state's adjutant general, Nicholas proudly noted, "military call by order of the Gov. of Virginia, 1st Company to arrive at the Penitentiary."[69]

Only a few months later, in January 1887, the first military activation of African Americans in a labor dispute occurred in Virginia. While newspaper accounts differ somewhat on the events at Newport News leading up to the strike of approximately 600 workers, the main emphasis seems to have centered on the demand for a wage increase of an additional ten cents per hour. At the time, there were three classes of workers toiling either along the wharf or on board the vessels in various stages of loading or unloading. These groups included the truckers, who handled the freight on the dock; the ships-hands, who received the materials from the dock on board ship; and the stevedores, who carefully arranged the freight in the hold and on the deck of the ships. Each group was dependent upon the other, but each was paid different wages.

Reportedly, the origins of the strike had begun in New York with similar circumstances involving requests for wage increases from the Old Dominion Steamship Company. That business paid below the standard of all other domestic steamship lines operating out of that port. After members of the Knights of Labor coordinated a work stoppage in the city, one of the organization's representatives "arrived at Newport News and immediately induced the longshoremen of the Old Dominion Steamship Company to go out on a strike."[70] On Thursday, January 6, after learning that their request for additional pay had been rejected, the dockworkers of the steamship company stopped work. Unable to replace its approximately 200 men on strike, the company sought relief by sending "a ship load of other men, gathered in New York, Jersey City and Brooklyn, . . . to break the strike."[71]

Events along the wharf began to unravel quickly for freight-handling businesses. Upon learning of the Old Dominion strike, the men of the Chesapeake

State Guard, May 21, 1887. Courtesy of John Listman.

and Ohio Railroad forwarded their demand for a similar increase in pay; once rebuffed, on Monday, January 10, they too joined the Old Dominion's workers in a labor stoppage. The next evening, at approximately 9:00 p.m., about 150 workers stormed Pier No. 2 in an effort to prevent further work from being conducted by their replacements. The men succeeded in forcing one ship to leave the port for Norfolk, one newspaper correspondent reporting, "the men helped themselves freely" to whiskey found on the dock, and "a reign of terror then began—fights, curses, screams, and yells all combining to make [the] night hideous." The violence spread to include the torching of a bathhouse owned by the Old Dominion Land Company and railroad warehouses. After this, a request for military assistance reached Gov. Fitzhugh Lee.[72]

Warwick County judge George Meredith Peek indicated to the governor that local civil authority was unable to stem the violence. He therefore requested "as soon as possible a sufficient force from the military of the State to preserve the peace and for the protection of property," further suggesting that he "send two companies, one of colored and one of white, and . . . give orders to a third company to hold itself in readiness for orders." Surprisingly, Governor Lee complied with Peek's suggestion, instructing Richmond's Companies A and B, 1st Regiment and the State Guard, one of the city's African American companies and under the command of Capt. Robert Austin Paul, to

Capt. Robert Austin Paul. From Northrop,
Penn, and Garland, *College of Life*, 72.

report to the Chesapeake and Ohio Railroad depot at midnight, armed and
equipped to move to Newport News. Additionally, at the suggestion of either
Col. Philip Haxall or Adj. Gen. James McDonald, the governor, through Maj.
Baker Perkins Lee at Hampton Roads, ordered the captains commanding the
African American units there, the Peninsula Guards and the Libby Guard, to
"proceed at daylight, or as soon thereafter as railroad transportation arrives,
with *arms and ammunition* to Newport News, where they will report to Brigadier General Anderson to aid in preserving the peace."[73] Lee had gone one
step further than Georgia's governor by not only mobilizing two of the state's
African American military companies to duty but also actually utilizing the
services of one of these units in a crisis.[74]

The morning of January 12 broke with ninety-five armed Virginia Volunteers, seventy-one white and twenty-four black, arranged along the waterfront. The quiet of the day had caused the two companies at Hampton to stand
down, and neither of them deployed to the scene of the crisis. Captain Paul's
unit was assigned to the coal pier, while the two white commands took up positions near the grain elevators and piers. That morning a State Guard sentry
reported to the officer of the guard that "he heard three shots up the railroad
and a cry of distress." Paul immediately sent a small detachment, followed by
a large body of the company under his command, "a considerable distance up

the road" but found nothing. The captain later reported that he thought the alarm "the work of some one anxious to create excitement."[75]

In a testament to the severity of the weather, described as "intensely cold—ground covered with snow and ice," each of Paul's militiamen received two blankets, having arrived with none.[76] The harsh weather, as well as the arrival of the military, probably played a role in the cessation of violence at Newport News. Remaining under arms for two days, the militiamen stood on alert until an agreement was eventually reached between the railroad and the leaders of the strike, identified as "Peter Allen, Frank Sampson, and two men by the name of Gaines."[77] For their participation, Paul's command received recognition from Maj. Joseph Virginius Bidgood. Writing to Col. Muscoe Livingston Spotswood, commanding the 1st Regiment, Virginia Volunteers, Bidgood reported, "this company rendered valuable service and met the approbation of our own troops," characterizing Paul as "a trusty officer" to be commended to the colonel and the governor.[78] Furthermore, the correspondent for the *Richmond Daily Times* published Bidgood's comment "that the colored troops . . . won well-deserved praise on all sides by their soldierly bearing and conduct."[79]

After the January snow thawed and the year 1887 progressed through spring and summer, the Petersburg Guard was once again activated in late August by order of the city's mayor, Thomas J. Jarratt.[80] Jarratt came under harsh criticism after imposing "an extortional fine and unprecedented sentence" upon Edward Ridley, "an unsophisticated colored man." Ridley, assaulted by a white woman, in an "unguarded moment" retaliated against her and then was beaten by three white men, Henderson Eanes, W. E. Wyatt, and a Mr. Badger. An African American magistrate, in turn, filed warrants for these three men to appear. When several African American citizens published a complaint against the mayor for his conduct in administering the case of Ridley, Jarratt issued warrants for libel against the signatories of the complaint as well as the editors of the *Petersburg Index-Appeal* and the city's black newspaper, *The Lancet*, for publishing such content. Days later, during the prosecution of a white doctor, Samuel Hinton, for his slapping of a black woman, an African American attorney, Alfred William Harris, demanded "that the same justice should be meted out in this case" as with Ridley, and if not, Harris "would not be responsible for the consequences, which might be serious."[81]

Mayor Jarratt, "apprehending the danger of a riot" generated by Harris's comments, ordered three of the city's militia companies to assemble at their armories "for prudential reasons" on the evening of August 30. The Petersburg

Grays and the R. E. Lee Battery—both white companies—and the African American troops of the Petersburg Guard received the order at 10:00 p.m.; seventy-five minutes later, the Guard had thirty-nine men answer the roll. The company, under the command of Capt. William F. Jackson, remained at its armory throughout the night and the following day, the men were released from duty at approximately 4:00 p.m. The *Richmond Dispatch* reported that "the determined action of the authorities last night in calling the military together and strengthening the constabulary force doubtless had a cooling effect," while the *Richmond Daily Times* opined that "reports sent from the city [were] greatly exaggerated."[82] Nevertheless, black militia companies had responded to the official call to duty by white civic authorities.

The Petersburg Guard was not the only African American uniformed militia company activated twice in emergency situations. The Carney Guard and the State Guard, both of Richmond, shared in this distinction.

In the early morning hours of January 31, 1888, a fire broke out in the large building operated by Joseph Davis & Company of Boston as a shoe factory at the state penitentiary. With inmates near the flames, and as the fire department arrived, prison guards opened cells and began to evacuate some of the convicts to the courtyard. The fire chief, fearing an outbreak of disorder beyond the control of the penitentiary's officials, sounded the military alarm, prompting not only a rush of the various militia companies to their armories but also the gathering of numerous bystanders to the prison. The response to the alarm was so quick that Brigadier General Anderson, 1st Brigade of Volunteer Infantry, stated, "'the men seemed to spring from the ground.'" The city's artillery battery, the Richmond Howitzers; the cavalry troop, the Stuart Horse Guards; and a total of seven infantry companies, which included three consisting of African Americans, responded to the alarm. The State Guard, commanded by Captain Paul, arrived with thirty-five men immediately following the arrival of the first white company and another small detachment. The Attucks Guard advanced on the scene with thirty-four men led by Captain Scott. Eventually, the Carney Guard, under the command of Captain Nicholas, also appeared, numbering twenty men. The *Richmond Dispatch* reported that "in an hour's time between three and four hundred militia were inside the penitentiary. Of this number about seventy-five were colored, who were not slow by any means in answering the call to duty."[83]

In the prison courtyard, as the white troops assembled into "a hollow square" formation, permitting defense on all four sides, the 1st Battalion's Major Johnson deployed his African American troops on the outside of the penitentiary walls. Following an assessment of the situation at approximately 8:45 a.m., the majority of the militiamen received orders to return to their armories, but two commands, one white and one black, remained behind. The white company, the Walker Light Guard, took up positions inside the prison yard, while the Carney Guard was detailed to keep "the roadway and the entrance to the Penitentiary clear of the crowd." Both militia units "were given their breakfast and dinner by the Superintendent" prior to their departure at approximately noon.[84]

As the men of the Carney Guard smartly marched away from the prison, none of them knew what their company might be doing in the future. With the coming of the 1890s, the state of Virginia never again activated any of its African American military organizations for duty, relegating them instead to parades, drill competitions, or target practices.

Nevertheless, these substantive examples in Virginia present clear evidence that state officials considered these companies useful in constabulary duties and apparently did not hesitate to employ them. Governor Lee, a former Confederate officer and nephew of Robert E. Lee, became the only chief executive in the South during this period to order not one, but two African American volunteer companies to respond to a riot. The Virginia state military made efforts to preserve the social protocol that segregated the companies from their white counterparts during these events, but it would have been almost impossible to strictly maintain that separation as the units raced to the scene or as they exited a train to march toward the emergency.

Conclusion

The record of employing black militia in crisis situations clearly supports the assertion that government and military officials in Georgia, Texas, and Virginia considered these companies as military organizations. Moreover, the fact that these assignments were made by former Confederates serving in significant political and military offices further reveals the unexpected flexibility of race relations, at least through the end of the nineteenth century. Although the willingness to officially order the black volunteers to public constabulary and other duties varied in each state, there also existed several similarities. Perhaps the most evident common trait centered on the level of inconsistency between how African American militiamen were utilized and trained in contrast to the favoritism shown to white militia organizations.

With the notable exception of Judge Sneed's specific request for African American militiamen to attend the execution at Augusta, and though the black troops in Savannah responded to the emergency military alarm when sounded there, citizens in Georgia never witnessed the arrival of black citizen-soldiers actually *used* as military troops. On multiple occasions, white citizens had observed black militiamen parading on the streets or watched their target contests or the celebratory firing of their firearms, but they had never seen them in a position of authority in a crisis. One exception might have been the involvement of Lieutenant Colonel Woodhouse and his junior officers at the docks in 1881. Due to the lack of contemporary reporting, however, it is not clear what those three African American officers were wearing when they met with the leaders of the strike. Assuming that each of the officers had donned their military uniform once the governor had placed them in a standby status, it remains plausible that every person involved as well as every spectator along the waterfront of Savannah did see three African Americans as not only military men but also as commissioned officers of the state of Georgia. The exceptional leadership of Woodhouse in that crisis, along with Major Deveaux and Captain Toomer, has virtually been forgotten, and long overdue is the credit each deserves for bringing calm to a volatile time, a moment ripe with the chance of hostilities, potential loss of life, and further destruction of property. Addressing Georgia's white elite, Woodhouse and his colleagues exercised similar diplomatic leadership for their continued efforts to obtain any amount of state-sponsored military field training in Georgia. Regrettably, none of their efforts have been recognized in the historical record.

Georgia officials may have considered initiating field training for the state's African American militia troops beginning in the 1880s, but the fact remains that they never actually authorized it. The military leadership adopted a "wait for next year" approach that may or may not have been deliberate in its effort to completely exclude its black troops. State officials, including military leaders, had supplied Georgia's black volunteers with arms, ammunition, and equipment. With the existing societal views toward segregating racial groups, separate training camps could have been possible, yet they did not take place.

Such contradictory measures also characterized the treatment of African American citizen-soldiers in Texas. There is no evidence of that state's civil or military officials activating any black troops, even when some opportunities presented themselves, such as the war with Spain or the disastrous 1900 Storm at Galveston. But Robertson County sheriff William Wyser and later Guadalupe County sheriff George Autry overcame any stigma of deploying armed black men to not only make use of the local African American militia company to uphold the law but also *required* the nearby white company to join forces with their African American colleagues. Both sheriffs needed troops during a tense situation, and to their credit, both chose those who were best disciplined and qualified to perform the duty required. Nevertheless, despite the absence of activations, Texas, out of these three southern states, was the only one that offered and funded field training for its African American militiamen, but then only sporadically throughout the 1890s.

Virginia held no state-sponsored, large-scale military field exercises for either its white or black militiamen. State officials chose instead to spend their meager funds to supply individual companies with arms, equipment, and uniforms plus cover operating expenses for state military advisors, company administrative costs, or individuals who were required by law to travel in conjunction with their military duties. Once again, Virginia, without a doubt, demonstrates clearly the best record of actually using their African American volunteers in a variety of situations by both its state and local government officials.

Most likely, nearly all of the six hundred or so striking workers at Newport News were African Americans, and probably many of those incarcerated at the state's prison at Richmond were black citizens. Social protocol would have obviously prevented deploying armed black militia had either of these groups been predominately white citizens; nonetheless, in the situation during the fire at the state prison, African American militiamen took charge of crowd control *outside* the walls, not inside, where one would expect their presence to be found guarding black prisoners. And at the time, the performance of these African American men from Richmond and Petersburg received positive praise from local newspapers and from the white military officers who submitted reports.

It remains surprising not only that white political leaders actually called forth black militia volunteers but also that, in all instances, African Americans were joined by white militia in performing the same duty at the same time and place. Some historians might argue that those white forces only ensured the appropriate behavior of the African American contingent, but throughout the highlighted episodes, the need for black troops to participate seemed to be the overriding factor. There is no doubt that personal relationships existed between many of the men involved in these individual events, but more importantly, white government and military leaders and citizens of both races appeared to have accepted the role of the black militia during this period.

What these events may show was the lack of a central criterion or common pattern in each state regarding when African American uniformed militia were deployed, either on the ground or as legally ordered reserve forces. Virginia had contributions from its black citizen-soldiers in the 1870s and 1880s, and there was activity in Georgia and Texas in the 1880s. Therefore, one might contend that the deterioration of racial relationships slowly occurred through the 1880s. But Texas held field exercises for its African American troops in the following decade, and in the East, training for black artillerymen at Flowersville, Georgia, occurred in 1897. These actions disclose a much cloudier and uneven historical picture regarding the treatment of black militiamen in the South. A lack of consistency in racial relationships, occurring on a swinging pendulum of acceptance, accommodation, and discrimination, endured throughout the late nineteenth century. And other notable social factors involving race also affected the experiences of African American citizen-soldiers in Georgia, Texas, and Virginia.

6

—∞—

Light, Bright, or White?

The Concept of Colorism and the Black State Volunteers

ON DECEMBER 8, 1870, Jefferson Wyly opened an account at the branch office of the Freedman's Bank and Trust in Atlanta. The registration information recorded provides valuable insight into Wyly's life. It may be the only document in existence that names his parents as well as other pertinent details, such as his residence on Decatur Street, in which he had been born and raised in Atlanta, and his employment in the city as a messenger for Hannibal Kimball, a powerful supporter of Georgia's sitting Republican governor, Rufus Bullock.[1] This bank register, used before the days of photographic identification cards, also described, surprisingly, the complexion of the depositor, which for Wyly is listed as "white." Two years later, he again deposited money at the bank, at which time his skin color was recorded as "almost white." After completing his three-year enlistment in the US Army, rising to the rank of sergeant prior to his discharge at Fort Davis, Texas, in May 1870, he had returned to Atlanta. There, Wyly had found employment, was saving for the future, and, with carefully cultivated relationships, was able to organize and command an African American volunteer militia company, the Atlanta Light Infantry.[2]

Captain Wyly's experiences and characteristics illustrated a confluence of factors that often came together in an officer who served in the African American component of Georgia's volunteer militia forces. For Wyly, these included an apparent desire for self-improvement, illustrated through bank deposits as well as his organizing of a militia company. Furthermore, his employment with Republican benefactors, his previous US Army service, and most notably his lighter skin color all seem to provide a glimpse into what produced for him a formula for success.

While unable to examine every single militia officer from the early 1870s to the early 1900s from Georgia, Texas, and Virginia, this chapter investigates similar qualities, experiences, and accomplishments from several high-ranking African American volunteer militia officers. More specifically, it analyzes and asserts that skin-color classification affected social status, as the larger white society may have perceived lighter skin as a sign of difference from darker African Americans. Depending on the state, this difference placed such individuals into a category of "other" that characterized them, in the context of the late-nineteenth-century United States, as more trustworthy and dependable. The role of skin color also could have played a part in an officer's ability to successfully build military, political, economic, and business relationships, the very alliances that contributed to the participation of African Americans as citizen-soldiers for over thirty-five years in those southern states.

The "Color" of Texas

Studying Ohio's black militia units, historian Lowell Dwight Black contended that those companies "were officered exclusively by mulattoes" and that the "Negro elite" maintained a "rigid class distinction" for social structure based upon skin color.[3] During roughly the same time period examined by Black, the muster rolls of African American volunteer militia companies in Texas reveal a very different color composition.

Commencing in 1880 and ending in 1899, when Texas no longer required categorizing physical traits in its annual reports, only five individuals were listed as either "yellow" or "light" who were elected to command their respective companies. Of these men, two were in Bryan, two in Seguin, and the other one in Galveston. Capt. Jacob Ray of Seguin was listed as "yellow" only on some of the early company rolls, this changed to "brown" for the last two years of his service. From the handwriting on the rolls, this alteration appears to be an example of a change in personnel with different terminology for skin-color determination. Ray's replacement, Horace E. Ferguson, who had previously served as a lieutenant, was the other officer classified as "yellow." Even though the Ireland Rifles of Seguin had more or less maintained someone of mixed race as their commanding officer, this does not appear to have translated into company longevity. Granted, many of the state's black militia companies struggled to sustain their membership, but skin color, which one might equate to more opportunity or better relationships with white benefactors, does not appear to be a factor in Texas. This is also true regarding Capt. Charles Mills of the Grant Guards at Galveston, who could only keep his company in service for five years, and Capt. J. D. Jackson of Bryan's Gregory Rifles, which existed for only two years.[4]

Bryan appeared to have the distinction of being the only location in the state that at any given time possessed a full complement of lighter-skinned officers. The Gregory Rifles from 1880 to 1881 elected J. D. Jackson as captain, who was listed as "light," with Lts. J. M. Monroe and M. J. Johnson both noted as "yellow." Following the dissolution of this company and the establishment of the Brazos Light Guard in 1882, the members of the new unit again elected mixed-race individuals for the three top commissioned ranks, but it would take an additional nine years for this to happen. Capt. Louis A. Johnson (described as "yellow") was initially elected as the commanding officer in 1891 and was reelected for each of the next three years. Henry Andrews and George Johnson (both "light") joined Captain Johnson as his lieutenants in 1894. The available muster rolls for the Light Guard from the years 1887–98 clearly illustrate the breakdown of the company's members by their perceived skin color. This demonstrates that within at least this organization in Bryan, preferential treatment for lighter-skinned African Americans did *not* occur when selecting the leadership of the company.[5]

The Brazos Light Guard consisted of a majority of lighter-skinned African American militiamen in 1894, when it reelected Johnson and gave him two mixed-race lieutenants to work with him. But Table 2 divulges that both dark- and light-skinned individuals served together in this company. It also illustrates the changing usage of skin-color terminology over the years. The word "dark" did not appear on the company's earliest rolls, with "black" used instead, but this changed in the 1890s before moving back toward "black" at the end of the century. The "other" category included two rather confusing descriptive terms on the 1887 muster roll—"freckled" and "reddish." And lastly, the term "mulatto," incorporating anyone who either appeared of mixed race or whose ancestry was known to be of such, was dropped in preference of additional stratification of lighter skin color. Perhaps some African Americans

TABLE 2. Brazos Light Guard membership numbers by "complexion" (skin color)

Complexion	1887	1894	1897
Black	21	–	28
Dark	–	19	9
Brown	–	–	10
Mulatto	10	–	–
Yellow	–	–	–
Light	–	14	–
Bright	–	6	–
Other	2	–	–

Note: A dash (–) indicates the term was not used by the company that year to describe complexion.

Source: Muster rolls, Brazos Light Guard, Texas Volunteer Guard, RG 401, Texas State Library and Archives Commission, Austin.

either choose to be "whiter" than others of mixed race or this is simply a case where the individual completing the muster roll understood that, at least in his mind, there was indeed a difference.[6]

The Sheridan Guards of Houston was the only company in the state that split into two "sections," beginning in 1896. It remains unknown if the two commanding officers had a personality conflict or if they possessed different political views, as might be interpreted by the actions of one section leader, who continued to march with the Houston Light Guard, a white company, as its drummer. Another possibility was that the operation of two sections provided the black community in the city with two company-size militia organizations under a different guise since Texas did not allow additional growth for African American companies. Without any record of the details or contemporary reports of this situation, the historian may never know.[7]

What is known is that both sections utilized different terminology in describing its members. In the first year, the recorder with Section A described

TABLE 3. Sheridan Guards—Sections A and B membership numbers by "complexion" (skin color)

Complexion	Section A			Section B		
	1896	1897	1898	1896	1897	1898
Black	1	34	12	18	20	19
Dark	1	–	–	–	–	–
Dark Brown	3	–	–	–	–	–
Brown	18	8	25	22	21	18
Mulatto	–	–	–	3	5	3
Quadroon	1	–	–	–	–	–
Coper [sic]	–	–	14	–	–	–
Yellow	3	2	–	–	–	–
Light Quadroon	1	–	–	–	–	–

Note: A dash (–) indicates the term was not used by the section to describe complexion.

Source: Muster rolls, Sheridan Guards, Texas Volunteer Guard, RG 401, Texas State Library and Archives Commission, Austin.

in greater detail the skin color of each member, while Section B consistently applied only three terms to identify its militiamen—"black," "brown," and "mulatto." Similar to the Brazos Light Guard in 1894, Section A documented a wider range of skin shades, but they, too, eventually settled on three, although not consistently. Throughout its brief tenure, Section A always had a "brown" commanding officer, Capt. Charles Green. Section B, initially led by John Sessums, who was identified as "black," chose a "brown" captain, James Taylor, two years later. The breakdown of complexion descriptive terms by member and by company section again demonstrates how color was interpreted and leads to conclusions concerning the influence of colorism on the successful outcome for elected officers.[8]

Table 3 shows that both sections of the Sheridan Guards contained members with a wide range of skin colors. In 1897, one might assert that the information illustrates deference to the lighter-skinned Green since there were an overwhelming majority of "black" members that year, but this is the only example found in all the muster rolls available from the state. Yet if one contends that light skin did equal better treatment and opportunity, as depicted by Section A in 1897, then the reverse could be claimed with the information presented for Section B.

With the majority of its membership described with light skin, these men selected a *black* captain to lead them, thus seemingly pointing to what one might classify as "reverse deference." Clearly, the most obvious conclusion drawn from the information in Table 3 is that there was no exclusiveness by either the lighter- or darker-skinned African Americans, at least in these two volunteer militia organizations.

The last supporting example is based on the Excelsior Guard of San Antonio. This company consistently elected a "dark" commanding officer. With the Lincoln Guards, the Excelsiors enjoyed the longest tenure in the Texas Volunteer Guard, thus, providing support to the assertion that lighter skin *did not* equate to preferential treatment from the surrounding white society. Table 4 can be used to illustrate the relationship between the individuals in the company of varying degrees of skin color with the eventual selection of leadership.

Beginning in 1882, the San Antonio company chose a "brown" US Army veteran, John F. Van Duzor, as captain. He was followed by another veteran of the Indian Wars, Capt. Simon Turner, who was always described as either "dark" or "black." Likewise, Turner's replacement, Jacob Lyons, who would eventually command the Battalion of Colored Infantry, was categorized as either "dark" or "brown," not "black." Robert George Ellis, the last commanding officer of the Excelsior Guard listed on muster rolls that still recorded physical characteristics, was consistently identified as "brown."[9]

Examining the African American volunteer militia companies of Texas, the membership or muster rolls have consistently illustrated a *lack* of colorism. The lack of company longevity with lighter-skinned African American officers seems to support the conclusion that skin color *did not* gain those men any advantages from white society. The scarce number of "light" officers at the company level demonstrates the same to be true within the black community as well. Conversely, the much longer tenure of service of several companies

TABLE 4. Excelsior Guard membership numbers by "complexion" (skin color)

Complexion	1883	1893	1897
Black	6	16	20
Dark	3	–	–
Brown	18	17	21
Mulatto	–	–	2
Light Brown	1	–	–
Yellow	4	3	6

Note: A dash (–) indicates the term was not used by the company to describe complexion.

Source: Muster rolls, Excelsior Guard, Texas Volunteer Guard, RG 401, Texas State Library and Archives Commission, Austin.

and the selection of "dark" or "black" commanding officers provides further support for this conclusion.

The last volunteer militia organization requiring examination involves the commanding officer and staff of the 1st Regiment, Colored Infantry, and its successor, the Battalion of Colored Infantry.

The state of Texas, recognizing the existence of eight African American infantry militia companies in 1880, ordered those organizations to "immediately proceed to make nominations for one colonel, one lieutenant-colonel and one major, . . . by convention, in which all the companies of the regiment are to be represented."[10] Unfortunately, of these three positions, only the skin color of Col. Andrew M. Gregory and Maj. P. H. Henderson have been determined. Gregory, an African Methodist Episcopal (AME) minister from North Carolina who may have arrived in Texas following the Civil War, was listed as a "mulatto" on the US census of 1880 but later recorded as "black" in 1900.[11] Henderson, born at Northampton, Virginia, enlisted and served for three years during the Civil War with Company I, 36th US Colored Infantry Regiment. His enlistment papers recorded his complexion as "light." Still a private when he obtained his discharge at Brazos Santiago, Texas, in 1866, Henderson soon made his way to Galveston, where he most likely assisted in establishing the Lincoln Guards in 1876; by 1879, he was in command of the company. Within two years, Henderson became the second-highest-ranking African American officer in Texas.[12]

In addition to the three field-grade officers, the regimental staff included several officers with the rank of captain who served as the regiment's adjutant, chaplain, commissary, quartermaster, or, initially, an assistant surgeon; a surgeon, with the rank of major, was added in 1883. From the regiment's inception in May 1880 to its reduction to a battalion in December 1886, ten men occupied these various staff positions. Of those individuals, only half have been positively identified, providing some evidence of their skin color and its possible influence on their becoming officers.

George W. Wilson was commanding the Roberts Rifles of Corpus Christi in December 1879, but within several years, he rose in the ranks of the regiment to become major and would initially command the Battalion of Colored Infantry. Like Henderson, Wilson had been born at Northampton, Virginia; enlisted in the US Colored Troops; and was mustered out in May 1866 at Galveston. But unlike Henderson, he was consistently listed as "black" throughout the historical records.[13] Another veteran, James H. King, who acted as the quartermaster officer for the regiment in 1880, is much more difficult to determine. When he enlisted in the US Colored Troops, his complexion was noted as "Dark Mulatto, Dark," suggesting that his skin tone was virtually "black." King's eyes were listed as "gray," so perhaps the enlisting officer viewed his eye color as proof of mixed race and recorded it the best way he could. But when King enlisted after the war in the 40th US Infantry, then later in the 24th US Infantry, both enlistment registers document his complexion as "yellow."[14] When Charles L. Madison obtained his commission as captain to join the regimental staff as chaplain in 1880, he was the pastor of the Austin AME Church; the census for that year listed him as "black."[15] The remaining two staff officers who were positively identified, Joshua Goins ttand Richard Allen, were both designated "mulatto." Allen, an active participant of the Republican Party in Texas and later chairman of its state committee, won a seat on the Houston Board of Alderman and later represented Harris County in the Texas House of Representatives in 1870–71 and again in 1873. At the time of his commission as a captain in the state militia, he was serving as an inspector and the deputy collector of customs at Houston.[16] Goins, a native of Ohio, served briefly as the chaplain of the regiment. He also served during the Civil War and, like King, had reenlisted in the US Army afterward. Serving three years in the 41st US Infantry Regiment, Goins was discharged at the expiration of his enlistment at Fort McKavett, Texas, in 1870. While his enlistment documents noted his complexion tas "yellow," the 1880 census for Ellis County, Texas, recorded him as a mulatto.[17]

While King's skin hue remains in doubt, and with information on only half of the officers available, the ability to arrive at any conclusions about the regimental staff as derived from skin color remains problematic. Still, one assumption can be inferred from this examination. While Henderson, a light-skinned African American, rose to the highest ranks in the black militia in Texas, so did his predecessor, Wilson, who had a darker complexion, thus signaling that, at least in Texas, colorism *did not* affect the promotion opportunities of individuals. For the regimental officer, or at least from what can be determined, his qualifications seem to center more on prior military service than on skin color.

The same is true for the command and staff officers of the Battalion of Colored Infantry. There were only four men who served as the major commanding the battalion from 1886 to the last available muster roll in 1903. Wilson and his successor, Jacob Lyons, were both Civil War veterans. Eugene Ogden Bowles had served briefly in the 24th US Infantry Regiment. And the battalion's last commanding officer, James Prentice Bratton, born in 1870, became its major without having any prior military service. All of these men are listed in field and staff muster rolls as either "dark" or "black"—the battalion was never led by a lighter-skinned African American. Similar to the regiment, the battalion staff always comprised men identified as having darker skin as well as those classified as "yellow" or "light." This again eliminates any argument of "mulatto exclusiveness" between African Americans who served in the Texas Volunteer Guard.[18]

To contrast the influence of colorism, or lack thereof, in the selection and service of African American officers in the Texas Volunteer Guard with their counterparts in Georgia and Virginia merits further discussion. The history of the last two states comprises much longer periods of racial interaction than Texas. Thus, their pasts include multigenerational and lengthier peri-

Rev. Joshua V. B. Goins. From Hall, *Hall's Moral
and Mental Capsule,* v.

ods of racial mixing, more entrenched legal codes governing the activities of
slaves and free persons of color, and the arrival of culturally diverse Caribbean
émigrés to the Eastern Seaboard. While to investigate the effects of colorism
on every African American volunteer militia organization in the states of
Georgia and Virginia over the course of thirty years would warrant a volume
unto itself, one can scrutinize the locations in each state where lived at one
time those men at the highest echelon of command. For Georgia, the infantry
battalions were located at Savannah, Atlanta, and Augusta; in Virginia, they
were at the cities of Richmond, Petersburg, and Norfolk.

Georgia's "Colored" Lieutenant Colonels

In antebellum Georgia, state law required free persons of color to identify a white guardian. Such relationships continued to have influence even in the post–Civil War years for leaders in the black militia.

The Georgia General Assembly in 1818 legislated that all free persons of color must register with the inferior courts of the county in which they resided.[19] By that time, the legal restraints on their activities had steadily increased through the years. In 1807, "an act for the better regulation of free negroes, in the cities of Savannah and Augusta," was passed that prevented any person within the city limits from hiring or renting "any house or tenement to any free negro, mulatooe, or mustezoe" without prior permission from the city council.[20] One year later, in order to eliminate "the dangerous tendency" of permitting "free negroes and persons of color to rove about the country in idleness and dissipation," the Georgia legislature permitted justices of the peace, supported by "three freeholders of the district," to hire out those individuals, ages eight to twenty-one, "*provided, such free persons or persons of color have no guardian.*"[21] By 1810, the Georgia assembly had codified the process of obtaining a guardian. Prior to the more informal steps that appeared to have existed in previous years, the free person of color had to apply to a white person, who in turn had to consent in writing to act as that person's guardian. Once completed, any judge of the state's superior or inferior courts could then legally appoint that individual to serve as guardian, placing them in charge of that free person of color's legal affairs. The state, however, did not *mandate* the guardian system until 1818, when the anxiety toward the number of free blacks residing in Georgia prompted the forced registration of all such persons and prevented entry into the state of any additional ones. Historian Janice L. Sumler-Edmond has argued, "although the system was intended to limit black independence, in reality it did not always have a detrimental impact on the free black population," and "it was not uncommon for a black ward to benefit from his or her relationship with the white guardian."[22]

The relationship that William Henry Woodhouse, with his complexion listed as "light" on the city of Savannah's registers of free persons of color, developed with his guardians may have contributed to his rise as Georgia's first lieutenant colonel of African descent. Young Woodhouse and his siblings were all represented by his mother's guardian, Robert W. Pooler. A West Point graduate, Pooler left the US Army to practice law in Savannah.

Later, he was elected to Georgia's House of Representatives, serving from 1823 to 1825; commanded a light artillery battery of the Georgia militia; and filled a variety of positions in several city and county courts. Pooler's death in 1853 caused Woodhouse to apply to another lawyer, John Elliott Ward. The mayor of Savannah at the time, Ward had served as the US attorney for the state, speaker of the Georgia House of Representatives as well as the president of the state senate, and a delegate to the Democratic National Convention in 1856. Pres. James Buchanan appointed him minister to China, but he returned to Savannah following Georgia's secession from the Union.[23]

Beginning on February 12, 1861, the *Savannah Daily Morning News* continuously printed an advertisement calling for "TWO THOUSAND able-bodied men for service of the State of Georgia to serve for three years. . . . Said recruits needed for such defense. . . . Musicians required as above. Apply to recruiting officer at Oglethorpe Barracks, Liberty Street, Savannah."[24] A carpenter by trade, Woodhouse enlisted as a musician for three months with the 25th Georgia Infantry Regiment at Tybee Island on October 1, along with several other mixed-race African Americans. He followed this initial service with a second enlistment in the Confederate army on January 1, 1862, this time for six months, and stood with the same regiment in the defenses at Thunderbolt, just across the Savannah River from Whitemarsh Island, Georgia. By the time his second term of service expired, Woodhouse, then at Cautson's Bluff, again volunteered. Continuing to serve as a musician, he enlisted for three years or the duration of the war in the regimental band of the 47th Georgia Infantry. Settling into camp life one and one-half miles from Savannah, Woodhouse served his first year in the army at a place known as Camp Williams before the regiment moved to Wilmington, North Carolina, in November 1862. That was where the record of his Confederate service ends.

The 47th Georgia Infantry Regiment's band comprised *only lighter-skinned* African Americans from the city of Savannah. Woodhouse served alongside his brother, Robert, and with Robert Burke, who later worked as a constable for Woodhouse when he was elected magistrate for Savannah's Fourth District. The band membership included two men with French surnames, Eugene Touchelet and Francis DeVersur, providing evidence of an émigré presence (or at least of their offspring). There were other family ties in the band as well. Woodhouse's family would marry into the Mirault family, whose cousins, Robert Low, Joseph Millen, and Robert Oliver, all marched with him in the band of the 47th Regiment. Following the war, Woodhouse became active in politics, served as a justice of the peace, helped establish and became the first superintendent "of a hospital for colored persons," served as an original member of the Mutual Benevolent Association, and was a petitioner for the creation of the Forest Light Infantry in 1872.[25]

Woodhouse served as the 1st Colored Battalion's commanding officer from August 5, 1880, to December 22, 1885.[26] His successor, Maj. John H. Deveaux, elected to the command on February 2, 1886, may also have benefited from his relationship with his guardian, Savannah mayor Richard D. Arnold. As it was with Woodhouse, Deveaux was identified as "light", as a registered free person of color and had served with Confederate forces. Both men were part of the mixed-race community in Savannah, which included a segment created upon the arrival of French émigrés from Saint-Domingue during or following the revolution led by Toussaint-Louverture.[27]

During the Civil War, Deveaux had joined the crew of the CSS *Georgia* when some members moved by rowboats in an effort to capture the USS *Water Witch* on the evening of June 2, 1864. He was not the only African American in the group. Moses Dallas piloted the boat that carried the expedition's leader, Lt. Thomas Pelot, who was killed during the boarding of the Union vessel.[28] Reportedly, Deveaux may have been saved by the officer; every Memorial Day, he made a pilgrimage to Pelot's final resting place in Laurel Grove Cemetery, where he placed flowers and paid the attendants to tidy the lieutenant's grave.[29]

By 1871, Deveaux had obtained an appointment to the position of clerk at the US Customs House at Savannah, most likely through his association with Richard W. White, "one of the most educated and prominent black politicians from Savannah."[30] Five years later, during an outbreak of yellow fever, Deveaux remained at his position with only two other clerks and the collector of customs, who soon took ill. When another clerk died, Deveaux singlehandedly kept the office "open during business hours and the entering and clearing of vessels; etc., attented [sic] to by him, until the Collector returned to duty, thus keeping the commerce of the port unbroken."[31]

Deveaux remained active in Republican Party politics, serving on the state executive committee and as a delegate to several national conventions.[32] His brother, James, often joined him as a delegate and would eventually work as an auditor for the Treasury Department in Washington, D.C., alongside Lyons.[33] In business, Deveaux, again with James and together with Louis B. Toomer and Louis M. Pleasant, established the African American

John Henry Deveaux. From Adams, *Republican
Party and the Afro-American*, n.p.

newspaper *Colored Tribune* in 1875. According to local Savannah historian
Charles Lwanga Hoskins, "white democratic printers refused to print the Republican leaning *Tribune* and it eased [*sic*] publication for a few years."[34] The
paper recommenced operations in 1886 under the banner *Savannah Tribune*,
with Deveaux as editor. Pres. Benjamin Harrison appointed him collector of
customs at Brunswick in 1889 and, according to historian Clarence Bacote,
"with the endorsement of Savannah white citizens and over the objections of
Brunswick whites."[35] His move to Brunswick prompted him to sell the *Tribune*
to Solomon Charles Johnson. Upon the election of Grover Cleveland, Deveaux resigned his collectorship but was once again considered for a position
by Pres. William McKinley. Appointed in 1898 for the port of Savannah, and

with the support of the mayor and the city council, he once again overcame protests from the Cotton Exchange and Board of Trade in the city. Deveaux also served as a director of the Wage Earners Loan and Investment Company and was active in fraternal societies, eventually serving as the Grand Master of the Grand Lodge of Prince Hall Masons of Georgia, a position he held for twelve years. He continued to serve as the collector for the port of Savannah, receiving his appointment from successive Republican presidents, until his sudden death on June 9, 1909.[36]

Four individuals—Jefferson Wyly, William Anderson Pledger, Floyd Henry Crumbly, and John Thomas Grant—were elected, at varying times between 1880 and 1899, to command the 2nd Colored Battalion, located at Atlanta. Wyly, who led the petition to form a battalion from the city's five infantry companies, served as its first commanding officer for approximately four years. Pledger, most likely born a slave at Jonesboro, Georgia, on February 16, 1851, moved to Atlanta following the end of the Civil War and found employment with the Western and Atlantic Railroad. Like his predecessor, he opened an account at the Freedman's Savings Bank. Pledger, unlike Wyly, was noted as having a "dark brown" complexion. He attended Atlanta University but left prior to graduation for Athens, where he established the *Athens Blade,* and in 1878 was commanding the city's African American militia company, the Athens Blues. Pledger utilized the paper to express his continued frustrations with Georgia's Republican leadership and the conditions of African Americans. He sought a political party led by a combination of white and black members, but through the years continually witnessed the inability of African Americans to break into leadership roles or to obtain the federal patronage that the party's white supporters enjoyed. Finally, at the state convention on April 21, 1880, Pledger received the nomination for the state chairmanship from his *Blade* coeditor, William Henry Heard.

Following the withdrawal of the other nominees—both men known for their work with the Freedmen's Bureau, sitting state chairman, John Emory Bryant, and African American Baptist minister William J. White—Pledger became the first black man to lead the state's Republican Party. His rise to leadership also led to the splintering of Georgia Republicans, with Pledger as the recognized leader of one faction and the other, the "lily-whites," led by future gubernatorial candidate Jonathan Norcross and US Marshal James Longstreet, a former Confederate lieutenant general.[37]

Pledger moved back to Atlanta, where he established two additional newspapers, the *Atlanta News* and the *Atlanta Age.* While he eventually lost the

William Anderson Pledger. From Washington, Williams,
and Wood, *New Negro for a New Century,* 43.

chairmanship of the state party, he later held the position of vice chairman. As a delegate, Pledger attended every Republican national convention from 1880 to 1900 and eventually received a presidential appointment as the surveyor of the Customs House at Atlanta. It was during this time that he was elected commanding officer of the 2nd Colored Battalion in 1883. When examined for the position, Pledger was found unfit to command and appears to have never been issued a commission by the governor. Even so, he was often referred to afterward as "colonel," which he either claimed as his lawful right due to the election results or had adopted later as an honorary rank. Smith Easley, another prominent Republican who ran against Pledger for the colonelcy, took the title of "major," although he, too, was never commissioned by the state. Both men continued their political activities, and Pledger, who studied law, was eventually admitted to the bar, He remained a tireless crusader for African American political, civil, and social rights until his death from tuberculosis on January 8, 1904.[38]

Lt. Col. John Thomas Grant succeeded Pledger as the elected commanding officer of the battalion on October 7, 1890. Grant, born a slave on June 4, 1862, at Monroe, Georgia, was raised on a plantation owned by Col. John Thomas Grant (born in 1813). Earning a fortune as a railroad engineer prior to the Civil War, the elder Grant was ruined financially following the economic destruction during the course of the conflict. Moving to Atlanta, Colonel Grant rebuilt his finances by rebuilding what the Union armies had destroyed.[39]

The younger Grant, known as Thomas, accompanied his benefactor to Atlanta. His mother, upon her deathbed, summoned "Marse John" to "give him" both Thomas and his brother, Richard, so the colonel could "take dem two boys and to make men out of 'em by makin' 'em wuk hard."[40] These two young men, both light -skinned African Americans, continued to work for the Grant family, which provided for the young Thomas's education at Atlanta University. Following the death of the "Colonel," Grant worked for his widow as a valet in the home on Peachtree Avenue. He did not possess the federal military experience that Wyly had brought to the command, nor was he as politically vocal, or volatile, as Pledger. It appears likely that he must have benefited from the patronage of his benefactor. Grant had commenced his state military career, which would span over ten years, as a private in the Fulton Guards in 1881. Soon elected as a second lieutenant in the Guards, he served continually as a lieutenant in this company until elected to its command on April 3, 1888. Grant was still serving as captain when he was elected lieutenant colonel of the battalion, a position he then held until his resignation on November 1, 1892, in order to pursue his business interests.[41]

The 2nd Battalion returned to its foundation of leaders having prior military service with Floyd Henry Crumbly, who was elected lieutenant colonel twenty-one days following Grant's resignation. Prior to this, he had served as Grant's adjutant.[42] Crumbly was born to a free mother and a slave father in Rome, Georgia, on May 10, 1859. His father, known as Robert "Crumley," was a Methodist minister who later represented Warren County in the Georgia Constitutional Convention of 1867–68. Before the Civil War, Crumbly's parents reportedly became separated, and he and his mother moved to Nashville, where she died in 1869. By 1870, he was reunited with his father and living in Griffen, Georgia, where the census taker, Thomas Allen, recorded the entire family as "mulatto."[43]

Floyd Henry Crumbly. From Carter, *Black Side,* 168d.

At the age of eighteen, Crumbly enlisted at Atlanta in the US Army for five years, serving with the 10th US Cavalry. He participated in a grueling eight-month campaign against the Chiricahuas known as Victorio's War in 1879–80. Crumbly rose through the ranks, becoming a sergeant in December 1880 prior to his discharge on November 16, 1881, at Fort Stockton, Texas. Returning to Atlanta, he worked as a grocery clerk before starting his own business in 1885. In time, he purchased the building where he operated his grocery store on Auburn Avenue. Crumbly's achievements in the black business community and Atlanta society echoed his success in the ranks of the military.[44]

With the assistance of other African American businessmen, including Henry Allen Rucker, Crumbly established the Georgia Real Estate Loan and Trust Company. He affiliated with the Grand Lodge of Prince Hall Masons of Georgia and worked as Deveaux's secretary for eight years. He also served as the adjutant of the Colored National Guard Association. Crumbly's reputation gained him a position on the board of directors of the Penny Savings Bank of Chattanooga, Tennessee, and the Carrie Steele Logan Orphanage of Atlanta. In 1895, he served as the director of the Negro Department at the Cotton States Exposition. The outbreak of the war with Spain ended his tenure as the 2nd Battalion's commanding officer.[45]

At Augusta, the 3rd Colored Battalion, formed in 1885, like its neighboring battalion in Savannah, only had two commanding officers during its history—Augustus Roberson Johnson and Isaiah Blocker. Johnson served the battalion from its conception until he resigned on September 20, 1892. He is first recorded on the decennial US Census for Richmond County in 1870 as a "black" seventeen-year-old schoolteacher; in 1880, he is listed as "mulatto"; then in 1900, he is again described as "black." With this conflicting evidence, it remains inconclusive if he would be considered either a light- or dark-skinned African American for the purpose of this investigation. Johnson remained a schoolteacher throughout his life and was the principal of Augusta's Mauge Street Grammar School when he died on October 21, 1908, following a two-month illness. His educational contributions spanned forty years in the city's schools, and he served sixteen years as the superintendent of Sunday school at Harmony Baptist Church.[46]

The battalion's second commanding officer, Isaiah Blocker, like Johnson, also taught in the public schools for African American children at Augusta and became a principal. According to the 1880 census, he, too, began early with his teaching career, at the age of nineteen. This same report documented the entire family as "mulatto." By 1899, the city of Augusta, in addition to its public schools, possessed a multitude of private educational facilities for African Americans, including Haine's Normal and Industrial Institute, the Paine Institute, the Walker Baptist Institute, and three academies, Nellieville, Weed, and Tolbert's. Augusta's black community certainly recognized the value of education toward improving one's standing in life.[47]

Blocker, like Crumbly in Atlanta, had served Lieutenant Colonel Johnson as an adjutant, obtaining his initial state commission from Gov. Henry McDaniel on September 8, 1885. He took the reins of battalion command on October 28, 1892, approximately one month following Johnson's resignation, and, also like Crumbly, led Augusta's African American militia volunteers until 1898. Neither Johnson nor Blocker possessed any military experience prior to their militia service. Focusing on education at an early age, each man devoted his entire life to teaching others in an effort to uplift their fellow African Americans. They most likely believed they were also accomplishing this goal as officers in Georgia's military. Their leadership and actions were recognized; this, more than the shade of their skin, led to their advancement.[48]

Georgia's Staff Officers and Company Commanding Officers

The absence of physical descriptions from the scattered Georgia company muster rolls during the 1890s prevents any detailed analysis of skin-color compositions as was possible with the African American militia volunteers in Texas. Nevertheless, exploring the skin color of the company commanding officers, who with their men voted for the various battalion commanders in their vicinity, and the individuals each lieutenant colonel chose for his staff offers an opportunity to relate complexion with those selection decisions.[49]

Woodhouse's initial staff for the 1st Colored Battalion at Savannah consisted mostly of officers with lighter skin, but there were two members who were darker—Robert H. Burke, a city constable, and James C. Bourke, a cemetery sexton. Those on the staff listed as "mulatto" included Deveaux, Toomer, Anthony Kirk Desverney, and Dr. Patrick Henry Coker. When Coker died in 1886, he was replaced by Dr. Thomas James Davis, a native of Jamaica who had received his education at English College on the island and at the University of Vermont. Davis, also of mixed race, in conjunction with several other physicians, including Dr. C. Bryan Whaley, formed the Southern Medical Association at Savannah in 1892. When he died in 1903, Davis was the superintendent of the city's Charity Hospital. The light-skinned Whaley replaced his late colleague on the battalion staff in 1904.[50]

The battalion's adjutant, Louis Toomer, was born a free person of color in Charleston, South Carolina. Described as "light," he was one of the founders of both Savannah's St. Stephen's Episcopal Church and the city's Republican Party. He assisted Deveaux, a fellow Episcopalian, in establishing the *Savannah Tribune*, worked as the editor for the *Savannah Weekly Echo*, and also ran for a position on the Board of City Commissioners in 1870, one of three African Americans to do so; none of them were elected. Toomer ran again for the Board of Education, lost, but was elected as a magistrate for the First District in 1877. At the annual meeting of the Grand Lodge of Georgia on December 27, 1876, he was elected as the Right Worshipful Deputy Grand Master, second in the state only to Deveaux. Upon his appointment to the battalion staff, Toomer was working as the superintendent of general delivery at the city's post office, where he had been employed since 1869.[51]

Desverney was Woodhouse's brother-in-law, worshiped with Deveaux and Toomer at St. Stephen's, and attended lodge meetings with Deveaux at the Eureka Lodge No. 1, Prince Hall Masons, serving for a time as its Grand Master. In addition to his personal connections with the 1st Battalion's top two officers, his position as a successful cotton shipper contributed to his appointment as the command's quartermaster. His only son, Edward Everette, later served as the battalion's last adjutant. The younger Desverney, educated in the city schools and at Virginia's Hampton Institute, worked over twenty years as a cotton broker. He also served on the board of a bank and that of Charity Hospital, was a member of the Masonic Lodge, and was part of a group that established the Carnegie Colored Library in the city. When he died at age forty-six in 1915, Desverney had approximately $50,000 in assets.[52]

Of the men who elected Woodhouse, consisting of the captains from the city's six infantry companies, one is listed as a "mulatto," three are categorized "black," and the other two—Daniel S. Youmans and J. H. Carter—are unknown. Capt. Louis M. Pleasant, the lighter-skinned African American and commanding officer of the Forest City Light Infantry, "became a leading Republican in the state and was recognized by national Republicans for his party loyalty and political shrewdness." Pleasant had also been one of the founders of the Colored Tribune with the Deveaux brothers and Toomer. According to historian Robert Perdue, Pleasant "was generally recognized by white Republicans for his leadership and control of Savannah Negroes," yet he was "more interested in pushing himself to the top than in the advancement of blacks."[53] Even so, Pleasant worked tirelessly for the Republican Party, attending at least five national conventions, and held a variety of federally appointed positions during Republican presidential administrations, including collector of customs at Savannah prior to Deveaux. In fact, it was surprising that Pleasant did not rise higher in the volunteer militia of the city, but his political aspirations and activities may have occupied much more of his time.[54]

Capt. Morris J. Cummings, a laborer; Capt. Prince A. D. Lloyd, a servant; and Capt. William H. Royall, Savannah's first African American undertaker, were all described as "black." Not much is known of Cummings or Lloyd. Royall, on the other hand, started one of the first African American businesses in the city of Savannah in 1878 after working for the Henderson Brothers, a white mortuary, during the yellow fever epidemic in 1876. He, too, was a Mason and was one of the signatories on the initial petition to the governor to establish the Savannah Light Infantry in 1877. He became the company's first commanding officer, a position he held until his election to major in 1890.[55]

Two men who may or may not have participated in the election of Woodhouse were the commanders of the city's artillery battery and cavalry troop.

The 1880 Census listed Captain Simmons of the Georgia Artillery as "black," while the military service record of Captain Jones of the Savannah Hussars documented his complexion as "yellow," a record supported by his later application at the Freedman's Bank, which recorded him as "light."[56]

As the command was passed from Woodhouse to Deveaux in 1886, and even before the deaths of Coker and Bourke, some staff positions had changed. Royall was elected as the major of the battalion on September 18, 1890, followed by Solomon Charles Johnson's appointment as commissary officer on December 12 of that same year. Johnson, a Savannah native, had a long association with the newspaper business. Starting as a young man delivering copies of the *Savannah Morning News,* he later worked as a printer at the *Echo* before joining Deveaux at the *Tribune,* where he eventually became editor and sole owner. His affiliation with Deveaux lasted until the lieutenant colonel's death in 1909. Johnson, most often listed as "black," was a member of the Prince Hall Masons and also served, as did Deveaux, as the Grand Master for Georgia. Two years after becoming commissary officer, Johnson was promoted to captain and battalion adjutant.[57]

A new staff position, the inspector of rifle practice, was created sometime in 1894 for the African American troops but may have remained unfilled in the 1st Battalion until October 20, 1899, when Dr. James Henry Bugg joined the staff. Surprisingly, the physician, at the time of the creation of the position, was a member of the executive committee of the Rifle and Gun Club of Savannah, a group of African Americans comprising "a number of the best shots in the city."[58] A native of Augusta, Captain Bugg graduated from Leonard Medical College at North Carolina's Shaw University. He initially began his medical practice at Lynchburg, Virginia, but in June 1892, he relocated to Savannah, where he joined the South East Georgia Medical Society and, like Davis before him, served as the superintendent of the Charity Hospital. Bugg, described on census reports as "black," was elected a city physician by the city council in 1897. During the last two years of its existence, he served as the commanding officer of the Savannah Light Infantry.[59] The staff officers who assisted Lieutenant Colonel Wyly during his tenure in command have not been identified.

The complexion of the staff officers of the 2nd and 3rd Colored Battalions likewise provide an opportunity to examine the possible presence of colorism at the highest levels of Georgia's African American volunteer militia. After taking command of the 2nd Colored Battalion in October 1890, Lieutenant Colonel Grant built a staff of five officers, who were all commissioned on

Dr. James Henry Bugg. From *Savannah Tribune,*
June 9, 1906.

January 21, 1891. At Augusta, Johnson's initial staff for the 3rd Colored Battalion only included two officers, each commissioned a day apart in September 1885. Some of the same men in each battalion continued to serve Crumbly and Blocker as each ascended to their respective commands. The pattern that emerges upon examination of the extant records remains similar to that at Savannah: the overwhelming number of men who held battalion staff positions at Atlanta and Augusta possessed lighter shades of skin color.[60]

With no second in command, the 2nd Colored Battalion had a total of five staff officers; of these, only one was described as "black" or "dark." Benjamin Franklin Hoyt, a native of Prattsville, Alabama, and a wheelwright by trade, served as the battalion's commissary officer. But Hoyt had replaced Christopher Columbus Wimbish, a lighter-skinned African American who resigned

Dr. Henry Rutherford Butler. From Kleizing and
Crogman, *Progress of a Race,* 550.

in April 1892; therefore, Grant initially possessed an entire staff of officers
categorized as "mulatto." While Crumbly also appointed a new battalion adjutant, William Brewster Pruden, he retained the rest of Grant's staff: Dr. Henry
Rutherford Butler, staff surgeon, Richard J. Henry, battalion quartermaster;
and Edward Randolph Carter, chaplain.[61]

Born April 11, 1862, at Fayetteville, North Carolina, Butler moved to Wilmington, where he studied under Dr. E. E. Green, before entering Lincoln University in Pennsylvania. Completing his courses in 1887, he began his medical
training at Meharry Medical College, graduating in 1890. Butler, with his former college classmate Thomas Heathe Slater, immediately moved to Atlanta,
where they became the city's first successful African American physicians.
Together, they operated Butler and Slater Pharmacy and an infirmary for
area black citizens. Butler was active in community affairs, wrote articles of
African American uplift for the *Atlanta Constitution,* established the Morris
Brown College School of Nursing, and served as the Grand Master of Georgia's Prince Hall Masons from 1900 until his death in 1931.[62]

Rev. Edward Randolph Carter. Courtesy of Edward
Randolph Carter and Andrew Jackson Lewis Collection,
Auburn Avenue Research Library on African American
Culture and History.

Henry was born at Jackson, Mississippi, on August 17, 1846, the son of
Brig. Gen. Patrick Henry and Anna Taylor, a slave. During the Civil War, he
worked as a servant for a Confederate officer until Henry deserted, returned
to Jackson, and then joined the crew of the troop carrier USS *Tarascon*. At
the end of the war, Henry moved to Selma, Alabama, where he organized a
Republican club. He refused several opportunities to serve at the national
and state level with the Republican Party. In 1870, Henry moved to Savannah
and started work with J. E. Johnston & Company, which administered the
insurance contracts of New York Life. He remained employed by the company
when it relocated to Atlanta in 1877. When Henry died in 1902, Deveaux acted
as one of his pallbearers, and Carter spoke at his funeral service.[63]

Born a slave on March 15, 1858, in Clarke County, Georgia, Carter received
a basic education and was apprenticed as a shoemaker by age thirteen. He

joined the church in 1875 and by 1880 was preaching at Stone Mountain Baptist Church. Two years later, he became the pastor of Atlanta's First Baptist Church, or Friendship Church, where he remained for sixty-one years. Carter completed his education at Atlanta Baptist Seminary in 1884 and two years later, with Augusta's Johnson as president, became vice president of the Georgia State Baptist Sunday School Convention. He went on to edit two Baptist journals, and as the minister "of one of the largest and influential Baptist churches in the State," he had "with each succeeding year grown in influence and power among his people."[64] A glance into Carter's attitude toward racial uplift can be found in his writing in 1894. Seeking to understand "how he may best serve his flock," Carter explained that he felt "encouraged enough not to despair, but to push forward under God's help with hope to become something and to yet make my people something," but he realized that "generations must come and go before this can be done."[65]

Lieutenant Colonel Blocker of the 3rd Colored Battalion in Augusta retained the services of Johnson's quartermaster officer, Henry Lucius Walker. First Lieutenant Walker, a lighter-skinned African American, received his commission on September 9, 1885. At that time, he not only was serving as the president of the (African American) State Teachers' Association but also was the principal at the Second Ward School in Augusta. Blocker added four more officers to his staff in the months after taking command: Rev. Charles Thomas Walker as chaplain, Nelson C. Redfield as adjutant, Robert F. Benefield as commissary officer; and Dr. George Nelson Stoney as battalion surgeon. Redfield resigned after only a year. He, Stoney, and Benefield were all light-skinned, whereas Reverend Walker possessed a darker complexion.[66]

Unlike Johnson before him, who concentrated exclusively on educators, Blocker's staff officers, with only two from the education field, point toward more inclusion from the black community. Benefield welcomed guests to the city's Commercial Club, with its "magnificent dining room, where 100 guests can be served at one time."[67] Redfield may have worked for Benefield as a waiter, but by the time of his commission, he was employed at the Planter's Hotel as a porter.[68]

The final two staff officers, a physician and a minister, held important positions in Augusta. Stoney, born at Aiken, South Carolina, received his education at the Avery Institute in Charleston; Howard University in Washington, D.C.; and the Chicago Medical School. In addition to medicine, he was active in a variety of fraternal orders, including the Masons and the Knights of Pythias, and served as a trustee of Paine College and as a director for the

Rev. Charles Thomas Walker. From Floyd,
Life of Charles T. Walker, 174.

Penny Savings Bank, the Georgia Mutual Insurance Company, and Augusta's YMCA.[69]

Born a slave in Hephzibah, Georgia, in 1858, Walker studied at the Augusta Institute for two years prior to being ordained in 1877. He founded Augusta's Tabernacle Baptist Church in 1885 and remained there except for his brief time as chaplain with the US Volunteers during the Spanish-American War and as pastor of Mt. Olivet Baptist Church in New York City. In addition to his pastoral duties in Augusta, Walker managed the business department of the *Augusta Sentinel* newspaper; authored the resolution calling for the creation of a normal school, Walker Institute; established the Tabernacle Old Folks Home; and assisted with the organization of the Augusta Exposition Company in 1893. In the introduction to a biography of Walker, Robert Stuart MacArthur wrote: "His racial characteristics are so strongly emphasized that the most bitter opponent of his race cannot attribute his acknowledged ability as thinker, writer and preacher to any interfusion of white blood in his veins. He is a Negro in every drop of his blood."[70]

This inquiry into the shades of skin color and the overwhelming presence, but not exclusively, of lighter-skinned officers at the highest levels of command in all three infantry battalions seems to strongly support that a color bias did not exist within the officer corps of the Georgia Volunteers, Colored.

With these results, one might expect that Georgia's lengthy history of slavery and racially diverse population, as shared by the Commonwealth of Virginia, would produce similar conclusions in the Old Dominion. The study of Virginia's staff officers and battalion commanders provides some insight as to whether this common history resulted in a similar composition of the officers of that state's African American militia organizations.

Virginia's "Colored" Battalion Officers

In Virginia, too, only had a handful of men rose to command a battalion of black infantry companies. The 1st Battalion, Colored Infantry at Richmond, organized June 16, 1876, may have been the first such African American military organization led by a black officer in the South. Its first commanding officer, Richard Henry Johnson, a native of the capital city, had enlisted in the 115th Regiment, US Colored Troops at the closing of the Civil War and achieved the rank of sergeant. Listed as "yellow" on his enlistment papers, Johnson most likely was at the initial gathering of veterans at the Union Eagle Hotel who formed the Richmond Zouaves in 1871. Obtaining the rank of captain with the Zouaves, Johnson led the company at Memorial Day services and at Grant's presidential inaugural parade. Either the company changed its name or a new company was formed in March 1873, with Johnson then in command of the Carney Guard. When the 1st Battalion formed, Johnson was elected not only its major but also the first African American in Virginia history to attain that rank. The Yorktown Centennial Celebration in 1881 may have been the highlight of his volunteer militia career as an officer, since Johnson resigned the next year, two years before his death in 1884. As in Georgia, the officer who succeeded him had previously served Johnson as the battalion's adjutant.[71]

Joseph Brown Johnson, described as "black," took the reins of the battalion on June 26, 1882, relinquishing them only when the battalion dissolved in 1899. Both Johnsons participated in the growing organized-labor movement in the city. Richard worked at the Patterson Tobacco Factory and served as an official in the Union Laboring Branch, while Joseph, an iron-foundry worker, eventually became the master workman for District Assembly 94, Knights

Dr. John C. Ferguson. From Kenney, *Negro in Medicine,* 53.

of Labor. In addition to his labor activities, Johnson was a Republican and assisted in establishing the first Masonic lodge at Manchester, Virginia.

Similar to other battalion commanding officers, Joseph Johnson inherited several men who had previously served on his predecessor's staff. For the 1st Battalion, these two men were John Graves, a "dark" tobacco factory worker, and Dr. John C. Ferguson, a "mulatto" physician, both commissioned on January 16, 1879.[72] Not much is known of Graves. Ferguson, a native of Virginia, received his primary education in Detroit, Michigan, where his father worked as physician for the city's First District. He attended Oberlin College in Ohio and graduated from the Detroit Medical College. Ferguson arrived in Richmond and quickly became involved in Readjuster politics, culminating in his appointment as the assistant superintendent of the Virginia Central Asylum

Dr. Samuel Henry Dismond. From Corey,
Baptist Home Mission Monthly, 202.

in 1882. As the battalion's surgeon, Ferguson worked closely with Dr. Samuel Henry Dismond, his assistant.

Born a slave in Appomattox County, Virginia, Dismond, looked for employment to support his widowed mother and siblings after the death of his father. Working during the day at Faulkner and Craighead Pharmacy, he spent the evening hours studying. Dismond graduated from the Richmond Institute in 1879 and from Howard University in 1883 as class valedictorian, with a degree as doctor of medicine and pharmacology. First Lieutenant Dismond joined the staff of the 1st Battalion on November 28, 1883, and ascended to the position of battalion surgeon upon the death of Ferguson in 1889. Beyond his militia service and medical practice, Dismond served on the Board of Trustees of the Hartshorn Memorial College and Virginia Union University and was a director of the YMCA in Richmond.[73]

Major Johnson filled three other staff positions in 1883—adjutant, Capt. Augustus C. Brown; quartermaster, 1st Lt. Ralph W. Brown; and battalion chaplain, Rev. Henry Haywood Mitchell. Captain Brown, a shoemaker, and

Rev. Henry Haywood Mitchell. Courtesy of African
American Collection, Columbus Public Library.

Lieutenant Brown, a porter, were listed as "black" in the census of 1880. Mitchell, the pastor of Richmond's Fifth Street Baptist Church at the time, had
been born in Canada to an escaped slave mother and British soldier in 1852,
according to family tradition. He studied at the Crozer Theological Seminary
and served as the secretary for the National Baptist Convention in 1884. He
resigned on August 1, 1887, to relocate.[74]

Mitchell was replaced as battalion chaplain by George E. Johnson in the
fall of 1887. Johnson, the pastor of the River View Baptist Church, remained
on staff until he was honorably discharged on April 29, 1899, "by disbandment
of the battalion."[75] With the exception of the minister and Dismond, Major
Johnson experienced a turnover of every officer on his staff over the next
few years. Two men, Henry A. Cobb and William Isaac Johnson, received
their commissions on March 10, 1890. They had worked together in the Richmond post office but later lost those positions. Cobb, listed as a "mulatto"
and a shoemaker by trade, initially entered Virginia's volunteer militia as a
first lieutenant in the Attucks Guard in 1885. He served for three years with

that company before resigning to take the same position in the newly formed L'Ouverture Guard.

When that company's first captain could not pass his examination, Cobb was promoted to the senior position, but the company failed to materialize. Major Johnson allowed him to keep his rank by bringing him on to his staff as adjutant, a position Cobb held until 1897. First Lieutenant Johnson served as the quartermaster officer and reportedly, like Cobb, had previously served in the L'Ouverture Guard. Upon his departure from the post office, he started a mortuary business that became so successful that he purchased a three-story building on Fonshee Street. Using the basement as a workshop, Johnson conducted his business on the first floor, his family lived on the second, and he subdivided the third floor into meeting rooms for rental income. Reportedly, his business was "as fine as any owned by the leading white undertakers in Richmond."[76]

The promotion of Dismond to battalion surgeon left an opportunity for another physician to join the staff as his assistant. Harrison Llewellyn Harris was born of a freeman and a slave mother in 1855 on what later became the Manassas battlefield. During the war, his family was moved to Alexandria, where Harris received his first education. Afterward, he worked for Frederick Douglass's newspaper the *New National Era* in Washington, D.C., and in 1882 graduated with a medical degree from Howard University. Harris, listed as "black," began his practice in Petersburg, where he also served on the Board of Health and as the city physician for African Americans from 1882 to 1888. In 1890, he opened a second office in Richmond and presided over the Negro Baptist Old Folks' Home. Like many of his colleagues, Harris was a member of the Prince Hall Masons. He served as the Grand Secretary of the Grand Lodge of Virginia for over three decades and published its historical textbook.[77]

On January 15, 1894, the battalion's subsistence officer, John Graves, died at Richmond. He was replaced in February by 1st Lt. William Hancock Anderson, who operated a successful publishing and supply business. Specializing in supplies for churches, schools, and fraternal societies, Anderson, consistently listed as "black," had completed studies in accounting and worked as a bookkeeper prior to establishing his own business in 1882. Entering military service for the first time, he served Major Johnson for three years and, upon the retirement of Captain Cobb, received a promotion to captain and the position of adjutant. During the war with Spain, he served in the 6th Virginia Volunteer Regiment, receiving an honorable discharge on January 26, 1899. A supporter of the Republican Party, he returned to Richmond and worked as a bailiff for

Harrison Llewellyn Harris. From Caldwell,
History of the American Negro, 19.

the US Circuit Court of Appeals. Anderson also served at one time as the
commander of the Department of the Potomac, United Spanish War Veterans.
Like so many other officers of the state volunteer militia organizations, he
was a Prince Hall Mason. Anderson published a Masonic directory in 1909.[78]

The 1st Battalion comprised not only men of both light and dark complex-
ions but also men who participated in the early labor movement in Richmond
as well as those considered by their occupations or professions as middle
class, such as ministers, physicians, or business proprietors. Leaders of the
2nd Battalion's companies at Petersburg and Norfolk shared such similarities
with those of the battalion in Richmond.

The 2nd Battalion, Colored Infantry was commanded by three different
individuals: William H. Palmer, William F. Jackson, and William Henry Johnson. Palmer a laborer at Norfolk's Navy Yard, was listed as "light" on his enlistment papers for the 36th Regiment of US Colored Infantry in 1863 but later

William Hancock Anderson. From Caldwell,
History of the American Negro, 171.

categorized as "black" by a census registrar. The early staff officers who served
under him while the battalion was headquartered in Norfolk, included a mail
carrier, Moses F. Jordan, as adjutant; Isaiah E. Whitehurst, quartermaster;
Jeffrey T. Wilson, who worked with Palmer in the Navy Yard, as commissary
officer; and battalion chaplain Elias Horace Bolden, a minister in the AME
Church. Reverend Bolden regularly attended the AME Virginia Conference
as a delegate and served on the board of trustees for both Wilberforce College
and Kittrell College. Of this group of men, Jordan was listed as a "mulatto,"
another's skin color is undetermined, and the other two were considered
"black." Jordan's position at the post office denotes political participation, as
does perhaps Wilson's employment. More importantly, this battalion was led
by an African American man from the laboring class.[79]

Palmer's death in 1887, coupled with the disbandment of several constitu-
ent companies, caused the temporary suspension of the 2nd Battalion until

William Henry Johnson. Courtesy of Maj. William
Henry Johnson Papers, James Hugo Johnston
Memorial Library, Virginia State University.

1891, when Jackson reorganized the command. He had joined the militia as an officer in the Petersburg Guard in 1878 and was elected captain of the company in 1883. Jackson died in 1894. The third and final commanding officer, also with previous militia service, was William Henry Johnson.

Commissioned a second lieutenant in the Petersburg Blues in 1884, Johnson was elected captain of the company the following year. Born a slave in 1858 at Petersburg, he learned the cooper's trade as a young man after the Civil War. With assistance from his parents and through his own labor, he attended Hampton Institute, graduating in 1878. Johnson was employed as a schoolteacher in Surry and Chesterfield Counties before returning to Petersburg, where he also taught school and was later a principal, eventually completing over fifty years in education in Virginia. Determining Johnson's skin color remains problematic since he was recorded as "black" in 1900, but ten years later, he was listed as "mulatto."[80]

Dr. Philip Lewis Barber. From Lamb, *Historical,*
Biographical, and Statistical Souvenir, 146.

Even though the battalion reorganized in 1891, by the time W. H. Johnson
took command in 1895, only one staff officer remained. That man, Dr. Philip
Lee Barber, joined Jackson's staff as the assistant surgeon in 1891 but was promoted to battalion surgeon eight months prior to the major's death. Born at
Winchester, Barber's family moved north during or after the Civil War. He received his education in Williamsport, Pennsylvania; studied at Storer College
at Harpers Ferry, Virginia; and in 1883 graduated with a medical degree from
Howard University. Relocating to Norfolk, Barber established his medical
practice, served as president of the city's African American YMCA, and was
vice president of the Home Loan and Building Association, Norfolk's first
black financial institution. Like Johnson, Barber's complexion was described
mostly as "black," but he was also noted as "mulatto."[81]

Dr. Charles R. Alexander became Barber's assistant on January 27, 1895.
He joined the staff at the same time as several other officers: John R. Stokes,
adjutant; William F. Clarke, quartermaster; W. T. Scott, subsistence officer;

and Rev. Hilliard Johnson, chaplain, who had served with the 10th Regiment, US Colored Infantry, as a corporal from 1863 to 1866. Every one of these men shared the same physical-description conflict as experienced with Johnson and Barber, being described as "black" at times and "mulatto" at others. Alexander, born at Bedford, Virginia, was educated at Shaw University, graduated from Leonard Medical College in 1891, and reportedly became "the first man of any race to receive 100 per cent in an examination before the Virginia Board of Medical Examiners."[82] Clarke, previously an officer in the Petersburg Guard for two years, only served on the staff for a year. Also receiving his medical education at Shaw University, he was a member of the board of directors for Petersburg's Harding Street YMCA, served at the local Red Cross, became a thirty-second-degree Mason, and served as assistant surgeon with the 6th Virginia Volunteers from June 1898 to January 1899.[83]

Conclusion

Studying and analyzing the classification of skin color remains a difficult endeavor. This difficulty contributes to the complexity of determining the existence of colorism, and its possible consequences, with the African American volunteer militia of Georgia, Texas, and Virginia. Using terms such as "yellow," "brown," "black," "dark," "light," or even "mulatto" are often interpreted differently by individuals across geographical space and time. For example, the illustration of John C. Ferguson of Virginia compared to those of the men who served as staff officers for Lieutenant Colonels Grant and Crumbly reveal a range of dissimilar physical features, although the records all describe them as "mulatto."

The results of this survey, however, consist of two separate and distinct conclusions, each one within the sphere of color—one white, the other black.

The contention that white society deemed an African American more acceptable and less threatening based on the lighter the skin color, or "whiteness," is *not* supported by the historical evidence from the state of Georgia. Although the three infantry battalions there possessed the highest percentage of lighter-skinned officers, this did not translate to any further longevity of their organizations, nor did it provide them with additional training, weapons, or freedom of movement.

Neither is this revealed in Texas or Virginia, where the longest-serving battalion commanders were dark-skinned African Americans. The white military and government officials of Texas organized training for their black troops at summer encampments. Despite segregation, Texas officials attempted to improve the military skills of black militiamen. Likewise, in Virginia, where the white adjutant general did not authorize camps of instruction for the state's African American forces, white state and city government personnel officially utilized their black volunteers on more occasions than counterparts in either Georgia or Texas, regardless of the militia officers' skin color.

Within these three states' black communities—more specifically, within the ranks of their African American volunteer militia units—in Georgia, at least, the enlisted men appear to have favored lighter-skinned individuals as battalion commanders. On the other hand, the number of men described as "black" who won elections as captains of companies seems to support the opposite conclusion, making it inconclusive to draw evidence of the influence of colorism within Georgia's militia.

In Texas and Virginia, however, the lack of discrimination within the African American rank and file confirms the absence of colorism within these two states. The elevation of regimental and battalion officers of dark skin color as well as the successful elections of company commanders of darker and lighter skin hues clearly reinforces this contention.

There is no doubt that the amount, or lack thereof, of "whiteness" in African Americans influenced society in the postemancipation southern United States of the late nineteenth century. While skin color may lead to the rise of inter- and intraracial discrimination, its effect on the African American militia volunteers in these three states appears minimal or difficult to determine. In Georgia, the skin color of volunteer militia officers ranged from Capt. Thomas Payce Beard ("white") of Augusta to Albany's Capt. Henry Bird ("dark"). Beard, a representative of Richmond County in the Georgia House of Representatives in 1868, was so light skinned that he "was deemed of 'indeterminate' race and not expelled with the other black legislators."[84] By contrast, Bird, "being a full blooded negro himself, . . . would never allow any but pure blooded negroes to enter the ranks of his company."[85]

Therefore, the most important conclusion to draw from this discussion centers on the *complexity* of racial relations both within and beyond the black communities of these three states rather than any simplicity of discrimination based upon the shade of one's skin. By examining the lives of these mostly forgotten African American leaders, men who ascended to the highest ranks of the volunteer militia in their state, some common characteristics are clearly identified. Many fostered relationships with reform-minded white southerners, including those with familial connections. Others participated in, and gave their strong support to, the Republican Party, leading to influential patronage positions in the community. But the single-most-obvious shared trait and apparent objective that these men possessed hinged on their efforts, almost in every social pursuit—political, educational, religious, business, and fraternal as well as military—to improve their condition in life as well as to lift up those around them.

It made no difference whether Charles Thomas Walker and some of his fellow officers had dark skin and John Henry Deveaux and others did not. What mattered to the enlisted men, and where applicable, to the junior officers, who elected these African American officers was their proven leadership. This trait, demonstrated in multiple ways in the local black communities that supported the militia companies, allowed these African American men to accomplish what would have been impossible prior to 1865. They established newspapers and numerous businesses; earned degrees in medicine, pharmacology, and law; opened hospitals; purchased property; and served in an array of federal government positions, from mail handler to overseeing the operations of a US Customs House. Often, serving in the US Army in the fight for freedom during the Civil War enhanced their status and sense of masculinity, which many of these men carried forward through their social status and recognized leadership in the state militias of Georgia, Texas, and Virginia.

The African Americans of all shades of skin who cast their ballots and chose their leaders were confident that the officers they selected would be the people best suited to uplift them as citizens, as Christians, and as men.

7

~~~

"Let Us Play the Man"

The Culture of Masculinity with the Black State Volunteers

Frank Leslie's Illustrated Newspaper published an insightful article together with what it referred to as an "animated sketch" on July 17, 1875. The suggestive illustration, titled *Our Colored Militia* and reportedly taken from real life, depicts an African American militiaman in his home on Sullivan Street, in the presence of his family, preparing for a parade. A vividly descriptive image, it clearly displays the trappings of nineteenth-century manhood embodied in militia participation for the man, as well as for those around him, as he prepares for New York City's Fourth of July parade. The accompanying article not only utilized the word "hero" in place of "man" in two different instances but also asserted that "the scene speaks of a new order of things, in which *masculine equality,* at least, is fully assured." *Leslie's* story not only clearly identified one of the most important motivations for African Americans to serve in the militia but also linked military participation with manhood.[1]

As discussed earlier, African American men communicated their desire to form military organizations through the language of citizenship and the rights heretofore associated with that status. State government officials had viewed them as soldiers by providing arms and supplies and, in some instances, by

Our Colored Militia. From *Leslie's Illustrated Newspaper,* July 17, 1875.

utilizing their services in times of emergency or civil disorder. Behaving in public as officially recognized citizen-soldiers confirmed black men in the culture of manliness in America in the late nineteenth century. They shaped this culture of manliness, gained prestige, earned status, and confirmed citizenship for themselves and other African Americans through their membership in their state's militia.

Active black militia organizations conducted various activities in the late nineteenth century that allowed their members to safely proclaim not only their newly granted constitutional rights as citizens but also their status as men. Studying their actions during those years in Georgia, Texas, and Virginia, reveals the underappreciated fluidity of race relations that initially allowed such events to occur. Unfortunately, these relationships were eliminated later in the century. While obviously illustrating the hardening of race relations, this also exposes the attempt to minimize the heightening awareness of masculinity within the African American male community.

Discussing Manhood and Masculinity

"Manhood" is defined as "the condition of being an adult male as distinguished from a child or female."[2] Especially in the nineteenth-century United States, to be considered a man, one had to possess the traits or characteristics that either society recognized as manly or that were accepted and placed upon an individual by himself as defined by his experience and culture. These traits or characteristics are defined as one's "manliness" or "masculinity."

In the antebellum South, both slaves and free black men, while neither children nor female, were rarely able to exhibit any characteristics of manliness in public. White men in the South, historians Craig Thompson Friend and Lorri Glover have argued, defined themselves by the ideals of "honor and mastery," further contending, "from the point of view of whites, enslavement equaled emasculation." In the antebellum years, most African Americans held as slaves remained encapsulated legally in a childlike status that prevented any social movement. Using this paradigm of "honor and mastery," active militia service (for whites) demonstrated a level of mastery through the elevation of one's social betters as officers, the possession of military firearms, and the wearing of lavish uniforms. Before 1865, legal restrictions kept blacks, for the most part, out of the militia, and any public display of manliness on their part could, and often did, result in violence. Honor, too, took part in the public ceremony, often in the form of paying tribute to those heroes who had sacrificed their lives in defense of the state or the nation. The participation of living veterans in these memorial events provided a connection to the most valued attribute of manliness—service in war. Of course, for black men who had rendered service in America's battles, this trait was incompatible with the culture of white manliness and quickly forgotten.[3]

Still, African American men did craft their own interpretation of what it meant to be a man even within the restrictive society that surrounded them. Friend and Glover asserted that slaves "carved out niches of masculinity in plantation artisan shops, as disciplinarians to their children, and through adept hunting and fishing."[4] Likewise, antebellum free black men defined their manhood by pursuing those trades and skills not open to women; by seeking out opportunities in education, including religious instruction; and by obtaining some degree of financial stability. Furthermore, in contrast to historian Harry S. Laver, who argued that for black men, "their direct participation in militia activities was out of the question," Georgia law allowed for free African Americans to participate in certain positions in the antebellum militia. The Savannah Volunteer Guards, *prior* to the Civil War, utilized two slaves (owned by members) and three free black men in their band.[5] And even during the war, some Confederate infantry units included African Americans as company or regimental musicians. The Sumter Light Guard of Americus, Georgia, later designated as Company K, 4th Georgia Infantry, had three black bandsmen in 1861.[6] At the same time, the 25th Georgia Infantry Regiment listed eleven African Americans from Savannah in its regimental band; a year later, nine of these same men were serving with the 47th Georgia Infantry's band. Surprisingly, in 1877, three of these veterans were listed in the city directory as members of the Savannah Volunteer Guards Band, whose African American members included a drum major, a band leader, and eleven others.[7] This remains a curious addition to the directory, especially since none of the men are listed as "colored," as they are later in the alphabetical listings. There is no doubt that those who performed and marched with the Savannah Volunteer Guards were employed by the battalion, as were the waiters and cooks who worked in the unit's armory building. Granted, playing a musical instrument is *not* the same as shouldering a rifle, but these men did wear military-style uniforms, could claim a level of manhood beyond the grasp of many black men in the community before African American militia companies formed, and surely enjoyed some level of satisfaction as they led the white troops in parades and public events.

The Confederacy's defeat not only ended slavery but also ushered in a new era of social, economic, and political uncertainty. These circumstances also brought gender insecurity for those who had defined their maleness through their mastery of women and the lower social classes, their ability in financial matters or with any holdings of land, and especially their ownership of slaves. Conversely, those who had accepted a modified version of the manly traits could now move more quickly into the realms of honor and mastery, which contributed to the existing uncertainty. As slavery had emasculated black men, the resounding defeat of 1865 accomplished the same for many of the South's white men. This prompted, Craig Thompson Friend asserted, a cultural shift in the traits that defined masculinity. Seeking to redefine themselves in the postwar society and to overcome their defeated status, southern whites modified the old tenets that composed the paradigm by paying tribute to the traits and characteristics of the immortalized Robert E. Lee. According to Friend, Lee epitomized a new model of manliness through his example of the "Christian gentleman—honorable, master of his household, humble, self-restrained, and above all, pious and faithful." Historian Karen Taylor has contended that the white men who accepted this model of the Christian gentleman "were often reformers and inclined to see nonwhite men as educable and therefore potentially redeemable, certainly in a religious sense and at least theoretically, in a political one."[8]

The Christian gentleman model also found meaning for African Americans whose lives became more centered in religion, in education, or in the local fraternal lodge. While they had to previously accept a somewhat-modified version of the cultural meaning of masculinity, they could now *expand* their definition of manliness within the sphere of the black community and push those boundaries into public spaces unavailable to them before 1865. Perhaps these men, too, like their Anglo-reformer counterparts, saw the white population in the same light—educable and redeemable—in their attitudes toward African Americans. Whatever the case, this model did provide for a "'race-neutral language' for masculinity" that could allow black men for the first time to display this characteristic in public settings.[9]

General Lee also remained at the center of another understanding of manhood. As the South's white population turned to the veneration of its military heroes from the war, the "masculine martial ideal" recognized these veterans as "models for a warrior-like and heroic manliness."[10] Not dissimilar to the earlier demonstration of honor, this interpretation also found significance with black men, especially those who had fought to win their freedom, and, surprisingly enough, even with those who had participated with Confederate troops during the war. While African Americans accepted this latter experience as part of the martial ideal, some whites, like their forefathers, forgot or dismissed black participation as outside the realm of manly prowess on the battlefield. Still, as discussed previously, other white southerners, mostly reformers, continued postwar relationships with those African Americans who had served with them during the conflict.

Militia service embodied the martial ideal following the end of the war, and for many black males, it served to symbolize and reinforce their position as a man in society. Legal statutes now allowed black men to form military companies, which further perpetuated the culture of manliness by indoctrinating its younger members in the warrior ethos and exposing them to comrades who had already proven their manhood on or near the battlefield. The race-neutral language of the Christian gentleman allowed them the opportunity to move beyond the "black sphere" into a more public, shared space in society, at least for a few years. The Christian gentleman model was often bolstered by religious sermons, including one delivered July 22, 1894, by Rev. Edward Carter as chaplain of the 2nd Battalion of the Georgia Volunteers, Colored.

Portraying in detail the historical example of European Jews, and especially British prime minister Benjamin Disraeli. According to Carter, Disraeli lived "not in the land where they [Jews] were recognized as men, and allowed every proper representation, but where they were ridiculously treated, sneered at, rebuked, and despised," but he rose "to so great a height of eminence and altitude of power and recognition." Carter faulted the political "partyism" of the day, with its "hot-headedness and incendiary speeches," which he concluded would "never bring peace." Instead, the reverend advocated patience and perseverance, appealing to the militiamen in attendance to "take the advice of the Mighty General of the armies of Isreal [sic], 'be of good courage, and *play the men for our people*, and for the cities of our God and the Lord, do that that seemeth good to them.'"[11]

"To play the man," many African American males sought to demonstrate their manly character through militia service. A sampling of the variety of public military activities in which they participated, such as parades, various public and memorial ceremonies, prize-drill competitions, and target practices, clearly illustrated how they sought to define themselves as men.

The Parade

Historian Shane White contended that for African Americans, parades acted as a means to "enter public life" and to proclaim to those who observed them that "we too are American workers and citizens."[12] For those who joined the militia, the parade not only gave them entrance into the public sphere but also was often combined with other military-type activities, such as a prize drill or target practice, steps serving to showcase their manhood through the martial ideal. Grand parades consisting of the various fraternal, church, labor, and military organizations from the black community occurred in many cities in Georgia, Texas, and Virginia from the 1870s to 1906. For African Americans, these larger and more community-inclusive marches often celebrated the birthday of Abraham Lincoln or other national leaders, the ratification of the Fifteenth Amendment to the US Constitution, or the most important revered holiday, the Emancipation Proclamation. Other important national events, such as George Washington's birthday, the Fourth of July, or Memorial Day, known as Decoration Day at the time, would also be celebrated, and sometimes the black community would join the larger white society in marking the importance of these days. Occasionally, just an individual black militia organization or two would simply take to the streets to acknowledge and commemorate a day. While smaller in scope, these exclusively military parades demonstrated through one group—the militia—the change in status of the black community since the end of slavery. More importantly, it highlighted African American manliness as exemplified in an official military ceremony.

A noteworthy example of this change occurred on the morning of May 25, 1877, when all of the existing African American military organizations in the city of Savannah, consisting of six infantry companies and one cavalry troop, gathered together in formation on South Broad Street. Under the command of the then–senior captain, W. H. Woodhouse, and preceded by the band of the Savannah Volunteer Guards, the men marched through the shaded streets to the extension at Forsyth Park. Once assembled into battalion formation facing the Confederate memorial, Capt. W. H. Bell, on horseback and accompanied by his fellow cavalrymen of the Savannah Hussars, departed for the residence of Judge Walter Scott Chisholm, having been selected to escort Governor Colquitt and his military staff to the parade ground. The governor, accompanied by a staff of seven officers, including Savannah's Col. Clifford Anderson, was received by a rolling volley fired by the infantry companies as he arrived to review the troops. According to a newspaper covering the integrated event, "In the presence of a large concourse of people, many of whom were whites," the Georgia governor reviewed the troops. Afterward, the men marched from the field to the armory of the Forest City Light Infantry, where the officers of the companies were then introduced one by one to the governor by Captain Woodhouse. Speaking briefly, Colquitt complimented the troops "upon their drill and appearance" and "was pleased to hear of their orderly conduct, and enjoining upon them to remember that a good *soldier* should also be a good citizen," reinforcing the manly ideals of humility, self-restraint, and faithfulness.[13]

One of the earliest parades of Virginia's first African American military unit, the Attucks Guard, occurred on August 4, 1873. Celebrating its second anniversary, the company also participated in target practice and evening entertainment. Just months earlier, this group of black militiamen had marched in President Grant's inaugural parade at Washington, D.C., with a fellow Virginia company, the Richmond Zouaves, and would soon return to the nation's capital in the fall of that year to take part in "an imposing parade."[14] This time, the Virginians, comprising 145 men of the Attucks Guard, Carney Guard, and Union Guard, accompanied by a 12-man brass band, marched through the streets of the nation's capital with six companies of African Americans militia of the District Battalion and the South Washington Band. Dressed in the standard state uniform of gray trousers and gray blouse trimmed in white and armed with Springfield breech-loading rifles, the men from Richmond and Manchester moved through the city of Washington, down Pennsylvania Avenue to the White House, and on to the executive residence before arriving at the baseball grounds, where several units jockeyed to win company guidons during a drill competition. Several years later, these three companies of African American Virginians would be joined in Washington by the Petersburg and Norfolk companies during the 1881 presidential inaugural parade for Pres. James Garfield.[15]

For African American men, serving in the state militia to march in a presidential inaugural parade, uniformed and armed, with other military organizations, both white and black, must have seemed the pinnacle of recognition of their rights as citizens, soldiers, and as men. While no African American state companies from Texas appear to have ever attended presidential ceremonies, those serving from Georgia made several excursions, although many years later, to represent their state and to demonstrate what they believed was African American progress.

The Georgia Cadets of Atlanta had to raise seven hundred dollars to send their forty-man company and fourteen band members to Pres. Benjamin Harrison's inaugural parade. The importance placed on attending the event became evident when the unit's members began to set aside a certain amount of their weekly wages, established a fundraising committee, and held benefits to bolster the organization's coffers. With "new uniforms, and ten new black shakos" on order, Capt. Moses Bentley understood that the companies would be placed in line of march according to when the state they represented came into the Union. In 1889, his company became the first African American military unit from Georgia to join in a procession down Pennsylvania Avenue.[16]

Several months after their return to Atlanta, a grand banquet was held for the Cadets. Rev. Joseph S. Flipper ushered in the evening's affair with compliments to Bentley's company regarding its "gallant appearance," stating, "by going to Washington it did more than any other company to represent the colored military of Atlanta." With the "most prominent and patriotic citizens" in attendance, Bentley, filled with the "convulsions of glory," proclaimed that "he would not only take his company to Washington, but to Europe" in an obvious display of manly bravado.[17] It would be almost ten years before another African American company would return to the nation's capital to do the same.

Macon's Capt. Sandy Lockhart and his company had the sole distinction of being the only African American military company from the South to march in review for President McKinley's inauguration in 1897. Wearing "caps which bore in large white letters across the front 'Georgia,'" Lockhart's men paraded fifty strong that day and returned to Washington four years later for McKinley's second inauguration, when they were joined by the black Georgia Artillery of Savannah. Within months, these same artillerymen would pay their final tribute to the fallen president by firing "half-hour guns from sunrise to sunset." The African American militia volunteers of Savannah not only paid their respects to McKinley as commander in chief but also to his military service to the country in two wars. To them, the departed president symbolized manhood through the martial ideal and provided a Republican "challenger" to the reputation of Lee.[18]

Some parades, historian Elizabeth Turner argued, "although peaceable and often joyous, brought with [them] a confrontational edge, emphatically stating a right to the streets, challenging notice by dominant groups."[19] Several instances occurred during the parades of African American military companies that revealed this complexity of racial relations.

On August 5, 1887, three companies of African American militiamen from Norfolk debarked from the ferry that had taken them to Portsmouth. They advanced in formation on the city streets to the train depot, where they had arranged transportation to a location for target practice. On the street, they encountered a Mr. E. A. Anderson, who attempted to pass through the company line. Stopped by Lt. George W. Foreman, who "took hold of his coat" and, according to Maj. William H. Palmer, "told him politely that he could not pass through," Anderson pulled a police baton from his coat and threatened the officer, who then allowed him to pass. The incident then escalated, as Foreman was stopped from boarding the train by Anderson, who had gained permission from the lieutenant's captain to have him accompany himself and the senior officer to the mayor's office, where the captain was reportedly needed to act as a witness to what occurred. Once at the Portsmouth mayor's office, Foreman was fined for disorderly conduct, paying five dollars. According to Major Palmer, the young lieutenant was informed by the white mayor that the militia had no authority over citizens during peacetime, and civilians could pass through the parading troopers. Palmer described Foreman. in a letter to Gov. Fitzhugh Lee, as "one of the most inoffensive officers in the command and have always shown himself to be an energetic, quiet and sober officer and soldier," pointing out that the entire affair "was a gross imposition upon the militia." Lee immediately forwarded the major's letter to the state adjutant general.[20]

James McDonald, in his eight-page response to the governor, wrote, "in my judgment, a grave misapprehension of the rights and privileges of military organizations exits in Portsmouth, and a wrong which should be redressed has been done to an officer who holds the commission of the State." The adjutant general detailed the section of the state's militia law that gave the right of any militia officer to hold and detain any individual who "interrupts, molests or insults by abusive word or behavior, or obstructs any officer or soldier while on duty, at any parade, drill or meeting for military improvement," and that, as a policeman, Anderson could only claim the right of way if he had been acting in the course of his legitimate duties. In closing, Adjutant General McDonald recommended that Lieutenant Foreman "be advised to take an appeal, if that be now allowable, from the decision of the mayor, and *that counsel be employed at the expense of the military. I want to see that his rights are cared for.*"[21]

Governor Lee must have communicated McDonald's recommendations and his review of the incident to Portsmouth mayor J. Thompson Baird, prompting a reply to the Virginia chief executive. Baird challenged Palmer's rendition of the event and, even though the mayor may have waived the fine, he boldly decried to the governor "that a sword in the hands of an epauletted man did not lift him in a plane above the civil law and so far that the civil law takes precedence of the military in times of peace—every good citizen will protect our volunteer soldiery; whose value is above estimation, but when they go beyond the law they *cannot be too quickly checked.*" McDonald seemed to have been correct in his assumption of the attitude toward military organizations in Portsmouth. Surprisingly, Baird made no mention in his letter to Lee concerning the African American troops, though it appears quite clear that Foreman's grabbing Anderson's coat to prevent him from crossing through the formation was the source of the contentious response by both the police officer and the mayor.[22]

City policemen were at the center of two other incidents, one on the streets of Savannah and the other at Macon, both occurring in 1895. Following the petition of Lieutenant Colonels Deveaux, Crumbly, and Blocker at the meeting of the Military Advisory Board on April 2 (as mentioned in chapter 5), the board concluded that, in order to move in this direction, a general inspection of the troops must occur, which was ordered by Georgia's adjutant general. Lt. Charles Booth Satterlee, US Army, on duty as the state's inspecting officer, received orders to proceed to Savannah for such an inspection, arriving in May. The *Savannah Tribune* characterized Satterlee as "showing much interest in his examination and inspection, and was earnest in giving valuable suggestions as to the details of the manual and drills, and administrative control."[23] It was during the lieutenant's inspection of the Colquitt Blues on the evening of May 16 that "a gang of toughs, in two vehicles drove ferociously through the streets and willfully drove into the company knocking down and injuring Sergeants West and Pinckney." Deveaux directed the company commander, Captain Carter, to take a squad and pursue the "toughs." Carter eventually captured the two drunk white men, James McGuire and C. W. Dyer, but not without further difficulty on the streets, as "Col. Deveaux received some bruises at the hands of the friends of McGuire and Dyer at Price and East Broad streets."[24] When the police arrived, both groups were arrested; charges were preferred against two policemen as well for their conduct during this scuffle. One of those officers may have been J. D. Reilly, who was later identified as having been "docketed some time ago for releasing a prisoner turned over to him on May 16th, for driving a vehicle into the Colquitt Blues." Reilly was chastised in the *Tribune* for the "very mild" suspension of twenty days without pay for this action and that of striking a prisoner while under arrest.[25]

The incident at Macon occurred in June 1895 as the Bibb County Blues were returning from a religious service in East Macon. Wearing their uniforms but not armed, the men of the company took to the sidewalks to simply avoid the muddy streets, with Captain Mason in the lead and the troops marching two abreast. City policemen named Bryan and Pluckett directed Mason to remove his men from the sidewalk. The captain refused and continued leading his men down the sidewalk. Plunkett called the duty sergeant to ask if the command could monopolize the sidewalk at the expense of all others and, after receiving a negative reply, promptly arrested Mason and took him to the police station. There, Duty Sergeant Long refused to lock up the captain until he received further instructions. Police lieutenant Carnes, in the process of writing a summons for Mason, withdrew it after the chief of police arrived and declared "that a military company had the same right to the sidewalk as other organized bodies in marching." Two days later, the Bibb County Blues captain received a summons. Represented by Marion Erwin, the US district attorney, Mason received a suspended fine for his actions. The *Macon Telegraph* reported that "the case was the first of its kind" and would "have considerable bearing on military organizations and other bodies of men who march on the sidewalks."[26]

These three events in Georgia and Virginia, while not numerous, illustrate a level of tension between the white civil authorities and the black military units even when, such as the example of the Colquitt Blues, the company was under the charge of a white officer. Therefore, one could make the argument that this was a simple matter of racial prejudice. Yet looking closer reveals that the common denominator in all three instances involved the presence of the police force. Policing in the late nineteenth century was recognized as a demanding job, and many of those who served had to be tough minded with enough physical strength, if required, to be capable of gaining compliance from those within their jurisdiction. The members of a city police force, especially those who walked a beat, possessed their own definition of manliness. White policemen embraced a sense of masculinity that, these three examples seem to indicate, conflicted with the presence of uniformed, often armed, African American men. These examples further illustrate that at least in Virginia in 1887, the black militia volunteers still enjoyed the confidence of the state governor and adjutant general. And, there were additional examples of this relationship.

In 1887, the city of Richmond gathered its military organizations, fraternal clubs, veterans groups, city departments, and even civic societies in a grand procession to celebrate the placement of the cornerstone for a new city hall. Local military organizations took precedence in the parade, led by Confederate veterans and followed by the 1st Regiment of Virginia Volunteers under the command of Major Bidgood. But instead of having additional white militia units following the entire regiment, the 1st Colored Battalion took the next place in line and was followed by the Richmond Howitzers and the Stuart Horse Guards. The battalion, comprising the African American infantry companies of Richmond and Manchester, was preceded by four mounted marshals for the parade and a "colored" drum corps. The *Richmond Dispatch* mentioned that the entire command was "complimented all along the route for their soldierly bearing," while the *Daily Times* reported that "the colored battalion came in for a just share of praise."[27] Later that year, the *Times* also reported that, on the occasion of the dedication of the imposing Robert E. Lee Monument, "the colored military were to have turned out, and were invited to do so, but when they assembled at the armory the ranks were so thin that it was decided by Captain Paul and the other officers not to do so."[28] Of course, it is tantalizing to contemplate the reason or reasons behind the low turnout by the African American troops. Obviously, Paul and other officers stood ready at the armory, but one is only left to speculate on the motivations of the absent men in this instance. Other situations reveal more clear conclusions.

That same year at San Antonio, Texas, during the annual Decoration Day parade, US Army troops led by Brig. Gen. David Sloan Stanley were followed in the procession by the city's African American company, the Excelsior Guard, city firemen, city police, and Union veterans who were members of the local Grand Army of the Republic (GAR) post. The *San Antonio Light* mentioned that the veterans of "the Grand Army wanted to take precedence, but the Excelsiors refused to yield."[29] The *Galveston Daily News* described this refusal more succinctly: "The Grand Army of the Republic, firemen and Excelsior Guards (colored) were in line, but the Grand Army men and firemen created a little sensation by breaking ranks at the corner of Houston and Soledad streets because they were placed behind the negro company." Not only did this group of white marchers break ranks but they also proceeded to another street corner with the intention of cutting off the black militiamen. The paper continued, "they succeeded temporarily, but by a private command from their captain the Excelsiors took the curbstone, marched in double-quick time and regained their place at the corner of Yturia and Commerce streets."[30] Placed in this position again, the fire companies left the parade, but there was no mention of the others departing the procession, leaving the impression that they remained in position and marched behind the African American company. While this instance of masculine assertiveness comes from the example of a parade, it clearly illustrated the importance and sense of status that Capt. Simon Turner placed in maintaining his company's position in this public display. Heightened by the meaning of Decoration Day, when honor, masculinity, and sacrifice were recognized, to have yielded their assigned position in the procession would have meant a loss in the black militiamen's sense of manhood.

The Decoration Day services not only honored those who had paid the ultimate sacrifice in military service but also served for the living, observers and troops alike, to connect somehow to that sacrifice by embracing the fallen soldiers' successful demonstration of manhood in war.

Memorializing the Heroes

While the origins of America's modern Memorial Day remain problematic for some, the designation of Decoration Day as May 30 was proclaimed by the head of the GAR, former Union major general John A. Logan, on May 5, 1868. With Union war dead buried in national cemeteries throughout the South, local GAR posts sought to commemorate those men who had paid the ultimate sacrifice in defense of the republic. For African Americans, Decoration Day gave meaning to Emancipation Day, for only through military victory was freedom assured, but it also meant much more. The observance of Decoration Day provided an opportunity for African Americans to participate publicly, along with other veterans, to recognize those men of African descent who had fought and died for freedom. And by honoring them, they reinforced the masculine ideal embodied through military service.

Historian Donald Shaffer argued that "former [African American] soldiers as a group were quite well regarded in the postwar black community, both for their manly valor and for helping to liberate their own people from bondage."[31] Militia participation at Decoration Day ceremonies allowed many of these veterans to continue to demonstrate their masculinity and, by association, to convey that culture of manliness to both the surrounding society and to those militiamen too young to have experienced the rigors of the war.

The first observance of what was termed "National Memorial Day" by African American militiamen in Virginia occurred under the auspices of the GAR's Sheridan Post No. 2 at Richmond on May 30, 1872. Both the Attucks Guard and the Richmond Zouaves, whose members, the "majority [of whom] have been soldiers," marched to the national cemetery, "where sleep hundreds of the brave soldiers of the Republic," to "participate in the beautiful rites."[32] By 1888, the entire 1st Battalion of Virginia's African American volunteers participated in a grand parade to the national cemetery, where they were addressed by their chaplain and the ministers of the Fourth Baptist Church and Second Baptist Church. After firing a salute, the men marched back to the city and joined a larger crowd from the black community at Richmond's "colored cemetery on Academy Hill," where a committee of prominent African Americans had carved out their own annual observance of the day.[33]

Often, for African American militia companies or battalions, the observance of Decoration Day only occurred if an appropriate location was within a reasonable train ride away. For the men at Macon, Georgia, this meant the federal cemetery at Andersonville; for those at Savannah and Augusta, their ceremonial location was Beaufort, South Carolina; the national cemetery at Marietta served as the center of remembrance for some companies headquartered at Atlanta. The frequency of participation by the various companies often differed, and many were not able to take part in these ceremonies until they had properly uniformed and equipped themselves or obtained arms from the state. At Savannah in 1883, the Forest City Light Infantry under Capt. Louis M. Pleasant appears to have been the first company to request permission to travel to Beaufort for Decoration Day.[34] Five years later, Capt. John Lark asked Governor Gordon "for permission to leave the state . . . in uniform and with arms to visit Beaufort" for Memorial Day exercises at the national cemetery there.[35] And in 1892, Georgia's adjutant general approved Lark's request, along with those from Capt. Robert G. Cummings of the Attucks Infantry and Capt. Thomas G. Walker of the Georgia Infantry, to travel "armed and equipped" to Beaufort for the annual observance.[36] By 1895, the participation of Savannah's African American active militia, often accompanied by a company or two from Augusta, in recognizing Memorial Day at Beaufort had become an annual event that continued until 1904, the year before their dissolution.

At Macon, the Lincoln Guards and the Bibb County Blues in 1888 invited Captain Bentley's Georgia Cadets from Atlanta to join them on an excursion to Andersonville "to participate in the decoration of the union soldiers' graves."[37] The following year, "the national department" awarded the E. S. Jones Post, GAR, of Macon the honor to arrange for the decorations of the graves at the cemetery. The Bibb County Blues failed to attend that year, however, citing either a controversy with the Lincoln Guards in failing to share the profits from the excursion tickets or, according to Capt. Lewis Moseley of the Blues, from the word that the "E. S. Jones post did not look with much favor upon the negroes taking part in the decoration exercises."[38] This was not the first such controversy occurring at the cemetery at Andersonville.

By 1893, the crowds for the annual observance had swelled to over four thousand from across the state, and two years later, the anticipated attendance had grown to over eight thousand. With the increase in participation, incidents of drunkenness and disorderly behavior also grew, causing the governor to order the Americus Light Infantry "to hold itself in readiness to go to Andersonville in response to a telegram from the sheriff that its services are needed."[39] The African American militia captains at Macon also issued a request through the local paper by asking those in the city's black community who planned to attend to "leave your flasks and bottles at home, and let us go peacefully and return as we have done heretofore, casting no shadow or cloud upon us as law breakers."[40]

Unfortunately, during the annual ceremonies in 1898, an African American woman and several men were shot and others cut with razors. Upon their return to Macon that year, a squad of the Lincoln Guards had a Mr. Ed Washington in custody. Washington, an African American who was reportedly intoxicated, had allegedly walked through the train cars snapping a loaded pistol at the excursionists and also cut another man with a razor. The *Atlanta Constitution* reported, "conservative negroes say they will never go again to Andersonville on Decoration day, as the conduct of many of the negro excursionists is outrageous and life is in jeopardy."[41] The inappropriate behavior of a few thus detracted from the manly image that the men in the militia volunteers wished to portray. Arguably, being placed in the rear position in parades did not contribute to black militiamen's sense of the martial ideal either, particularly if following cavalry units; during the opening parade of the Cotton Exposition and International Exposition, Lieutenant Colonel Crumbly and his men had to march behind Troop B, Governor's Horse Guards.[42] Seeking to eliminate such indignities, the men turned their efforts toward events that highlighted their masculinity through military skill in a very open, public setting, thus leaving no questions in the minds of the spectators.

The Prize Drill

On a weekly basis at a simple building in the city that served as an armory, the men of the various African American active militia companies typically would gather to retrieve their arms and accoutrements. Standing at attention in their uniforms, the company would practice the assorted rifle positions or drill movements from the appropriate instruction manuals, a basic military skill meant to require the men to coordinate and move together as one. These regular drills embraced the martial ideal, created racial and male solidarity, and prepared the company for a time when they might be called forward to use their skills to protect their community, county, or state. As they became more proficient in the manual of arms and the school of the squad and company, and in constant need of financial support, many of the companies would challenge their brother organizations in drill competitions. These events were not the same as the summer encampments, where practical field training occurred under the auspices of US Army personnel. The prize drill was instead a very public and, at times, animated affair.

The first prize drill strictly for African Americans was slated for late May 1878 at Savannah but was planned entirely by a group of Augusta citizens led by Augustus Johnson. In his invitation to Governor Colquitt, Johnson explained that the purpose of the drill was "to deepen the interest felt by the colored companies of our State in military affairs."[43] His committee could only contact eighteen of the existing companies since it remained unable to learn the names of the other units. The grand prize was a sword and scabbard with the inscription, "Awarded the Best Drilled Company in the State of Georgia by the Citizens of Augusta"; sent to Captain Woodhouse at Savannah, he had it placed on exhibit at S. P. Hamilton's jewelry store on Broughton Street. The judges for the contest were not other African Americans, but instead high-ranking white officers, "Col. E. W. Anderson, of Savannah, Capt. J. O. Clark, of Augusta and Capt. George L. Mason, of Macon."[44]

Once the drill commenced on May 27, nine companies—two from Augusta, one from Macon, and four from Savannah—competed for the honor and recognition of being the best in drill. The *Savannah Morning News* reported that Governor Colquitt, along with Col. Isaac W. Avery, one of the secretaries of the executive department, and John B. Baird, at that time the governor's military secretary, would "review the *brigade* at the Park extension." The newspaper also recognized Woodhouse as the "senior officer, . . . who will have command of the *regiment*," thus informing its readers of the presence of a large body of African American troops assembled in the center of Savannah. With language consistent with the ethos of the Christian gentleman, the article noted that Woodhouse provided a set of strict rules that would be observed during the contest. These regulations not only stated that the drill would be judged using the most current edition of *Upton's Tactics,* the standard US Army manual, but also reminded each officer to not "use profane language or abuse his men while on drill."[45]

In scenes repetitive from the year before, Woodhouse, "acting as Colonel," led the seven infantry companies from South Broad Street to the extension at Forsyth Park. Meanwhile, at the Pulaski House, the Savannah Hussars, with sabers at attention, waited for the governor and his staff to mount and then escorted the party to the park. Following a review of the troops, the governor, his official party, and the commanding officer and staff of Savannah's 1st Regiment gathered at the armory of the Forest City Light Infantry. Of the several speeches delivered, many touched on masculinity. Governor Colquitt appealed to the group in attendance "to let their fine soldierly appearance and bearing represent in their characters that chivalry and virtue, and in their conduct that subordination to law and exercise of manhood that alone made a people prosperous, happy and respected." And Colonel Anderson "wished that in the coming prize drill, as in all contests, they might win the laurels due to martial worth."[46]

As the drill commenced that afternoon, the *Savannah Morning News* estimated the number of spectators at "seven thousand persons" and recorded, "it was almost impossible to keep the people from pressing upon the companies, they were thus greatly impeded in making evolutions for want of space." Eventually, the Chatham Light Infantry of Savannah, followed closely by the Douglass Light Infantry of Augusta, was named the winner of the event. Deveaux, chosen to award the sword and scabbard on "behalf of the noble-hearted ladies and gentlemen of Augusta," intermingled his presentation with acknowledging the importance of the event. Delivering a message of mutual interest, encouragement, and recognition of progress, the Republican leader emphasized how the governor's attendance signaled the importance of the event and hailed the "gentlemen of the Chatham Light Infantry" for their "proficiency and discipline," and noting also how "the efforts of your competitors" made their triumph "more honorable and glorious."[47]

The "honor" and "glory" of the prize drill at Savannah caught the attention of the Atlanta companies, who soon after persuaded the managers of the North Georgia Stock and Fair Association to offer cash prizes for the best three companies in the state in what was deemed the "championship of the world."[48] Captain Wyly of the Atlanta Light Infantry invited the Savannah companies, but Woodhouse declined to attend at this time due to financial reasons, yet insisted on accepting the challenge at a later date. Despite their absence, the contest took place on the last day of the fair at Oglethorpe Park, with officers of the 13th US Infantry Regiment serving as judges. Only two companies from Atlanta and the Douglass Infantry from Augusta competed in the event. The *Atlanta Constitution* printed that "there was nothing in the drilling to excite any especial interest" and commented that even the winning company "while being under much better training than their competitors, were still deficient in many of the nice points in the manual of arms."[49]

In 1879, the Columbus Volunteers, with its city's black fire company, traveled to Atlanta to participate in a parade and, for the militia company, a prize drill. The city's residents thus witnessed two forms of African American demonstrations of manliness—the military and the fire companies. The day began with the parade, which included other visitors from the city of Columbus and terminated on Marietta Street in front of the Georgia Capitol. With only the Georgia Cadets and Washington Guards from Atlanta and the Columbus Volunteers taking part, the drill contestants showed "astonishing skill in the handling of their weapons." The individual winner, Pvt. Tom Hicks, "was the recipient of considerable applause."[50]

Two years later, Texas held its first gathering of African American troops in 1881 at the Houston fairgrounds. Although this event had the characteristics of an encampment without the supervision of state or federal military authorities, it did allow the spectators that would normally attend a prize drill. The Davis Rifles of Houston hosted the two black active militia companies from Galveston and the Roberts Rifles from Corpus Christi. As the various companies sought out new fundraising opportunities beyond their own locale, these prize-drill contests were sometimes combined with civilian-sponsored events or merged into larger, out-of-state affairs, such as the reunion of the

Colored National Guards Association at Columbus, Ohio, in 1882 and the gathering at Atlanta in 1883.[51] All of these experiences, no matter the form, served to demonstrate African American manhood through the public display of military skills.

The Georgia Cadets of Atlanta was the only African American company from its state to attend the "reunion" at Columbus, Ohio. Some of the militiamen's fellow citizens from the city gathered at the train depot to see them off. During the course of their departure, the *Atlanta Constitution* took notice of one "old darkey" who exclaimed, "'golty, doesn't dey look like dey was big men shore 'nuff.'"[52] With companies from Ohio, Tennessee, and Missouri represented, the opening parade in Columbus "presented a fine appearance," with the soldiers in their "new gaudy uniforms, military caps and the huge bearskins of the Georgia Cadets."[53] Without the required number of members per company to conduct a prize drill, an "exhibition drill" took place followed by a "sham battle," illustrating the same level of manliness as a competitive event would garner. The Cadets were also present at the "National Guard union" at Atlanta the following year, although that time only Georgia companies from Atlanta, Rome, and Columbus participated in the prize drill conducted at the "old barracks at Jamestown."[54]

Without a doubt, the most ambitious and controversial prize drill took place in the United States in May 1887, the so-called National Drill. Invitations to the event, to be held under the shadow of the Washington Monument and organized to observe the centennial of the US Constitution, were extended to companies across the country. By March, the planning committee had received 226 responses representing thirty-six states. But when three invitations were accepted by African American infantry companies, several white active militia organizations leveled a protest with the National Drill Association, which then stood by the decision to admit the black companies. Virginia Adjutant General Anderson visited the head of the association and the manager of the drill and "expressed emphatically as approving the position of the committee with reference to allowing colored companies to participate in the drill."[55] Anderson was joined in his support by the adjutant general of North Carolina, but once learning of no possibility of a reversal, the entire contingent of white militia from Alabama withdrew; the Lomax Rifles of Mobile later reversed their decision and participated in the event.[56]

One of Virginia's African American companies, the State Guard, led by Captain Paul, by this time was well acquainted with drill competitions. The group had taken first place in three of the four contests it had entered begin-

Attucks Guard, May 21, 1887. Courtesy of John Listman.

ning in 1879. It was joined by the Attucks Guard under Captain Scott, the senior African American company from the state but much more inexperienced
in drill contests. The two black companies accompanied the Virginia Brigade,
under the command of the state's adjutant general, Charles Anderson, but
they may have been bivouacked in an isolated position from the white militiamen in order to maintain the expectations of social decorum existing at that
time. Therefore, while Scott's and Paul's companies had received support from
Anderson to be included with the state's military contingent, signaling his
approval of their organizations, the adjutant general could not alter prevailing
racial attitudes.[57]

Initially, sixty-eight companies entered the drill competition to be judged
for "their especial fitness" by a group of regular US Army officers appointed
by Gen. Phil Sheridan.[58] Still, when the week of the drill had passed, only
forty-two of them had taken the field, including infantry and Zouave companies, light artillery and machine-gun batteries, and young cadets from several colleges across the country. Even though the Virginia Brigade had won
championships in its home state, it could only accumulate 249.6 points out
of a possible score of 820. Only two companies finished behind them—the
Attucks Guard and Company C, 2nd Connecticut State Guard. The African
American company from Washington, D.C., finished with 435.6 points, but
the winners, the Lomax Rifles of Mobile, amassed 753 points to earn the grand

prize of five thousand dollars.[59] The Washington *Bee,* the capital city's black newspaper, reported that the companies "from Virginia acquitted themselves much better on dress parade than in the prize drill."[60] Despite the results of the competition, all three African American companies had proudly competed with white units from all across the United States and actually had proven themselves superior in drill over several of them.

On Wednesday, June 1, "a general parade of all the troops through the principal streets of the city" took place. During periods of adjustment often seen in long, winding columns, some officers entertained the crowds that lined the streets with movements from the manual of arms. Two companies, the Vicksburg Southrons and the Memphis Zouaves, which had been placed behind a company from the District of Columbia comprising African Americans, withdrew from the procession. In a rather surprising observation, the *National Tribune* recorded that "the actions of these companies was generally condemned, for it was the opinion of the majority of the other Southern organizations that there was no occasion for drawing the color line."[61] The *Bee* decried the absurdity of the companies' withdrawal, exclaiming, "it is a little strange that men who have picked cotton with Negroes, played marbles with Negroes, fought over a hoe cake with Negroes, gone in swimming with Negroes and often even nursed at a Negro mammy's breast should raise such a howl about walking with them in a military parade."[62]

The National Drill reveals the level of complexity of racial relationships in 1887 as they existed across city and state boundaries. Absent were any African American military organizations from either Texas or Georgia. Texas sent two white infantry companies from San Antonio, which according to the final scoring were well prepared for the contest. Georgia sent none, although Captain Bentley did volunteer his company to act as an escort for the governor if he decided to attend. And Virginia, of course, sent its entire 1st Regiment of infantry, an artillery battery, a cavalry troop, and two black infantry companies, though only those from Richmond and one of which had already proven itself reliable in the incident at Newport News.[63]

Moreover, the placement of Virginia's African American militia volunteers' campsite on the field of Camp George Washington emphasizes that, while these men could enter the public arena, their space within it was strictly defined. The white militia units of Montgomery, Alabama, who had declined to participate, declared that they did not "object to the negroes having all the po-

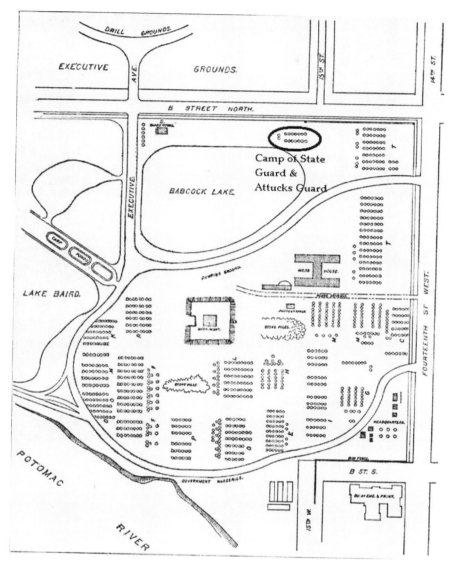

Camp George Washington. From *Washington Evening Star,* May 21, 1887.

litical rights under the law." What they objected to was "anything bordering on social equality," which strongly supports the contention that black masculinity was a component in their objection to the presence of the African American troops from Richmond.[64]

Reinforcing the Man

Although excluded from taking part in the ranks of the state volunteers, black women succeeded in playing a role that reinforced the manly traits of their men in uniform. Historian William Fitzhugh Brundage has argued that "the ceremonial roles open to black women required not only a reserved, feminine demeanor but also tacit support for the ideals that black men profess—concerns principally associated with the male public sphere."[65] Occupying this traditional gender role, these women were a common sight at public events and ceremonies, attended frequent armory-hall dances, and often accompanied the men on the numerous excursions hosted by the militia companies. Some even acted as "sponsors" for their local militia unit during the summer encampments, as in one example reported by the Austin Daily Statesman in 1892.[66] It remains unclear exactly what these women did, especially since a part of camp life involved cooking and cleaning for the soldiers. They may have assisted the camp surgeon with his duties; fulfilling again a traditional gender role available to them. If so, they could have nurtured those not strong enough—that is, not manly enough—to ward off camp sickness back to a condition of strength and vigor—the very definition of a man.

Black women further reinforced the cult of masculinity for African American militiamen by honoring them with one of its symbols—a flag. Men had fought and died for the possession of their enemy's flag or to protect their own on the battlefields of the Civil War. The loss of a unit's flag clearly revealed that the soldiers had not been manly enough to protect it, a defeat that signaled, in gender terms, their emasculation. As the troops, acting as Christian gentlemen, honored womanhood, they received in turn the recognition of their manhood from their ladies. During the summer encampment held at Austin, Texas, in 1892, the sponsor for the Capital Guards, Martha McKinley, daughter of Dr. John F. McKinley, had "made a beautiful flag" that she presented "to the company which has so much honored her." This cultural behavior extended across geographical space and was practiced by women in Georgia and Virginia as well.[67]

The earliest mention of a flag given to an African American company in Virginia occurred within months of the organization of the Attucks Guard of Richmond in 1871. A "ladies committee," organized to support the company, labored for six months to raise the necessary funds to purchase the flag.[68] The flag ceremony was filled with masculine symbolism. Occurring on April 9, 1872, Prof. John M. Langston of Howard University, not a member of the ladies committee, presented the banner to Capt. Robert L. Hobson, commanding the company. The ladies had not only honored the men of the company with their gift but also recognized the martial ideal personified in both Langston, an educator and civil rights advocate who had fought against slavery and recruited colored troops for the war, and Hobson, a Civil War veteran. Similar flag presentation ceremonies followed in Georgia at Savannah, Augusta, and later Atlanta.[69]

Days prior to their departure for Savannah to participate in the celebration of Charles Sumner's birthday, Captain Beard, commanding the Douglass Infantry of Augusta, conducted a prize drill to ready his men for a competition with Savannah's Forest City Light Infantry.[70] Immediately preceding the drill contest, the company stood at attention on "the green under the trees near McIntosh street, where a stage had been erected," to receive their new flag. The presenter was not a leader in the African American community but a fourteen-year-old mixed-race girl, Cecelia Barefield, who, according to a newspaper account, "made a very creditable speech." Although only a teenager, she stated "that the donors of the flag had selected her to present it to the company as a slight testimonial of their regard for them as *men* and their confidence in them as soldiers."[71] The flag, made of "heavy silk, buff on one side and blue on the other," was bordered in "fine gold fringe." The buff side displayed "the coat of arms of Georgia painted in oil," while the blue side contained the national coat of arms and, "above and below" it, the inscription "'Douglass Infantry, Organized August 5th, 1873.'"[72] Barefield elaborated upon the symbolism of the new banner:

> The name which the company bore was a good one, and they should strive to do it *honor.* On one side of the flag was the eagle. Might they emulate it in its lofty qualities, and excel in all those *noble* traits that make a *good citizen* and a *true soldier.* On the other side was the coat of arms of Georgia. Established upon the eternal rock of truth, overshadowed by the Constitution, and supported and upheld by Wisdom, Justice and Moderation, might they always be guided by the great principles therein contained, and thus demonstrate to the world their capacity to discharge all of the duties devolving on the citizen and the soldier.[73]

Upon the receipt of the flag, Beard recognized the substantial monetary aid given to the company by both the city's white citizens and the black community, then immediately commenced the drill competition. The entire ceremony was witnessed by members of the white citizenry of Augusta. More importantly, the judges of the drill contest consisted of several white officers, including Lt. Col. Wilberforce Daniel and members of his staff. These judges exercised a level of influence—and control—over the interpretation of black masculinity through their selection of *"the best drilled man,"* who would receive as his reward a white plume, the symbol of courage.[74]

Two years later, the men of the Union Lincoln Guards at Savannah received "a most beautiful banner" at the celebration of their fourth anniversary.[75] On July 31, the Guards, accompanied by a large procession, marched to the house of Georgiana Kelly, described as a "venerable and patriotic lady," to receive new company colors from the United Daughters of Lincoln. The flag was made of blue silk with heavy gold fringe attached to its edges. Unlike the symbolism of the flag presented to the Douglass Infantry, this banner's theme centered more on the nation instead of the state of Georgia. One side of the new ensign depicted Lady Liberty holding a sword in her right hand while she raised in her left a set of scales containing the Emancipation Proclamation and the Civil Rights Act. The phrase "implements of war and of peace showing also the results of industry" encircled the female figure.[76] The other side of the flag contained a portrait of Pres. Abraham Lincoln beneath a representation of the US Capitol surrounded by a wreath of stars, denoting the states of the Union, with the motto *E Pluribus Unum.* Deveaux presented the flag to the company on behalf of the United Daughters of Lincoln. The choice of Deveaux to present the cherished symbol of the company remains strikingly similar to the selection of Langston at Richmond. Both men had committed themselves to the uplift of African Americans, Langston as a professor at Howard University and Deveaux as a supporter of Savannah's city schools, in which both his wife and daughter worked as teachers. In fact, Kelly herself had previously been employed as an educator. Each man, Deveaux and Langston, remained steadfast in the fight for civil and political rights, and each of them epitomized the martial ideal from their involvement and experience during the Civil War.[77]

The Georgia Cadets of Atlanta celebrated their tenth anniversary on February 22, 1889. Still under the command of its original captain, Moses Bentley, the company was initially scheduled to "be presented with a handsome flag" by a young female student of Morris Brown College, but the men received the banner from Emma Brown Steele instead. During the presentation ceremony, held at historic Big Bethel AME Church on Auburn Avenue, Bentley's men listened to an address given by Rev. Joseph Simeon Flipper. Although his words went unrecorded, the choice of Flipper embodied a firm foundation in manhood interpreted through the Christian gentleman and the martial ideals. The minister had founded a militia company in his hometown of Thomasville and held a commission from the governor before arriving in Atlanta. More importantly, he was the brother to US Army officer Henry Ossian Flipper, the first African American graduate of the US Military Academy at West Point. Although by this time his older brother already had been dismissed from the army, the assembled militiamen, and Joseph Flipper himself, most likely still held his accomplishment in high esteem and agreed with Henry's claim of innocence.[78]

Many of these flag-presentation ceremonies included parades, drill competitions in the manual of arms, and often a public marksmanship contest—again, all of these to fortify the manliness of the men exhibited through military skill.

Target Practice

Of all the skills associated with martial ability and manly prowess, successful marksmanship was highly celebrated. When Virginia Adjutant General McDonald submitted his annual report to Gov. Frederick William Mackey Holliday on November 1, 1879, he listed every volunteer militia organization in the state and accounted for all military stores received and issued to the various commands. McDonald also commented on a variety of military topics, including the "indispensability of target practice." Noting changes in tactics and the improvements in weapons technology that now allowed troops to "engage at wide distances and take advantage of all natural or improvised means of covering" themselves, he advocated "that the whole training and teaching of the soldier converge on the one object of making his fire effective." It was, McDonald argued, "the only means in time of peace of acquiring the coolness, confidence and skill, which are the culmination and sine qua non of a soldier's education."[79]

Georgia, too, recognized the need to properly train its active militia in the proper use of firearms. The Military Advisory Board in 1889 reported its concern regarding the neglect of rifle practice in the state. According to the board, only those commands, or members thereof, that purchased ammunition took an active interest in target practice. Its members recommended that the state appropriate $2,500 annually for ammunition "in order to ascertain what should be the true amount to accomplish the end desired." The ten-member board also advocated mandatory firearms training ten times a year, with scores recorded "so that said reports can be condensed, and in this way, the efficiency of the force be largely increased."[80] Two years later, Georgia eventually approved $63.35 for targets and an unrecorded amount of ammunition for one company to practice at Tybee Island, near Savannah.[81]

In Texas, the records for its Volunteer Guard are less revealing on the need for weapons proficiency. In fact, there is no mention of it in the annual reports of the state's adjutant general, John A. Hulen, until 1906. At that time, the only firing range owned by the state for the Guard's use was at Camp Mabry in Austin. Active militia organizations functioning in distant El Paso or Laredo took advantage of the federal ranges in those locations and enhanced their marksmanship with the assistance from regular US Army personnel. The state provided ammunition, but the lack of adequate facilities constituted the large obstacle to improved proficiency for the Texas Volunteer Guard.[82]

Hulen's newfound emphasis on target practice may have coincided with the poor performance of the Volunteer Guard rifle teams in national competitions. Texas finished thirtieth in a field of thirty-seven teams competing in the National Rifle Match at Sea Girt, New Jersey, in the fall of 1905. The adjutant general excused this performance with the comment, "the Texas team had a great deal less practice than any other team taking part in the match." One year later, the Texans placed twenty-eighth, but this was in a field of forty-one competitors, signaling virtually no improvement. Yet again, the adjutant general was optimistic. Through the competition, Hulen asserted, "the National match would be the means of greatly increasing the interest of the Guardsmen in rifle shooting, and ... would gain a great deal of valuable information, which they would be able to impart to their organizations at home."[83]

These three examples clearly demonstrated that the state military officials of Georgia, Texas, and Virginia had not placed any emphasis on marksmanship until many years after the reorganization of the states' militia forces. Therefore, one might contend that target practice did not equate to a soldier's manliness or martial quality prior to this. But the historical record reveals that the troops, especially African Americans, competed consistently years before these states' adjutant generals began to discuss the need for rifle practice.

Often, the demonstration of marksmanship skills, as with the other displays of manliness, took place within the public sphere. Target-shooting competitions began early in the history of the militia organization and, for those who could afford it, would become an annual event. The Attucks Guard of Richmond celebrated their second anniversary with a dinner, a parade, and target practice at Peterson's Garden on the Grove Road on August 4, 1873. A local news correspondent, who later regretted his inability to attend the event, noted, "the muster roll of this company embraces the names of seventy-five men" and its members "deservedly hold a high rank among the citizen soldiery of the commonwealth."[84] And when Virginia began to consistently record the activities of its militia companies, beginning in 1884, some of the African American organizations reported not only their annual participation in target practice but also having initiated this training years earlier. One such company, the Flipper Guard of Petersburg, commanded by Capt. James E. Hill, reported in his "annual record of [the] company" that his men had participated in their "*Sixth* Annual Target Practice" on January 1, 1886, signaling their early and consistent interest in rifle training.[85] Ten years later, and like their neighbors to the south, the Carney Guard of Richmond included a shooting competition as part of their anniversary celebration. Recognizing twenty-four years as part of the Virginia Volunteers, the company awarded the best-shot award to 1st Sgt. Charles E. Steward, who "put a bullet through the bull's eye."[86]

The occasion of the fourth anniversary of the Forest City Light Infantry at Savannah yielded one of the city's first shooting competitions by its African American citizen-soldiers. On May 8, 1876, Captain Woodhouse marched his company from the city to an area known then as Eastville for the contest. The winner, Sgt. Robert Williams, received "a handsome white plume" for being the best shot, but unlike the reporting in Richmond, the last-place participant was clearly identified in the news story. A Private Habersham was named as "the fortunate winner of a large tin cup, for having made the worst shot." In an obvious effort to publicly humiliate the young soldier and shame him toward improving his shooting skills, Habersham definitely had his manhood called into question.[87]

Days later at Augusta, the Douglass Infantry held "their annual target excursion" across the Savannah River at Shultz Hill, near the city of Hamburg, South Carolina.[88] Described as an "excursion," the event most likely was attended by members of the city's black community, again reinforcing the culture of manliness demonstrated through martial skills and manly competition. This community may have also allowed the company to liberally award lavish prizes to the winners of the shooting contest.

Captain Beard presented a gold medal to the best shot from the enlisted ranks, Sgt. G. H. Grimes, while the runner up, Pvt. Samuel McNeil, received a silver goblet. Beard received a gold pen as the winning officer, a silver medal was awarded to Henry Jackson from the company's "drum corps," and a wine set was bestowed upon the victorious Benjamin Lumpkin, an honorary member. Furthermore, the members of Beard's company competed for the favor of their "lady honorary members," thus seeking not only to prove their manliness through shooting competition but also reinforcing the concept of honor as an important component within the definition of masculinity. Sergeant Grimes, once again triumphant, gathered the first prize in honor of Miss Emma Harper, while Pvt. H. Wright took second place for Miss Fredy Ridley. Lexius Henson accepted the first award from Captain Beard "with an appropriate speech."[89] The following year, the Douglass Infantry traveled to Aiken, South Carolina, for their annual target practice, then seemingly would not return to Shultz Hill until 1885, an annual tradition that extended well into the 1890s and expanded to include the entire 3rd Battalion, Georgia Volunteers, Colored.[90]

These early rifle-shooting competitions seem to conflict with historian Ehren Foley's argument that, "for most companies the presentation of their skill was not an individual, but rather a collective exhibition, more closely associated in its social meaning with a parade or drill." Granted, target practices often occurred in conjunction with parades or prize-drill competitions, but the identification of individuals as the victors in these contests clearly captures much more than social significance. These were serious events highlighting the martial skill that defined the masculinity of the participants within their organization. While not "the highly individualized and standardized sharp-shooting competitions that would characterize the professionalism of the militia service later in the century," they were definitely more than social events and were recognized as such.[91] Following "an exhibition drill and a target practice" between African American militiamen from Atlanta and Athens in 1880, the *Atlanta Constitution* clearly identified Abe Clark of the Governor's Volunteers as the winner of the best three shots and Wash Newton of the Atlanta Light Infantry as having the best single shot. The newspaper concluded that "the shooting generally was very good, and in some case considerable skill was manifested."[92]

Individual companies, sometimes full battalions, of black militiamen from across Georgia, Texas, and Virginia continued to instruct their members in the proper use of firearms throughout the 1880s and 1890s. Documentation is lacking for the Texas companies, but the scant ordnance returns there do record the yearly use of ammunition for target practices. Still, as with the annual camps of military instruction, which military officials in Texas conducted for their African American volunteers and those in Virginia did not, Georgia instituted organized rifle instruction at Camp Northen, near Griffin, in 1892. Georgia also created the office of the inspector general of small-arms practice, established qualifying scores of a range of marksmanship classifications, and even named inspectors for the majority of the commands across the state. The exclusion of all African American militia organizations from all these improvements clearly demonstrates a contrast between providing those units with firearms and ammunition and instructing them in their use. So, while the state of Georgia did recognize them as military organizations, military officials hesitated to increase their skill with firearms, which at the time would have raised the martial ability—and thus the masculinity—of these men to a par with, or even exceeding that of, their white counterparts.[93]

Conclusion

From the 1870s to 1906, the existing social structure in the United States often relegated African American troops to the rear of the parade, not only because of race but also because of the organizational seniority of the white companies. In the South, ex-Confederate veterans took the place of honor in parades in recognition of their service during the Civil War. That recognition was founded in their successful demonstration of manhood in war. Even in the segregated society in which they lived, black military units could assert their manhood. Their very inclusion in any parades during those years, to officially wear a uniform and to march with a rifle under the command of officers elected by their company's rank and file all signaled some public recognition and progress.

Furthermore, activities highlighting the martial arts, such as drill or shooting competitions, within the very open and public sphere contributed to the culture of masculinity. And, at other times, the African American companies, or a battalion, would conduct activities that excluded everyone except those in military uniform. All of these steps built toward both an internal and an external culture of manhood.

The black community often reinforced the definition of manhood through recognizable and accepted symbols, such as providing a company flag or deciding what prize would be given to a champion, the man who had triumphed over all other men. The winners had their names published in the local newspaper, while the individual who performed most poorly received a dose of public humiliation in an effort to motivate him to improve and to spur his growth toward manhood. But the years ahead would prove difficult for African American citizen-soldiers, even more so for African American men who continued to value and exhibit their masculinity.

8

~~~

Conclusion

Manhood Lost

CONGRESS DECLARING WAR against Spain on April 25, 1898, and President McKinley's subsequent call for 125,000 volunteers, generated an outpouring of patriotic responses and offers to serve from the African American state militia volunteers in the states of Georgia, Texas, and Virginia. Not only could these men prove their loyalty to their state and nation in hopes of curbing the deterioration of their civil and political rights, but they also could, if given the opportunity, verify their manliness on the field of battle. The subsequent racial strife that occurred in and near many of the training camps contributed to the further erosion of the racial accommodations and small victories won over the years by the African American militia volunteers. Still, even with this violence, many black soldiers sustained their organizations past 1898, asserted their rights as citizens, and demonstrated their masculinity through military service into the new century. The dissolution of their individual local commands came years after the war ended. Other factors, including the introduction of a federal law mandating militia efficiency and the achievements of *black men* seen as a challenge to white men each played a role in the demise of the African American militia volunteers.

While the African Americans who served in the state militia organizations remained intertwined with the black US Volunteer regiments in considering the war with Spain, with some of the national troops having previously served in state forces, this study is not an examination of those wartime servicemen. Yet the actions of black state militia volunteers demonstrated their intention to prove themselves as good citizens, as patriots, and, more importantly, as men.

The years prior to the declaration of war had witnessed both some successes and disappointments for the African American militia volunteers and the larger black community. The US Supreme Court had ruled in favor of "separate but equal" public-education systems in *Plessy v. Ferguson;* mob violence and the heinous crimes of lynching against African Americans (particularly males) had reached a peak across the nation, especially in the South; and discriminatory laws, known as the Black Codes, continued to multiply. At the local level, some African American had politicians suffered defeats, among them John Mitchell Jr., who lost his seat on Richmond's city council to a white man, while others had persisted, including John Deveaux, who continued to oversee the operations of the US Customs House at Savannah. Before his departure, Mitchell, along with Maj. Joseph Johnson and others, convinced the city government in 1894 to approve funding for an armory on Leigh Street for Johnson's 1st Battalion of Colored Infantry.[1]

In Georgia in 1897, the Georgia Artillery conducted successful field training six miles from Savannah, and plans were underway for a new armory at Cuyler and New Houston Streets for the city's African American battalion. Macon's Lincoln Guards marched in President McKinley's inauguration parade but were, according to the *Atlanta Constitution,* the "only colored company from the South" to do so. To the west, Texas coordinated field training for its singular African American battalion throughout the 1890s. These setbacks and achievements, which have thus far defined the experience of the African American militia volunteers, continued through the war with Spain and into the new century.[2]

"The Manhood of the Negro"

On April 23 at Savannah, two days prior to Congress declaring war, the Savannah Tribune reported that the city's "colored citizens are loyal to the flag and stand ready and willing to defend it," asserting that "in no state will they be found more loyal than [in] Georgia."[3] In Atlanta, Lt. Col. Floyd Crumbly, commanding the 2nd Battalion, informed the Atlanta Constitution that he "'took occasion to question the men and found that fully 75 per cent of them are willing to go to the front.'" Crumbly further stated that he was unaware of how many of his men had been exposed to yellow fever, "'but we can stand the climate of Cuba better than any one else,'" noting that the majority of the state's African American volunteers come from Savannah "'and are already partially acclimated.'"[4] Others were not so optimistic. John Mitchell Jr., editor of the Richmond Planet, reminded his readers "that he had risked his life many times in his crusade against lynching, . . . [but now] had no desire to prove his bravery in a war of aggression." He questioned if the Cubans would be "better off under an American administration than under Spanish rule."[5]

The outset of the war also brought a mixed reaction by the governors of Georgia, Texas, and Virginia. Neither Texas nor Georgia called forth any of their existing African American militia volunteer companies for wartime duty. This early decision elicited condemnations from those currently serving in state militia organizations, including Capt. Robert Ellis of San Antonio's Excelsior Guard. Using the language of manhood, the captain boldly expressed his frustration to Adj. Gen. W. H. Mabry by characterizing the governor's decision not to muster the state's African American militia "as a disgrace." Ellis further conveyed his opinion that "now that the time has come when we can show to the world what we can do and what we are willing to do, we have to wait and let white men come from all over the state and fill out the white company's and most of them are men that have never taken any interest in the state guards."[6] Mabry responded with the hollow excuse that "the number of men required was secured before the colored battalion was reached."[7]

Learning of the president's call for troops, Georgia governor William Atkinson sent his personal secretary to convey his support of recruiting African Americans from the state into the command of US Army major general John Rutter Brooke, then stationed at the training camp at Chickamauga Park.[8] Without any previous proper field training or rifle practice, Governor Atkinson knew that the state had not properly prepared its African American volunteers; Crumbly disagreed. The lieutenant colonel argued that the men "residing in Atlanta, Augusta and Savannah can safely be relied upon as being practically immunes from the contagions of Cuba," admitting that they only "had some instructions in field and camp duties in a limited way but are well informed in the manual of small arms." Crumbly also reminded the secretary of war that many of these "loyal citizens" who have "enjoyed special educational advantages" were capable to serve as commissioned officers.[9]

Even Capt. John Simmons believed his men were ready when he tendered the services of his seventy-eight-man artillery battery to the governor.[10]

Only Virginia governor James Hoge Tyler could withstand the political firestorm that surrounded his decision to muster in eight companies of black troops with their existing officers to form a two-battalion regiment following President McKinley's call for an additional 75,000 troops in May 1898. Unfortunately, he selected Richard Croxton as the regiment's commanding officer, who then called for reexaminations of some of its African American officers. This act prompted the resignations of some officers, including the 2nd Battalion's Maj. William Johnson. The replacement of these experienced men with white officers prompted many of the black troops to resist by refusing to drill, an act that prompted Virginia's white press to dub the command the "Mutinous Sixth." The black press hailed them as patriots, declaring "the day is dawning when *colored men know how to assert their manhood* and resent insult tendered to their dignity." Far from mutinous, this editor believed that the men's actions upheld the "principle that brought on the Revolution of 1776" and deemed them the "Grand, Glorious, Immortal Sixth."[11]

The organization of ten US Volunteer regiments by federal law in May 1898 created additional opportunities for African Americans to serve, especially those already in uniform in the Georgia and Texas militias. Days later, Georgia's Judson Lyons, the register of the Treasury and a Republican Party national committeeman, along with former US representative John Lynch of Mississippi, urged the president "to recognize the services of the colored volunteers by assigning them to one or more of the immune regiments provided for under existing law." Lyons, like Crumbly, argued that "nearly all of these men are trained soldiers and they have endured yellow fever."[12] Months later, when the president forwarded his request for "25,000 colored troops from the nation at large" because "of the special adaptability of colored troops for service under the condition of a tropical climate," even more requests and recommendations for officer appointments flooded McKinley's office.[13]

These letters not only revealed the high level of patriotism expressed by Georgia's serving black militia officers but also illustrated a continuation of the uplift movement and the desire to publicly demonstrate their masculinity through military service. The *Baptist Home Mission Monthly* supported the elevation of black men into the officer ranks, arguing, "it is very important that they [African Americans] should be made to feel that their citizenship is not a mere name, but a solid reality; that citizenship means manhood."[14]

Judson W. Lyons. From Washington, Williams, and
Wood, *New Negro for a New Century,* 113.

Following his meeting with McKinley, Lyons continued to play a vital role
in recommending and successfully obtaining commissions for many of Georgia's militia officers. He received several requests from his Augusta associates,
including Capts. Ansel Golphin and John Lark; Golphin included a letter
of support from his former lieutenant colonel, Augustus Johnson.[15] Third
Battalion staff officers Rev. Charles Walker and Surgeon George Stoney both
received a personal endorsement from Lyons directly to the president, and
both served in the war, Walker as a chaplain in the 9th US Volunteer Infantry
Regiment, and Stoney as the assistant surgeon in the 10th US Volunteers.[16]
Joining Stoney in the 10th "Immunes" as first lieutenants were former 2nd
Battalion lieutenant colonels Crumbly and Grant of Atlanta. Crumbly raised
his own company and requested, through Lyons, to serve jointly with Grant,
having "been personal friends for 20 years."[17]

Savannah Light Infantry's Capt. Henry Nathanial Walton obtained a letter
of support from former Confederate officer Emmitt F. Ruffin. The southern
veteran espoused Walton's military knowledge, strength of character, and

Henry Nathanial Walton.
Courtesy of *AncestryUSA*.

support of the military organizations to Lyons. Emphasizing his own participation in four wars, Ruffin believed he was certainly "able to judge of one's
fitness who desires to make his avocation of life a military one."[18] Initially,
Walton's command remained at Savannah as part of Lieutenant Colonel Deveaux's 1st Battalion of Colored Infantry. Deveaux's written exchange with the
state's acting adjutant general regarding new arms for the battalion in April
1898 pointed to the use of his command as a defensive force against possible
Spanish incursions into the port city.[19]

Postwar

The preparations for the war with Spain and the conflict itself strained African
American manpower in the state militia organizations. The war's demands
also heightened racial conflict between white and African American men as
each sought to maintain their definition and position of masculinity. The resignations from the 6th Virginia Volunteer Regiment hinged on an insult to the
honor and dignity of those who had already been found qualified as officers by

Virginia's military officials. The conflicts that arose within the training camps and with the local communities were arguably disputes of masculinity, with black men attempting to publicly display their self-worth and maintain their honor. The mustering out of the 6th Virginia ended the African American contribution to that state's militia volunteers.[20]

The elimination of the black militia organizations in Virginia was not repeated in either Georgia or Texas. Both of those states maintained their prewar organizations during the war, but multiple newspaper accounts highlighted the so-called ill-disciplined African American troops in the regular and volunteer regiments. Therefore, it is quite surprising that the governments of these southern states did not follow the Old Dominion's lead. Instead, both sought to reorganize their African American commands.

The Georgia Adjutant General's Office announced in General Order No. 2, dated February 23, 1899, that the state's inspector general would "make a thorough inspection of the State Troops beginning March 1 or as soon thereafter as practicable."[21] These inspections, "which . . . [would be] of the most rigid nature," eventually led to the dissolution of the majority of the African American military units in the state, supposedly due to their being "farcical as organizations, and uniformed travesties on the name of soldiery."[22] Those that survived continued to participate in the military activities as they had previously while the state attempted to improve the overall standing of its militia volunteers. Many of these instituted improvements were equally applied to both white and African American troops, such as armory rents, which began in 1900, and required properly recorded and submitted enlistment rolls and extending the length of enlistment from one to two years. Another improvement was not without controversy. On the one hand, the position of inspector of rifle practice was finally filled in the 1st Battalion, but on the other, military officials still prevented African Americans from qualifying. Again this demonstrated an unease of contributing to the elevation of black men, thereby, heightening their manliness in relation to white contemporaries. An example of this occurred when Col. George T. Cann, inspector general of rifle practice for the Georgia Volunteers, expressed his disgust with reported "complaints about members of the Georgia Volunteers, colored, in Savannah parading with a sharpshooter's badge." Cann asked Adjutant General John Kell if "any qualifications have been established" for the African American contingent and if his office was "permitting a member of the Georgia Volunteers, colored, to wear insignia as badges for marksmanship." Kell responded that "no colored marksmen or sharpshooters have qualified" and that the government only authorized those badges as set forth in the state's military regulations.[23]

Some black companies further sought to improve themselves by discharging those men who failed to maintain the proper military standard. Some had legitimate reasons why they could no longer serve, such as a business concern or a physical ailment, while others failed to consistently participate, were insubordinate, or in other way were unsuccessful in upholding the martial ideal of manhood. Capt. Lewis Mosely of the Maceo Guards at Augusta discharged twelve men, eight dishonorably, in the company's first year of existence. Capt. J. H. Carter at Savannah, who carried forty men on the 1900 enlistment roll of the Colquitt Blues, the following year eliminated a total of forty-six men, mostly for nonparticipation, indicating not only high turnover but also potential problems with a lack of interest or dissatisfaction with leadership.[24]

The legislation that guided the reorganization of the Georgia Volunteers in 1899 also demoted the commanding officer of the 1st Battalion of Colored Infantry to the rank of major. The law reduced battalion commanders to major since the rank of lieutenant colonel was now reserved for those who acted as the second in command of the larger regimental organizations. Deveaux easily won election as major of the battalion in January 1900, yet by the end of 1901, the general assembly overwhelmingly approved to restore him to his former rank. This bipartisan step supports the contention that, even after the violence of the war years, Deveaux still garnered respect in political and military circles in the state.[25]

Throughout the first few years of the new century, Georgia's African American militia volunteers experienced some achievements and disappointments. They continued to parade to celebrate a variety of anniversary events, participated in annual Memorial Day observances, and still traveled out of state, though for the first time they were ordered to do so without "ball cartridges." In Texas, this instruction, too, began to be issued to African American troops in travel orders. Both states' inspectors general kept an annual schedule of unit assessments and reported the results to their respective adjutant general.

In his annual report to the governor in 1900, Georgia's adjutant general, "with no cause for prejudice or bias," reported that he failed "to see where the Georgia State Troops, Colored, are or can be of any service to the State, from a military standpoint."[26] Still, his subordinate, Col. William Obear, the same inspector general who recommended the dissolution of African American military organizations in 1899, reported that the 1st Battalion's "troops under Major Deveaux's supervision have made marked improvement in the past twelve months, and from a disorganized, indifferent number of companies, they are now a compact battalion whose administration, drill and discipline is a credit to the State and to themselves."[27] One year later, Inspector General Obear recorded that the "Colored Troops" had the highest average attendance at inspection, with 73 percent reporting present.[28] This attendance was accomplished even though the average enlistment that year was eighty-eight men—the state only provided uniforms for fifty of them.

The passage of the national law in 1903 "to promote the efficiency of the militia," commonly referred to as the Dick Act, provided for federal supervision, better arms and equipment, and consistent training for the National Guard, or organized militia. The regular army detailed inspecting officers to the various states to survey the efficiency of their military forces. By 1905, the 1st Battalion, Colored, at Savannah had been reduced to only five infantry companies, three in the city, one at Macon, and the Maceo Guards of Augusta.[29] The military secretary of the US War Department forwarded to the Georgia adjutant general the findings from that year's report, which included the comment, "I am informed that they would be useless in a local riot or emergency on account of their race," for every African American company in Savannah. Moreover, the state's inspector general had recommended that Macon's Lincoln Guards be disbanded. In contrast, the Maceo Guards were singled out: "as far as efficiency is concerned, I think they could be depended upon in case of domestic emergency."[30]

By the time this report reached the adjutant general's office, the Georgia legislature a month earlier had already voted 106 to 6 to disband the state's African American military commands. Prior to the vote, Rep. Pleasant Alexander Stovall of Chatham County, in a letter to the state inspector for rifle practice, Walter E. Coney, argued *against* the dissolution of the troops, asserting: "You all are making a mistake in trying to disband the colored military companies. The way I look at it, this will have a distinctly bad effect on the colored troops, who ought to be encouraged as far as possible."[31] Coney may have begun his lobbying campaign to disband the black troops after receiving a letter from one of his rifle-range instructors, A. J. Scott. The instructor recorded that the governor had informed him, "if the legislature did not disband the negro troops that he [the governor] was not going to be responsible any longer for their non-equipment, and if, the negroes remained in the service that he was going to use this year's appropriation to equip them." Scott continued, "we have been making excuses for the non equipment of these troops to the Govt., or Army Inspectors each year and the legislature has passed it by without giving any attention to it whatever; so we have either got to get them out or send a lot of good money and equipment to them."[32]

Months later, on the floor of the Georgia House of Representatives, the debate against the bill was led by Joseph Hill Hall of Bibb County. He cautioned the assembly that "legislation against the negro because he is a negro was a very dangerous principle" since "it might be applied also to a certain class of whites." Both Hall and Stovall worried about federal repercussions, yet they also agreed that opportunities for the use of African American troops remained possible. Hall asserted, "there were occasions on which the negro troops might well perform duty for the state."[33] And Stovall, who characterized the commands as "among the best negro citizens in the state," argued that "they were law-abiding and were ready to perform any service they might be called upon to do." Those supporting the disbandment brought forth the argument of not "having any negro officer outranking white officers under any circumstances," as they interpreted would happen under the requirements of the 1903 Dick Act.[34] In opposition, Stovall argued that those members had overreacted since no "Democratic Governor, or even President [Theodore] Roosevelt would do anything which would degrade a Southern Soldier by putting over him a negro officer."[35] Even though men such as Stovall and Hall argued in favor of maintaining the African American troops, they both cited the possible loss of federal appropriations as the reason for their opposition to the bill. They both also saw, however, the possibility of actually utilizing the black militia volunteers, contrary to most of their associates, like James Tift Mann, the chairman of the House Committee on Military Affairs, who argued that African American units "are entirely unfit for service and could never on any occasion, be of any service to the State."[36] Although two years had elapsed since Congress had passed the Dick Act, this dispute can arguably be summed up as a conflict of manliness exasperated by the potential loss of local or state control over the military organizations. The opposition to black officers outranking white officers or commanding white troops, the presence of black men in uniform to quell a riot that might contain white men, and, of course, the provisioning of the African American troops with the same equipment and arms, training them during summer months, or instructing them in the proper use of firearms all had the potential to make some of these black troops nearly equal to, and as such just as manly as, their white counterparts.

The state of Texas did not need legislative action to disband its African American militia. Lack of appropriations and training contributed to their demise company by company over the years, and state officials finally dissolved the last units on January 1, 1906. Although acknowledging that "the colored companies made an exceptionally good show at drills and parades, and cared for their arms and equipment as well as the average white company," Adj. Gen. John Hulen still mustered out the entire battalion "on account of the inadvisability of having both white and colored troops in such a small organization as the State maintains." He admitted that "the men seem to take considerable interest in their organizations" and could maintain sufficient enlisted strength, but he considered the officers as "not equal to the positions held by them," "were too fond of the 'show' feature, and spent much of their time in wrangling and in dissension."[37] With this statement, Texas ended over thirty-five years of African American service in its militia volunteer forces.

Legacy

During a tumultuous period of American history, stigmatized for its white supremacy; racial violence, intimidation, and discrimination; economic uncertainty; labor strife; and increasing urbanization, groups of African American men from Georgia, Texas, and Virginia successfully petitioned the Democratic governors of their respective states to sanction them to form armed, uniformed volunteer militia companies. Over the course of thirty-five years, beginning in 1871, African Americans could, and did, maintain those state-sponsored military organizations. Their experiences, coupled with the documented actions of government and military officials from these three states, illustrated a more complex narrative of the late nineteenth-century American South than others have acknowledged. Examining numerous records and experiences contributes to a more complete and understanding of race relations during those decades.

The very presence of armed, uniformed black troops in southern cities supports the contention that racial relationships remained flexible enough during this period to allow for such organizations. Black militiamen were led by their own African American officers, duly elected by each unit's members. For a time, many black junior officers were examined by higher-ranking African American officers as to their qualifications. These military companies did not operate unofficially or clandestinely. On the contrary, they were highly visible to their fellow citizens and clearly active in the public sphere, whether parading down Pennsylvania Avenue in Washington, D.C., to celebrate a presidential inauguration; performing military movements on Alamo Square in

San Antonio, Texas; or firing rifles and cannons at the Park Extension in the center of Savannah, Georgia.

The existence of racial accommodation in society, however minor, toward African American militia companies can also been seen through the actions of the three state governments and their military officials to *arm, equip, and train* these black troops. Granted, the black companies often received the oldest weapons and equipment in the state's inventory, but documents clearly demonstrated that even so, some of the rifles were taken from them and issued to white units. Some African American companies in Georgia and Texas, though not all, appear to have shouldered the same models and types as their white counterparts, while in Virginia, the black militiamen eventually received the same arms. The example of assigning weapons must be understood within the context that all state troops remained consistently underfunded, inconsistently trained, and unevenly equipped. In addition to firearms, the historical records clearly illustrate that ammunition was issued to the African American commands over the years, and it was used not only in ceremonial salutes but also in target practice and competition. The participation of some African American militia organizations in field training, especially under the auspices of experienced military leadership, whether sponsored by the state or an association, placed them clearly in the public sphere, with most having to travel armed and uniformed over the rail network to their destinations. Moreover, these events always involved a closing military review of the troops open to civilians.

More importantly, however, these preparatory steps combined with white government officials ordering actual deployment of these African American commands in a constabulary role. Such official actions contribute succinctly in overturning the notion that African American militia units were merely social or ceremonial organizations. There can be no doubt that state and local officials viewed these black militiamen as members of bona fide military organizations.

Understanding that this condition of racial relationships may be attributed to paternalism, business interests, or concerns of federal intervention in southern states' treatment of their newest citizens does not detract from the militia's existence in the South, demonstrated by the continued presence of African American state troops in the region. The ability of black militia units to openly muster, parade, practice with their weapons, and travel on official trips within the state and beyond its borders calls into question the traditionally accepted termination of Reconstruction in 1877. Clearly, the events analyzed in this study should encourage a careful reconsideration of when and how we should classify the end of Reconstruction as well as any stereotype of ending black engagement in public life in the 1870s.

First, the governors and military officers of Georgia, Texas, and Virginia exhibited not only varying degrees of neglect and discrimination against black militias but also varying levels of accommodation. As described by *Savannah Tribune* editor Solomon Johnson, some white officials were "broad minded and willing to give a helping hand" toward their state's African American militia volunteers.[38] For example, one could argue that Virginia and Texas officials were more progressive than those in Georgia in their management of their black militia volunteers, especially since both eventually armed their African American troops with improved .45-caliber breech-loading rifles. The adjutant general of Texas authorized and supervised black militia field-training exercises for several years, and Virginia's Brig. Gen. Charles Anderson remained the only southern adjutant general to send black troops to the National Drill in 1887. Surprisingly, all three states had incidents of calling forth their black militia volunteers. Some historians might dismiss the smaller activations or even discount the importance of them all, but with the acknowledged interpretation of race relations that existed during this time, even the thought of using black state troops in the South would have seemed completely unacceptable to many whites at the time. Therefore, the so-called reconstruction of the southern states occurred at different rates—to sweepingly consent to the year 1877 as its ending is to misunderstand the more complex picture.

Second, investigating the legislative actions paired with the military treatment of African Americans clearly divulges a pattern of increasing restrictions over the course of this thirty-five-year period, especially in Georgia, parallel to the rise of "Jim Crow." This pattern, however, remained slow, and state laws made allowances, or what might be characterized as concessions, to its black military at times. This fact points squarely to the ability of some African Americans to successfully employ political persuasion and to the presence of continued support by some prominent leaders in white society. Lastly, even though Georgia, Texas, and Virginia during these years had been "redeemed" by the Democratic Party, African Americans who traditionally supported the Republican Party were not politically prostrate. Local black politicians still won elections and held office during this period. At the state level, African Americans remained influential in elections by supporting one Democratic candidate over another, and nationally, their support of the Republican Party continued to generate patronage positions in government. This employment, in turn, meant local influence and financial rewards, attributes that supplemented the various activities characterized as components of the African American uplift movement.

This uplift movement clearly included African American membership in military organizations. Not only did belonging to official volunteer militia companies demonstrate to the surrounding community their position as citizens in society, but it also enabled these men to publicly display their masculinity and martial spirit. Achieving and maintaining manhood remained one of the strongest motivations for militia membership among males in southern society as a whole. Unmistakably visible in many of the lives of the African American military leadership, the manly ideal can be seen in the teachings of the Masons and the morality lessons of Christian churches and was invariably linked with good citizenship, which the black community took very seriously.

This concept of masculinity also assists in explaining the militia participation of former military veterans, both North and South. Historians understand the motivations of African Americans fighting to end slavery, but those who fought also did so for their status as men. It was obvious that substantive military experience in the Union army was widely respected among African Americans. Even those black men who accompanied Confederate regiments during the Civil War established a soldierly creditability that can be viewed through the framework of manhood, yet they have been largely ignored and mostly relegated to the status of personal servants or conscripted laborers in the historical narrative. By contrast, this study found antebellum free men of color enrolling in areas of Confederate service allowed by law. Even if they were *not* fighting for the preservation of slavery or for states' rights, these African Americans in Georgia arguably sought to enhance their status as a man through their presence with Confederate fighting units. Laying aside any matter that they were coerced, some of these same black men in the postwar period continued to associate with the reorganized white militia organizations that they had marched off to war with in 1861 or sought official recognition as members of the state militia now open to them. In both instances, during the Civil War and afterward, the actions of these African Americans support the contention that their involvement bolstered their status as men and their manliness within southern and American society. It was this central desire to demonstrate that manhood that cemented the relationship between the two groups of African American veterans who later joined together in a common cause with other black volunteers in the state militia.

Moreover, significant values of manhood, specifically honor and self-discipline, became necessary for African American men to demonstrate publicly during this period that witnessed lynching as the punishment for those black men who allegedly could not control themselves. The request by African American commanders for the involvement of high-ranking white state military officials and governors to inspect their troops in the presence of the entire community, both black and white, illustrates an opportunity for the militiamen to exhibit the prestigious traits of manliness and good citizenship. Ironically, this public display of martial skill and masculinity may have also contributed in a negative way toward the erosion of civil rights of black men of all classes and, with other factors, played a role in the eventual dissolution of the African American militia.

Finally, the brief examination of colorism attempted to ascertain if intraracial discrimination existed within the "colored" military organizations of Georgia, Texas, and Virginia. The results seem to indicate that there was no color exclusivity within the militia organizations of these three states. This study also considered an interracial aspect, whether the presence or dominance of lighter-skinned officers made the African American militia more palatable to white society. In the context of the late nineteenth century, with its racial perceptions that categorized newly arriving European immigrants as "both white and racially distinct from other whites," African Americans who appeared as "less black" still remained, culturally and politically, black citizens.[39]

The survey of the higher-ranking officers was severely hampered by the lack of consistency in terminology and the difficulty surrounding the exact definition of "mulatto." If the term simply indicates the physical appearance of a mixed-race individual, it cannot be utilized to determine how light or dark skinned those officers were. A person with straight hair or facial features that some would characterize as more closely resembling a white person, but who possessed a darker complexion, could be described as a mulatto just as someone with lighter skin and the physical features that might be related to an ethnically African person. Even the classifications of "quadroon" and "octoroon," which seem to define a lighter and much lighter shade of skin color, do not provide clear understanding of what would constitute shades of light or dark. The photographs used in this study help demonstrate the levels of difficulty in determining how arbitrary the characterization "mulatto" was applied. The influence or presence of colorism may have existed in individual militia companies, as supported by Capt. Henry Bird's stated membership goals, but more research is required in order to understand how far reaching and diverse this practice may or may not have been, particularly in cities where more than one military organization existed.

As a companion to the need for further research on colorism, so, too, should more studies be commenced regarding the rise and behaviors of the African American middle class as well as a comparative study of the black and white militia within one or more states. Hinging directly into the values of good citizenship and manhood, the middle class espoused the virtues of social acceptability and individual responsibility through thrift, morality, marital integrity, cleanliness, good manners, and education. The numerous members of the Prince Hall Masonic Order, government officials or employees, educators, physicians, and businessmen found within the ranks of the militia leadership, combined with the attitudes toward self-improvement and virtuous behavior, illustrates the strong presence of the middle class guiding the affairs of the African American state volunteer organizations. Their stories found among the pages of directories and self-published biographies, such as the Rev. Edward Carter's *The Black Side* (1894), reinforce the significance of those virtues for personal respect and a successful life.

The provisioning, arming, and training provided to the white men of a state's military organizations compared to those for its black troops will reveal even more clearly the inadequate and discriminatory treatment of African Americans. Moreover, if viewed over the course of a similar thirty-five-year period, is the treatment in other states widely disparate, or does it become more acute as the years progress? And, in what ways did the consequences of the social and economic issues affecting the black community transfer to the African American militia volunteers? Conversely, are any of these same issues illuminated by studying those white militia commands that failed to receive proper equipment, obtained poor marks during inspections, or were disbanded? To date, only singular histories of either white or African American state militia volunteers have been published, indicating an important void in the scholarship of citizen-soldiers of the United States.

Overall, the activities of armed, uniformed African Americans in state-sponsored military organizations clearly illustrate the complexity of race relations in the postemancipation South. Even though eliminated in all three states by 1906, the ability of these men to sustain their organizations for as long as they did—thirty-five years in Georgia—surrounded by the society in which they lived, and with only minimal assistance from the state marks a significant achievement in African American history too long ignored by scholars.

The apparent lack of intraracial and class conflict and the ability of enlisted men to elect their own leaders characterizes the African American militia as one of the most open and democratic organizations in the black community. Recognizing the importance of good citizenship and the virtues of middle-class respectability, these military organizations, as an integral part of the uplift movement, provided African American men with prestige and the opportunity to publicly demonstrate their desire for self-improvement as men through the military arts. When their military organizations were disbanded, African American men sought out other means to fulfill that public display of masculinity and citizenship. But for those who had served their states faithfully, nothing could define those attributes more concisely than militia membership.

Describing the dissolution of Georgia's African American military organizations, Solomon Johnson's assertion that "no greater injustice could ever be inflicted upon any class of citizens" can be applied as well to the black men of Texas and Virginia.[40]

APPENDIX A

General Rules Governing the 2nd Battalion, Georgia Volunteers, Colored

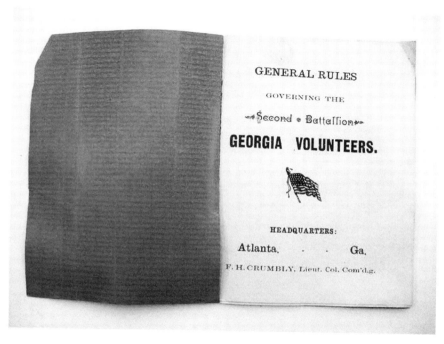

Title page of *General Rules Governing the Second Battallion.*
Courtesy of RCB-41412, Georgia Archives.

HEADQUARTERS 2D BATTALLION [*SIC*] GEORGIA VOLUNTEERS, ATLANTA, GA., MARCH 1, 1893.

In order that there may be progress made in the management and discipline of the company composing the 2nd Battalion, Georgia Volunteers, and for the creation of more interest and an increased desire of the soldiers to excel in their duties, that they may better enjoy the benefits to be derived from their connection with the army of the State, and for the special purpose of placing into the hands of every soldier the uniform drills as adopted by the Advisory

Board and approved by the Commander-in-chief of the State's army, known
as drill cards Nos. 1, 2, 3, 4 and 5 respectively treating upon the following
drills to wit: Infantry drill regulations, school of the soldier without arms,
school of the soldier with arms, school of the company, the squad, the platoon,
[and] the company acting alone. I would state that the authorities of the State
expect that the colored troops shall make proficiency in every respect equal
to that of any other class of the armed force of the State, and in addition to
being provided with the same facilities as other troops are favored with[,] it
is absolutely necessary that the attention of all officers be particularly directed to a prompt and full enforcement of these drill regulations and the rules
herein given. The commanding officer of this Battallion desires to press on
the minds of all, more particular the commissioned officers, the importance
of rendering him their continuous support. His efforts to succeed to make
the Battallion just what it should be in drill and discipline must be supported
by the officers; in the performance of duty there should not appear the least
signs of the least dissatisfaction from any military standpoint; all military duty
should be performed with dignity, candor and with determination. Officers of
companies should know that the success of the company is in a large measure
due to their ability to drill and direct company affairs; the men will at all times
expect the officers to do well what they attempt to do; officers are regarded
by the men as models for their guidance, hence officers ought to have an
understanding of their duties. The members of company ought not to elect
one of their comrades to be an officer over them because he is a favorite, or a
clever fellow; such men as have executive ability only ought to be elected to
executive places.

The interest to the State may at some time require the service of an officer
in a place and under circumstance which will necessitate the exercise of the
wisest judgment in connection with the orders he may be under, and upon
his acts may greatly depend the success of the State in protecting life, property
and the enforcement of the law.

GENERAL RULES.

1. There shall be at least two (2) meetings of the company each
   month in the year.
2. All officers and non-commissioned officers are required to be
   present at each regular meeting of the company.

3. The Lieutenants must diligently assist the Captain in his effort to carry into effect all orders, rules and regulations, and particularly the drills and the performance of all his duties as required by law.

4. The company shall be divided into squads under the immediate charge of the sergeants who shall, in addition to keeping a squad roll, have the resident address of each member of his squad in order that he may be summoned to the armory for duty in the shortest possible time; also that the trooper may receive the attention of this comrades in case of sickness or other auses.

   The chiefs of squads will be held responsible for the efficiency of the members thereto belonging in the drills and duties of the soldier.

5. The 1st sergeant of the company must, when forming the company before reporting to the officer in command, call the company roll and report the number of absentees; any trooper absent from the company for thirty days without lawful excuse of sickness or absence from the city shall be tried for conduct to the prejudice of good order and military discipline, or fined $1.00; the first sergeant shall at all times know the resident address of every member of the company. He shall confer with the company commander as often as possible and keep him informed of the conduct of the men while bearing arms. He shall fearlessly discharge every duty assigned him by his superior officers and require the strictest obedience from all non-commissioned officers and members of the command under him.

6. All non-commissioned officers must be respected and obeyed by all soldiers placed under their control.

7. No officer or soldier has a right to dictate to his superior officer. All duties assigned by a superior must be promptly executed.

8. No officer or non-commissioned officer shall directly or indirectly curse or use any profane language in the discharge of his duty to those under his charge; any officer so doing shall be charged with conduct unbecoming an officer or a gentleman.

9. No officer is allowed to conspire against another officer or encourage troopers in criticizing the acts of his fellow officer under liability of general charge trail by a general court marshal [sic] as required by article of war.

10. No man who has served in one company of this Battallion shall be received by an officer into any other company except he exhibits evidences of an honorable discharge from the company in which he had formerly served as required by article of war.

11. Enlisted officer will carefully examine all applicants for enlistment and see that none are admmitted [*sic*] except sound, healthy, moral and well formed men. Special attention must be paid to eyesight, sense of hearing, and ability to use well his arms, fingers and legs.

12. There shall be regular business meetings held in each company.

13. The soldiers shall pay not less than twenty-five cents each month as monthly dues for the payment of hall rents, lights, etc.

14. There shall be a company fund in each company of the Battallion of all monies paid into the company whatsoever.

15. There shall be a company treasurer elected by ballot by a majority of all the votes cast; he shall hold in charge all company funds; he shall receive the same from the company clerk, give his receipt therefor, pay it out by order of the company, by warrant signed by the secretary and approved by the company commander, and not otherwise; for the faithful performance of his duty he shall execute a satisfactory bond as may be agreed upon by the company commander. He shall be exempt from monthly dues.

16. There shall be a company clerk who shall be elected by a majority vote of all present for a term of one year, he shall receive all monies from the troopers for dues and taxes and fines, and such other monies as may belong to the company, turn it over to the treasurer, take his receipt for the same, keep a just and true account between the members and the company, and notify all members of their arrearages. He shall keep the records of the company and perform such clerical duties from time to time as the company commander may direct; he shall at all times by record be prepared to render an account of the financial condition of the company; he shall issue no warrants for money not passed upon and approved by the company, except for hall rent and lights, and that must be reported at next company meeting. For service rendered he shall be exempt from monthly dues. He shall attend all company meetings.

17. All dues, fines and assessments should be paid at company armory on meeting nights.

18. At the death of a comrade the entire membership of the company will be assembled at company armory by the company commander and marched under arms to the place where the deceased comrade lie in state and will attend the funeral as required by the usages of the army of the United States.

19. At the death of a comrade each trooper of the company to which he belonged shall be assessed 50 cents to defray the expense of said funeral.

20. Thirty ($30.00) dollars shall be allowed for funeral expense, provided the finance of the company does not justify a greater sum, and the increased amount voted out by the company.

21. Companies may give entertainments for the benefit of its treasury. All funds must be turned over to the treasurer by the secretary and his receipt taken and recorded.

22. Company commanders will carefully direct the management of all funds voted out by the company, see to it that it is appropriated as ordered by the company, and that there be no encouragement given in the slightest way to any financial misconduct on the part of any member of his command.

23. The ladies belonging to families of members of companies may be elected as company aides, and may be very helpful in the success of entertainments. They may also have monthly meeting, and have charge of the department of refreshments for the benefit of the company; all fund thus derived to be turned over to the clerk of the company and by him delivered to the treasurer; as an evidence of appreciation for their valuable services they should be allowed to wear gold badges bearing the name of the company and Battallion to which it belongs.

24. Each trooper shall wear cross rifles and the letter of his company, and figure two (2) the number of this Battallion on his fatigue cap.

25. Fatigue uniforms should be used on all occasions unless otherwise ordered by the commanding officer of the Battallion.

26. There shall be held not less than one officers' meeting each month in the year; at such meetings none but commissioned offices shall be present. The commander of the Battallion will be the presiding officer; the adjutant will record the proceedings; any improvements in the active management of the Battallion may be recommended and

discussed; the commander will be the judge on all general issues. If complaint is offered against a fellow officer in all candor and soldierly respect to the officer complained of, and a possible adjustment of the difference between the officers may be reached, the commander will hear the grievance and endeavor to bring about a satisfactory understanding in the case. If the charge be one within the purview of the general regulations of the army of the State, the same bearing relation to the laws governing the Army of the United States, the commander will himself, or cause to be preferred, the proper charges and specification against the disobedient officer and forward the same through proper military channel to the Adjutant General, and request the detail of a court martial for the trial of the case.

27. Officers under charge awaiting trial will be considered as being under arrest and will be relieved temporarily from duty.

28. No trooper will be allowed to fall into line with his company without having his shoes blacked, his uniform and brasses in clean condition, and, unless otherwise ordered by the company commander, he must have on white gloves when handling his gun.

29. No trooper will be allowed to use profane or disrespectful language to his superior, or comrade, while in company armory. Any enlisted man violating this section will be liable to a court martial and a dishonorable discharge from the army of the State.

30. Enlisted men nor officers are allowed to chew tobacco, smoke, or drink any spirituous liquors while on duty; nor shall they speak to any person whatever except in the discharge of duty while in the performance of the same. Any officer or enlisted man violating this section are liable to punishment.

31. Company commanders will at all times use their best endeavors to protect the reputation of their company by honest dealing in all business matters.

32. Whenever a company has a fund on hand and a comrade is sick and in need the company must render him financial aid of not less than two ($2.00) dollars nor more than four ($4.00) dollars per week.

33. The company may, whenever the treasury will justify, make such reasonable contributions to the widows and orphans of their dead comrade as its ability will allow.

34. It is the indispensible duty of all comrades to in private life pay respect and willing obedience to the law of the city, county, State and

United States, that whenever he is called upon to enforce the laws he may do so with effect.

35. No gambler, murderer or convict shall enlist in the service of the State army.

36. Company commanders will report to the tax collecting authorities all men who are carried on the company rolls, also all who are dropped from time to time by reason of discharge, death, etc.

37. Company commanders are strictly required to pay proper respects to the Governor, his staff, the City Mayor, the Judiciary and Magistrates, and at all times to promptly respond to the call of the proper authorities in the enforcement of law and order in all matters without regard to race, color, or condition, and to perform all duties fearlessly and discreetly.

38. Company commanders will see to it that all property belonging to the government of Georgia, or of the United States is protected against invaders; all camp and garrison equipages, ordinance [sic] and ordinance [sic] stores, and all public property, not herein mentioned, shall be protected by the military.

39. The officers of the Battallion should inform themselves on the geographical map of the State, and their duties as officers in the field, in the camp and on the march.

40. There shall be a company orderly in each company whose duty it shall be to prepare the armory for company meetings and perform such other duties as he may be ordered by the company commander. For such service he shall be exempt from all duties and paid such salary as the company may vote [and] agree upon.

Asking a prompt compliance with these rules and recommendations, I am respectfully your obedient servant,

F. H. Crumbly, *Lieutenant Colonel commanding.*

The foregoing rules have been spread on the records of the Battalion.

W. B. PRUDEN, First Lieutenant and acting Adjutant,

Second Georgia Battalion.

APPENDIX B

Constitution of the Maceo Guards of Augusta, Georgia

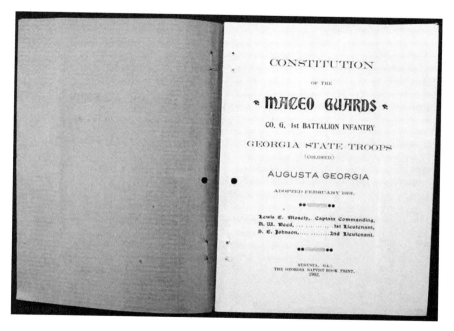

Title page of *Constitution of the Maceo Guards.*
Courtesy of RCB-41409, Georgia Archives.

PREAMBLE

In order to acquire a full knowledge of the military art, and to perfect ourselves in the drill and discipline of the citizen solder, we, the enlisted strength of this command, hereby form ourselves into a military association, and to more readily promote our object, and for our civil government, as well as to perfect our military organization by rules supplementary and subsidiary to those provided by the State of Georgia for the government of the militia, we adopted the following Constitution:

ARTICLE I.

The name of this Company shall be "Maceo Guards," (Co. G, 1st Battalion Infantry, G. S. T., Colored).

ARTICLE II.

Art. 14—Regulations for the government of the volunteer forces of the State of Georgia.

ARTICLE III.

1. The commissioned and non-commissioned officers of the company shall be chosen agreeably to the rules and regulations that now, or may hereafter govern the Georgia State Troops, but the Treasurer shall be chosen at the annual meeting on the 4th Wednesday night of November. The 1st sergeant, in the discretion of the Captain, will act as Secretary. The Quarter Master Sergeant will serve as Armorer.

2. The Captain of the Company shall be the President thereof [ex-officio], and in case of his death, absence, resignation, or other disability, the next commissioned officer in rank present shall preside, and the duties of the President shall be the same as a similar officer in like organizations.

3. It shall be the duty of the Treasurer to collect all fines, dues, and assessments; to pay all bills, upon the order of the President, which are countersigned by the Secretary; to receive, safely keep, and pay over, when properly required, all money of the Company; to keep correct accounts of all receipts and expenditures; as well as an account with each member; to report quarterly the condition of the finances; to allow his books to be open to the inspection of each member; and to give bond, if required, with good and sufficient sureties, in the penal sum of . . . . for the faithful performance of his duties.

4. It shall be the duty of the Secretary, in addition to keeping the minutes of the proceedings of each meeting for the transaction of business, to keep an account of all the military meetings and parades in an orderly book, which shall be brought to each meeting, and be, at all times, open to general inspection; and he shall also keep a muster roll, which he shall call at the time named for assembling, and shall note and report, as soon as possible, to the Treasurer, all fines and assessments, and those upon who they are to be levied. An assistant may be had to distribute orders or notifications to the member, of special meetings or parades.

5. It shall be the duty of the Armorer to provide, at the expense of the company, all needful utensils etc.; to keep the arms, accoutrements, and military apparatus of the company in safety and good order; to keep record of all the property in his charge, and of its condition, reporting a copy of the same at each quarterly meeting, keeping it open, meanwhile, for the inspection of the members, and, during the absence or inability of Armorer, the Assistant Armorer shall take his place.

6. In consideration of the faithful performance of the duties appertaining to the several offices, the Secretary, Treasurer and Armorer shall be exempt from dues.

ARTICLE IV.

1. There shall be appointed by the President, at the annual meeting, the following standing committees, namely: On Finance, Music, Sick and Examination, to consist of three members each, and of each of the committees the Captain shall be a member ex-officio.

2. The Duties of the Finance Committee shall be to act, when instructed, as a committee of Ways and Means; inspect the books and accounts of the Treasurer; assist him in collecting amounts due to the company; audit his account previous to his quarterly report; to take charge of his business in case of his absence or inability and to attend generally to the financial affairs of the company.

3. The duty of the Music Committee shall be to engage, on the most advantageous terms, the music necessary for the parades and drills of the company; to audit all bills for said music, and to report them to the following meeting of the company.

4. The duty of the Sick Committee shall be to visit all members, who may be sick, and any member who reports himself sick, shall make an immediate report to the President, that he may sign an order on the Treasurer for the relief fund; and no member shall be entitled to the relief fund, who has not been confined to his room for at least one week.

5. The duty of the Examining Committee shall be to examine into the personal character and physical condition of all persons proposed as candidates for membership, and report the results of the examination to the company; the committee will further require all applicants for membership to file their applications in writing.

ARTICLE V.

1. Each and every member, excepting the Secretary, Treasurer and Armorer, shall pay to the treasury of the company the sum of 25 cents per month, for relief funds, and pay in addition such sums as shall be necessary of parades, etc., and each and every member shall be subject to the following fines, namely: For absence from any Squad Drill or company Drill, fifty cents; or absence from Company Meetings, 25 cents; for absence from Annual Meeting, one dollar; for retiring from meeting without leave, fifty cents; and no fines or assessments shall be commuted or remitted except for good cause, and by a vote of the company.

ARTICLE VI.

1. The commissioned officers of the company shall form a "Board of Control," with authority to do and perform all acts which it may be necessary to do and perform for the benefit of the company, when, from the nature of the case, it shall be impracticable to call the company together to act, and shall report their action, at the next meeting of the company.

ARTICLE VII.

1. No member shall be admitted to the ranks until he shall be deemed by his drill officer to be sufficiently expert in the school of the soldier, and any member whom the commanding officer shall, at any time judge to be deficient in military discipline, shall be remanded to a drill officer for further instruction.

ARTICLE VIII.

1. Any member intending to be absent from the city for more than thirty days, must apply to the commandant for a furlough, and, having obtained it, he shall be exempt from all fines and assessments until his return; and any member neglecting to obtain a furlough shall be liable to all fines and assessments which may be incurred during his absence.

ARTICLE IX.

1. Any member making written application to [the] commandant, accompanied by a certificate from the Treasurer that he has paid all his debts to the company, may, by a vote of the company, by consent of the Governor (Article 16, State Regulations) be transferred. And if any member shall be guilty of any act discreditable to himself or the company (Article 15 Reg.) And any member

absenting himself from six successive drills or meeting without a satisfactory excuse to the commanding officer, his name shall be erased from the roll.

ARTICLE X.

1. The regular meetings of this company shall be on the second Wednesday night of each month. Drill one night in each week, and the hour for meetings and drills shall be, from the 1st of September to the 1st of March inclusive, at 8 o'clock p.m., and during the rest of the year at 8:30; but special meetings or drills may be called by the Captain, if he so determine.

ARTICLE XI.

1. To perpetuate the principles which led to the establishment of this company, and in honor of its founders, the 16th of November shall be celebrated as its anniversary, in such manner as may be directed by a majority of the members of the company.

ARTICLE XII.

Arrangement of Business.

1. Roll Call; 2. Reading the Minutes; 3. Report of Standing Committee; 4. Report of Special Committee; 5. Unfinished Business; New Business; Collection of Fines, Dues, etc.

ARTICLE XIII.

1. On the death of any member of this company, who was in good standing at the time of his death, the President on being informed thereof shall order the Treasurer to pay out the sum of twenty-five dollars for the purpose of paying the funeral expenses of such deceased member.

ARTICLE XIV.

Any member in arrears for three (3) months dues shall not receive any benefits.

ARTICLE XV.

1. This Constitution shall not be altered, amended or abrogated, except by a vote of two-thirds of the members present at a stated meeting next after that at which said amendment or alteration shall have been proposed in writing.

LEWIS E. MOSELY, Captain Commanding.

NOTES

Abbreviations

RG   Record Group

GAM   Georgia Archives, Morrow

LVA   Library of Virginia, Richmond

NARA   National Archives and Records Administration, Washington, DC

TSL   Archives and Information Division, Texas State Library and Archives Commission, Austin

TVG   Texas Volunteer Guard

Chapter 1

1. See James Michael Russell, *Atlanta, 1847–1890: City Building in the Old South and the New* (Baton Rouge: Louisiana State University Press, 1988); John Dittmer, *Black Georgia in the Progressive Era, 1900–1920* (Urbana: University of Illinois Press, 1977); William A. Link, *Atlanta, Cradle of the New South: Race and Remembering in the Civil War's Aftermath* (Chapel Hill: University of North Carolina Press, 2013); Ronald H. Bayor, *Race and the Shaping of Twentieth-Century Atlanta* (Chapel Hill: University of North Carolina Press, 1996); Peter J. Rachleff, *Black Labor in Richmond, 1865–1890* (Urbana: University of Illinois Press, 1989); Allison Dorsey, *To Build Our Lives Together: Community Formation in Black Atlanta, 1875–1906* (Athens: University of Georgia Press, 2004); Edward J. Cashin and Glenn T. Eskew, *Paternalism in a Southern City: Race, Religion, and Gender in Augusta, Georgia* (Athens: University of Georgia Press, 2001); and Robert L. Perdue, *The Negro in Savannah, 1865–1900* (New York: Exposition, 1973).

2. According to historian John Dittmer, the two men ended their relationship following the Atlanta riot of 1906, which, according to Du Bois, "illustrated the failure of Booker T. Washington's accommodationist philosophy." See Dittmer, *Black Georgia*, 192.

3. The governors of Kansas, Illinois, Virginia, Ohio, North Carolina, Alabama, and Massachusetts did activate African American companies from their state military organizations to serve in the war with Spain.

4. Bruce A. Glasrud, ed., *Brothers to the Buffalo Soldiers: Perspectives on the African American Militia and Volunteers, 1865–1917* (Columbia: University of Missouri Press, 2011). Historian Jennifer Keene has contended that Glasrud "settles for the unsatisfying approach of simply summarizing the main points of each individual essay," thus

"leaving it solely to the reader to draw connections and trace the evolution of the field over time, the contradictions or tensions among the various essays, and possibilities for future research." See Jennifer Keene, "Uncovering the Unknown Soldier: Black Militias, 1865–1917," review of *Brothers to the Buffalo Soldiers: Perspectives on the African American Militia and Volunteers, 1865–1917,* ed. Bruce Glasrud, H-Net, April 2012, http://www.h-net.org/reviews/showrev.php?id=33096 (accessed June 28, 2013). Out of the eleven essays in Glasrud's collection, only two feature research directed solely on the peacetime activities of the black militia. The view that African American militia companies survived because they served mostly as ceremonial and fraternal organizations permeates the literature.

5. Roger Dryden Cunningham, "They Are as Proud of Their Uniforms as Any Who Serve Virginia: African American Participation in the Virginia Volunteers, 1872–99," *Virginia Magazine of History and Biography* 110, no. 3 (2002): 293–338. An example of Black treatment in wartime service is Cunningham, "'A Lot of Fine, Sturdy Black Warriors': Texas's African American 'Immunes' in the Spanish American War," *Southwestern Historical Quarterly* 108, no. 3 (2005): 345–67.

6. Roger D. Cunningham, *The Black Citizen-Soldiers of Kansas, 1864–1901* (Columbia: University of Missouri Press, 2008), xvi.

7. Frances Smith, "Black Militia in Savannah, Georgia, 1872–1905" (master's thesis, Georgia Southern College, 1981).

8. Charles Johnson, *African American Soldiers in the National Guard* (Westport, CT: Greenwood Press, 1992), 92. Johnson's research covers the entire United States, including all of the former Confederate states—except Arkansas—that possessed black militia organizations from the 1870s to the early 1900s.

9. Gregory Mixon, *Show Thyself a Man: Georgia State Troops, Colored, 1865–1905* (Gainesville: University Press of Florida, 2016), 9–10.

10. Michael Kimmel, *The History of Men: Essays in the History of American and British Masculinities* (Albany: State University of New York Press, 2005).

11. Earnestine Jenkins and Darlene Clark Hine, eds., *A Question of Manhood: A Reader in U.S. Black Men's History and Masculinity,* 2 vols. (Bloomington: Indiana University Press, 2001), 1:xvi.

12. Marline Kim Connor, *What Is Cool?: Understanding Black Manhood in America* (New York: Crown, 1995), 9.

13. Simone Drake, "'So I Decided to Quit and Try Something Else for a While': Reading Agency in Nat Love," in *Fathers, Preachers, Rebels, Men: Black Masculinity in U.S. History and Literature, 1820–1945,* ed. Timothy R. Buckner and Peter Caster (Columbus: Ohio State University Press, 2011), 160–83.

14. Gail Bederman, *Manliness and Civilization: A Cultural History of Gender and Race in the United States, 1880–1917* (Chicago: University of Chicago Press, 1995).

15. Ibid., 21.

16. Mike O'Brien, "Manhood and the Militia Myth: Masculinity, Class, and Militarism in Ontario, 1902–1914," *Labor / Le Travail* 42 (Fall 1998): 115.

17. Ibid., 141.

18. Ehren K. Foley, "'To Make Him Feel His Manhood': Black Male Identity and Politics of Gender in the Post-Emancipation South" (Ph.D. diss., University of South Carolina, 2012).

19. Trina Jones, "Shades of Brown: The Law of Skin Color," *Duke Law School Public Law and Legal Theory Working Paper Series* no. 7 (October 2000): 1487–1557 (quote, 1497).

20. Willard B. Gatewood Jr., *Aristocrats of Color: The Black Elite, 1880–1920* (Bloomington: Indiana University Press, 1990), 180–81.

21. Sarah Bartlett, "Brown Fellowship Society (1790–1945)," BlackPast, September 14, 2010, http://www.blackpast.org/aah/brown-fellowship-society-1790-1945 (accessed Nov. 23, 2015).

22. Gatewood, *Aristocrats of Color,* 14.

23. Elijah Horace Fitchett, *The Free Negro in Charleston, South Carolina* (Chicago: University of Chicago, 1950); James B. Browning, "The Beginnings of Insurance Enterprise among Negroes," *Journal of Negro History* 22, no. 4 (October 1937): 422–24; Robert L. Harris Jr., "Charleston's Free Afro-American Elite: The Brown Fellowship Society and the Humane Brotherhood," *South Carolina Historical Magazine* 82, no. 4 (October 1981): 289–310 (quote, 300–301). See also Kevin R. Johnson, ed., *Mixed Race in America and the Law: A Reader* (New York: New York University Press, 2013).

24. Dittmer, *Black Georgia,* 93.

25. Perdue, *Negro in Savannah,* 90; Dittmer, *Black Georgia,* 61.

26. Quoted in Charles Lwanga Hoskins, *W. W. Law and His People: A Timeline and Biographies* (Savannah: Gullah, 2013), 65.

27. Department of Commerce, Bureau of Census, *Negro Population in the United States, 1790–1915* (Washington, DC: GPO, 1918), 207–8.

28. Muster rolls, Austin City Rifles, Capitol Guard, Brenham Blues, Brazos Light Guard, Gregory Rifles, Roberts Rifles, Jim Blaine Rifles, Cochran Greys, Cochran Blues, Lone Star Rifles, Grant Rifles, Lincoln Guards, Davis Rifles, Sheridan Guards, Excelsior Guard, Ireland Rifles, and Hubbard Rifles, TVG, RG 401, TSL.

Chapter 2

1. For clarity, the end of "Reconstruction" in Georgia as stated here recognizes the seating of the state's US senators and Georgia's readmission to the Union on July 15, 1870. *The Code of the State of Georgia* as stated here includes the following: Richard H. Clark, Thomas R. R. Cobb, and David, Irwin, eds., *The Code of the State of Georgia,* rev. ed. (Atlanta: Franklin Steam Printing House, 1868), hereafter cited as *1868 Irwin's Code*; Richard H. Clark, Thomas R. R. Cobb, David Irwin, George N. Lester, and Walter B. Hill, eds., *The Code of the State of Georgia,* 2nd ed. (Macon: J. W. Burke, 1873), hereafter cited as *1873 Irwin's Code*; Nathaniel E. Harris, ed. *A Supplement to the Code of Georgia Containing the Public Acts Passed by the General Assembly since 1873 and the Constitution of 1877* (Macon: J. W. Burke, 1878); George N. Lester, Christopher Rowell, and Walter B. Hill, eds., *The Code of the State of Georgia,* 4th ed. (Atlanta: J. P. Harrison, 1882); John L. Hopkins, Clifford Anderson, and Joseph Rucker Lamar, eds. *The Code*

of the State of Georgia Adopted December 15, 1895, vol. 1 (Atlanta: Foote & Davies, 1896); and Howard Van Epps, ed., *Supplement to the Code of the State of Georgia,* vol. 4 (Nashville: Marshall & Bruce, 1901), hereafter cited as *1901 Supplement.*

2. *1868 Irwin's Code,* 205, 209; *1873 Irwin's Code,* 179–82 (emphasis added). James Milton Smith (1823–1900) was born in Twiggs County, Georgia; educated as a lawyer; and elected a judge three months prior to Georgia's secession from the Union. Opting to serve as a soldier instead, he was elected captain of Company D, 13th Georgia Infantry Regiment and then major of the regiment on July 8, 1861. Later promoted to lieutenant colonel, Smith was severely wounded at the Battle of Cold Harbor on June 27, 1862, prior to taking command of the regiment as colonel on September 17, 1862. Smith resigned his commission upon winning a seat in the Confederate Congress in 1863. See Keith Hulett, "James M. Smith (1823–1890)," *New Georgia Encyclopedia,* August 4, 2006, http://www.georgiaencyclopedia.org/articles/government-politics/james-m-smith-1823-1890 (accessed March 31, 2015); "Smith, James M.," Compiled Service Records of Confederate Soldiers Who Served in Organizations from the State of Georgia, RG 109, NARA (hereafter cited as Compiled Service Records of Confederate Soldiers, Georgia, RG 109, NARA).

3. Hans Peter Mareus Neilsen Gammel, *The Laws of Texas, 1827–1897,* 10 vols. (Austin: Gammel Book, 1898), 6:185–90, 7:468–69; *Acts and Joint Resolutions Passed by the General Assembly of the State of Virginia at Its Session of 1870–71* (Richmond: C. A. Schaffter, Superintendent of Public Printing, 1871), 318.

4. *Acts and Joint Resolutions,* 318.

5. Gammel, *Laws of Texas,* 6:187.

6. Sidney Herbert, *A Complete Roster of the Volunteer Military Organizations of the State of Georgia* (Atlanta: James P. Harrison, 1878), n.p. Herbert's work provides a glimpse into the organization of the volunteers of Georgia. But since there are no corresponding materials to confirm or deny his information, one could question its accuracy.

7. Ibid. Further investigation is needed to determine the catalyst for these revisions of the law. Most likely, the poor performance of militia organizations during the Great Railroad Strike of 1877 prompted legislators, the governor, and state military officials to improve the condition of the widely dispersed, largely unregulated groups of Georgia Volunteers.

8. *Acts and Resolutions of the General Assembly of the State of Georgia, 1884–85* (Atlanta: State Printer, 1886), 74–75 (hereafter cited as *Acts and Resolutions, 1884–85*).

9. William H. Clark to Adj. Gen. John A. Stephens, September 25, 1885, RCB-41578, RG 22, GAM. John Alexander Stephens (1838–87) was the nephew of former Confederate vice president and Georgia governor Alexander H. Stephens. During the Civil War, he was a second lieutenant in Company D, 1st Georgia Regulars, rising to the rank of captain. He was captured and held as a prisoner at Camp Chase, Ohio. Educated as a lawyer, Stephens practiced at Crawfordville and Atlanta. He served as adjutant general for the state of Georgia from 1882 to 1886, resigning due to poor health. See "Georgia's Patriotism and Gratitude," *Confederate Veteran* 14, no. 10 (October 1906): 442–43; "Unit Information—1st Georgia Regulars," Compiled Service Records of

Confederate Soldiers, Georgia, RG 109, NARA; and "Death of Col. John A. Stephens," *New York Times*, April 24, 1887.

10. Clark to Stephens, September 25, 1885.

11. Henry Dickerson McDaniel (1836–1926), born at Monroe in Walton County, Georgia, graduated from Mercer University and practiced law prior to the Civil War. Initially voting against secession at the state convention in 1861, he eventually voted in favor of Georgia leaving the Union and enlisted in the 11th Georgia Infantry Regiment in July 1861. Rising to the rank of major, McDaniel was captured at Hagerstown, Maryland, after suffering a gunshot wound in the abdomen during the retreat from Gettysburg. He spent the remainder of the war as a prisoner at Johnson Island, Ohio, until released upon taking the oath of allegiance to the United States on July 25, 1865. McDaniel served as a Georgia state legislator and senator prior to his election as governor to fill the remainder of the term of Alexander H. Stephens, who died in office in 1883. He won the election to a full term as governor in 1884. See Robert E. Luckett, "Henry McDaniel (1836–1926)," *New Georgia Encyclopedia*, September 30, 2006, http://www.georgiaencyclopedia.org/articles/government-politics/henry-mcdaniel-1836-1926 (accessed March 31, 2015); and "McDaniel, H. D./McDaniel, Henry D. (28)/McDaniel, Henry D.," Compiled Service Records of Confederate Soldiers, Georgia, RG 109, NARA.

12. Thornton Turner, William Gaines, and Rolla Ferrell to Gov. Henry D. McDaniel, February 15, 1886, RCB-41414, RG 22, GAM.

13. "The Colored Companies," *Savannah Tribune*, February 15, 1896.

14. *Report of the Adjutant General of the State of Georgia for the Year 1896* (Atlanta: Franklin Printing, 1897), 4 (hereafter citied as *Adjutant General of Georgia, 1896*).

15. Allen Daniel Candler (1834–1910) was born at Auraria in Lumpkin County, Georgia, and graduated from Mercer University in 1859. Teaching school prior to the Civil War, he enlisted as a private in Company H, 34th Georgia Infantry Regiment in May 1862 and rose to the rank of captain by October. Fighting in Tennessee, Mississippi, Kentucky, and Georgia, Candler was promoted to lieutenant colonel and transferred to the 4th Georgia Reserves in May 1864 after losing the sight in his left eye from a wound suffered at the Battle for Jonesboro. Surrendering in May 1865, Candler was later a Georgia state representative, state senator, US representative, and secretary of state for Georgia prior to his election as governor in 1898, serving until 1902. See Robert E. Luckett, "Allen D. Candler (1834–1910)," *New Georgia Encyclopedia*, May 4, 2006, http://www.georgiaencyclopedia.org/articles/government-politics/allen-d-candler-1834-1910 (accessed March 31, 2015); "Candler, Allen D.," Compiled Service Records of Confederate Soldiers, Georgia, RG 109, NARA; "Candler, Allen Daniel (1834–1910)," *Biographical Directory of the United States Congress,* http://bio-guide.congress.gov/scripts/biodisplay.pl?index=c000109 (accessed April 3, 2015).

16. "Patriotic Negroes," *Macon (GA) Telegraph*, March 31, 1898; "Negroes Must Go," *Baltimore Sun*, March 27, 1899.

17. *1901 Supplement*, 147–51.

18. Pleasant A. Stovall to Maj. Walter E. Coney, August 15, 1905, RCB-15620, RG 22, GAM.

19. "Ill Feeling Grows," *Dallas Morning News,* October 24, 1903.

20. "An Act to Abolish the Colored Troops of the State of Georgia from the Militia of this State," RCB-35736, RG 22, GAM.

21. *Report of the Adjutant General of Texas, December, 1886* (Austin: Triplett & Hutchings, State Printers, 1886), 28 (hereafter cited as *Adjutant General of Texas, 1886*). The battalion in 1886 consisted of the Excelsior Guard of San Antonio, Lincoln Guard of Galveston, Roberts Rifles of Corpus Christi, and the Valley City Guard of Columbus. Wilburn Hill King (1839–1910) enlisted twice during the Civil War, once with the Missouri State Guard at the outset, and again in Texas after he had been medically discharged due to wounds. Elected an officer in both states, King later rose to the rank of colonel of the 18th Texas Infantry Regiment. Wounded again at the Battle of Mansfield, King would end the war as a divisional commander. He served as Texas adjutant general from 1881 to 1891. See David S. Walkup, "King, Wilburn Hill," in *The New Handbook of Texas,* ed. Ronnie C. Tyler, 6 vols. (Austin: Texas State Historical Association, 1996), 3:1108–9.

22. *Report of the Adjutant General of Texas, 1890–1891* (Austin: Henry Hutchings, State Printer, 1892), 85–86 (emphasis added; hereafter cited as *Adjutant General of Texas, 1890–91*). Capt. Richard I. Eskridge, 23rd US Infantry, assigned as inspecting officer of the encampment, made this recommendation. See Alwyn Barr, "The Texas 'Black Uprising' Scare of 1883," *Phylon* 41, no. 2 (2nd Qtr.1980): 179–86; and Barr, "The Black Militia of the New South: Texas as a Case Study," *Journal of Negro History* 63, no. 3 (December 1978): 153–60.

23. Based on the number of rifles or muskets issued to the companies, the white companies averaged about fifty-eight men per infantry unit, while the African American companies numbered about fifty-five men per infantry unit. The cavalry commands appear to have averaged about fifty men each, while it is difficult to determine the number of troops serving in the artillery companies. If an average of fifty-four men (the average between fifty and fifty-eight) is used for the artillery units, then the white troops of Virginia numbered approximately 2,690 men and the black militiamen 880, in addition to battalion staff officers for each group.

24. *Acts and Resolutions of the General Assembly of the State of Georgia, 1878–79* (Atlanta: James P. Harrison, State Printer, 1880), 103, 105 (emphasis added; hereafter cited as *Acts and Resolutions, 1878–79*).

25. Ibid., 104.

26. Ibid., 107.

27. Clifford W. Anderson to Adj. Gen. Stephens, August 29, 1884, RCB-41414, RG 22, GAM (original emphasis). Clifford Wallace Anderson (1848–1901), a native of Savannah, enlisted at the age of sixteen in the 5th Georgia Cavalry and served briefly in the ranks before joining the staff of the regimental commander (and his father), Col. Robert Houstoun Anderson, later a brigadier general, as a courier and assistant aide-de-camp. The younger Anderson "was one of these selected to carry cartel surrender between Johnston and Sherman in April 1865." Following the end of the war, he returned to Savannah, entered into business, and joined the state volunteers in 1872 as a private. Rising to the rank of colonel and command of the 1st Volunteer Regiment, Anderson later resigned his command but remained active as an aide-de-camp on the

staff of several Georgia governors until his retirement on March 28, 1892. See "Clifford W. Anderson," Indigent Pension, 1897, RG 58, GAM; "Roll of Retired Officers," *Report of the Adjutant General of the State of Georgia from January 1, 1899, to October 17, 1900* (Atlanta: Franklin Printing, 1900), 112 (hereafter cited as *Adjutant General of Georgia, 1899–1900*); and Virginia Military Institute, "Clifford Wallace Anderson," Historical Roster Database, http://www9.vmi.edu/archivesroster/ArchiveRoster.asp?page=details&ID=3191&rform=search (accessed October 13, 2014).

28. "Cannot Be Colonel," *Atlanta Constitution,* February 29, 1884. Pledger was one of eight men in Georgia examined for the rank of lieutenant colonel.

29. *Savannah Tribune,* quoted in Henry Lewis Suggs, *The Black Press in the South, 1865–1979* (Westport, CT: Greenwood, 1983), 120.

30. "A Colored Colonel," *Atlanta Constitution,* September 8, 1880. John Benjamin Baird (1850–97) had previously served as the superintendent and deeper of public works prior to his assignment as adjutant general in 1879, serving until 1882. He had been too young to serve in the Civil War. See *Appletons' Annual Cyclopaedia and Register of Important Events of the Year 1879,* 19 vols. (New York: D. Appleton, 1885), 4:421; "John B. Baird's Funeral," *Washington Evening Times,* September 3, 1897. Wilberforce Daniel (1836–97), on the other hand, served as an officer in both the 63rd Georgia Infantry Regiment and the 12th Georgia Light Artillery. After the war, he worked as a cotton merchant at Augusta, served as Richmond County sheriff, and was on the state Democrat's Executive Committee. Daniel led the Independent Battalion, Georgia State Militia at Augusta in 1878 until Governor Gordon selected him as an aide-de-camp in 1887, a position that also placed him on the Military Advisory Board. See "Daniel, Wilberforce," Compiled Service Records of Confederate Soldiers, Georgia, RG 109, NARA; Herbert, *Complete Roster,* n.p.; "State Democratic Executive Committee," *Atlanta Constitution,* July 19, 1882; and Arthur Eugene Sholes, comp., *Sholes' Directory of the City of Augusta, 1883* (Augusta: A. E. Sholes, 1883), 195.

31. "Colored Colonel," *Atlanta Constitution,* September 8, 1880.

32. William Garrard (1836–1918) was educated at the Military University of Alabama and enlisted in Company I, 31st Alabama Infantry Regiment as sergeant major, rising to first lieutenant. He took command of Company K, 23rd Alabama Infantry Regiment and, in 1863, was selected to join the staff of Brig. Gen. Edmund Pettus as assistant adjutant and inspector general. After the war, he studied law at the University of Kentucky and then moved to Savannah, where he served on the city council and later as the city attorney. Garrard enrolled as a private in the Savannah Volunteer Guards in 1873. Promoted to lieutenant colonel, he was serving in this capacity when taking command of the 2nd Georgia Volunteer Infantry in 1898 during the war with Spain. Garrard retired from military service in 1900. "Garrard, William N.," Compiled Military Service Records of Confederate Soldiers Who Served in Organizations from the State of Alabama, RG 109, NARA; *Adjutant General of Georgia, 1899–1900,* 115; James Clark Fifield, *The American Bar: Contemporary Lawyers of the United States and Canada* (Minneapolis: James C. Fifield, 1918), 112.

John Flannery (1835–1910), born in County Tipperary, Ireland, served as a captain during the Civil War with the 1st Georgia (Olmstead's) Regiment. After the conflict, he worked as a cotton merchant and banker at Savannah. "Flannery, John," Compiled

Service Records of Confederate Soldiers, Georgia, RG 109, NARA; William Harden, *A History of Savannah and South Georgia*, 2 vols. (Chicago: Lewis, 1913), 2:1078–80.

33. Clifford W. Anderson et al. to Adj. Gen. Stephens, February 17, 1886, RCB-41578, RG 22, GAM.

34. W. A. Pledger to Gov. McDaniel, February 2, 1884, RCB-41414, RG 22, GAM.

35. Adj. Gen. Stephens to A. R. Johnson, July 14, 1885, VOL1-1709, RG 22, GAM.

36. John McIntosh Kell (1823–1900) was born at Laurel Grove plantation in McIntosh County, Georgia. He entered the US Navy as a midshipman in 1841, served during the war with Mexico (1846–48), and accompanied Commodore Perry to Japan in 1853. Upon Georgia's secession from the Union, he offered his services to the Confederate States Navy and served as executive office of the CSS *Sumter* and CSS *Alabama*. Kell served as adjutant general of Georgia from 1887 to his death in 1900. "Georgia's Patriotism and Gratitude," *Confederate Veteran* 14, no. 10 (October 1906): 442–43; John McIntosh Kell, *Recollections of a Naval Life, including the Cruises of the Confederate States Steamships "Sumter" and "Alabama"* (Washington, DC: Neale, 1900); Norman C. Delaney, *John McIntosh Kell of the Raider Alabama* (Tuscaloosa: University of Alabama Press, 2003); *Adjutant General of Georgia, 1896*, 9.

37. A. R. Johnson to John M. Kell, March 31, 1890, RCB-37046, RG 22, GAM (original emphasis).

38. Hugh T. Reed, *Upton's Infantry Tactics, Abridged and Revised, embracing the Schools of the Squad and Company, Skirmishers, Inspection, Etc.* (Baltimore: A. W. Reed, 1882). This manual, named after Union Civil War hero Emory Upton, includes detailed instructions for the teaching of soldiers. These included the manual of arms, squad and company movements, skirmishing, inspections, musters, honors, salutes, and battalion activities. The manual of arms included instructions on how to present arms, order arms, trail arms, right shoulder arms, port arms, carry arms, fix and unfix bayonets, inspect (cartridge) boxes, how to load, ready, aim, fire, carry, recover, and how to execute these actions by squad, by file, and by rank, lying down or kneeling. There are additional instructions on the use of swords—draw, present, carry, return, and inspection.

39. Adj. Gen. Kell to Thomas Grant, February 27, 1892, VOL1-1721, RG 22, GAM; Adj. Gen. Kell to Floyd H. Crumbly, February 27, 1892, ibid.; *Acts and Resolutions, 1878–79*, 107; Adj. Gen. Kell to Joseph H. Hammond, August 4, 1890, VOL1-1705, RG 22 GAM; Adj. Gen. Kell to William H. Royall, August 25, 1890, ibid.; Adj. Gen. Kell to Lymus A. Washington, July 13, 1891, VOL1-1706, ibid.

40. *Acts and Resolutions, 1878–79*, 107.

41. *Acts and Resolutions of the General Assembly of the State of Georgia, 1892* (Atlanta: George W. Harrison, State Printer, 1892), 81 (hereafter cited as *Acts and Resolutions, 1892*).

42. *Report of the Adjutant and Inspector-General of the State of Georgia for the Year 1893* (Atlanta: Franklin Printing, 1893), 17.

43. *Acts and Resolutions, 1892*, 81.

44. Ibid.

45. Asst. Adj. Gen. [illegible] to Isaiah Blocker, December 12, 1896, VOL1-1729, RG 22, GAM.

46. Adj. Gen. Kell to Julius Maxwell, March 3, 1894, VOL1-1723, RG 22, GAM.

47. William L. Grayson to Adj. Gen. Kell, March 22, 1898, RCB-41473, RG 22, GAM.

48. William S. Rockwell to the Adj. Gen. Kell, October 26, 1897, RCB-41473, RG 22, GAM.

49. John Jenkins to Acting Adj. Gen. Oscar J. Brown, May 1, 1898, RCB-41473, RG 22, GAM.

50. Ibid.

51. W. G. Harrison to the Adj. Gen. Kell, October 4, October 8, 1898, RCB-41473, RG 22, GAM; Jordan F. Brooks to Adj. Gen. Kell, January 17, 1900, RCB-41418, ibid. (emphasis added). The annual report of the adjutant general for 1899–1900 lists both First Lieutenant Thomas and Captain Simmons with their respective commands.

52. John P. Ross to Adj. Gen. Kell, February 16, 1899, RCB-41418, RG 22, GAM.

53. *Adjutant General of Georgia, 1899–1900*, 110.

54. "Roster of Commissioned Officers Georgia Volunteers," *State of Georgia Adjutant General Records*, vol. 6, *1877–99* (Atlanta, n.d.), 63–201, RG 22, GAM, microfiche (hereafter cited *Georgia Adjutant General Records, 1877–99*). Those governors included James M. Smith, Alfred H. Colquitt, Alexander H. Stephens, James S. Boynton, and Henry D. McDaniel.

55. Gammel, *Laws of Texas*, 9:1041.

56. *Rules and Regulations for the Government and Discipline of the Texas Volunteer Guard* (Austin, 1895), 80–81.

57. Ibid., 83–84.

58. *Report of the Adjutant General of the State of Texas for 1895–96* (Austin: Ben C. Jones, 1897), 28 (hereafter cited as *Adjutant General of Texas, 1895–96*); *Report of the Adjutant General of the State of Texas for 1899–1900* (Austin: Von Boeckmann, Schutze, 1900), 201 (hereafter cited as *Adjutant General of Texas, 1899–1900*); *Biennial Report of the Adjutant General of Texas for the Years 1903 and 1904* (Austin: Von Boeckmann, Schutze, State Printers, 1904), 48.

59. *Acts and Joint Resolutions, 1870–71*, 318–21.

60. *Report of the Adjutant-General of the State of Virginia for the Year 1896* (Richmond: J. H. O'Bannon, Superintendent of Public Printing, 1896), 63 (hereafter cited as *Adjutant General of Virginia, 1896*).

61. Ibid., 69.

62. The adjutant general's 1887 report mentions that the inspector general, during his tour of inspection that year, formed boards at Petersburg, Danville, Staunton, and Norfolk. See *Report of the Adjutant-General of the State of Virginia for the Year 1887* (Richmond: A. R. Micou, Superintendent of Public Printing, 1887), 57 (hereafter cited as *Adjutant General of Virginia, 1887*).

63. *Report of the Adjutant-General of the State of Virginia for the Year 1886* (Richmond: A. R. Micou, Superintendent of Public Printing, 1887), 50 (hereafter cited as *Adjutant General of Virginia, 1886*).

64. Ibid., 41.

65. Joseph Lane Stern (1848–1932), born in Caroline County, Virginia, served briefly as a telegrapher in Gen. Robert E. Lee's headquarters on the Virginia Central Railroad. Graduating from Washington and Lee University in 1870, he moved to Richmond to practice law, joining Company C, 1st Virginia Infantry on April 12, 1871. Stern became

assistant inspector general of the Virginia Volunteers in 1884, with the rank of lieutenant colonel, and later served as adjutant general on several different occasions until his retirement in 1922. Marshall Wingfield, "General Jo Lane Stern," in *A History of Caroline County, Virginia* (Baltimore: Genealogical Publishing, 2009), 215–21.

66. *Adjutant General of Virginia, 1886,* 50.

67. Ibid.

68. *Adjutant General of Virginia, 1887,* 11.

69. Ibid., 10.

70. Ibid., 57.

71. Ibid., 55.

72. *Report of the Adjutant-General of the State of Virginia for the Year 1894* (Richmond: J. H. O'Bannon, Superintendent of Public Printing, 1894), 57 (hereafter cited as *Adjutant General of Virginia, 1894*). Charles Jeffries Anderson (1848–1925) graduated from the Virginia Military Institute in 1869 (the same class as Georgia's Clifford W. Anderson). During the Civil War, as a cadet in Company A, he took part in the Battle of New Market in 1864. Beginning in 1870, "he began an active commercial career in Richmond." One year later, he enrolled in the Virginia Volunteers, serving initially as a captain and later succeeding former Confederate general Fitzhugh Lee as brigadier general in command of the 1st Brigade in 1885. Anderson occupied this position until his appointment as adjutant general in 1893, serving in that role until 1898. He also served on Richmond's city council and as a member of the House of Delegates and the state senate. Lyon G. Tyler, *Men of Mark in Virginia: Ideals of American Life,* 5 vols. (Washington, DC: Men of Mark, 1907), 2:13–14; Virginia Military Institute, "Charles J. Anderson," Historical Roster Database, http://archivesweb.vmi.edu/rosters/record.php?ID=3190 (accessed April 3, 2015).

73. *Adjutant General of Virginia, 1894,* 58.

74. *Adjutant General of Virginia, 1896,* 37.

Chapter 3

1. *1868 Irwin's Code,* 210.

2. Ibid., 211.

3. "Georgia," *New Orleans Commercial Bulletin,* July 14, 1870. See Eric Foner, *Freedom's Lawmakers: A Directory of Black Officeholders during Reconstruction* (New York: Oxford University Press, 1993), 37–38.

4. Richard D. Goodman to Gov. Smith, April 10, 1872, OVER-561, RG 22, GAM; "'Union Lincoln Guards' (Colored)," *Georgia Adjutant General Records, 1877–99,* 361.

5. A. W. Stone to Gov. Smith, n.d., OVER-561, RG 22, GAM; "'Forest City Light Infantry' (Colored)," *Georgia Adjutant General Records, 1877–99,* 307. See also Thomas G. Dyer, *Secret Yankees: The Union Circle in Confederate Atlanta* (Baltimore: Johns Hopkins University Press, 2001), based on the diary of Cyrena Stone, Amherst Stone's wife.

6. James B. Lewis to Gov. Smith, April 22, 1872, NEWS-253, RG 22, GAM; "Chatham County, Georgia," 1870 US Census, Population Schedules, RG 29, NARA (hereafter cited as Ninth Census, 1870); Alexander Abrams, comp., *Directory of the City of Savannah for 1870* (Savannah: J. H. Estill, Publisher and Printer, 1870), 167.

7. "A Record of Honor," *Savannah Tribune,* June 15, 1901; "An Honorable Record," ibid., May 4, 1901.

8. W. E. Hunter, M. H. Prehlieu, and James Houston to Gov. Smith, April 25, 1872, NEWS-253, RG 22, GAM.

9. William Yates to Gov. Smith, November 3, 1873, DOC-2816, ibid.

10. Ibid.

11. "Matters and Things Laconically Noted," *Savannah Morning News,* August 4, 1875; "Union Delmonico Guards," ibid., November 8, 1877; Herbert, *Complete Roster,* n.p. Alfred Holt Colquitt (1824–94) was born in Walton County, graduated from the College of New Jersey (later Princeton University) in 1844, and admitted to the bar two years later. After serving as a staff officer in the war with Mexico, Colquitt relocated to Macon to practice law. A licensed Methodist minister, he entered politics and was elected to the US Congress. Entering Confederate service as a captain, Colquitt was elected colonel of the 6th Georgia Infantry Regiment in May 1861 and then promoted to brigadier general a year later. Participating the battles with the Army of Northern Virginia until 1863, he later took his command to the Carolinas and Florida before returning to Virginia to defend Petersburg. After the war, Colquitt served as governor from 1876 to 1882 and a US senator from 1883 to his death in 1894. Barton Myers, "Alfred H. Colquitt (1824–1894)," *New Georgia Encyclopedia,* March 3, 2006, http://www.georgiaencyclopedia.org/articles/government-politics/alfred-h-colquitt-1824-1894 (accessed February 16, 2016).

12. Perdue, *Negro in Savannah,* 17; Lucian Lamar Knight, *A Standard History of Georgia and Georgians,* 2 vols. (Chicago: Lewis, 1917), 2:828–32. While Knight wrote disparaging of Bradley, he did characterize African Americans Henry M. Turner, Tunis Campbell, and Moses Bentley "as good and true men." See also Olive Hall Shadgett, *The Republican Party in Georgia from Reconstruction to 1900* (Athens: Georgia University Press, 1964); and Foner, *Freedom's Lawmakers,* 17–18, 37–38, 215–16.

13. William S. Basinger to Gov. Smith, July 11, 1872, DOC2-894, RG 22, GAM. William Starr Basinger (1827–1910) became a member of the Savannah Volunteer Guards Battalion in 1851. When the Civil War began, the Guards became the 18th Georgia Battalion, with Basinger as a second lieutenant. In 1862, he took command of Company A and participated in all the engagements of the command, surrendering with the remnants of the unit on April 9, 1865. He was incarcerated at the Old Capitol Prison and Johnson's Island before obtaining his release. Basinger returned to Savannah, reassociated with the Volunteer Guards in 1872, and was leading the battalion when he left state military service in 1882. He was a lawyer and, in 1885, became the president of the North Georgia Agricultural College at Dahlonega, serving until 1894. *Adjutant General of Georgia, 1899–1900,* 113; William Starr Basinger Papers, 1835–1932, Wilson Library, University of North Carolina, Chapel Hill.

14. John Screven to Governor Smith, September 1872, DOC-2815, RG 22, GAM. John Screven (1827–1900) was the son of James P. Screven, a former mayor of Savannah, state senator and railroad president. Young Screven was born and raised in Savannah, obtained an education at Franklin College (later the University of Georgia), and studied law at Heidelberg, Germany. Admitted to the bar in 1849, he was elected as justice of the inferior court at Savannah in 1852, holding that position until 1866.

Screven joined the Savannah Volunteer Guards, also in 1852, and became president of
the Atlantic and Gulf Railroad in 1859; he took a leave of absence to fight for the Confederacy. At the beginning of the war, Screven led a line company of the 18th Battalion
of Georgia Infantry, rose to the rank of lieutenant colonel, and was in command of the
inner defensive lines around Savannah in 1864. After the war, Screven served as a state
representative and as mayor of Savannah (1869–73), remaining active in military, civic,
fraternal, veterans, and social affairs. Harden, *History of Savannah and South Georgia*,
2:595–605; Allen D. Candler and Clement A. Evans, eds., *Georgia: Comprising Sketches
of Counties, Towns, Events, Institutions, and Persons, Arranged in Cyclopedic Form*, 3
vols. (Atlanta: State Historical Association, 1906), 3:260–61; *National Cyclopaedia of
American Biography*, 13 vols. (New York: James T. White, 1892), 2:229; "Screven, John,"
Compiled Service Records of Confederate Soldiers, Georgia, RG 109, NARA.

15. Screven to Gov. Smith, October 4, 1872, RCB-2812, RG 22, GAM.

16. "Matters and Things Laconically Noted," *Savannah Morning News*, October 25,
1875.

17. George McCarthy to Gov. Alfred H. Colquitt, April 28, 1879, DOC-2834, RG 22,
GAM.

18. "Roundabout in Georgia—Savannah News," *Atlanta Constitution*, November 23,
1878; George McCarthy, Charles Atkins, and Adam Brown to Gov. Colquitt, March
25, 1881, RC-41414, RG 22, GAM; "'Lone Star Cadets' (Colored)," *Georgia Adjutant
General Records, 1877–99*, n.p.; "'Georgia Artillery' (Colored)," ibid., 362. See also
Herbert, *Complete Roster*, n.p.; and Francis Bernard Heitman, *Historical Register of
the United States Army from Its Organization, September 29, 1789 to September 29, 1889*
(Washington, DC: National Tribune, 1890), 30, 90. Charles Johnson does not indicate
if any other state possessed a black artillery battery. See *African American Soldiers in the
National Guard*.

19. William H. D'Lyon to Gov. Colquitt, July 10, 1878, DOC-2834, RG 22, GAM.

20. Herbert, *Complete Roster*, n.p.; "Matters and Things Laconically Noted," *Savannah Morning News*, August 20, 1878.

21. "Our Military on Parade," *Savannah Tribune*, May 25, 1889; Garrard to Adj. Gen.
Stephens, February 8, 1886, RCB-14578, RG 22, GAM; *Report of the Adjutant and
Inspector-General of the State of Georgia for the Year 1889* (Atlanta: W. J. Campbell, State
Printer, 1890), 6 (hereafter cited as *Adjutant and Inspector-General of Georgia, 1889*).

22. *Acts and Resolutions, 1884–85*, 74–75.

23. Garrard to Adj. Gen. Stephens, February 8, 1886, RCB-41578, RG 22, GAM.

24. *Acts and Resolutions, 1878–79*, 103.

25. Resolution of the Union Lincoln Guards, July 8, 1880, RCB-41414, RG 22, GAM;
Resolution of the Chatham Light Infantry, July 5, 1880, ibid.; Resolution of the Forest
City Light Infantry, July 9, 1880, ibid.; Resolution of the Savannah Light Infantry, July
6, 1880, ibid.; Resolution of the Colquitt Blues, July 5, 1880, ibid.; Resolution of the
Lone Star Cadets, July 6, 1880, ibid.

26. William H. Woodhouse et al. to Gov. Colquitt, December 10, 1877, DOC2-894,
RG 22, GAM.

27. Woodhouse and Louis B. Toomer to Gov. Colquitt, July 14, 1880, RCB-41414, RG
22, GAM.

28. Headquarters, 1st Batt., Inf. G.S.T. Col'd, General Order 4, August 4, 1900, RCB-41393, RG 22, GAM.

29. "The Georgia Cadets Grand Parade," *Savannah Weekly Echo,* December 2, 1883.

30. "Our Military on Parade," *Savannah Tribune,* May 25, 1889; "Emancipation Day Celebration," ibid., January 6, 1894. It is unclear if the Chatham Zouaves were commonly referred to as the "Young Chathams" or if this was indeed a different company.

31. "Disturbance in East Savannah," *Savannah Morning News,* August 20, 1878; "The Hunter Rifles—The Alleged Disturbance in East Savannah," ibid., August 21, 1878.

32. King Thomas to David G. Cotting, July 10, 1872, DOC-2811, RG 22, GAM; Robert Wilson to Gov. Smith, October 27, 1872, DOC-2812, ibid.; James H. Carter to Gov. Smith, October 10, 1873, ibid.; Benjamin Day to Gov. Smith, November 6, 1873, DOC-2816, ibid.; Day to Gov. Smith, July 16, 1874, RCB-37023, ibid.

33. Smith, "Black Militia in Savannah, Georgia," 23.

34. Perdue, *Negro in Savannah,* 3; Dorsey, *To Build Our Lives Together,* 122; Donald Lee Grant, *The Way It Was in the South: The Black Experience in Georgia* (Secaucus, NJ: Carol, 1993), 298; B. I. Diamond and J. O. Baylen, "The Demise of the Georgia Guard Colored, 1868–1914," *Phylon* 45, no. 4 (4th Qtr., 1984): 311–13.

35. *Testimony Taken by the Joint Select Committee to Inquire into the Condition of Affairs in the Late Insurrectionary States: Georgia,* 2 vols. (Washington, DC: GPO, 1872), 2:1036.

36. Ibid., 1037. Henry McNeal Turner (1834–1915) was born in South Carolina. After the Civil War, he continued organizing efforts for the African Methodist Episcopal Church, rising to the position of bishop of the church. Turner, living at Macon, won election from Bibb County to the Georgia House of Representatives in 1868. He was known as "one of the most influential African American leaders in late nineteenth-century Georgia" and a vocal advocate for the "Return to Africa" movement. Stephen Ward Angell, "Henry McNeal Turner (1834–1915)," *New Georgia Encyclopedia,* September 3, 2002, http://www.georgiaencyclopedia.org/articles/history-archaeology/henry-mcneal-turner-1834-1915 (accessed February 10, 2016).

37. *Testimony Taken by the Joint Select Committee,* 2:1036.

38. Ibid., 611, 1040. Born a slave in South Carolina, Thomas Allen (1844–1923), a shoemaker by trade, learned to read and became a Baptist minister. He represented Jasper County in the Georgia House of Representatives in 1868. Edmund L. Drago, *Black Politicians and Reconstruction in Georgia: A Splendid Failure* (Baton Rouge: Louisiana State University Press, 1982), 21, 39, 93, 701; Foner, *Freedom's Lawmakers,* 4; Grant, *Way It Was in the South,* 105–6; William E. Montgomery, *Under Their Own Vine and Fig Tree: The African-American Church in the South, 1865–1900* (Baton Rouge: Louisiana State University Press, 1995), 97, 156–57, 163, 304; Vital Statistics Registers, City of Savannah Health Department, Savannah, GA.

39. Nat D. Sneed et al. to Gov. Smith, April 18, 1872, DOC-2810, RG 22, GAM; Sneed to Col. Alexander, May 3, 1872, ibid.; "Richmond County, Georgia," Ninth Census, 1870; W. L. McBride to Gov. Smith, May 29, 1872, DOC-2810, RG 22, GAM; "Roster of Commissioned Officers Georgia Volunteers," *Georgia Adjutant General Records, 1877–99,* 63.

40. D'Lyon to Gov. Smith, October 20, 23, 1873, DOC-2816, RG 22, GAM.

41. A. O. Bacon et al. to Gov. Smith, June 9, 1874, DOC-2819, RG 22, GAM.

42. "'Central City Infantry' (Colored)," *Georgia Adjutant General Records, 1877–99,* 348.

43. Wesley Simmons to Gov. Smith, November 3, 1873, DOC-2816, RG 22, GAM.

44. M. H. Mason to Gov. Smith, August 5, 1875, DOC-2824, RG 22, GAM; Herschel V. Johnson to Gov. Smith, August 19, 1875, ibid.; John W. Robinson to Gov. Smith, August 23, 1875, ibid.; Salem Dutcher to Gov. Smith, August 24, 1875, ibid.

45. "SANDERSVILLE TRIALS," *Atlanta Constitution,* September 4, 1875.

46. Thomas P. Beard to Gov. Smith, September 20, 1873, NEWS-253, RG 22, GAM.

47. Wilberforce Daniel et al. to Gov. Colquitt, February 4, 1878, DOC-2834, RG 22, GAM.

48. "Roster of Commissioned Officers Georgia Volunteers," 63–201.

49. Ibid.

50. Ibid.; C. M. Wiley to Adj. Gen. Stephens, July 12, 1884, RCB-41414, RG 22, GAM.

51. "Roster of Commissioned Officers Georgia Volunteers," 63–201; William C. Yancey to Gov. Smith, August 24, 1874, DOC-2820, RG 22, GAM.

52. "Roster of Commissioned Officers Georgia Volunteers," 63–201; "'Augusta Cadets' (Colored)," *Georgia Adjutant General Records, 1877–99,* 343; Herbert, *Complete Roster,* n.p.

53. F. Marion Sheppard to Gov. Colquitt, May 3, 1880, RCB-41414, RG 22, GAM.

54. "COLORED MILITARY," *Atlanta Constitution,* June 5, 1883; Herbert, *Complete Roster,* n.p.

55. "Marietta Light Infantry col'd (Independent)," *Georgia Adjutant General Records, 1877–99,* n.p.

56. Green E. Ellis to Adj. Gen. Baird, June 15, 1881, RCB-41414, RG 22, GAM.

57. *Acts and Resolutions, 1878–79,* 104.

58. Louis M. Pleasant et al. to Gov. Colquitt, July 14, 1880, RCB-41414, RG 22, GAM; "Application for Organization," June 15, 1880, NEWS-253, RG 22, GAM; Jefferson Wyly et al. to Gov. Colquitt, September 29, 1880, NEWS-253, RG 22, GAM.

59. A. R. Johnson to Adj. Gen. Stephens, January 30, 1886, RGB-41578, RG 22, GAM.

60. John Neibling to Adj. Gen. Stephens, May 21, 1884, RGB-41578, RG 22, GAM; Neibling to Adj. Gen. Stephens, December 9, 1884, RGB-41414, ibid.

61. J. S. Mason to Gov. Gordon, June 21, 1888, RCB-41395, RG 22, GAM; S. Don Dryer to Gov. Northen, August 25, 1892, RCB-41405, ibid. In an effort to attain recognition in Georgia's militia, Mason, after complimenting the governor, former Confederate general John Brown Gordon, wrote: "We the young colored men composing a part of the citizens of this grand old commonwealth, have organized ourselves into a military company in honor of our executive head, namely, the Gordon Cadets. . . . [W]e will by being named for so admirable and amiable character so good a citizen so perfect a gentleman feel satisfied that success will be ours." For biographical information on Gordon, see W. Todd Groce, "John B. Gordon (1832–1904)," *New Georgia Encyclopedia,* December 10, 2004, http://www.georgiaencyclopedia.org/articles/government-politics/john-b-gordon-1832-1904 (accessed February 11, 2016). For Northen, see Casey P. Cater, "William J. Northen (1835–1913)," *New Georgia Encyclopedia,* August 12, 2005, http://www.georgiaencyclopedia.org/articles/government-politics/william-j-northen-1835-1913 (accessed February 13, 2016). See also William J. Northen

Papers, 1865–1929, GAM; and William J. Northen Family Papers, 1790–1959, Richard B. Russell Library, University of Georgia, Athens.

62. See Appendix B for the *Constitution of the Maceo Guards* (Augusta: Georgia Baptist Book Print, 1902).

63. *Adjutant General of Georgia, 1899–1900*, 7, 13, 127 (emphasis added); Special Orders No. 283, November 16, 1900, RCB-37020, RG 22, GAM. Phill Glenn Byrd (1861–1939), whose name is sometimes given as "Phillip" or "Phil," was born at Walesca, Georgia, on February 3, 1861, and received his education at the North Georgia Military College in Dahlonega, graduating in 1880. He enlisted in the Rome Light Guards that same year and served one year. Byrd worked as a newspaper editor before returning to the Georgia Volunteers as the captain of the Hill City Cadets, commanding the unit from 1891 to 1894. Appointed an aide-de-camp for Governor Northen in 1894, Byrd served in that position until January 1, 1899, when he became Adjutant General Kell's assistant. When Kell died in October 1900, Byrd became Georgia's adjutant general but resigned one month later due to health concerns and business interests that took him to Costa Rica. Byrd fell from his horse on the morning of August 12, 1938 and died from complications eleven months later. Initially buried in Costa Rica, his body was returned to the United States in 1954 and reinterred at Myrtle Hill Cemetery in Rome, Georgia. *Adjutant-General Report of Georgia, 1899–1900*, 62; Reports of American Citizens Abroad, 1835–1974, General Records of the Department of State, RG 59, NARA; "Gen. Phill Glenn Byrd," Find-a-Grave, January 4, 2011, http://www.findagrave.com/cgi-bin/fg.cgi?page=gr&GSln=byrd&GSfn=phill&GSmn=glenn&GSbyrel=all&GSdyrel=all&GSob=n&GRid=63731800&df=all& (accessed February 11, 2016).

64. Richard Lowe, *Republicans and Reconstruction in Virginia, 1856–70* (Charlottesville: University Press of Virginia, 1991), 170–79, 181, 183–89.

65. Virginius Dabney, *Richmond, Virginia: The Story of a City*, rev. ed. (Charlottesville: University Press of Virginia, 1990), 237.

66. Ibid., 220–40; Don H. Doyle, *New Men, New Cities, New South: Atlanta, Nashville, Charleston, Mobile, 1860–1910* (Chapel Hill: University of North Carolina Press, 1990), 15. See also Steven J. Hoffman, *Race, Class, and Power in the Building of Richmond, 1870–1920* (Jefferson, NC: McFarland, 2004).

67. "LOCAL NEWS—Military Items," *Daily State Journal* (Richmond, VA), April 18, 1871.

68. *Acts and Joint Resolutions*, 318.

69. Joseph Lane Stern, *Roster Commissioned Officers Virginia Volunteers, 1871–1920* (Richmond: Davis Bottom, Superintendent of Public Printing, 1921), iv.

70. "Local Matters—Military," *Daily State Journal* (Richmond, VA), July 28, 1871; "The Attucks Guard," ibid., January 25, 1872; "Injustice to the Attucks Guard," ibid., November 16, 1871.

71. "The Attucks Guard," *Daily State Journal* (Richmond, VA), January 25, 1872.

72. Stern, *Roster Commissioned Officers*, 280–81; "Local Notes," *Daily State Journal* (Richmond, VA), March 20, 1872. Hobson received his commission on February 17, 1872, and like Reid was a US Colored Troops (USCT) veteran. Reid later commanded the Douglass Guard at Danville, Virginia, from 1879 to 1883. See Stern, *Roster Commissioned Officers*, 286.

73. *Annual Report of the Adjutant General of the Commonwealth of Virginia for the Year 1873* (Richmond: R. F. Walker, Superintendent of Public Printing, 1873), 2 (hereafter cited as *Adjutant General of Virginia, 1873*). William Harvie Richardson (1795–1876) commanded a company of Virginia militia during the War of 1812 and was the first secretary of the commonwealth, serving from 1832 to 1852. Richardson organized the Virginia State Library in 1828 and acted as its first librarian to 1852. In 1841, he was appointed as Virginia's adjutant general and as a member of the Board of Visitors of the Virginia Military Institute, continuing to serve in both capacities until his death in 1876. Virginia did not have an adjutant general during the post–Civil War hiatus of militia service from 1865–1870. Virginia Military Institute, "William Harvie Richardson," Historical Roster Database, http://archivesweb.vmi.edu/rosters/record.php?ID=11649 (accessed February 11, 2016); "Richardson, William H.," Compiled Service Records of Volunteer Soldiers Who Served during the War of 1812, RG 94, NARA.

74. Edward King, *The Great South* (1875; repr., New York: Arno and the *New York Times*, 1969), 581.

75. *Annual Report of the Adjutant General of the Commonwealth of Virginia for the Year 1876* (Richmond: R .F. Walker, Superintendent of Public Printing, 1876.), 4 (hereafter cited as *Adjutant General of Virginia, 1876*). Not much is known of the Attucks Jr. Guard or if the "Jr." designates its membership as younger men or cadets or simply denotes a second company with the same name.

76. *Adjutant General of Virginia, 1873*, 2–3; King, *Great South*, 592 (quote).

77. Stern, *Roster Commissioned Officers*, 275; *Adjutant General of Virginia, 1876*, 4.

78. *Adjutant General of Virginia, 1876*, 4.

79. Stern, *Roster Commissioned Officers*, 272, 285; *Annual Report of the Adjutant-General of the State of Virginia for the Year Ending November 1, 1879* (Richmond: R. E. Frayser, Superintendent Public Printing, 1879), 19–22 (hereafter cited as *Adjutant General of Virginia, 1879*). The Flipper Guard was named for US Military Academy graduate and US Army officer Henry Ossian Flipper.

80. *Annual Report of the Adjutant-General of the State of Virginia for the Year 1879–80* (Richmond: R. F. Walker, Superintendent Public Printing, 1880), 19–22 (hereafter cited as *Adjutant General of Virginia, 1880*); *Annual Report of the Adjutant-General of the State of Virginia for the Years 1884 and 1885* (Richmond: Rush U. Derr, Superintendent Public Printing, 1885), 23 (hereafter cited as *Adjutant General of Virginia, 1884–85*). The African American men of Norfolk chose the successful military leader of Carthage (Africa), Hannibal Barca, as its inspiration, while the L'Ouverture Guard chose Gen. Francois-Dominique Toussaint-Louverture, the black military leader of the successful 1791 slave rebellion on the French colony of Saint Domingue, who ended slavery on the island and created the independent state of Haiti.

81. *Adjutant General of Virginia, 1884–85*, 27; Ruth Coder Fitzgerald, *A Different Story: A Black History of Fredericksburg, Stafford, and Spotsylvania, Virginia* (N.p.: Unicorn, 1979), 210.

82. *Adjutant General of Virginia, 1894*, 30–32.

83. General Order No. 13, Adjutant General's Office, State of Texas, June 19, 1876, RG 401, TSL; Bonds, A–K, ibid.; *Report of the Adjutant General of the State of Texas. Austin,*

December 31, 1880 (Galveston: News Book & Job Office, 1881), 7–8, 24 (hereafter cited as *Adjutant General of Texas, 1880*). The entry of the Coke Rifles might have been an error since they are still listed in the 1880 and 1882 adjutant general reports. Much is unknown about many of these early companies due to the loss of historical records in the burning of the state capitol in November 1881. In addition to the Frontier Battalion, by 1876, Texas recognized twenty white infantry companies, one infantry battalion, and one artillery battery in addition to its black militia. See Doyle, *New Men, New Cities,* 15; Kenneth Mason, *African Americans and Race Relations in San Antonio, Texas, 1867–1937* (New York: Garland, 1998); Lawrence D. Rice, *The Negro in Texas, 1874–1900* (Baton Rouge: Louisiana State University Press, 1971); David G. McComb, *Galveston: A History* (Austin: University of Texas Press, 1986); and Earle B. Young, *Galveston and the Great West* (College Station: Texas A&M University Press, 1997).

84. Rice, *Negro in Texas,* 13–15, 101. See also Maud Cuney-Hare, *Norris Wright Cuney: A Tribune of the Black People* (1913; repr., New York: Simon & Schuster Macmillan, 1995); Carl Moneyhon, *Edmund J. Davis: Civil War General, Republican Leader, Reconstruction Governor* (Fort Worth: Texas Christian University Press, 2010); Foner, *Freedom's Lawmakers,* 5–6, 55; Alwyn Barr and Cary D. Wintz, "Allen, Richard," in Tyler, *New Handbook of Texas,* 1:112–13; and Merline Pitre, "Cuney, Norris Wright," ibid., 2:446.

85. *Adjutant General of Texas, 1880,* 24.

86. The adjutant general of Texas ordered all volunteer companies to stand inspection in 1885 and those unable to muster were disbanded.

87. Title LXIV, Militia Law, *The Revised Statutes of Texas* (Galveston: A. H. Belo, 1879); *Adjutant General of Texas, 1880,* 24; "Exhibit No. 7: Annual Return of Militia in the State of Texas for Year Ending December 31, 1882," *Report of the Adjutant-General of the State of Texas, December 31, 1882* (Austin: E. W. Swindells, State Printer, 1883), n.p. (hereafter cited as *Adjutant General of Texas, December 1882*); Special Order No. 43, July 25, 1883, Adjutant General's Office, State of Texas, Folder 1012, RG 401, TSL; General Order No. 10, September 10, 1883, Folder 984, ibid.; *Report of the Adjutant-General of the State of Texas. September, 1884* (Austin: E. W. Swindells, State Printer, 1884), 4-6 (hereafter cited as *Adjutant General of Texas, 1884*); Barr, "Texas 'Black Uprising' Scare," 179–86; "Exhibit No. 4: List of Companies of Texas Volunteer Guard Organized and Disbanded since Annual Report of December 31, 1884," *Adjutant General of Texas, 1886,* n.p. Two national events may have contributed to the near simultaneous military actions in Georgia and Texas—the poor showing by state militias in the Great Railroad Strike of 1877 and the US Supreme Court ruling in 1883 that overturned the Civil Rights Act of 1875. See Robert V. Bruce, *1877: Year of Violence* (Indianapolis: Bobbs Merrill, 1959); Nick Salvatore, "Railroad Workers and the Great Strike of 1877: The View from a Small Midwest City," *Labor History* 21, no. 4 (1980): 522–45; and Lawrence Goldstone, *Inherently Unequal: The Betrayal of Equal Rights by the Supreme Court, 1865–1903* (New York: Walker, 2011), 118–29.

88. *Adjutant General of Texas, 1886,* 15.

89. *Adjutant General of Texas, 1890–91,* 85–86. For biographical information on Woodford Haywood Mabry, see chapter 4, note 65. For Richard Isaac Eskridge, see chapter 5, note 44.

90. *Report of the Adjutant General of the State of Texas 1889–1890* (Austin: Henry Hutchings, State Printer, 1890), 42–43 (hereafter cited as *Adjutant General of Texas, 1889–90*).

91. *Report of the Adjutant General of the State of Texas 1892* (Austin: Ben C. Jones, State Printer, 1893), 92 (hereafter cited as *Adjutant General of Texas, 1892*).

92. *Adjutant General of Texas*, 28; *Report of the Adjutant General of the State of Texas 1893–1894* (Austin: Ben C. Jones, State Printer, 1895), 22, 28 (hereafter cited as *Adjutant General of Texas, 1893–94*); *Adjutant General of Texas, 1895–96*, 29; John Sessums to General Mabry, July 23, 1896, RG 401, TSL; *Adjutant General of Texas, 1899–1900*, 122. Sessums wrote to Adjutant General Mabry on the printed stationary of "Richard Cocke, Brig. Gen'l. Commanding, Headquarters Second Brigade, Texas Volunteer Guard." For internal strife in Sheridan Guards from August to December 1896, see correspondence in Adjutant General's Office of Texas Records, TSL.

93. *Adjutant General of Texas, 1899–1900*, 203. Richard Cocke (1861–1919) was born at Bellville, Texas, and educated at the Texas Military Institute at Bastrop. The son of a physician, he moved to Houston to start his own business and joined the Houston Light Guard. By the time he turned twenty-eight years old, he was a colonel in the Texas Volunteer Guard. In 1895, Cocke was promoted to brigadier general and given the command of the 2nd Brigade. As a lieutenant colonel, he commanded the 3rd Texas Volunteer Infantry during the war with Spain. "Col. Richard Cocke Dies Following Brief Illness," *Houston Post*, January 19, 1919.

94. *Report of the Adjutant-General of the State of Texas for 1901–1902* (Austin: Von Boeckmann, Schutze, State Printers, 1902), 191 (hereafter cited as *Adjutant General of Texas, 1901–2*).

95. Pete Williams to Adj. Gen. King, July 23, 1890, RG 401, TSL; *Adjutant General of Texas, 1892*, 28.

96. A. O. George to Adj. Gen. Mabry, August 22, 1893, RG 401, TSL; A. O. George to Gov. Cuberson [*sic*], June 21, 1895, ibid.

97. Tony Smith to Adj. Gen. Mabry, May 28, 1895, RG 401, TSL.

98. Smith to Adj. Gen. Mabry, May 12, 1896, RG 401, TSL.

99. *Adjutant General of Texas, 1901–2*, 191.

100. Lee A. Leonard to Adj. Gen. Mabry, June 12, August 3, 14, 1896, RG 401, TSL.

Chapter 4

1. *1868 Irwin's Code*, 221.

2. *Acts and Resolutions of the General Assembly of the State of Georgia, Passed at Its Session in July and August, 1872* (Atlanta: W. A. Hemphill, State Printers, 1872), 59.

3. *Acts and Resolutions of the General Assembly of the State of Georgia, Passed at the Regular January Session 1873* (Atlanta: W. A. Hemphill, State Printers, 1873), 70.

4. General Orders No. 39, War Department, Adjutant General's Office, Washington, March 21, 1873, copy in RCB-14199, RG 22, GAM.

5. Ibid.

6. The dollar amounts listed here are calculated using the annual appropriation of $200,000 divided by the total seats in the US House of Representatives, multiplied

by the number of representatives for each state—Georgia, Texas, and Virginia—then multiplied by the inclusive eight-year period 1862–69. *Biographical Directory of the United States Congress, 1774–Present,* http:/bioguide,congress.gov.

7. R. M. Hill to S. C. Williams, May 26, 1874, DOC-2819, RG 22, GAM.

8. This determination is made using the $5,908 annual funding for Georgia compared to six thousand men, which is the estimated strength of ten companies with an average of forty men each, multiplied by the cost of a musket.

9. T. B. Higginbotham of the Rome Star Guards reported that his company was "drilling with old muskets and shot guns." The Union Lincoln Guards of Savannah reported using "29 Guns Springfield" and "26 Guns Enfield" as late as 1877. RCB-41414, RG 22, GAM; and DOC-3324, ibid. The cost of a musket is based upon Adj. Gen. Stephens to Lt. Col. J. H. Deveaux, March 31, 1886, VOL1-1709, ibid.

10. "Wiley, Jefferson," US Army, Register of Enlistments, 1798–1914, RG 94, NARA.

11. "Woodhouse, W. H.," Compiled Service Records of Confederate Soldiers, Georgia, RG 109, NARA. Woodhouse was later elected as the first African American lieutenant colonel in Georgia history.

12. "List of Companies to which Arms Have Been Issued with Amount and Kind of Ammunition and Equipments," *Georgia Adjutant General Records, 1877–99,* n.p.,. Macon's Lincoln Guards are incorrectly noted as the "Union" Lincoln Guards on this list. It is unknown if Fraction had any previous military experience.

13. Ibid. (emphasis added).

14. N. D. Sneed to Gov. Smith, September 5, 1873, DOC-2815, RG 22, GAM. Sneed, a member of the African Methodist Church, was active in the uplift movement, taking part in the Equal Rights and Educational Association of Georgia in 1866. *Proceedings of the Equal Rights and Educational Association of Georgia* (Augusta, GA: Loyal Georgian, 1866).

15. Sneed to Gov. Smith, September 19, 1873, DOC-2815, RG 22, GAM.

16. Ibid. (original emphasis).

17. Frank Disroon to Gov. Smith, October 3, 1873, DOC-2816, RG 22, GAM.

18. "Rev. Turner and His Tools," *Savannah Morning News,* March 5, 1874. There is a strong possibility that Sneed worked behind the scenes with this convention. Turner, not associated with the militia per se, remained a leader in the state, and both he and Sneed were active socially and politically. They also associated with the African Methodist Episcopal church and had resided in Macon during the same period.

19. Ibid. John Holbrook Estill (1840–1907), a native of Charleston, South Carolina, worked in his father's printing business. At the age of nineteen, he moved to Savannah, where he later became part owner of the *Evening Express* and enrolled in the city's Oglethorpe Light Infantry. In 1861, this company became Company B, 8th Georgia Infantry Regiment. Engaged at First Manassas, Estill was severely wounded, resulting in a medical discharge in 1862. Returning to Savannah, he opposed Union forces approaching the city and was captured. After the war, he reentered military service as an officer in the Georgia Volunteers, commanding the city's Company F (Johnston Light Infantry), 1st Regiment. In 1880, Estill was promoted to lieutenant colonel and joined the staff of Governor Colquitt. In addition to Colquitt, he advised the next four Geor-

gia governors before being placed on the retired list on July 31, 1895. Estill edited the *Savannah Morning News,* was active in various Confederate veteran organizations and the Masonic Order, and served on the board of the Bethesda Orphanage in the city. "Estill, John Holbrook," Compiled Service Records of Confederate Soldiers, Georgia, RG 109, NARA; *Adjutant General of Georgia, 1899–1900,* 114; "John Holbrook Estill," *Confederate Veteran* 16, no. 5 (May 1908): xxxv.

20. "Applications for Arms—not granted—1877, 1878, 1879, 1880," January 10, 1880, RCB-41414, RG 22, GAM.

21. *Acts and Resolutions, 1878–79,* 108.

22. The biography of Jackson McHenry, written by Rev. Edward R. Carter, described the captain of the Volunteers as an "enterprising and progressive citizen" who succeeded in business, ran for Atlanta City Council, and was active in Republican politics. He served as a delegate to district and state Republican Party conventions, worked for H. I. Kimball, and later received an appointment in the Atlanta Customs House. In 1889, he traveled to Indiana with other African American leaders to pay their respects to Benjamin Harrison at his home. E. R. Carter, *The Black Side: A Partial History of the Business, Religious, and Educational Side of the Negro in Atlanta, Ga.* (Atlanta, 1894), 178–80; "Jack Is Back," *Atlanta Constitution,* February 17, 1889.

23. When the Civil War commenced, Moses Henry Bentley "went to the front with his young master." Reportedly, Bentley and his brother, Dr. William Patterson, bore the dying Col. Francis Bartow of Georgia from the field at Manassas. A controversial figure, Bentley was a Democrat who, while serving as the messenger of the general assembly, shot and killed an African American representative in the capitol. Later pardoned, he operated a successful barber shop in Atlanta. There is also some evidence that he participated in repulsing a riot, but it remains unclear if he did this as the captain of the Cadets or if he led an ad hoc group of men during this incident. Even though he resigned in 1892, Bentley's grave marker in South-View Cemetery in Atlanta retains his military title. "Remarkable Negro Passes from Life," *Atlanta Constitution,* November 16, 1906; M. H. Bentley to Gov. W. J. Northen, December 31, 1892, RCB-41405, RG 22, Georgia Archives.

24. "Douglass Infantry, Report for 1876," DOC-2827, RG 22, GAM; "Douglass Infantry, Report 1877," DOC-3324, ibid.

25. D. Johnston to Adj. Gen. Stephens, June 23, 1883, RCB-41414, RG 22, GAM.

26. "Distribution," VOL1-1701, RG 22, GAM; A. F. Golphin to Adj. Gen. Stephens, June 9, 1885, RCB-41578, ibid.

27. A. R. Johnson to Adj. Gen. Kell, July 20, 1888, RCB-41395, RG 22, GAM. See also A. R. Johnson to Adj. Gen. Kell, August 23, 1888, ibid.

28. "Union Lincoln Guards, Report for 1876," DOC-3324, RG 22, GAM; "Lincoln Guards, Savannah, Ga. Report of 1877," DOC-2828, ibid.; "1887 Annual Report of the Union Lincoln Guards, Savannah, Ga.," RCB-41395, ibid.; "1888 Annual Report of the Union Lincoln Guards, Savannah, Ga.," ibid. The various descriptions listed on the line "Number of Arms received from State" can be found on numerous annual reports; see RCB-41395, RG 22, GAM.

29. Missing for 1890 is the paperwork of McHenry's Governor's Volunteers. Again, discounting the artillery and cavalry commands, this represents the best performance to date with reporting requirements.

30. Annual reports for all African American commands, 1890, RCB-41406, RG 22, GAM; *The Organized Militia of the United States—Statement of the Condition and Efficiency for Service of the Organized Militia from Regular Annual Reports and Other Sources Covering the Year 1897* (Washington: GPO, 1898), 78 (hereafter cited *Organized Militia 1897*); *The Organized Militia of the United States in 1895* (Washington, DC: GPO, 1896), 52.

31. Acting Adj. Gen. Oscar J. Brown to Deveaux, December 9, 1897, VOL1-1725, RG 22, GAM.

32. Acting Adj. Gen. Brown to Deveaux, April 21, 1898, RCB-41576, RG 22, GAM. The acting adjutant general ordered forty-five rifles for the Savannah Light Infantry, fifty for the Colquitt Blues, four-seven for the Lone Star Cadets, and forty for the Union Lincoln Guards.

33. Isaiah Blocker to Acting Adj. Gen. Brown, March 30, 1898, VOL1-1725, RG 22, GAM.

34. Ibid.

35. Acting Adj. Gen. Brown to Blocker, March 31, 1898, VOL1-1725, RG 22, GAM.

36. Blocker to Acting Adj. Gen. Brown, April 2, 1898, RCB-41473, RG 22, GAM.

37. *Acts and Resolutions of the General Assembly of the State of Georgia, 1900* (Atlanta: George W. Harrison, State Printer, 1900), 83; Inspector General Obear to Deveaux, December 19, 1900, RCB-41576, RG 22, GAM.

38. Deveaux to Inspector Gen. Obear, December 20, 1900, RCB-41576, RG 22, GAM; Deveaux to Inspector Gen. Obear, March 20, 1901, ibid.; Bill of Lading, Central of Georgia Railway Company, January 16, 1901, ibid.

39. "Supplement to Report on Annual Inspection of troops, Dec. 31/01," February 24, 1902, RCB-41393, RG 22, GAM. Inspector General Obear further commented in his report: "The personnel of the colored troops is now of the very best.... [N]one but reliable, sober, industrious men are accepted as recruits.... [O]fficers are educated, reliable men, carefully selected, who have the respect and confidence of the white people in the cities where they are located as well as of the colored race."

40. Assistant Adjutant General of the United States to the Adjutant General, State of Georgia, May 31, 1904, RCB-41409, RG 22, GAM.

41. See Muster rolls, Brenham Blues, Excelsior Guard, and Gregory Rifles, TVG, RG 401, TSL.

42. Muster rolls, Bryan Light Infantry, TVG, RG 401, TSL. Capt. Jeff Young took command of the Bryan Light Infantry in 1895, still possessing thirty stands of arms that he described as "very good."

43. Muster rolls, Austin City Rifles, TVG, RG 401, TSL (emphasis added). John B. Jones (1834–81) enlisted in the famed 8th Texas Cavalry, better known as Terry's Texas Rangers, but left to become the adjutant for the 15th Texas Infantry Regiment. When the war ended, he had risen to the rank of major and was serving as a brigade adjutant.

In 1874, Gov. Richard Coke appointed him to command the Frontier Battalion. Five years later, Gov. Oran Roberts allowed him to retain that command and to serve concurrently as the state's adjutant general. Jones held that position until his death in Austin in 1881. Thomas W. Cutrer, "Jones, John B.," in Tyler, *New Handbook of Texas*, 3:986.

44. Milton Hill and G. Williams to Adj. Gen. W. H. Mabry, May 1891, TVG, RG 401, TSL.

45. Muster roll, Jim Blaine Rifles, TVG, RG 401, TSL.

46. Muster rolls, Brenham Blues, TVG, RG 401, TSL.

47. Muster rolls, Lincoln Guards, TVG, RG 401, TSL. For biographical information on Wilburn Hill King, see chapter 2, note 21.

48. Muster rolls, Davis Rifles, Cochran Blues, and Bryan Light Infantry, TVG, RG 401, TSL. There is much mystery surrounding Houston's Sheridan Guards, which unlike any other volunteer company, black or white, operated with two sections, A and B, each with its own set of officers. Capt. Charles Green, a native of Massachusetts and quite possibly a Civil War veteran who listed his occupation as a junk dealer, commanded Section A, while Sessums, only a first lieutenant, led Section B. Sessums appears not to have reported to Green and completed his own set of muster rolls. It is unknown if this anomaly of organization occurred due to friction within the black community, influence from the city's white citizens, or simply a ploy to get more men in uniform and under arms than the state would approve at the time. The Sheridan Guards were replaced by the Cocke Rifles in Houston on November 29, 1899.

49. Muster rolls, Lincoln Guards, TVG, RG 401, TSL.

50. L. P. Sieker to Adj. Gen. King, October 1889, RG 401, TSL. Sieker (1848–1914), known as "Lam," joined Capt. W. W. Parker's company of Virginia Light Artillery in the Army of Northern Virginia. Moving to Texas after the war, he enrolled in 1874 in Company D, Frontier Battalion (i.e., the Texas Rangers), and continued his service until 1905. He also served as the state's assistant adjutant general from 1889 to 1895. Harold J. Weiss Jr., "Seiker, Lamartine Pemberton," in Tyler, *New Handbook of Texas*, 5:1043.

51. Muster rolls, Lincoln Guards, TVG, RG 401, TSL.

52. Ibid. Taylor, born in Kentucky, served as a corporal in the 5th Kentucky Volunteer Infantry Regiment, USA, from 1863 to 1865 and then with the 9th US Cavalry Regiment from 1867 to 1872. *Adjutant General of Texas, 1899–1900*, 202.

53. Muster rolls, Hawley Guards, Texas National Guard, RG 401, TSL.

54. Ordnance Returns, Lincoln Guards, TVG, RG 401, TSL.

55. Other examples of African American volunteer militia organizations should be examined by scholars to determine if this became a shared experience across Texas.

56. The Springfield Model 1873 (M1873), commonly known as the "Springfield Trapdoor" for its distinctive hinged breechblock, became the first standard-issue breech-loading rifle in the US Army. Used from 1873 to 1892, the rifle measured almost fifty-two inches in length and fired a .45-70 cartridge. Springfield's Model 1884 had the same dimensions and fired the same ammunition as the M1873 but was equipped with a round-rod bayonet and a new rear sight, considered by some to be the identifying feature of the weapon. The description of "Model 1878" is somewhat confusing since

the Springfield Armory only made one thousand Hotchkiss-designed rifles with that designation for testing. Sharps produced a single-shot Model 1878 for military use, but it remains unclear if the state of Texas purchased any of these for its militia organizations. Since the Sharps only measured forty-eight and five-eighths inches in length, it would have stood out in a formation of men armed with both the standard US Army rifles and these shorter ones. Lastly, another explanation may simply involve the annual production run of rifles at the Springfield Armory for 1878, identified by their serial number. John Charles Davis, "U.S. Army Rifle and Carbine Adoption between 1865–1900" (master's thesis, US Army Command and General Staff College, 2007); Douglas C. McChristian, *Uniforms, Arms, and Equipment: The U.S. Army on the Western Frontier, 1880–1892,* 2 vols. (Norman: University of Oklahoma Press, 2007); John Walter, *Rifles of the World,* 3rd ed. (Iola, WI: Krause, 2006).

57. Muster rolls, Capital Guards, TVG, RG 401, TSL; *Adjutant General of Texas, 1892,* 86.

58. Muster rolls, Excelsior Guard, TVG, RG 401, TSL.

59. "Simon Turner," Indian Wars Pension Files, 1892–1926, RG 15, Department of Veterans Affairs, Washington, DC.

60. Muster rolls, Excelsior Guard, TVG, RG 401, TSL.

61. Sieker to Adj. Gen. King, September 3, 1887, RG 401, TSL.

62. Ordnance reports, Excelsior Guard, TVG, RG 401, TSL.

63. Muster rolls, TVG, RG 401, TSL.

64. Robert G. Ellis to Adj. Gen. Mabry, November 13, 1897, RG 401, TSL.

65. Woodford Haywood Mabry (1856–99) served as Texas adjutant general from January 22, 1891, to May 5, 1898. The son of a noted Confederate cavalry colonel, Mabry was educated at the Virginia Military Institute, graduating in 1875. As adjutant general, he improved the Texas Volunteers and the Frontier Battalion and secured funding for a permanent training site at Austin and named in his honor. Mabry died of malaria near Havana, Cuba, during his service as colonel of the 1st Texas Infantry Regiment. Virginia Military Institute, "Woodford Haywood Mabry," Historical Roster Database, http://archivesweb.vmi.edu/rosters/record.php?ID=1965 (accessed July 14, 2015); "Woodford H. Mabry," *Texas Military Forces Museum,* http://www.texasmilitaryforcesmuseum.org/hallofhonor/mabry.htm (accessed July 14, 2015); Claudia Hazlewood, "Mabry, Woodford Haywood," in Tyler, *New Handbook of Texas,* 4:360.

66. R. H. Bruce to Adj. Gen. Mabry, August 26, 1891, RG 401, TSL.

67. Muster rolls, Excelsior Guard, TVG, RG 401, TSL.

68. *Adjutant General of Texas, 1890–91,* 85.

69. E. O. Bowles, John F. Van Duzor, John H. Martin, and Ed Thomas to Adj. Gen. Mabry, August 15, 1896, RG 401, TSL. Martin, also known as John H. Minton, obtained his freedom on April 19, 1861, and enlisted two years later at the age of sixteen at Baltimore, Maryland, in the 4th USCT. Mustered out in 1866, Martin reenlisted and served in both the 25th and 40th US Infantry Regiments before retiring as a first sergeant. "Minton/Martin, John H.," Compiled Military Service Records, US Colored Troops, RG 94, NARA; "Martin, John H.," Civil War Pension Files, ibid.

John Francis Van Duzor (1851–1921) enlisted for five years on February 15, 1872, at Albany, New York, as a private in Company B, 24th US Infantry Regiment. Promoted to corporal in 1876, Van Duzor left the army as a sergeant at Fort Duncan, Texas, with an excellent character rating. He served as captain of the Excelsior Guard and then as battalion adjutant for the Colored Battalion. After his retirement from the Texas Volunteer Guard, he found employment as a notary public. "Vanduzer, J. F.," *Register of Enlistments, 1798–1914*; *Adjutant General of Texas, 1883*, 15; *Adjutant General of Texas, 1888*, 22; *Adjutant General of Texas, 1889–90*, 42; "J. F. VanDuzor," Standard Certificate of Death, Municipal Archives & Records, City of San Antonio, TX.

70. Muster rolls, Excelsior Guard, TVG, RG 401, TSL.

71. Stern, *Roster Commissioned Officers*, iv. These "rifles" were probably smoothbore muskets that must have been either .69- or .70-caliber models dating to 1822 and used by some Confederate troops in the 1860s. The term "Napoleon" was commonly used to describe the Model 1857 12-pounder (describing the weight of the solid shot) smoothbore light gun-howitzer developed by the French and named for Emperor Napoleon III. Its accuracy, durability, and versatility made it one of the most effective artillery weapons of the American Civil War. The 6-pounder brass gun refers to the Model 1841 smoothbore bronze cannon that performed well in the Mexican War but was found less effective on the battlefields of the Civil War due to its smaller bore diameter, resulting in less hitting power. The 3-inch Ordnance rifled muzzleloader "was the second most common rifled field gun in the Union and Confederate armies," with some arguing that it became the most popular of the war because of its accuracy and reliability. Curt Johnson and Richard C. Anderson Jr., *Artillery Hell: The Employment of Artillery at Antietam* (College Station: Texas A&M University Press, 1995), 21–26; Dean S. Thomas, *The Confederate Field Manual with Photographic Supplement* (Arendtsville, PA, 1984), 18–21, 52.

72. *Adjutant General of Virginia, 1873*, 2. For biographical information on William Harvie Richardson, see chapter 3, note 73.

73. *Adjutant General of Virginia, 1873*, 3.

74. *Adjutant General of Virginia, 1876*, 4. McDonald also served on the Board of Visitors for the Virginia Military Institute from 1876 to 1882 and acted as Virginia's adjutant general from 1888 until his death in 1893. Virginia Military Institute, "James McDonald," Historical Roster Database, http://archivesweb.vmi.edu/rosters/record.php?ID=12042 (accessed July 16, 2015).

75. *Adjutant General of Virginia, 1879*, 5–11.

76. Henry Davenport Northrop, Joseph R. Penn, and Irvine Garland, *The College of Life or Practical Self-Educator: A Manual of Self-Improvement for the Colored Race* (N.p., 1896), 79–80.

77. *Adjutant General of Virginia, 1880*, 8–22.

78. *Adjutant General of Virginia, 1884–85*, iv.

79. Ibid., 75–76.

80. Ibid., 52. The two African American volunteer infantry companies were the State Guard at Richmond and the Libby Guard at Hampton.

81. *Adjutant General of Virginia, 1886*, 59; *Adjutant General of Virginia, 1894*, 68; *Adjutant General of Virginia, 1896*, 51. In 1886, the attendance at inspection for Virginia's white militia organizations ranged from 66.8 percent to 86.4 percent, giving them an

average of 76.4 percent compared to the black troops, who managed to get 63 percent of their membership to stand inspection that year. But in both 1894 and 1896, the black militiamen outperformed their white counterparts,. The white troops mustered 82.08 percent of their members (compared to 84.6 percent of black troops) in 1894 and 83.5 percent (versus 90.5 percent) in 1896.

82. *Report of the Adjutant-General of the State of Virginia for the Year 1888* (Richmond: J. H. O'Bannon, Superintendent of Public Printing, 1888), 32–33, 36. No historical record has been located that catalogs the existing inventory required, if any, to remain on hand for each company.

83. *Adjutant General of Virginia, 1894,* 41, 57.

84. *Adjutant General of Virginia, 1896,* 62–70.

85. *Organized Militia 1897,* 320–25.

Chapter 5

Unnumbered note: Title quote from Nathan T. Humphry to Adj. Gen. Kell, May 25, 1890, RCB-37046, RG 22, GAM.

1. John Screven to Gov. Smith, September 1872, DOC-2815, RG 22, GAM.

2. "Arrival of General Grant," *Savannah Morning News,* January 2, 1880 (emphasis added). Louis Henry de Montmollin (1846–84) was the son of John Samuel de Montmollin II and Marie Madeline Henriette de Rossignol de Beleanse. His father owned plantations in Georgia, Florida, and South Carolina and was president of the Savannah Mechanics Bank. Too young for service in the Civil War, Louis was a "student-at-law" with the firm of Hartridge & Chisholm at Savannah in 1871. He later practiced law in Savannah, was appointed as a commissioner in the Fifth US Circuit Court, and served on the city council. Thomas M. Haddock, comp., *Haddock's Savannah, Ga., Directory and General Advertiser* (Savannah: J. H. Estill, 1871), 132; *Register of Officers and Agents, Civil, Military, and Naval, in the Service of the United States* (Washington, DC: GPO, 1877), 316.

3. "Arrival of General Grant," *Savannah Morning News,* January 2, 1880.

4. John F. Wheaton to Gov. Colquitt, September 20, 1881, RCB-41414, RG 22, GAM; "Savannah's Laborers," *Atlanta Constitution,* September 20, 1881.

5. "Savannah's Laborers," *Atlanta Constitution,* September 20, 1881.

6. Special Order No. 85, Executive Department, State of Georgia, RCB-41414, RG 22, GAM.

7. Special Order No. 86, Executive Department, State of Georgia, September 22, 1881, RCB-41414, RG 22, GAM.

8. "Savannah's Strike," *Atlanta Constitution,* September 22, 1881.

9. "The Mob Charged," ibid., September 23, 1881.

10. Ibid.

11. Telegrams, J. H. Estill to Gov. Colquitt, September 22, 23 (2), 27, 1881, RCB-41414, RG 22, GAM; "Fatal Rioting," *Washington Evening Critic,* September 23, 1881.

12. "Only Two Hangings—Anderson Jones," *St. Paul (MN) Daily Globe,* January 21, 1882; "Editorial Notes," *Brenham (TX) Weekly Banner,* January 26, 1882; "General

Intelligence—Executed," *Dallas Daily Herald,* January 21, 1882; "Late News Items," *Iola (KS) Register,* January 27, 1882; "Hinrichtung," *Der Deutsche Correspondent* (Baltimore), January 21, 1882; "The Execution To-Day," *Augusta (GA) Chronicle,* January 20, 1882; "A Life for a Life," *Augusta Chronicle,* January 21, 1882. *Hinrichtung* is German for "execution," as translated in Friedrich Köhler, *Dictionary of the English and German Languages* (London: H. Grevel, 1892), s.v. "Hinrichtung."

13. Claiborne Snead (1836–1909) enlisted April 26, 1861, in Company G, 3rd Georgia Infantry Regiment, eventually rising to the rank of lieutenant colonel and command of the regiment. Wounded twice and serving throughout the war in the Army of Northern Virginia, Snead was taken captive at Gettysburg, later released, and eventually surrendered with his regiment at Appomattox Court House. After the war, he served as the judge for the Superior Court of Richmond County and was elected as a state senator. Thomas W. Loyless, comp., *Georgia's Public Men, 1902–1904* (Atlanta: Byrd Printing, n.d.), 70–71; Claiborne Snead, grave marker, Magnolia Cemetery, Augusta, GA.

14. "Savannah in Flames," *Atlanta Constitution,* April 7, 1889; "Savannah's Signal," ibid., September 22, 1889; *Acts and Resolutions, 1884–85,* 74–79. John Schwarz (1839/40–1908) was a native of Zweibrückener, Germany, and immigrated to New York in 1855, later relocating to Savannah, where he worked as a baker. He served in the 32nd Georgia Infantry Regiment during the Civil War for a year and a half before being tasked with operating the steam bakery at Savannah for the Confederacy. After the war, Schwarz associated with the city's ethnic German American militia company, the German Volunteers, which had originally organized in 1846. He later commanded the company prior to his promotion to major, 1st Regiment, Georgia Volunteers, a position he held until 1894. Schwarz was active in civic and business affairs in the city of Savannah and, as a Democrat, held a position on the city council in 1869–73, 1877–83, 1887–89, and again in 1899–1901. He served as mayor for one term, 1889–91, and then as Chatham County sheriff. *Memoirs of Georgia Containing Historical Accounts of the State's Civil, Military, Industrial and Professional Interests, and Personal Sketches of Many of Its People,* 2 vols. (Atlanta: Southern Historical Association, 1895), 2:413–14; Passenger Lists of Vessels Arriving at New York, New York, 1820–97, RG 36, NARA; "Swartz, J," Compiled Service Records of Confederate Soldiers, Georgia, RG 109, ibid.; "Funeral of Major Schwarz," *Atlanta Constitution,* May 22, 1908; Candler and Evans, *Georgia,* 3:254–55.

15. "The Mayor and the Military," *Savannah Tribune,* September 28, 1889.

16. George A. Mercer to Adj. Gen. Kell, March 13, 1895, RCB-41389, RG 22, GAM.

17. George Mercer estimated the crowd at between 2,500 and 3,000 people in his March 2, 1895, report to the adjutant general, while the *Savannah Tribune* believed the "tremendous crowd," to number "about 2000 assembled." George A. Mercer to Adj. Gen. Kell, March 13, 1895, RCB-41389, RG 22, GAM; "Ex-Priest Slattery and Wife Lectured under the Protection of the Police," *Savannah Tribune,* March 2, 1895. Born at Savannah, George Anderson Mercer (1835–1907) was educated in that city and in Connecticut. He graduated from Princeton and then earned a law degree from the University of Virginia. At the outbreak of the Civil War, Mercer enlisted as a corporal in Savannah's Republican Blues, rose to the rank of captain, and was captured at Ma-

con in 1865. Returning to Savannah, he resumed his law practice; served as captain of the Republican Blues, Georgia Volunteers, for fifteen years; then assumed command of the 1st Regiment as colonel. He was active on the boards of the Savannah Medical College, Chatham Academy, Telfair Academy, and the Georgia Historical Society and also served as a delegate to the Democratic convention in 1892. *Memoirs of Georgia,* 2:402–3.

William Washington Gordon (1834–1912), also a native of Savannah, graduated from Yale University in 1854 and joined the Georgia Hussars, one of the city's cavalry troops, in 1857. This command later became part of the 6th Virginia Cavalry. Promoted to captain, Gordon served on the staff of Mercer's father when he was wounded at Lovejoy Station, Virginia. He later surrendered with Confederate lieutenant general Joseph Wheeler's cavalry in April 1865. Gordon, who represented District 1 in the Georgia General Assembly from 1883 to 1890 was an officer of Merchant's National Bank, president of the Savannah Cotton Exchange, and colonel in the Georgia Volunteers. Later, as brigadier general, US Volunteers, he was a member of the Military and Naval Commission that supervised the transfer of Puerto Rico to the United States from Spain. *Memoirs of Georgia,* 2:389; "Roll of Retired Officers," *Adjutant General of Georgia, 1899–1900,* 112–13.

18. John H. Deveaux to Capt. Robert G. Guillard, March 9, 1895, RCB-41389, RG 22, GAM. The officers reporting for duty were Deveaux and his battalion adjutant, Solomon Johnson; Capts. E. A. Williams, Nelson Law, Henry N. Walton, James H. Carter, and Lymus A. Washington; and Lts. P. Y. Giles, C. C. Blake, W. H. Haynes, J. C. Beatty, and F. C. Pierce. Joining them were fourteen sergeants, fifteen corporals, and 141 men.

19. "Ex-Priest Slattery and Wife Lectured under the Protection of the Police," *Savannah Tribune,* March 2, 1895. Those reported to have an arrest record were Pat Scully, Thomas Hogan, John Duffy, Florence Sullivan, James McBride Jr., J. W. Foughner, Ed Morrinsey, Batty Winters, and T. J. Houliham.

20. Mercer to Adj. Gen. Kell, March 13, 1895, RCB-41389, RG 22, GAM.

21. *Report of the Adjutant-General of the State of Georgia for the Year 1895* (Atlanta: Franklin Printing, 1896), 7.

22. Clifford W. Anderson to Adj. Gen. Stephens, August 29, September 10, 1884, RCB-41414, RG 22, GAM.

23. Charles H. Olmstead to Gov. McDaniel, October, 1886. RCB-41578, RG 22, GAM (original emphasis). Charles Hart Olmstead (1837–1926), born at Savannah, was commissioned as a major in the 1st Georgia Infantry Regiment in May 1861, rising to the rank of colonel and command of the regiment. During the Civil War, he directed the defenses at Fort Pulaski, where he was captured and then imprisoned at Fort Columbus, New York, and at Fort Johnson on James Island, South Carolina. Later exchanged, Olmstead participated in the defense of Charleston before leading troops in the Army of Tennessee during the battles for Atlanta, at Franklin, and at the surrender of Gen. Joseph E. Johnston at Greensboro, North Carolina, in 1865. Returning to Savannah, Olmstead was active in military and civic affairs until his death at age eighty-nine. Charles Hart Olmstead Papers, Georgia Historical Society, Savannah; Charles H. Olmstead Papers, Louis Round Wilson Library, University of North Carolina, Chapel Hill.

24. "Annual Report of the Adjutant General, General J. McIntosh Kell, for the Year 1888" (unpublished report), RCB-41395, RG 22, GAM.

25. *Adjutant and Inspector-General of Georgia, 1889*, 39–53.

26. Cummings to Adj. Gen. John Baird, May 25, 1882, RCB-41414, RG 22, GAM; Royall to Adj. Gen. John A. Stephens, June 27, 1883, ibid.; Lloyd to Adj. Gen. Stephens, July 16, 1884, ibid.; Bell to Adj. Gen. Stephens, June 18, 1885, RCB-41578, ibid.; Lloyd to Adj. Gen. Stephens, June 20, 1886, ibid.; Maxwell to Adj. Gen. John M. Kell, May 12, 1887, RCB-41395, ibid.; Deveaux to Adj. Gen. Kell, August 14, 1888, ibid.; Lark to Adj. Gen. Kell, July 24, 1889, ibid.

27. The first two state-wide prize drills occurred in 1878, the first at Savannah in May, followed by one at Atlanta in October. "The Colored Military," *Savannah Morning News,* May 8, 1878; "The Colored Military," ibid., May 27, 1878; "The Colored Military," *Atlanta Constitution,* October 27, 1878; "At the Park," ibid., October 27, 1878; "Colored Military," ibid., June 5, 1883; "The Prize Drill," ibid., June 6, 1883; "Off to Columbus," ibid., August 15, 1882; "Through the City," ibid., July 22, 1886; "Through the City," ibid., July 25, 1886. Reportedly, fifteen companies were scheduled to participate in an encampment at Macon in June 1882, but no record of this event occurring has been located. "The Colored Encampment," *Atlanta Constitution,* May 2, 1882; "Southern Gleanings," *Panola Weekly Star* (Sardis, MS), May 27, 1882; "Southern Gleanings," *Milan (TN) Exchange,* May 27, 1882; "Southern Gleanings," *St. Landry Democrat* (Opelousas, LA), June 2, 1882; "A Colored Military Encampment," *Atlanta Constitution,* August 31, 1886; *Acts and Resolutions, 1888–89*, 24–25.

28. The number of troops may have been more than these reported since neither the Forest City Light Infantry nor the Chatham Light Infantry, both of which stated they would attend, reported the number of personnel going to the events.

29. *Report of the Adjutant and Inspector-General of the State of Georgia for the Year 1890* (Atlanta: W. J. Campbell, State Printer, 1890), 29–35 (hereafter cited *Adjutant and Inspector-General of Georgia, 1890*); Olmstead to Adj. Gen. Kell, May 20, 22, 1890, RCB-37046, RG 22, GAM. The special order Olmstead mentioned has not been located.

30. I. C. Levy to Adj. Gen. Kell, April 15, 1891 (with attached undated newspaper clipping), RCB-41401, RG 22, GAM.

31. A. R. Johnson to Adj. Gen. Kell, February 22, 1892, RCB-41405, RG 22, GAM.

32. Adj. Gen. Kell to A. R. Johnson, March 1, 1892, VOL1-1721, RG 22, GAM.

33. The roster for Company F, 2nd Regiment, Georgia Volunteers listed "3 musicians and 4 cooks, all negroes," while the morning report for Camp Northen contained a handwritten note stating, "this company had two colored men enlisted, which is not authorized by law, per diem for them is deducted above." "Roster of Co. F, 2nd Regt. Ga.," n.d. (contained within the reports from 1892 encampment), RCB-41412, RG 22, GAM; "Statement of Daily Strength—Muster Roll by Inspector General of Troops in Attendance at Camp Northen, May 23 to May 30: 2nd Regiment of Infantry," n.d. (contained with papers from 1894 encampment), RCB-41389, ibid.

34. "Aimed at the Guard," *Atlanta Constitution,* April 3, 1895.

35. Deveaux, Blocker, and Crumbly to the Military Advisory Board, February 1897, RCB-41473, RG 22, GAM. See also the discussion of Georgia's effort to replace unserviceable rifles in chapter 4.

36. Oscar J. Brown to J. C. Simmons, July 23, 1897, VOL1-1729, RG 22, GAM; Brown to Jackson McHenry, March 11, 1898, VOL1-1725, ibid.

37. Simmons to Adj. Gen. Kell, September 1, 1897, RCB-41389, RG 22, GAM. Some of the skills Simmons listed were "the care of health, of arms and equipment, pitching and breaking camp, guard duty, and proper police duty, and the march."

38. Ibid.; *Adjutant General of Georgia, 1896,* 50; "Artillery Has Returned," *Atlanta Constitution,* August 20, 1897 (quote); "Returned from Camp Kell," *Savannah Tribune,* August 21, 1897.

39. *Adjutant General of Texas, 1889–90,* 18, 86. The Brazos Light Guards and the Lincoln Guards received seventy-five cents per man per day while traveling.

40. The *Dallas Morning News* reported 221 men in the procession, while the opening day's morning report counted 179 men but failed to note the 24 (or 25) men of the Harvey Brass Band of San Antonio, who were not officially associated with the Texas Volunteer Guard. "Alamo City Advises," *Dallas Morning News,* September 25, 1890; Battalion of Colored Infantry, Morning Report, September 24, 1890, RG 401, TSL.

41. "Colored Encampment," *San Antonio Daily Light,* September 24, 1890.

42. Ibid.; "Alamo City Advices," *Dallas Morning News,* September 25, 1890; *Adjutant General of Texas, 1889–90,* 88. Killed by British troops in the Boston Massacre on March 5, 1770, Crispus Attucks is recognized as the first African American to die in the struggle for American rights. The battalion's adjutant, Thomas J. Dilwood, a native of Boston, may have had a hand in suggesting Attucks as the camp name.

43. General Order No. 2, 1st Battalion, Colored, TVG, September 24, 1890, Adj. Gen. Correspondence, RG 401, TSL.

44. *Report of the Adjutant General for 1889–90,* 90. Richard Isaac Eskridge (1840–1903), a native of Missouri, served first in the 2nd Iowa Volunteer Infantry, then with the 2nd Missouri Cavalry, USA, rising to the rank of captain prior to the end of the Civil War. Obtaining a commission in the US Army following the war, he served with the 14th US Infantry and was recognized for "conspicuous gallantry in charging a large band of Indians strongly fortified" in California in 1867. Eskridge also served as a battalion commander in the 23rd and the 10th US Infantry Regiments. During the war with Spain, he was wounded in action at Santiago, Cuba, an injury that would eventually force his retirement in 1901 as a full colonel. *Official Army Register for 1901* (Washington, DC: GPO, 1900), 315; "Col. Eskridge Dies in Manila," *Salt Lake Herald,* September 3, 1903; Francis Bernard Heitman, *Historical Register and Dictionary of the United States Army,* 2 vols. (Washington, DC: GPO, 1903), 1:408; "Sketches of the Lives of Some of the Leaders Who Dared the Foe in Cuba and Were Shot Down," *New York Times,* July 5, 1898.

45. "At Camp Attucks," *San Antonio Daily Express,* September 28, 1890.

46. *Adjutant General of Texas, 1890–91,* 82.

47. Cailloux was described by historian Stephen J. Ochs as "a thirty-eight-year-old Afro-Creole . . . lauded as the nation's first black military hero, one of the first black men to hold an officer's commission in the United States Army, and a member of the first black regiment to be officially mustered into the Union army and to engage in a major battle." Captain Cailloux, killed while moving "in advance of his troops urging them to follow him" at the Battle of Port Hudson, Louisiana, on May 27, 1863,

commanded a company of the Native Guards regiment of New Orleans. Ochs, *Black Patriot and a White Priest*, 144.

48. *Adjutant General of Texas, 1890–91*, 85–86.

49. Ibid., 8. Hunter Liggitt (1857–1935) was born in Pennsylvania, graduated from the US Military Academy in 1875, and served with the 5th US Infantry Regiment through the war with Spain. He was president of the Army War College in 1910; a member of the General Staff; commanded the 4th Brigade, 2nd Division; and when the First World War commenced, was the commanding officer at Fort McKinley in the Philippine Islands. During that war, he acted as Gen. John Pershing's chief of staff, was commanding general of the First and Third Armies, and received the Distinguished Service Medal. Returning to the United States, Liggitt took charge of IX Corps at San Francisco until his retirement in 1921 as a lieutenant general. *Official Army Register for 1921* (Washington, DC: GPO, 1922), 1185; Heitman, *Historical Register and Dictionary of the United States Army*, 1:632.

50. "The Colored Encampment," *Austin Daily Statesman*, August 27, 1892.

51. "Colored Encampment," *San Antonio Daily Express*, September 16, 1893.

52. *Adjutant General of Texas, 1893–94*, 42.

53. *Adjutant General of Texas, 1895–96*, 4.

54. Louis Taylor to Adj. Gen. Mabry, September 16, 1897, RG 401, TSL.

55. J. A. Wilkins to Adj. Gen. Mabry, September 22, 1897, RG 401, TSL. Capt. Robert G. Ellis had worked diligently with Mabry to obtain free transportation over several railroad lines for his company. He finally arrived in Brenham on September 22 with forty-one men.

56. "Yellow Jack in Texas," *San Antonio Light*, September 22, 1897.

57. Rice, *Negro in Texas*, 270.

58. "Hangman's Day," *Galveston Daily News*, April 17, 1880; "State Specials," *Dallas Daily Herald*, April 17, 1880; *Adjutant General of Texas, 1878*, 28; *Adjutant General of Texas, 1880*, 24. Charles Partin Salter (1830–99) was born in Georgia and moved Texas in 1853, settling near Sterling in Robertson County. He amassed a great fortune in cotton and, at the outbreak of the Civil War, enlisted in the Robertson's Five-Shooters, commanded by Capt. William P. Townsend, before enrolling with Company E of Col. Charles Leroy Morgan's Confederate cavalry regiment. In 1863, Salter was tasked by the Confederate government to oversee operations of a wool mill and cotton sales across the border with Mexico. When the war ended, he returned to Robertson County, worked to bring the Houston and Texas Central Railroad to Calvert, and served on the city council and in the Texas legislature as a state representative from 1872 to 1874. Aragom Storm Miller, "Salter, Charles P.," *Handbook of Texas Online*, http://www. tshaonline. org./handbook/online/articles/fsa93 (accessed February 5, 2016); "Salter, Charles P.," Civil War Muster Rolls Index Cards, RG 401, TSL; Janet B. Hewett, ed., *Texas Confederate Soldiers, 1861–1865*, 2 vols. (Wilmington, NC: Broadfoot, 1997), 2:299.

William Quincy Wyser (1847–95), at age fifteen, accompanied his older brothers into Confederate service with Brown's Texas cavalry regiment. Following the end of conflict, he and his brother, Addison, became law-enforcement officials in Robertson County, he as sheriff and city marshal, Addison as a staffer in the county jail. "Robertson County," *Galveston Daily News,* November 8, 1878; "Texas Town Topics," *Houston Post,* March 8, 1894; "Mortuary—W. Q. Wyser," *Galveston Daily News,* April 18, 1895; "Wyser, Alice S.," Widow's Application 50591, Confederate Pensions Applications Records, TSL.

59. "A Brutal Fiend," *Seguin (TX) Record,* August 27, 1889. Herrera is listed as "Jesús Herrera," "Jesús Gonzalez," or "Alyo Perez" in various newspaper accounts.

60. "A Foul Murder," *Fort Worth Daily Gazette,* August 23, 1889; "Munck's Murderer," *San Antonio Light,* August 23, 1889; "Probably True," ibid., August 26, 1889; "Another Death," *Neu Braunfelser Zeitung,* August 29, 1889 (translation provided by Sophienburg Museum, New Braunfels, TX); Muster and pay roll, Company D, "Ireland Rifles," September 10, 1889, TVG, RG 401, TSL. George Monroe Autry (1842–1907), born in Mississippi, enlisted in the 34th Mississippi Infantry Regiment in March 1862; saw action at Corinth, Stones River, and Chickamauga; and was captured at Lookout Mountain in November 1863. Imprisoned at Rock Island, Illinois, Autry was exchanged in March 1865 and was on his way home when he heard the news of Lee's surrender. Following the war, he moved to Texas, first to Houston, then to Seguin, where he served as sheriff from 1888 to 1894. "Autrey," and "Capt. George Monroe Autrey," *Confederate Veteran* 16, no. 3 (March 1908): 239, 357.

61. "A Brutal Fiend," *Seguin (TX) Record,* August 27, 1889.

62. "'Misapprehension of 'Language versus Facts,'" *Seguin (TX) Record,* September 3, 1889.

63. *Adjutant General of Virginia, 1873,* 2–3; Cunningham, "They Are as Proud of Their Uniforms," 322.

64. "The Conservative Excursion to Petersburg," and "The Conservative Demonstration in Petersburg Last Night," *Daily State Journal* (Richmond, VA), October 24, 1873. The *Daily State Journal* was considered a Republican Party newspaper.

65. "Fear! Fear!! Fear!!!," *Daily State Journal* (Richmond, VA), November 4, 1873. Robert William Hughes, the Republican nominee for Virginia governor, ran against Democratic opponent and former Confederate general James Lawson Kemper. "Major R. W. Hughes Nominated for Governor," *New York Times,* July 31, 1873.

66. Cunningham, "They Are as Proud of Their Uniforms," 322. Cunningham's article contains additional information and quotations from the *Petersburg Rural Messenger,* the *Petersburg Appeal-Index,* and the *Richmond Daily Dispatch.* The newspapers complimented Hill and his company's actions, indicating that they were actually on the streets. *Adjutant General of Virginia, 1873,* 3.

67. *Adjutant General of Virginia, 1873,* 2.

68. "A Big Shake," *Richmond Dispatch,* September 1, 1886.

69. "Virginia's Visit," *Richmond Dispatch,* September 2, 1886; Muster roll, Company B, First Battalion Infantry, Colored, Virginia Volunteers, November 1, 1886, RG 46, LVA.

70. "The Strike at Newport News," *New York Times,* January 11, 1887. For additional information on the involvement and growth of the Knights of Labor in Virginia, see Rachleff, *Black Labor in Richmond.*

71. "The Labor Situation," *Bradstreet's* (New York City), February, 5, 1887; "The Old Dominion Strike," *New York Standard,* January 22, 1887; "The Strike at Newport News," *New York Times,* January 11, 1887.

72. "Newport News," *Richmond Daily Times,* January 13, 1887 (quote); "Military Moving," *Richmond Dispatch,* January 12, 1887; "Serious Strike at Newport News," *Shenandoah Herald* (Woodstock, VA), January 14, 1887.

73. "Military Moving." "Troops Sent to Newport News," *New York Times,* January 12, 1887 (emphasis added).

74. George Meredith Peek (1839–96), born at Hampton, Virginia, received his education at the Hampton Academy and the University of Virginia. During the Civil War, he served in both the Confederate army, as a staff officer in the 26th Alabama Infantry Regiment, and the Confederate navy, mostly as a professor of cadets. After the war, Peek briefly worked as superintendent of Warwick County schools, then organized the Bank of Hampton. He later accepted the position of judge, which he held until his death in 1896. Robert Alonzo Brock, *Virginia and Virginians,* 2 vols. (Richmond: H. H. Hardesty, 1888), 2:688–89; "Hon. George Meredith Peek," *Baltimore Sun,* January 9, 1896.

Baker Perkins Lee (1830–1901) was selected to fill the unexpired term of Peek's judgeship in 1896. Lee had been a major in the Confederate army during the war and afterward studied law and worked in the newspaper business at Hampton. Serving several terms in the state legislature and as county judge, Lee received an appointment as collector of customs at Newport News during the first Cleveland administration. Lyon G. Tyler, ed., "The Lee Family of York, Virginia," *William and Mary Quarterly* 24, no. 1 (July 1915): 46–54; "Judge Baker P. Lee Dead," *Richmond Times,* September 3, 1901.

Philip Haxall (1840–97), the son of a prominent Richmond businessman, enlisted in the 4th Virginia Cavalry and served briefly with the unit before his appointment to a staff position with the rank of captain, first with Brig. Gen. Joseph Reid Anderson, then with Brig. Gen. Beverly Holcombe Robertson. He was wounded twice during the conflict. After the war, Haxall formed and commanded the Stuart Horse Guards, a militia cavalry unit, at Richmond from 1883 to 1885. He was later appointed to serve on Governor Lee's staff, with the rank of colonel. Haxall also served until his death as the president of the Haxall Mills, a flour-milling company his father had founded. Brock, *Virginia and Virginians,* 2:288; "Death of Captain Haxall," *Norfolk Virginian,* February 12, 1897; "Capt. Philip Haxall Dead," *Richmond Times,* February 12, 1897.

75. *Adjutant General of Virginia, 1886,* 49 (includes period to March 1, 1887); "Newport News," *Richmond Daily Times,* January 13, 1887.

76. *Adjutant General of Virginia, 1886,* 46.

77. "Newport News," *Richmond Daily Times,* January 13, 1887; "Newport News," ibid., January 14, 1887; "The Newport News Rebellion," ibid., January 15, 1887.

78. *Adjutant General of Virginia, 1886,* 46–47.

79. "Newport News," *Richmond Daily Times,* January 14, 1887. Muscoe Livingston Spotswood (1850–1928) graduated at the top of his class at the Virginia Military Institute in 1872 and later obtained a law degree from the University of Virginia. He practiced in the legal profession in Richmond, where he also reached the rank of colonel of Virginia Volunteers, commanding the 1st Regiment from 1885 to 1890. [Virginia Mili-

tary Institute], *Register of Former Cadets: Centennial Edition* (Roanoke, VA: Roanoke Printing, 1939), 72–73; *Adjutant General of Virginia, 1886, 6.*

Joseph Virginius Bidgood (1841–1921) left his studies at William and Mary to enlist in the 32nd Virginia Infantry Regiment. He saw action during the Seven Days' Battles around Richmond before receiving promotion to sergeant major and then to adjutant of the regiment. He participated in the engagements at Harpers Ferry, Sharpsburg, and Fredericksburg before being captured near Petersburg. Bidgood refused to take the oath of loyalty to the Union, resulting in his incarceration at Point Lookout prison until June 1865. After the war, he served in both the infantry and the cavalry arms of the Virginia Volunteers, served as the state's lieutenant governor under Fitzhugh Lee, and held several positions in the Virginia Division of the United Confederate Veterans. Clement A. Evans, ed. *Confederate Military History,* 13 vols. (Atlanta: Confederate Publishing, 1899), 3:724.

80. Thomas J. Jarratt (1817–95), born in Sussex County, Virginia, served in Company D, 3rd Battalion of Virginia Reserves and participated in the defense of Petersburg. After the Civil War, he worked as a commission merchant in the city, was elected to the city council, and later served as mayor from 1882 to 1888, winning as part of the Readjuster-Republican coalition. Brock, *Virginia and Virginians,* 2:646; Edward Pollock, *Historical and Industrial Guide to Petersburg, Virginia* (Petersburg: T. S. Beckwith, 1884), 150; "Jarratt, T. J.," Compiled Service Records of Confederate Soldiers Who Served in Organizations from the State of Virginia, RG 109, NARA.

81. "A Test Prosecution," *Richmond Dispatch,* August 28, 1887; "To Arms!," ibid., August 31, 1887. Alfred William Harris (1853–1920), born in Fairfax County, worked as a newspaper editor in Alexandria before reading law in Petersburg. He graduated from Howard University in 1881 and returned to Petersburg to practice law a year later. As part of the Readjuster-Republican ticket, he was elected to the general assembly, won reelection three times (serving eight years), and authored the bill to create the Virginia Normal and Collegiate Institute (now Virginia State University). Harris remained loyal to Virginia governor William Mahone and even opposed other African Americans in the Republican Party, yet he fought against white Republicans who tried to force African Americans out of political office. In 1889, he received the position of special inspector for the Newport News Customs House and remained active in local politics. Michael Woods, "Harris, Alfred W. (1853–1920)," *Encyclopedia of Virginia,* http://www.encyclopediavirginia.org/Harris_Alfred_W_1853-1920#contrib (accessed September 16, 2015); Luther Porter Jackson, *Negro Office-holders in Virginia, 1865–1895* (Norfolk, VA: Guide Quality, 1945), 20.

82. Muster roll, Petersburg Guard, Separate Company, Virginia Volunteers, n.d., RG 46, LVA; "Petersburg Quiet," *Richmond Dispatch,* September 1, 1887; "All Quiet," *Richmond Daily Times,* September 1, 1887. For additional quotes from the *Petersburg Appeal-Index* and the *Richmond Daily Dispatch,* see Cunningham, "They Are as Proud of Their Uniforms."

83. "Convicts in Peril" (quotes) and "Disastrous Fire," *Richmond Daily Times,* February 1, 1888. The *Daily Times* reported that Captain Paul had twenty-seven men under his command when he arrived.

84. "Convicts in Peril" and "Disastrous Fire," *Richmond Daily Times,* February 1, 1888.

Chapter 6

1. Hannibal Ingalls Kimball (1832–95) was born in Oxford County, Maine, the son of a successful wheelwright. Kimball continued in his father's profession and combined it with carriage making. With his brothers, he established a company at New Haven, Connecticut, but after it failed he moved to Colorado to work for a mining company. There, Kimball met George Pullman, who contracted with him to establish the Pullman Company's sleeping-car lines in the South. Initially choosing to locate in Nashville, Kimball changed his mind and centered the company in Atlanta in 1867. Around this time, he was part of a group of businessmen who convinced the Georgia legislature to relocate the state capital to the city. He built and later sold the first structure used as the Georgia Capitol, incorporated Atlanta's water company, and became active in Republican politics as well as other numerous civic and business affairs that promoted the city. Kimball was a close friend and supporter of Governor Bullock as well as Henry Grady of the *Atlanta Constitution.* At one time, he was president of nine different railroad companies and built two hotels in the city, both known as the Kimball House. The first building was reported to be "equal in all respects to the fifth [*sic*] Avenue Hotel in New York and far superior to anything in the South." Leonard Allison Morrison, *A History of the Kimball Family in America from 1634 to 1897* (Boston: Damrell & Upham, 1897); Wallace Putnam Reed, *History of Atlanta Georgia, with Illustrations and Biographical Sketches of Some of Its Prominent Men and Pioneers* (Syracuse, NY: D. Mason, 1889), 162–68.

2. Record for Jefferson Wyly, December 8, 1870, Registers of Signatures of Depositors in Branches of the Freedman's Savings and Trust Company, 1865–74, RG 105, NARA (hereafter cited as Registers of Signatures of Depositors, 1865–74); Record for Jefferson Wyley, September 21, 1872, ibid.; "Wiley, Jefferson," Register of Enlistments, 1798–1914, RG 94, ibid.; Wyly to Gov. Smith, April 30, 1874, DOC-2819, RG 22, GAM. In 1872, Wyly worked as a messenger in the "treasurer's office W. and A. R. R.," but three years later he had worked his way into a position as a porter for the railroad. The treasurer of the Western and Atlantic Railroad, William C. Morrill, was also the president of both the Citizens Bank of Georgia and the Atlanta Rolling Mill Company. Morrill acted as one of Wyly's sureties when he obtained his company's firearms from the state. The other two men who signed the bond for Wyly were Beverly W. Wrenn, general passenger agent for the Kennesaw Route of the Western and Atlantic, and David G. Wylie, yardmaster for the railroad. "Light Infantry in Law," *Atlanta Constitution,* April 24, 1877; Arthur Eugene Sholes, comp., *Sholes' Directory of the City of Atlanta for 1877* (Atlanta: A. E. Sholes, 1877), 252, 354, 356.

3. Lowell Dwight Black, "The Negro Volunteer Militia Units of the Ohio National Guard, 1870–1954: The Struggle for Military Recognition and Equality in the State of Ohio" (Ph.D. diss., Ohio State University, 1976), 183, 188. Unfortunately, Black does not specifically state "light skinned mulattoes" and leaves the reader to assume his meaning based on later comments. Roger Cunningham fails to discuss the concept of color and its effect on the various African American volunteer militia organizations in Kansas. See Cunningham, *Black Citizen-Soldiers of Kansas.*

4. Muster rolls, Austin City Rifles, Capitol Guard, Brenham Blues, Brazos Light Guard, Gregory Rifles, Roberts Rifles, Jim Blaine Rifles, Cochran Greys, Cochran Blues, Lone Star Rifles, Grant Rifles, Lincoln Guards, Davis Rifles, Sheridan Guards, Excelsior Guard, Ireland Rifles, and Hubbard Rifles, TVG, RG 401, TSL.

5. Muster rolls, Gregory Rifles and Brazos Light Guard, TVG, RG 401, TSL.

6. Muster rolls, Brazos Light Guard, TVG, RG 401, TSL.

7. Muster rolls, Sheridan Guards, TVG, RG 401, TSL.

8. Ibid.

9. Muster rolls, Excelsior Guard, TVG, RG 401, TSL.

10. "From the State Capital," *Galveston Daily News,* May 5, 1880. The eight companies listed are the Coke Rifles, San Antonio; Austin City Rifles, Austin; Lincoln Guards, Galveston; Hubbard Rifles, Waco; Brenham Blues, Brenham; Roberts Rifles, Corpus Christi; Salter Rifles, Calvert; and the Davis Rifles, Houston. All three ranks were filled by serving company commanders—Captain Gregory of Waco as colonel, Capt. Henry Riley of San Antonio as lieutenant colonel, and Captain Henderson of Galveston as major.

11. "Robertson County, Texas," Tenth Census of the United States, 1880, Records of the of the Bureau of the Census, RG 29, NARA (hereafter cited as Tenth Census, 1880); "Lavaca County, Texas," Twelfth Census of the United States, 1900, ibid. (hereafter cited as Twelfth Census, 1900).

12. *Adjutant General of Texas, 1880,* 24; *Report of the Adjutant General of the State of Texas. Austin, February 28, 1882* (Galveston: A. H. Belo, Printer, 1882), 21; "Henderson, Pearson," Compiled Military Service Records, US Colored Troops, RG 94, NARA; "Henderson, Preston," US Civil War Pension Index: General Index to Pension Files, 1861–1934, RG 15, ibid. Henderson's first name is a source of controversy, having been given as "Pearson," "Person," "Preston," and "Priest" (and possibly others) in various records and accounts.

13. "List of Companies Complying with Militia Law Revised Statutes," Roster of Texas Volunteer Guards, January 1, 1882 (unbound), RG 401, TSL; *Adjutant General of Texas, 1880,* 24; *Adjutant General of Texas, February 1882,* 21; *Adjutant General of Texas, 1886,* 28; "Wilson, George," Compiled Military Service Records, US Colored Troops, RG 94, NARA. Wilson is identified as "black" on his enlistment documents and on federal census records. See "Nueces County, Texas," Ninth Census, 1870; and "Nueces County, Texas," Tenth Census, 1880.

14. "King, James H.," Compiled Military Service Records, US Colored Troops, RG 94, NARA; "King, James H.," Register of Enlistments, 1798–1914, ibid.

15. *Adjutant General of Texas, 1880,* 24; Charles D. Morrison and Joseph V. Fourmy, comp., *Morrison and Fourmy's General Directory of the City of Austin for 1881–82* (Austin: E. W. Swindells, 1881), 117; "Travis County, Texas," Tenth Census, 1880.

16. *Adjutant General of Texas, February 1882,* 21; *Adjutant General of Texas, 1883,* 14; *Adjutant General of Texas, 1884,* 14; Foner, *Freedom's Lawmakers,* 5–6.

17. *Adjutant General of Texas, 1884,* 14; "Goins, Jashua," Register of Enlistments, 1798–1914, RG 94, NARA; "Ellis County, Texas," Tenth Census, 1880. Goins's occupation on the 1867 enlistment register was "dis'd soldier," and his inclusion in the 1890

special census of veterans supports his participation in the American Civil War. "Ellis County, Texas," US Bureau of the Census, *1890 Special Census of Civil War Union Veterans and Widows* (Washington, DC: GPO, 1890).

18. Muster rolls, Field & Staff, Battalion Colored Infantry, TVG, RG 401, TSL; Muster-in roll, 1st Battalion, Colored, Texas National Guard, ibid.; "Larne, Jacob," Compiled Military Service Records, US Colored Troops, RG 94, NARA; *Adjutant General of Texas, 1901–2,* 198, 200.

19. Lucius Q. C. Lamar, comp., *A Compilation of the Laws of the State of Georgia, Passed by the Legislature since the Year 1810 to the Year 1819, Inclusive* (Augusta, GA: T. S. Hannon, 1821), 811–17.

20. Augustun Smith Clayton, comp., *Laws of the State of Georgia, Passed by the Legislature since the Political Year 1800, to the Year 1810, Inclusive* (Augusta, GA: Adams & Duyckinck, 1812), 462–63.

21. Ibid., 655–56 (emphasis added).

22. Janice L. Sumler-Edmond, *The Secret Trust of Aspasia Cruvellier Mirault* (Fayetteville: University of Arkansas Press, 2008), 5.

23. Registers of Free Persons of Color, 1817–1864, City of Savannah, Research Library and Municipal Archives, Savannah, GA; George W. Cullum, *Biographical Register of the Officers and Graduates of the U.S. Military Academy at West Point, N.Y.* (Cambridge, MA: Riverside, 1891), 142; "Ward, John Elliott," in Candler and Evans, *Georgia,* 3:521; M. Foster Farley, "John Elliott Ward, Mayor of Savannah 1853–1854," *Georgia Historical Quarterly* 53, no. 1 (March 1969), 69–77; "John Elliott Ward Dead," *New York Times,* December 1, 1902.

24. "Wanted," *Savannah Daily Morning News,* February 12, 1861. The newspaper printed this same advertisement a total of forty-nine times from February 12 to August 23, 1861.

25. "Woodhouse, William," Compiled Service Records of Confederate Soldiers, Georgia, RG 109, NARA (Woodhouse has a service record in both the 25th and the 47th Georgia Infantry Regiments); "The Magistrates' Election," *Savannah Morning News,* January 8, 1877; Sumler-Edmond, *Secret Trust,* 55–57; A. W. Stone to Gov. Smith, [n.d.], 1872, NEWS-253, RG 22, GAM; Arthur Eugene Sholes, comp., *Sholes' Georgia State Gazetteer and Business Directory for 1879 and 1880* (Atlanta: A. E. Sholes, 1879), 710; Charles L. Hoskins, *Yet with a Steady Beat: Biographies of Early Black Savannah* (Savannah: C. L. Hoskins, 2001), 233; untitled article, *Savannah Tribune,* September 23, 1876. The 1860 US Census for Chatham County, Georgia, classified every future member of the 47th Regiment's band as lighter-skinned individuals.

26. "The Colored Battalion," *Savannah Morning News,* August 7, 1880; John H. Deveaux to Adj. Gen. Stephens, December 22, 1885 RCB-41578, RG 22, GAM; Adj. Gen. Stephens to Deveaux, December 31, 1885, ibid.

27. Registers of Free Persons of Color, 1817–1864, City of Savannah; Deveaux to Adj. Gen. Stephens, January 7, 1886, RCB-41578, RG 22, GAM. The 1828 register lists a "Catherine Deveaux," born about 1785, from Antigua. That same year, the register provides evidence to the origins of the Mirault family in Saint-Domingue.

28. "The Capture of the U.S. Steamer 'Water Witch' in Ossabaw Sound, Ga., June 2–3, 1864," *Georgia Historical Quarterly* 3, no. 1 (March, 1919): 11–27.

29. Alexander A. Lawrence, "The Night Lieutenant Pelot Was Killed aboard the 'Water Witch,'" *Georgia Review* 4, no. 3 (Fall 1950): 174–76; "Deveaux, John," Naval Records Collection of the Office of Naval Records and Library, RG 45, NARA.

30. Perdue, *Negro in Savannah*, 52. Richard W. White, Thomas S. Walsh, and Deveaux held the clerk positions at Savannah in 1871. *Register of Officers and Agents, Civil, Military, and Naval, in the Service of the United States* (Washington, DC: GPO, 1872), 96 (hereafter cited as *Register of Officers and Agents, 1872*). White became the first African American to serve as clerk of the Superior Court of Chatham County. Perdue, *Negro in Savannah*, 53.

31. "Our Leader Dead," *Savannah Tribune*, June 12, 1909. See also Charles L. Hoskins, *The Trouble They Seen: Profiles in the Life of Col. John H. Deveaux, 1848–1900* (Savannah: C. L. Hoskins, 1989).

32. Shadgett, *Republican Party in Georgia*, 166–73.

33. *Register of Officers and Agents, Civil, Military, and Naval, in the Service of the United States* (Washington, DC: GPO, 1878), 48. Deveaux maintained steady employment at the Treasury Department as a clerk in the Auditor's Office until 1905.

34. Hoskins, *W. W. Law and His People*, 57.

35. Clarence A. Bacote, "Negro Officeholders in Georgia under President McKinley," *Journal of Negro History* 44, no. 3 (July 1959): 217–39 (quote, 228).

36. "Our Leader Dead," *Savannah Tribune*, June 12, 1909; Perdue, *Negro in Savannah*, 52.

37. Record for William Anderson Pledger, March 22, 1871, Registers of Signatures of Depositors, 1865–74. See also Herbert, *Complete Roster*; Shadgett, *Republican Party in Georgia*; and Ruth Currie McDaniel, "Black Power in Georgia: William A. Pledger and the Takeover of the Republican Party," *Georgia Historical Quarterly* 62, no. 3 (Fall 1978): 225–39. William J. White (1831–1913) was born a slave. He, like Johnson and Blocker, sought advancement through education, working first with the Freedmen's Bureau, then in 1867 helping found the Augusta Baptist Institute, which later moved to Atlanta and became Morehouse College. White, as pastor of Harmony Baptist Church, worked closely with Johnson. He also worked for the newspaper *Colored American* and edited the *Georgia Baptist*. In 1869, he received a presidential appointment as internal revenue assessor at Augusta but resigned in 1880. A critic of Booker T. Washington, White remained active in Republican politics and was a lifelong proponent of African American rights. Foner, *Freedom's Lawmakers*, 228–29.

38. *Register of Officers and Agents, 1872*, 169; "The Color Line in Georgia," *New York Times*, March 26, 1884; "Through the City," *Atlanta Constitution*, July 21, 1883; "Cannot Be Colonel," ibid., February 29, 1884.

39. Thomas Grant to Adj. Gen. Kell, September 26, 1892, RCB-41405, RG 22, GAM; "Records of Volunteer Officers," *United States Army and Navy Journal and Gazette of the Regular and Volunteer Forces* 37, no. 7 (October 14, 1899): 145; Thomas H. Martin, *Atlanta and Its Builders: A Comprehensive History of the Gate City of the South*, 2 vols. (Atlanta: Century, 1902), 2:657–58.

40. "Julia Cole," in *Slave Narratives: A Folk History of Slavery in the United States from Interviews with Former Slaves*, 17 vols., ed. Benjamin A. Botkin (Washington, DC: GPO, 1941), pt. 1, 4:232–36 (quote, 235). Julia Cole, described by the interviewer as "yellow-

ish gingercake in color," stated that her brothers were Grants but that she and her sister were Johnsons.

41. Grant to Adj. Gen. Kell, September 26, 1892, RCB-41405, RG 22, GAM; Grant to Gov. Northen, November 1, 1892, ibid.; "Records of Volunteer Officers," 145; Ralph Lane Polk, comp., *Atlanta City Directory for 1889* (Atlanta: R. L. Polk, 1889), 554. Grant operated his own coal-supply company in Atlanta.

42. *Adjutant Report for Georgia, 1896*, 52; Adj. Gen. Kell to Crumbly, February 27, 1892, VOL1-1721, RG 22, GAM.

43. Carter, *Black Side*, 60–63; Foner, *Freedom's Lawmakers*, 54; Frank Lincoln Mather, *Who's Who of the Colored Race*, vol. 1 (Chicago: n.p., 1915), 82; "Spaulding County, Georgia," Ninth Census, 1870.

44. "Crumbly, Floyd," Register of Enlistments, 1798–1914, RG 94, NARA; Mather, *Who's Who of the Colored Race*, 82; Carter, *Black Side*, 60–63; Dan L. Trapp, *Victorio and the Mimbres Apaches* (Norman: University of Oklahoma Press, 1974), 218–51. See Appendix A for *General Rules Governing the Second Battallion*.

45. Carter, *Black Side*, 60–63; Mather, *Who's Who of the Colored Race*, 82; "What the Negro Is Doing," *Atlanta Constitution*, April 11, 1897; Acting Adj. Gen. Phill G. Byrd to Crumbly, March 25, 1899, VOL1-1726, RG 22, GAM. Henry Allen Rucker (1852–1924) was born a slave. He became a businessman in Atlanta, rose in Republican politics, and was appointed by President McKinley the collector of internal revenue in Georgia in 1897, a position he held until 1911. Gregory Mixon, "The Making of a Black Political Boss: Henry A. Rucker, 1897–1904," *Georgia Historical Quarterly* 89, no. 4 (Winter 2005): 485–504.

46. A. R. Johnson to Gov. Northen, September 20, 1892, RCB-41405, RG 22, GAM; "Richmond County, Georgia," Ninth Census, 1870; "Richmond County, Georgia," Tenth Census, 1880; "Richmond County, Georgia," Twelfth Census, 1900; "A. R. Johnson Died Yesterday," *Augusta Chronicle*, October 22, 1908.

47. "Richmond County, Georgia," Tenth Census, 1880; T. J. Maloney, comp., *Maloney's 1899 Augusta City Directory* (Augusta: Maloney Directory., 1899), 95–96. The 1870 census listed Blocker as "mulatto." "Richmond County, Georgia," Ninth Census, 1870.

48. *Adjutant Report for Georgia, 1896*, 52.

49. The muster rolls available at the Georgia Archives consist of most of the organizations from the early 1890s to 1898–99. None of the enlistment rosters contain any descriptions of personal features.

50. Henry Alphonsus Goette, comp., *Goette's Savannah City Directory for 1904* (Savannah: H. A Goette, 1903), 57.

51. Hoskins, *Yet with a Steady Beat*, 166–67; "Grand Lodge F. A. M. for the State of Georgia," *Savannah Tribune*, December 30, 1876; "Toomer, Louis," Registers of Free Persons of Color, 1817–64, City of Savannah.

52. Hoskins, *Yet with a Steady Beat*, 296–99.

53. Perdue, *Negro in Savannah*, 62.

54. "Chatham County, GA," Tenth Census, 1880; Hoskins, *Yet with a Steady Beat*, 322–23; Shadgett, *Republican Party in Georgia*, 166–73. Pleasant later worked for Deveaux as an inspector of customs.

55. Tenth Census, 1880; Twelfth Census, 1900; Woodhouse to Gov. Colquitt, July 21, 1877, NEWS-253, RG 22, GAM; Resolution, July 6, 1880, RCB-41414, ibid.; Adj. Gen. Kell to Deveaux, October 2, 1890, VOL1-1705, ibid.; "Eureka's Re-Union," *Savannah Tribune,* February 18, 1893.

56. "Beaufort County, South Carolina," Tenth Census, 1880; "Franklin Jones," Compiled Military Service Records, US Colored Troops, RG 94, NARA; Record for Franklin Jones, 1867, Registers of Signatures of Depositors, 1864–74.

57. Hoskins, *Yet with a Steady Beat,* 288–93; "Roster of Commissioned Officers Georgia Volunteers" *Georgia Adjutant General Records, 1877–99;* Deveaux to Adj. Gen. Kell, December 12, 1890, RCB-37046, RG 22, GAM; Mather, *Who's Who of the Colored Race,* 157; A. B. Caldwell, *History of the American Negro, Georgia Edition,* 2 vols. (Atlanta: A. B. Caldwell, 1920), 2:347–49. The adjutant general sent Johnson's commission as first lieutenant three days after his nomination. Adj. Gen. Kell to Deveaux, December 15, 1890, VOL1-1705, ibid.

58. "Rifle and Gun Club," *Savannah Tribune,* March 10, 1894.

59. "Dr. J. H. Bugg Died on Visit to Old Home," *New York Age,* August 14, 1920; *Goette's Savannah City Directory for 1904,* 57; "Richmond County, GA," Tenth Census, 1880; "Chatham County, GA," Twelfth Census, 1900; "Another City Physician," *Savannah Tribune,* June 19, 1897; "A New Physician," ibid., June 18, 1892.

60. "Roster of Commissioned Officers Georgia Volunteers."

61. *Adjutant General of Georgia, 1895,* 57; "Roster of Commissioned Officers Georgia Volunteers"; Shadgett, *Republican Party in Georgia,* 171–73; "Death of C. C. Wimbish, a Well-Known Negro," *Atlanta Constitution,* October 21, 1915. Wimbish was commissioned a captain on August 22, 1878, to command the Capital Guards at Atlanta. An active supporter of Republican politics, he served as a delegate to at least four national conventions from 1888 to 1900. First employed as a mail carrier, Wimbish later received appointments as collector and as surveyor of customs at Atlanta before returning to the post office. His sons, Hugh and Christopher Columbus Jr., both served as officers during World War I. Christopher Jr. studied at Howard and Northwestern University Law School and served as a state senator. Christopher Wimbish Papers, 1870–1962, Chicago History Museum.

62. "Lincoln Graduates in the Medical Profession," *Lincoln University Herald* 21, no. 2 (February 1917): 1; "Henry Rutherford Butler, M.D., 1862–1931," *Journal of the National Medical Association* 51, no. 2 (September 1959): 406–8; D. W. Culp, ed., *Twentieth Century Negro Literature; or, A Cyclopedia of Thought on the Vital Topics Relating to the American Negro* (Atlanta: J. L. Nichols, 1902), 220.

63. "The New York Life in Georgia," *Insurance Times* 37 (November 1904): 463; Edward R. Carter, *Biographical Sketches of Our Pulpit* (1888; repr., Chicago: Afro-Am, 1969), 100–102; "Aged Negro Who Handled Millions Is Now Dead," *Atlanta Constitution,* September 18, 1902; "Many Attend Funeral of Faithful Negro," ibid., September 19, 1902.

64. Carter, *Biographical Sketches of Our Pulpit,* vi(c).

65. Carter, *Black Side,* v.

66. Arthur Eugene Sholes, comp., *Sholes' Directory of the City of Augusta, 1886* (Augusta: A. E. Sholes, 1886), 22. At the time the 3rd Colored Battalion was formed, its

commanding officer, Johnson, was the principal at the First Ward School, Walker was the principal at the Second Ward School, and Blocker served as principal at the Third Ward School. The Fourth Ward School's principal was Richard R. Wright, who later served as the president of Georgia Industrial College (now Savannah State University).

67. *Year Book of the Augusta Georgia Chamber of Commerce* (Augusta: Augusta Chronicle Job Printing, 1908), n.p. Benefield's exact responsibilities at the club are unknown, but his obituary stated that "no man in his line stood higher than he did, having been connected with the hotel life at this town for about fifty years." "Notes among the Colored People," *Augusta (GA) Chronicle*, September 28, 1919.

68. "Richmond County, Georgia," Tenth Census, 1880; Ralph Lane Polk, comp., *R. L. Polk's Augusta City Directory 1888* (Atlanta: R. L. Polk, 1888), 356.

69. "Death Yesterday of Geo. N. Stoney Prominent Negro," *Augusta (GA) Chronicle*, October 6, 1926.

70. Silas Xavier Floyd, *Life of Charles T. Walker, D.D., "The Black Spurgeon"* (Nashville: National Baptist, 1902), 7.

71. "Johnson, Richard H.," Compiled Military Service Records, US Colored Troops, RG 94, NARA; "Local News—Military Items," *Daily State Journal* (Richmond, VA), April 18, 1871; "National Memorial Day," ibid., May 30, 1872; "The Grand Procession," *Washington Evening Star*, March 3, 1873; Stern, *Roster Commissioned Officers*, 281; Virginia, Deaths and Burials Index, 1853–1917, AncestryInstitution, http://search.ancestryinstitution.com/search/db.aspx?dbid=2558 (subscription site; accessed December 11, 2015).

72. "Representatives Elect," *Journal of United Labor* 6, no. 9 (September 10, 1885): 1076; "Richmond City, Virginia," Eighth Census of the United States, 1860, Records of the Bureau of the Census, 1790–2007, RG 29, NARA ; "Richmond City, Virginia," Ninth Census, 1870; "Richmond City, Virginia," Tenth Census, 1880; *Adjutant General of Virginia, 1884–85*, 21; "Manchester News and Gossip," *Richmond Planet*, June 20, 1871. See also Rachleff, *Black Labor in Richmond*, 87–89, 127, 138–40, 145.

73. John A. Kenney, *The Negro in Medicine* (Tuskegee, AL: Tuskegee Institute Press, 1912), 9–10; *Journal of the Common Council from January 14, 1873 to January 13, 1874* (Detroit: Daily Post Book & Job Printing, 1874), 9; Daniel Smith Lamb, comp., *A Historical, Biographical, and Statistical Souvenir* (Washington, DC: R. Beresford, 1900), 163; C. H. Corey, "Samuel H. Dismond, M.D.," *Baptist Home Mission Weekly* 20, no. 6 (June 1898): 202–3; "Dr. Dismond's Demise," *Richmond Planet*, March 12, 1898; Stern, *Roster Commissioned Officers*, 275. No record of Dismond's skin color has been located.

74. "Richmond City," Tenth Census, 1880; *Adjutant General of Virginia, 1884–85*, 21; "Alumni of Crozer Theological Seminary," *Bulletin of the Crozer Theological Seminary* 1, no. 1 (October 1908): 73; John Henry Chataigne, comp., *Chataigne's Directory of Richmond, Va., 1884–85* (Richmond: J. H. Chataigne, 1884), 376; "Rev. Henry Haywood Mitchell, Sr.," AncestryUSA, Public Family Trees, http://trees.ancestryinstitution.com/tree/1851768/person/598116253 (subscription site; accessed December 11, 2015); "Our History," National Baptist Convention, USA, http://www.nationalbaptist.com/about-us/our-history (accessed December 11, 2015); Stern, *Roster Commissioned Officers*, 284.

75. Stern, *Roster Commissioned Officers*, 281.

76. G. F. Richings, *Evidences of Progress among Colored People* (Philadelphia: George S. Ferguson, 1904), 488–89 (quote); "Henrico County, Virginia," Tenth Census, 1880; John Henry Chataigne, comp., *Chataigne's Directory of Richmond, Va.* (Richmond: J. H. Chataigne, 1882), 265; Chataigne, *Chataigne's Directory of Richmond, Va., 1884–85*, 313; *Adjutant General of Virginia, 1895*, 23; John Henry Chataigne, comp., *Chataigne's Directory, 1895–96* (Richmond: J. H. Chataigne, 1896), 431; *Register of Officers and Agents, Civil, Military, and Naval, in the Service of the United States* (Washington, DC: GPO, 1881), 694 (hereafter cited at *Register of Officers and Agents, 1881*); Stern, *Roster Commissioned Officers*, 274, 282. Joseph Stern stated that Johnson was a first lieutenant with the company in 1880, yet official documents fail to support this information, showing that the L'Ouverture Guard was organized on February 2, 1888. Officer's Rosters, 1878–1897, RG 46, LVA.

77. *American Medical Directory* (Chicago: American Medical Association, 1921), 1518; "Deaths," *Journal of the American Medical Association* 75, no. 24 (December 11, 1920): 1662; A. B. Caldwell, *History of the American Negro, Virginia Edition* (Atlanta: A. B. Caldwell, 1921), 18–20; Lamb, *Historical, Biographical, and Statistical Souvenir*, 175. See also Harrison L. Harris, M.D., *Masonic Text-Book: A Concise Historical Sketch of Masonry and the Organization of Masonic Grand Lodges, and Especially of Masonry among Colored Men in America* (Petersburg, VA: Masonic Visitor, 1902).

78. Caldwell, *History of the American Negro, Virginia*, 170–72; "Richmond City," Twelfth Census, 1900; "Richmond City," Thirteenth Census of the United States, 1910, Records of the Bureau of the Census, RG 29, NARA (hereafter cited as Thirteenth Census, 1910); "Richmond City," Fourteenth Census of the United States, 1920, ibid. (hereafter cited as Fourteenth Census, 1920); Stern, *Roster Commissioned Officers*, 272; *Adjutant General of Virginia, 1894*, 24; Officer's Rosters, 1878–1897, RG 46, LVA.

79. Israel LaFayette Butt, *History of African Methodism in Virginia; or, Four Decades in the Old Dominion* (Hampton, VA: Hampton Institute Press, 1908), 133, 174, 203; "Palmer, William H.," Compiled Military Service Records, US Colored Troops, RG 94, NARA; *Register of Officers and Agents, 1881*, 691; *Register of Officers and Agents, Civil, Military, and Naval, in the Service of the United States* (Washington, DC: GPO, 1887), 452; *Register of Officers and Agents, Civil, Military, and Naval, in the Service of the United States* (Washington, DC, GPO, 1891), 571; *Adjutant General of Virginia, 1884–85*, 23.

80. Maj. William Henry Johnson Papers, Special Collections and Archives, James Hugo Johnston Memorial Library, Virginia State University, Petersburg; *Twenty-Two Years' Work of the Hampton Normal and Agricultural Institute* (Hampton, VA: Normal School Press, 1891), 111–12; Officer's Rosters, 1878–1897, RG 46, LVA. See also William Henry Johnson, *History of the Colored Volunteer Infantry of Virginia, 1871–99* (Richmond: Virginia Historical Society, 1923).

81. *Adjutant General of Virginia, 1895*, 23; Stern, *Roster Commissioned Officers*, 273; Lamb, *Historical, Biographical, and Statistical Souvenir*, 146; "Claimed by Death," *New Journal and Guide* (Norfolk, VA), October 17, 1925; "Lycoming County, PA," Ninth Census, 1870; "Norfolk, VA," Twelfth Census, 1900.

82. Rev. J. A. Whitted, D.D., *A History of the Negro Baptists of North Carolina* (Raleigh: Edwards & Broughton Printing, 1908), 161.

83. Caldwell, *History of American Negro, Virginia,* 170–72; "Dr. Wm. F. Clarke," *Petersburg (VA) Progress-Index Appeal,* July 17, 1954; "Petersburg City," Tenth Census, 1880; "Petersburg City," Twelfth Census, 1900; "Petersburg City," Thirteenth Census, 1910; "Petersburg City," Fourteenth Census, 1920; Stern, *Roster Commissioned Officers,* 274; *Adjutant General of Virginia, 1895,* 24; "Johnson, Hilliard," Compiled Military Service Records, US Colored Troops, RG 94, NARA; "Johnson, Hilliard," General Index to Pension Files, 1861–1934, RG 15, ibid.; Officer's Rosters, 1878–1897, RG 46, LVA.

84. Foner, *Freedom's Lawmakers,* 15.

85. "A Faithful Negro Dead," *Thomasville (GA) Times-Enterprise,* May 15, 1894. Henry Bird accompanied Capt. Thomas Nelson as a body servant during the Civil War. According to his obituary, he served as the captain of Albany's Colquitt Guards from 1879 to his death in 1894. As for Nelson, he served briefly as the surgeon of the 4th Georgia Infantry Regiment before raising his own cavalry troop, Nelson's Independent Georgia Cavalry, in 1862. In June 1864, he was promoted to major of Scouts and Guards. Nelson was killed one month later as lieutenant colonel of the 6th Georgia Cavalry Regiment. "Nelson, Thomas M.," Compiled Service Records of Confederate Soldiers, Georgia, RG 109, NARA.

Chapter 7

Unnumbered note. The title quote refers to a sermon delivered by Edward Randolph Carter in the summer of 1894 to members of the 2nd Battalion, Georgia Volunteers, Colored. See Carter, *Black Side,* 284–91.

1. *Our Colored Militia,* (illustration), *Frank Leslie Illustrated Newspaper,* July 17, 1875, 333; "The Morning of the Parade," ibid., 338 (emphasis added).

2. *Merriam-Webster's Collegiate Dictionary,* 11th ed. (Springfield, MA: Merriam-Webster, 2008), s.v. "manhood."

3. Craig Thompson Friend and Lorri Glover, eds., *Southern Manhood: Perspectives on Masculinity in the Old South* (Athens: University of Georgia Press, 2004), xi. See also Edward L. Ayers, "Honor," in *New Encyclopedia of Southern Culture,* 13 vols., ed. Ted Ownby and Nancy Bercaw (Chapel Hill: University of North Carolina Press, 2005), 13:134–6; and E. Anthony Rotundo, "Learning about Manhood: Gender Ideals and the Middle-Class Family in Nineteenth-Century America," in *Manliness and Morality: Middle-Class Masculinity in Britain and America, 1800–1940,* ed. J. A. Mangan and James Walvin (Manchester, UK: Manchester University Press, 1987), 35–48.

4. Friend and Glover, *Southern Manhood,* xiii.

5. Harry S. Laver, "Refuge of Manhood: Masculinity and the Militia Experience in Kentucky," in Friend and Glover, *Southern Manhood,* 5; William S. Basinger, "The Savannah Volunteer Guards from 1858 to 1882," MS982—Savannah Volunteer Guards Records, Georgia Historical Society, Savannah, 75. The narrative lists Joe Parkman and Dave Ellison as slaves belonging to George W. Davis and William Battersby, respectively, and Louis, Jack, and Joe Verdery as free blacks.

6. See *Portrait of Unidentified Members of the Sumter Light Guard, Company K, 4th Georgia Infantry, near Barracks in Americus, Georgia,* April 26, 1861, Image VIS 170.987.001, Kenan Research Center, Atlanta History Center.

7. The Savannah Guards Battalion was one of the oldest militia organizations in Georgia, founded in 1802. The 25th Georgia Infantry Regiment's eleven African American musicians, led by Robert Lowe, can also be found in the regimental band for the 47th Georgia Infantry Regiment, minus Robert Burke and Joseph Millen; Burke (a constable), Lowe (a brick mason), and William Woodhouse (a justice of the peace), however, are listed in the 1877 city directory with drum major Sido Brown (a porter), Charles Lawton (a barber), S. Myralt (Simon Mirault, a brick mason), F. A. Myralt (Francis A. Mirault, a cotton-press worker), N. A Cuyler (Nelson A. Cuyler, a bricklayer), J. Atkinson (James Atkinson, a laborer), W. A. Gary (William A. Geary, a porter), C. Gary (Charles Geary, a barber), and H. Gary (Haily Geary, a laborer). Muster rolls, Field and Staff Band, 25th Georgia Infantry, 47th Georgia Infantry, Compiled Service Records of Confederate Soldiers, Georgia, RG 109, NARA; George H. Rogers, comp., *Rogers City Directory of Savannah* (Savannah: George H. Rogers, 1877), 271; "Chatham County, Georgia," Tenth Census, 1880.

8. Karen Taylor, "Reconstructing Men in Savannah Georgia, 1865–1876," in *Southern Masculinity: Perspectives on Manhood in the South since Reconstruction,* ed. Craig Thompson Friend (Athens: University of Georgia Press, 2009), 3. Taylor could have also included the military as well as education in this assessment.

9. Friend, *Southern Masculinity,* xi.

10. Ibid.

11. Carter, *Black Side,* 284–91 (emphasis added).

12. Shane White, "'It Was a Proud Day': African Americans, Festivals, and Parades in the North, 1741–1834," *Journal of American History* 81 (June 1994): 13–50. See also David Waldstreich, *In the Midst of Perpetual Fetes: The Making of American Nationalism, 1776–1820* (Chapel Hill: University of North Carolina Press, 1997). While both White and Waldstreich examined parade activity during an earlier period in US history, the meanings and purposes remained the same from the 1870s to 1906.

13. "Review of the Colored Military by the Governor of Georgia," *Savannah Morning News,* May 26, 1877 (emphasis added). It is important to recall that Governor Colquitt was a former Confederate brigadier general.

14. "Military Visitors from Richmond, Virginia," *Washington Evening Star,* October 7, 1873.

15. "The Grand Procession," *Washington Evening Star,* March 3, 1873; "The Twentieth President," *Jeffersonian Republic* (Stroudsburg, PA), March 9, 1881.

16. "The Colored Companies," *Atlanta Constitution,* January 19, 1889; "The Two Negro Companies," ibid., February 17, 1889; "On to Washington," ibid., March 1, 1889. There is some indication that Captain McHenry's Governor's Volunteers may have attended the inauguration too, but there is no confirmation of this.

17. "From Our Notebook—The Inspiration Do Come," *Atlanta Defiance,* reprinted in *Atlanta Constitution,* April 20, 1889.

18. "To See the Majah," *Atlanta Constitution,* March 2, 1897; "Back from Washington," ibid., March 8, 1897; "Off for the Inauguration," *Macon (GA) Telegraph,* March 1, 1901; "The Lincoln Guards," *Atlanta Constitution,* March 12, 1901; *Inaugural Souvenir, 1901* (Washington, DC: Press of W. F. Roberts, 1901); "Was Observed in Savannah," *Atlanta Constitution,* September 20, 1901. The souvenir booklet does not contain numbered

pages, but counting from the outside front cover, page 81 contains the listing of the Georgia Artillery, and page 64 has a photograph of the members of the "Prominent Colored Members of Inaugural Committee."

19. Elizabeth Hayes Turner, *Women, Culture, and Community: Religion and Reform in Galveston, 1880–1920* (New York: Oxford University Press, 1997), 250.

20. William Palmer to Gov. Fitzhugh Lee, September 12, 1887, Executive Papers of Gov. Fitzhugh Lee, 1885–89, LVA (hereafter cited as Lee Papers).

21. Adj. Gen. James McDonald to Gov. Fitzhugh Lee, September 23, 1887, Lee Papers (emphasis added).

22. J. Thompson Baird to Gov. Fitzhugh Lee, September 29, 1887, Lee Papers (original emphasis). John Thompson Baird (1839–1905) enlisted as a private in the 61st Virginia Regiment and rose to rank of first lieutenant. He lost his left leg at Davis's Farm in 1864 and, after the war, returned to Portsmouth, where he was a businessman prior to his election as mayor, a position he held for twenty-three years. See "Mayor J. Thompson Baird," *Confederate Veteran*, 13, no. 7 (July 1905): 373.

23. "Military Inspection," *Savannah Tribune*, May 18, 1895. Charles Booth Satterlee (1855–99), a Pennsylvania native, graduated from West Point in 1876 with a commission as an artillery officer. On May 20, 1891, Adjutant General Kell reported that Satterlee had arrived "for duty in connection with the militia of this State" and that same day appointed him "to act as Assistant Adjutant and Inspector-General." *Report of the Adjutant and Inspector-General of the State of Georgia For the Year 1891* (Atlanta: Franklin Printing House, 1892), 4. Three years later, Kell commended "to him [Satterlee], more than any other man, is the State indebted for the measure of excellence attained and so generally recognized." *Report of the Adjutant-General of the State of Georgia For the Year 1894* (Atlanta: Franklin Printing House, 1894), 19. Thus, the Military Advisory Board, in their assignment of Satterlee to inspect the African American units, signaled their genuine intent of evaluating and improving the condition of those troops.

24. "Outrageous Assault," *Savannah Tribune*, May 18, 1895.

25. "Soldiers vs. Citizens," *Atlanta Constitution*, May 17, 1895; "A Light Punishment," *Savannah Tribune*, July 6, 1895.

26. "Arrested the Captain," *Macon (GA) Telegraph*, July 1, 1895.

27. "Done, Yet Just Begun," *Richmond Dispatch*, April 6, 1887; "A Happy Day," *Richmond Daily Times*, April 4, 1887.

28. "In Honor of Lee," *Richmond Daily Times*, October 28, 1887.

29. "Decoration Day," *San Antonio Daily Light*, May 30, 1887.

30. "Decoration Day," *Galveston Daily News*, May 31, 1887.

31. Donald R. Shaffer, *After the Glory: The Struggles of Black Civil War Veterans* (Lawrence: University Press of Kansas, 2004), 59. For more information on the activities of the GAR, see Nina Silber, *The Romance of Reunion: Northerners and the South, 1865–1900* (Chapel Hill: University of North Carolina Press, 1993); and Stuart McConnell, *Glorious Contentment: The Grand Army of the Republic, 1865–1900* (Chapel Hill: University of North Carolina Press, 1992).

32. "Local News," *Daily State Journal* (Richmond, VA), April 18, 1871; "National Memorial Day," ibid., May 30, 1872.

33. "National Cemetery," *Richmond Dispatch,* May 31, 1888. There is no mention of any participation by the GAR at the national cemetery event. Several observances were held by the white citizens of Richmond at Hollywood Cemetery and on the Seven Pines battlefield.

34. Louis M. Pleasant to Gov. McDaniel, May 18, 1883, RCB-41414, RG 22, GAM.

35. John Lark to Gov. Gordon, May 7, 1888, RCB-41395, RG 22, GAM.

36. Adj. Gen. Kell to Lark, Cummings, May 14, 1892; Adj. Gen. Kell to Walker, May 23, 1892, VOL1-1721, RG 22, GAM.

37. "Military Excursion," *Atlanta Constitution,* May 20, 1888; "Things about Town," ibid., May 24, 1888.

38. "The E. S. Jones Post," *Atlanta Constitution,* May 18, 1889; "At Andersonville," ibid., May 31, 1889.

39. "On to Andersonville," *Atlanta Constitution,* May 24, 1895.

40. "Decoration Day," *Macon (GA) Telegraph,* May 24, 1895.

41. "Another Riot at Andersonville," *Atlanta Constitution,* May 31, 1898.

42. "The Gates Open," *Macon (GA) Telegraph,* September 19, 1895.

43. "The Colored Military," *Augusta (GA) Chronicle,* May 5, 1878. The committee consisted of ten "influential colored men of Augusta," including Johnson (the principal of the First Ward school), Judson W. Lyons (a lawyer), James S. Harper (a mail agent), Isaac W. White (a letter carrier), and Richard L. Newsome (a cabinet maker). Two others appear to have been Peter Johnson and Robert Battey, both blacksmiths. Polk, *Polk's Augusta City Directory 1888, 1889,* and *1891;* Walter Howard, comp. *Howard's Directory of Augusta, Summerville, and Turpin Hill, Georgia, and Hamburg, S.C., 1892–93* (Augusta: Chronicle Job Printing, 1892). Battey was listed in the city directories as Robert R. and Johnson as Peter F., but the *Chronicle's* article listed them as R. T. Battey and F. P. Johnson. The other three members of the committee, C. L. Gardner, W. H. Herschal, and C. C. Singleton, were not listed in any of the city directories from 1888 to 1893.

44. "The Prize for the Colored Troops," *Savannah Morning News,* May 22, 1878. This article identified "Theus' jewelry store" as the location where the sword was displayed, but no such store was listed in the 1886 city directory, though it did list an establishment operated by Thomas N. Theus with S. P. Hamilton, which was registered as a watch, clock, and jewelry business. See Sholes, *Sholes' Directory of the City of Savannah, 1886,* 80, 93, 308. "E." in Anderson's name is a typographical error, and the *Morning News* should have printed "C. W. Anderson" for Col. Clifford W. Anderson, 1st Volunteer Regiment of Georgia. The other two mentioned were Capt. James O. Clarke, Clarke Light Infantry, and Capt. George L. Mason, Macon Guards. Herbert, *Complete Roster,* n.p.

45. "The Colored Military," *Savannah Morning News,* May 27, 1878.

46. "A Grand Day among the Colored People," *Savannah Morning News,* May 28, 1878.

47. Ibid.

48. "The Colored Military," *Savannah Morning News,* October 21, 1878.

49. "At the Park," *Atlanta Constitution,* October 27, 1878. The newspaper further stated, "the contest was creditable to them all," considering there were "limited op-

portunities for attaining skill in military evolutions are considered." The Douglass Light Infantry "was by long odds the best drilled of the three." See also "By Telegraph," *Savannah Morning News,* October 28, 1878.

50. "The Colored Parade," *Atlanta Constitution,* July 11, 1879; "The Prize Drill," ibid., July 15, 1879. Hicks, winner of a gold medal, had also won the year before at the North Georgia Stock and Fair.

51. "Colored Military Encampment," *Galveston Daily News,* June 12, 1881; "Stray Notes," ibid., June 24, 1881. The chairman of the planning committee, P. H. Henderson, received his commission as lieutenant colonel of the regiment on June 26, 1881, immediately following this event.

52. "Off to Columbus," *Atlanta Constitution,* August 15, 1882.

53. "Colored Troops," *Ohio State Journal* (Columbus), August 16, 1882.

54. "The Prize Drill," *Atlanta Constitution,* June 6, 1883. Governor McDaniel reviewed the city's companies—the Fulton Guards, Governor's Volunteers, Georgia Cadets, and Atlanta Light Infantry—along with the Rome Star Guards and the Columbus Volunteers. Captain Hill's Fulton Guards won the competition with a score of 92 out of 100, followed closely by Captain McHenry's company, which scored 90.

55. "To-day's Telegraphic News—The National Drill," *Alexandria (VA) Gazette,* April 6, 1887; "The National Drill," *Atlanta Constitution,* April 6, 1887. Two of those three "colored" companies were from Virginia—the State Guard and Attucks Guard, both from Richmond. See also Roger Dryden Cunningham, "Breaking the Color Line: The Virginia Militia at the National Drill, 1887," *Virginia Cavalcade* 49, no. 4 (2000): 178–87.

56. "The National Drill," *Atlanta Constitution,* March 16, 1887; "The Nigger in Line," ibid., April 3, 1887.

57. "Soldiers of Camp Washington," *Washington Evening Star,* May 21, 1887.

58. "The Coming Great National Drill," *Washington Evening Star,* May 21, 1887.

59. "The National Drill," *Alexandria (VA) Gazette,* May 31, 1887.

60. "The National Drill," *Washington Bee,* June 4, 1887.

61. "Washington Gossip," *National Tribune* (Washington, DC), June 2, 1887.

62. "The National Drill, *Washington Bee,* June 4, 1887.

63. The Belknap Rifles and San Antonio Rifles placed third and fifth, respectively, in the competition and took home a combined total of two thousand dollars in prize money. "The National Drill," *Alexandria (VA) Gazette,* May 31, 1887; Bentley to Gov. Gordon, April 16, 1887, RCB-41395, RG 22, GAM.

64. "The Nigger in Line," *Atlanta Constitution,* April 3, 1887.

65. William Fitzhugh Brundage, *The Southern Past: A Clash of Race and Memory* (Cambridge, MA: Harvard University Press, 2008), 83.

66. "The Colored Encampment," *Austin Daily Statesman,* August 25, 1892. The article recorded, "the following sponsors are in attendance on the camp and are the recipients of many attentions from the wearers of the brass buttons: Miss Lily Downs of Seguin, sponsor for the Ireland Rifles. Miss Martha McKinley of Austin, sponsor for the Capital City Guard. Miss Mary Howard of San Antonio, sponsor for the Excelsior Guard."

67. "The Colored Encampment," *Austin Daily Statesman,* August 27, 1892. John Franklin McKinley (1859–1918), born and educated in Tennessee, resided in Nashville

after completing his medical training at Meharry College. Moving later to Austin, McKinley met and married the daughter of arguably the state's most recognized African American Republican, Norris Wright Cuney. McKinley later moved again, this time to Chicago, where he lectured "on diseases eye, ear, nose and throat in Walden University" and worked as a "laryngologist and rhinologist" at Lakeside and Provident Hospitals. Walter R. McDonough, comp., *1905 Chicago Medical Directory* (Chicago: Chicago Medical Society, 1905), 208–9; *Directory of Deceased American Physicians, 1804–1929*, 2 vols. (Chicago: American Medical Association, 1993), 2:1042.

68. "Movement in Behalf of the Attuck's [*sic*] Guard," *Daily State Journal* (Richmond, VA), October 11, 1871.

69. "Local Matters—Flag Presentation," *Daily State Journal* (Richmond, VA), April 9, 1872. John Mercer Langston (1829–97), born in Virginia, was the son of a white Revolutionary War veteran and a free woman of mixed race; he was orphaned at age four. Moving to Ohio, he later graduated from Oberlin College and took an interest in law. Unable to gain entrance to law school because of his race, Langston read law and was admitted to the bar in 1854. He became a prominent attorney, bought vast tracts of property in Oberlin, and joined Frederick Douglass in the abolition movement, often traveling with him throughout the North and serving as president of the Ohio Anti-Slavery Society. During the Civil War, he assisted hundreds of men into the US Colored Troops. His postwar activities included president of the National Equal Rights League, inspector general of the Freedmen's Bureau, first dean and founder of the law school at Howard University, US minister to Haiti, and first president of the Virginia Normal and Collegiate Institute (now Virginia State University); he even assisted Sen. Charles Sumner in drafting the Civil Rights Act of 1875. Langston won a contested election for and served as US representative from Virginia's Fourth District. He published his autobiography in 1894 and died three years later of a stroke. John Mercer Langston, *From the Virginia Plantation to the National Capitol; or, The First and Only Negro Representative in Congress from the Old Dominion* (Hartford, CT: American Publishing, 1894); William Cheek, "A Negro Runs for Congress: John Mercer Langston and the Virginia Campaign of 1888," *Journal of Negro History* 52 (January 1967): 14–34; Luis-Alejandro Dinnella-Borrego, "From the Ashes of the Old Dominion: Accommodation, Immediacy, and Progressive Pragmatism in John Mercer Langston's Virginia," *Virginia Magazine of History and Biography* 117, no. 3 (2009), 215–49.

70. "The Douglass Infantry," *Augusta (GA) Chronicle*, May 10, 1874; "Off for Savannah," ibid., May 19, 1874; "Letter from South Georgia—Colored Jubilee," ibid., May 21, 1874.

71. "The Douglass Infantry," *Augusta (GA) Chronicle*, May 13, 1874 (emphasis added).

72. "A Handsome Flag," *Augusta (GA) Chronicle*, May 6, 1874.

73. "The Douglass Infantry," *Augusta (GA) Chronicle*, May 13, 1874 (emphasis added).

74. Ibid. (emphasis added). The flag cost $200, and the money was raised in three evenings under the supervision of Mrs. Lexius Henson. The Hensons, an African American family, operated a "first class restaurant" on Ellis Street in Augusta featuring "wine, liquors, cigars, etc." Arthur Eugene Sholes, comp., *Sholes' Directory of the City of Augusta, 1883* (Augusta: A. E. Sholes, 1883), 96. Mr. Henson was also considered one of the "Augusta black intellectuals" on par with Augustus R. Johnson and Richard R.

Wright, who later founded Savannah State College. Mary Magdalene Marshall, "'Tell Them, We're Rising!': Black Intellectuals and Lucy Craft Laney in Post–Civil War Augusta, Georgia" (Ph.D. diss., Drew University, 1998), 1; "Douglass Infantry," *Augusta (GA) Chronicle,* May 10, 1874. See also Henry Smith Williams, ed., *The Historians' History of the World,* 25 vols. (London: Hooper & Jackson, 1908), 11:398; and Alicia Lefanu, *Henry the Fourth of France,* 4 vols. (London: A. K. Newman, 1826), 2:148.

75. "Anniversary Celebration," *Savannah Tribune,* July 29, 1876.

76. "The Union Lincoln Guards—Flag Presentation," *Savannah Tribune,* August 5, 1876.

77. Georgiana Kelly (c.1819–86), a native of Georgia, was a free person of color and either the sister or wife of Jeremiah Kelly, a wheelwright, who was also free. By 1870, she had accumulated $3,000 in real estate and $150 in personal property and later worked as a teacher. Kelly died on February 5, 1886, at the reported age of sixty-seven from gangrene of her foot. "Chatham County, Georgia," Ninth Census, 1870; Register of Free Persons of Color for the Year 1863 under the New Code, City of Savannah, Research Library and Municipal Archives, Savannah, GA, 6–7; Vital Statistics Registers, 1803–1966, City of Savannah Health Department, Savannah, GA.

78. "The Colored Contingent," *Atlanta Constitution,* February 22, 1889; "On Washington's Birthday—How It Was Celebrated," ibid., February 23, 1889. Emma Brown married Robert Steele on April 5, 1872, in Atlanta. Steele was referred to as the "Prince of Barbers" and maintained a patronage of white customers consisting "of the best of that race in this city," according to Rev. Edward Randolph Carter, who also characterized him as "a Christian gentleman" who gave generously toward the black community. Steele was a member of the Masonic lodge and Atlanta's Afro-American Historical Society, also serving as a trustee, with Lieutenant Colonel Crumbly, on the board of the Carrie Steele Logan Orphanage, named for and operated by his mother. Carter, *Black Side,* 187–89.

Joseph Simeon Flipper (1859–1944), born into slavery as the son of Festus and Isabella Flipper, began his formal education at age eight, completed studies at Atlanta University, and taught school for many years until obtaining a license to preach in 1879. Flipper organized the Thomasville Independents, Georgia State Militia. By 1882, he was a trustee at Morris Brown College. Assigned to Big Bethel AME Church in 1886, he served for four years, transferred to another church, and then returned to Morris Brown as a dean, becoming president of the institution in 1904. Flipper became a bishop in 1908; his many other accomplishments in education and the ministry are too numerous to mention. "Joseph Simeon Flipper," *Journal of Negro History* 30, no. 1 (January 1945), 109–11. For further reading on Henry Flipper, see Henry Ossian Flipper, *The Colored Cadet at West Point: Autobiography of Lieut. Henry Ossian Flipper, USA* (New York: Homer Lee, 1878); Theodore D. Harris, ed., *The Western Memoirs of Henry O. Flipper, 1878–1916* (El Paso: Texas Western College Press, 1963); and Charles M. Robinson III, *The Fall of a Black Army Officer: Racism and the Myth of Henry O. Flipper* (Norman: University of Oklahoma Press, 2008).

79. *Adjutant General of Virginia, 1879,* 29–30.

80. *Adjutant and Inspector-General of Georgia, 1889,* 52.

81. *Adjutant and Inspector-General of Georgia, 1890,* 48–50.

82. John Augustus Hulen (1871–1957), a native of Missouri, moved as a child to Gainesville, Texas. He attended military schools in Virginia and Missouri and worked in the railway business, a career that was often interrupted by military service. Hulen enlisted as a private in his hometown Gainesville Rifles in 1887, was promoted to lieutenant in 1889, and then elevated to captain of a cavalry troop in 1893. He served with this last organization as a brevet lieutenant colonel during the war with Spain. Hulen did not see action until he received a commission as a captain in the 33rd US Volunteers and served in the Philippines, where he was awarded the Silver Star. Upon his return to Texas, Governor Lanham promoted him to brigadier general and appointed him adjutant general, a position he held until 1907. During his life, Hulen served as a delegate at the Democratic National Convention in 1932, was on the board of Texas Technological College (now Texas Tech University), commanded a brigade that patrolled the Texas-Mexico border in 1916, and then took charge of a brigade of the 36th US Division during World War I, earning the Distinguished Service Cross and two Croix de Guerre during the Meuse-Argonne offensive. Finally, while only a ceremonial appointment, Pres. Franklin Roosevelt appointed Hulen regional salvage manager of the War Production Board, a position he held throughout the Second World War. Jimmy M. Skaggs, "Hulen, John Augustus," in Tyler, *New Handbook of Texas,* 3:778–79.

83. *Report of the Adjutant General of Texas for Two Years ending December 31, 1906* (Austin: Von Boeckmann-Hines, 1907), 13–17 (1st quote, 15; 2nd quote, 17; hereafter cited as *Adjutant General of Texas, 1906*). Georgia's rifle team in 1905 placed nineteenth, while Virginia did not compete. At the 1906 National Match, Georgia came in twenty-fourth, and Virginia placed last. All the rifle teams from these three states comprised white troops.

84. "The City News," *Daily State Journal* (Richmond, VA), August 2, 1873.

85. Muster roll, Flipper Guard, Separate Company, Virginia Volunteers, September 27, 1886, RG 46, LVA (emphasis added).

86. "Target Practice," *Richmond Planet,* April 4, 1896.

87. "Anniversary Parade,—Prize Drill, ect. [sic]," *Savannah Tribune,* May 13, 1876. The historic neighborhoods of Eastville, Collinsville, and the Meadows are now known as the Benjamin Van Clark neighborhood and is bordered by Anderson, Bee, Wheaton, and Harmon Streets. See Benjamin Van Clark Neighborhood Documentation Project, Record Series 6112-003, City of Savannah Research Library and Municipal Archives, Savannah, GA.

88. Shultz Hill, named for Henry Shultz, who founded a town along the river in 1821, is located northwest of the original city of Hamburg. In July 1876, the city gained notoriety as the site of racial violence that culminated in the murder of several African American residents and the wanton destruction of their property. While there is evidence supporting the participation, or at least complacency, of Augusta's white militia troops, there is none supporting the involvement of the city's African American companies.

89. "The Douglass Infantry," *Augusta (GA) Chronicle,* May 23, 1876. The year before, both the Lincoln Guards and the Forest City Light Infantry of Savannah celebrated the passage of the Fifteenth Amendment with African American militia organizations from South Carolina. That celebration, according to an eyewitness report, "passed off

... with the utmost good order and decorum," and "the colored volunteers behaved well in every respect." "The Colored Troops," ibid., May 21, 1875.

90. Beard to Gov. Colquitt, May 10, 1877, DOC2-894, RG 22, GAM; "Cutting in Carolina," *Augusta (GA) Chronicle,* May 21, 1885. This news article described the actions of an African American citizen from Hamburg who seriously injured two members of the Lincoln Guards with a knife. One of the individuals at the center of this was a "Doc" Adams, who had previously attempted to establish a militia company in Augusta. See G. A. Snead to Gov. Smith, May 25, 1872; D. L. Adams to Gov. Smith, May 29, 1872; DOC-2810, RG 22, GAM; and Foley, "To Make Him Feel His Manhood," 185–86.

91. Foley, "To Make Him Feel His Manhood," 185.

92. "The Colored People," *Atlanta Constitution,* August 8, 1880.

93. *Adjutant General of Georgia, 1893,* 103–9.

Chapter 8

1. "New Armory," *Richmond Planet,* October 19, 1895. On lynching in Georgia, *Lynching in the New South: Georgia and Virginia, 1880–1930* (Urbana: University of Illinois Press, 1993); and William D. Carrigan, *The Making of a Lynching Culture: Violence and Vigilantism in Central Texas, 1836–1916* (Urbana: University of Illinois Press, 2006).

2. "Off to See the Majah," *Atlanta Constitution,* March 2, 1897; "Forward! March!," *Macon (GA) Telegraph,* March 1, 1897. The Savannah City Council approved the sale of property to the 1st Battalion for one dollar but did not approve any additional funding to erect the structure.

3. "The Colored Troops," *Savannah Tribune,* April 23, 1898. The title of this section borrows from "The Manhood of the Negro," *Baptist Home Mission Monthly* 20, no. 9 (September 1898): 336. The article advocated the importance of African American officer appointments.

4. "Negro Soldiers Want to Fight," *Atlanta Constitution,* May 25, 1898. Here, Crumbly was demonstrating the same racial thinking that later gave rise to the creation of "immune" regiments of black US Volunteers for duty in Cuba.

5. Ann Field Alexander, "'No Officers, No Fight!': Sixth Virginia Volunteers in the Spanish-American War," *Virginia Cavalcade* 47, no. 4 (Autumn 1998): 178–91 (quote, 180).

6. "Capt. Ellis Kick," *San Antonio Light,* May 1, 1898.

7. "Mabry's Reply," *San Antonio Light,* May 5, 1898.

8. "Negroes Anxious to Fight," *Atlanta Constitution,* April 28, 1898. John Rutter Brooke (1838–1926) was born in Pennsylvania and entered the army as a captain in the 4th Pennsylvania Infantry Regiment during the Civil War. He was later promoted to colonel of the 53rd Pennsylvania and took part in the Peninsula Campaign. Participating in the Battles of Sharpsburg, Fredericksburg, Chancellorsville, and Gettysburg, where he was wounded in the Wheat Field fighting. Returning to duty, Brooke was critically wounded at Cold Harbor and thereafter was unfit for field duty. After the war, he commanded the 37th US Infantry Regiment. In 1897, Brooke was a major general, commanding the camp at Chickamauga. He fought under Nelson Miles in the Puerto Rico Campaign and was the island's first governor before being named governor of

Cuba following the evacuation of Spanish forces from that island. See "John Rutter Brooke," www.arlingtoncemetery.net/jrbrook.htm. (accessed January 5, 2016).

9. "Negroes Anxious to Fight," *Atlanta Constitution*, April 28, 1898.

10. Crumbly to Secretary of War, May 18, 1898, RG 94, NARA; Simmons to Atkinson, April 29, 1898, RCB-41473, RG 22, GAM. Crumbly had written President McKinley three days after the declaration of war and offered to raise a regiment, providing ten letters of recommendation from, among others, the mayor of Atlanta, the state's official government printer, four prominent Atlanta businessmen, and his previous commanding officer from the 10th US Cavalry Regiment.

11. "Mutiny in the Sixth," *Richmond Dispatch*, November 3, 1898; "Sixth Virginia" *People's Defender*, reprinted in "The Silence Broken," *Richmond Planet*, November 19, 1898 (emphasis added). For further reading concerning the experiences of the 6th Virginia Volunteers, see Willard Gatewood Jr., "Virginia's Negro Regiment in the Spanish-American War: The Sixth Virginia Volunteers," *Virginia Magazine of History and Biography* 80, no. 2 (April 1972), 193–209; Gatewood, *"Smoked Yankees" and the Struggle for Empire: Letters from Negro Soldiers* (Fayetteville: University of Arkansas Press, 1987); Ann Field Alexander, *Race Man: The Rise and Fall of the "Fighting Editor" John Mitchell Jr.* (Charlottesville: University of Virginia Press, 2002); and Alexander, "No Officers, No Fight." Alexander points out that at least one African American soldier, Zachary Fields, whose company commander, Capt. E. W. Gould, had been slated for reexamination, wrote his wife that he was glad to get white officers.

12. "Georgia Negroes Now Have a Chance to Volunteer," *Atlanta Constitution*, May 24, 1898.

13. Alger to Garrett Hobart, President of the US Senate, to Thomas Reed, Speaker of the House, July 2, 1898, RG 94, NARA.

14. "Manhood of the Negro," 336.

15. Lark to Lyons, July 18, 1898, RG 94, NARA; Johnson to Lyons, July 14, 1898, ibid.; Golphin to Lyons, July 14, 1898, ibid.

16. Lyons to the President of the United States, June 28, 1898, RG 94, NARA. For the chaplain's experiences in Cuba, see Floyd, *Life of Charles T. Walker*, 83–87. See also Cunningham, "'A Lot of Fine, Sturdy Black Warriors,'" 345–67. Two of Galveston's former militia volunteer officers also obtained positions in the 9th US Volunteers— Burnett Mapson, company first sergeant, and Wallace Seals, second lieutenant. Lyons also recommended William Pledger for paymaster. A month later, the president's secretary reminded McKinley of Lyons's earlier letter concerning Pledger, who Lyons characterized as "a worthy and useful man." J. A. Porter, Secretary to the President, to the President, July 29, 1898, RG 94, NARA. See also William Hilary Coston, *The Spanish-American War Volunteer: Ninth United States Volunteer Infantry Roster, and Muster, Biographies, Cuban Sketches* (Middletown, PA., 1899).

17. Service records, Crumbly to Lyons, June 27, 1897, RG 94, NARA. For further reading on Georgia's contribution to the 10th US Volunteers, see Russell K. Brown, "A Flag for the Tenth Immunes," in Glasrud, *Brothers to the Buffalo Soldiers*, 209–21. Brown's account again supports the contention of the public display of masculinity through the presentation ceremony of the company flag.

18. Ruffin to Lyons, November 29, 1898, RG 94, NARA. Emmitt F. Ruffin served as a captain in the Confederate Signal Corps in the military district encompassing South Carolina to Georgia. According to his lengthy four-page letter to Lyons, he also had accompanied William Walker into Nicaragua in 1855–56. Following Lee's surrender, Ruffin traveled to Europe and fought with Austrian forces during the Austro-Prussian War (1866) before moving once again, this time to South America, where he joined the Peruvian navy and participated in the first two years of the War of the Pacific involving Chile, Peru, and Bolivia.

19. There is a series of letters between Deveaux and Acting Adj. Gen. James B. Erwin from April to July 1898 coordinating the delivery of newer .45-caliber rifles and shipment details of the battalion's old .50-caliber Springfields. See RCB-41414, RG 22, GAM.

20. The minutes of Virginia's Military Board fail to record any discussion of the elimination of the African American volunteers, nor has any written record been found in Adjutant General Tyler's papers. The minutes of Richmond's public school board record that the city council approved a resolution to convert the 1st Battalion Armory into a school. See Minutes of Military Board of the State of Virginia, RG 46, LVA; J. Hoge Tyler Family Collection, 1802–1956, Carol M. Newman Library, Virginia Polytechnic Institute and State University, Blacksburg; and Thirtieth Annual Report of the Superintendent of the Public School of the City of Richmond, Va., for the Scholastic Year Ending July 31, 1899, in *School Reports, City of Richmond, 1899–1903* (Richmond: Ware & Duke, Printers, 1900), 10.

21. General Order No. 2, February 23, 1899, RCB-41418, RG 22, GAM.

22. Deveaux to Kell, September 15, 1899, RCB-41418, RG 22, GAM (1st quote); *Adjutant General of Georgia, 1899–1900*, 13 (2nd quote). The "Act to Provide for the Reorganization, Discipline, Enlistment and Protection of the Military Forces of this State," approved by the general assembly on December 20, 1899, reflected the results of the inspector general's recommendations by limiting African American participation to seven infantry companies and one artillery battery. *Acts and Resolutions of the General Assembly of the State of Georgia for 1899* (Atlanta: Geo. Harrison, State Printer, 1900), 60.

23. Cann to Kell (and Kell endorsement), March 16, 1899, RCB-41418, RG 22, GAM.

24. Carter to Adjutant General, January 26, 1901, RCB-37024, RG 22, GAM; Carter to Adjutant General, November 3, 1901, ibid.; Mosely to Adjutant General, September 10, 1901, ibid.; "Enlistment of Colquitt Blues at Savannah Ga., 1900," NEWS-253, ibid.; Circular No. 5, RCB-45966, ibid.; W. J. Pinkney to Adjutant General, September 1, 1900, RCB-41418, ibid.

25. Acting Adjutant General to Deveaux, January 15, 1900, RCB-41418, RG 22, GAM; Deveaux to Obear, April 2, 1900, OVER-561, ibid.; *Acts and Resolutions of the General Assembly of the State of Georgia 1901* (Atlanta: Franklin Printing, 1901), 84.

26. *Adjutant General of Georgia, 1899–1900*, 13.

27. Ibid., 127.

28. *Report of the Adjutant-General of the State of Georgia from December 1st, 1901, to September 30th, 1902* (Atlanta: Geo. W. Harrison, State Printer, 1902), 30.

29. The Fulton Guards of Atlanta, and the Chatham Light Infantry and the Georgia Artillery of Savannah were recommended for disbandment since, according to the inspector general, they had failed to improve during their ten-day probationary period. The Military Board dissolved the Savannah companies on April 18, followed by the Guards on May 12, 1904. "State Gossip Caught in Capitol Corridors," *Atlanta Constitution*, April 1, 1904; "Gossip at the Capitol," ibid., April 20, 1904; "Ten Companies on Probation," ibid., April 29, 1904; "Better Militia Service Recommended, More Work for Obear," ibid., January 19, 1905.

30. War Department Military Secretary to Adjutant General of Georgia, September 16, 1905, RCB-15521, RG 22, GAM.

31. Stovall to Coney. August 7, 1905, RCB-15620, RG 22, GAM. The six representatives voting against this measure included "Representative Rogers of McIntosh, the colored member." "Would Abolish Negro Troops," *Atlanta Constitution*, August 15, 1905. Pleasant Alexander Stovall (1857–1935) was born at Augusta and educated at the University of Georgia. He began a career in the newspaper business with the *Augusta Chronicle* before moving in 1891 to Savannah, where he founded and served as editor of the *Savannah Press* until 1931. Serving on the military staff of Governors Northen and Atkinson, Stovall was appointed to the Board of Trustees of the University of Georgia by Governor Gordon. In 1892, he was elected chairman of the state Democratic Party. According to his obituary, Stovall was a close friend of Woodrow Wilson, who as president appointed him ambassador to Switzerland in 1913, where he remained until 1919. Author of two books, Stovall is buried at Augusta, Georgia. Candler and Evans, *Georgia*, 3:388–89; "Pleasant Alexander Stovall," Find-a-Grave, www.findagrave.com (accessed January 20, 2016).

32. Scott to Coney, March 7, 1905, RCB-15620, RG 22, GAM.

33. "Would Abolish Negro Troops," *Atlanta Constitution*, August 15, 1905. Joseph Hill Hall (1852–1922) was the son of Georgia Supreme Court justice Samuel Hall. The younger Hall was born in Crawford, Georgia; educated at the University of Georgia; and admitted to the bar in 1874. Relocating to Macon, he practiced law prior to his successful election as state representative for Bibb County in 1898. Candler and Evans, *Georgia*, 2:184–85.

34. "Would Abolish Negro Troops."

35. Stovall to Coney, August 15, 1905, RCB-15620, RG 22, GAM.

36. Mann to Coney, July 13, 1905, RCB-15620, RG 22, GAM. James Tift Mann (1880–1926) held the prestigious position of chairman of House Military Affairs Committee at the young age of twenty-five. Born at Albany, Georgia, he received his education at the University of the South at Sewanee, Tennessee, and studied law at the University of Georgia. Mann joined the militia as a private in 1900 and two years later was commanding his company. He is credited with securing a $100,000 appropriation bill and the disbandment of the African American troops. By 1906, Mann was a lieutenant colonel and serving as the judge advocate general of the Georgia National Guard. Candler and Evans, *Georgia*, 2:524–25.

37. *Adjutant General of Texas, 1906*, 10.

38. Untitled article, *Savannah Tribune*, August 26, 1905.

39. Matthew Frye Jacobson, *Whiteness of a Different Color: European Immigrants and the Alchemy of Race* (Cambridge, MA: Harvard University Press, 1998), 6. Jacobson argued that race remained an organizer of power, a mode of perception of differences, and in instigator of the struggles associated with those. See also David R. Roediger, *Working towards Whiteness: How America's Immigrants became White—The Strange Journey from Ellis Island to the Suburbs* (New York: Basic Books, 2005); and Alexander Saxton, *The Rise and Fall of the White Republic: Class Politics and Mass Culture in Nine-teenth-Century America* (London: Verso, 1990).

40. Untitled article, *Savannah Tribune*, August 26, 1905.

BIBLIOGRAPHY

Primary Sources

ARCHIVES

Archives and Information Division, Texas State
Library and Archives Commission, Austin

Comptroller's Office, Confederate Pension Applications Records, 1899–1979
Record Group 401, Records of the Texas Adjutant General's Department

Auburn Avenue Research Library on African American Culture and History, Atlanta

Edward Randolph Carter and Andrew Jackson Lewis Collection
Selena Sloan Butler Collection

Carol M. Newman Library, Virginia Polytechnic
Institute and State University, Blacksburg

J. Hoge Tyler Family Collection, 1802–1956

Chicago History Museum, Research Center, Chicago

Christopher C. Wimbish [Jr.] Papers, 1870–1962

Columbus Public Library, Columbus, OH

African American Collection

Earl Gregg Swenn Library, College of William & Mary, Williamsburg, VA

Fitzhugh Lee Papers, 1866–87

Georgia Archives, Morrow

Henry Dickerson McDaniel Family and Business Papers, 1822–1947
William J. Northen Papers, 1865–1929
Record Group 1, Governor Records, 1877–1902
Record Group 2, Secretary of State Records, Elections Division, 1860–2012
Record Group 22, Defense Records, Adjutant General, 1861–1975
Record Group 34, Revenue Records, Property Tax Unit, 1793–2000
Record Group 37, Legislative Records, House and Senate, 1800–2006
Record Group 58, Confederate Pension Applications, 1879–1960

Georgia Historical Society, Savannah

Charles Hart Olmstead Papers, 1861–1921
Savannah Volunteer Guard Manuscript Collection

James Hugo Johnston Memorial Library, Virginia State University, Petersburg
Major William Henry Johnson Papers, 1884–1935

Kenan Research Center, Atlanta History Center, Atlanta
Atlanta History Photograph Collection

Library of Virginia, Richmond
Executive Papers of Governor Frederick W. M. Holliday, 1878–81
Executive Papers of Governor William E. Cameron, 1882–85
Executive Papers of Governor Fitzhugh Lee, 1885–89
Executive Papers of Governor Philip W. McKinney, 1889–93
Executive Papers of Governor Charles T. O'Ferrall, 1894–97
Executive Papers of Governor James Hoge Tyler, 1860–1901
Executive Papers of Governor Andrew Jackson Montague, 1854–1938
Governor Gilbert Carlton Walker Executive Papers, 1869–73
James Lawton Kemper Papers, 1804–1951
Record Group 46, Office of the Adjutant General, Department of Military Affairs,
    State Records Collection

Louis Round Wilson Library, University of North Carolina, Chapel Hill
Charles H. Olmstead Papers, 1837–1926
William Starr Basinger Papers, 1835–1932

Municipal Archives & Records, City of San Antonio, TX
Birth and Death Records

National Archives and Records Administration, Washington, DC
Record Group 15, Records of the Veterans Administration, 1867–1935
Record Group 29, Records of the Bureau of the Census, 1790–2007
Record Group 36, Records of the United States Customs Service, 1745–1997
Record Group 45, Naval Records Collection of the Office of Naval Records and
    Library, 1861–1942
Record Group 59, General Records of the Department of State, 1789–1976
Record Group 94, Records of the Adjutant General's Office, 1780s–1917
Record Group 105, Records of the Bureau of Refugees, Freedmen, and Abandoned
    Lands, 1861–79
Record Group 109, War Department Collection of Confederate Records, 1825–1900

Research Library and Municipal Archives, Savannah, GA
Records of Health Department, Vital Statistics Registers, 1803–1966
Registers of Free Persons of Color, 1817–64
W. W. Law Photograph Collection, 1868–2002

Richard B. Russell Library for Political Research and Studies, University of Georgia, Athens

Joseph M. Terrell Papers, 1861–1912
William J. Northen Family Papers, 1790–1959

GOVERNMENT PUBLICATIONS

United States

Botkin, Benjamin A., ed. *Slave Narratives: A Folk History of Slavery in the United States from Interviews with Former Slaves.* 17 vols. Washington, DC: GPO, 1941.

Department of Commerce, Bureau of Census. *Negro Population in the United States, 1790–1915.* Washington, DC: GPO, 1918.

Heitman, Francis Bernard. *Historical Register and Dictionary of the United States Army.* 2 vols. Washington, DC: GPO, 1903.

Official Army Register for 1901. Washington, DC: GPO, 1900.

Official Army Register for 1921. Washington, DC: GPO, 1922.

Official Register of Officers of Volunteers in the Service of the United States. Washington, DC: GPO, 1900.

The Organized Militia of the United States in 1895. Washington, DC: GPO, 1896.

The Organized Militia of the United States—Statement of the Condition and Efficiency for Service of the Organized Militia from Regular Annual Reports and Other Sources Covering the Year 1897. Washington DC: GPO, 1898.

Registers of Enlistments in the United States Army, 1798–1914. Vol. 68. Washington, DC: GPO, 1956.

Register of Officers and Agents, Civil, Military, and Naval, in the Service of the United States. Washington, DC: GPO, 1872.

Register of Officers and Agents, Civil, Military, and Naval, in the Service of the United States. Washington, DC: GPO, 1877.

Register of Officers and Agents, Civil, Military, and Naval, in the Service of the United States. Washington, DC: GPO, 1878.

Register of Officers and Agents, Civil, Military, and Naval, in the Service of the United States. Washington, DC: GPO, 1881.

Register of Officers and Agents, Civil, Military, and Naval, in the Service of the United States. Washington, DC: GPO, 1887.

Register of Officers and Agents, Civil, Military, and Naval, in the Service of the United States. Washington, DC: GPO, 1891.

Testimony Taken by the Joint Select Committee to Inquire into the Condition of Affairs in the Late Insurrectionary States: Georgia. 2 vols. Washington, DC: GPO, 1872.

US Bureau of the Census. *1890 Special Census of Civil War Union Veterans and Widows.* Washington, DC: GPO, 1890.

———. *Ninth Census of the United States: Population Schedules.* Washington, DC: GPO, 1870.

Georgia

Acts and Resolutions of the General Assembly of the State of Georgia, Passed at Its Session of July and August 1872. Atlanta: W. A. Hemphill & Co., State Printer, 1872.

Acts and Resolutions of the General Assembly of the State of Georgia, Passed at the Regular January Session 1873. Atlanta: W. A. Hemphill & Co., State Printer, 1873.

Acts and Resolutions of the General Assembly of the State of Georgia, 1878–79. Atlanta: James P. Harrison, State Publisher, 1880.

Acts and Resolutions of the General Assembly of the State of Georgia, 1884–85. Atlanta: James P. Harrison, State Publisher, 1885.

Acts and Resolutions of the General Assembly of the State of Georgia, 1892. Atlanta: George W. Harrison, State Publisher, 1892.

Acts and Resolutions of the General Assembly of the State of Georgia, 1899. Atlanta: George W. Harrison, State Publisher, 1900.

Acts and Resolutions of the General Assembly of the State of Georgia, 1900. Atlanta: George W. Harrison, State Publisher, 1900.

Acts and Resolutions of the General Assembly of the State of Georgia 1901. Atlanta: Franklin Printing, 1901.

Clark, Richard H., Thomas R. R. Cobb, and David Irwin, eds. *The Code of the State of Georgia.* Rev. ed. Atlanta: Franklin Steam Printing House, 1868.

Clark, Richard H., Thomas R. R. Cobb, David Irwin, George N. Lester, and Walter B. Hill, eds. *The Code of the State of Georgia.* 2nd ed. Macon: J. W. Burke, 1873.

Clayton, Augustun Smith, comp. *Laws of the State of Georgia, Passed by the Legislature since the Political Year 1800, to the Year 1810, Inclusive.* Augusta, GA: Adams & Duyckinck, 1812.

Incoming Correspondence, Governor James Milton Smith, 1872–1877. Atlanta: Georgia Department of Archives and History, 1973.

Report of the Adjutant and Inspector-General of the State of Georgia for the Year 1889. Atlanta: W. J. Campbell, State Printer, 1890.

Report of the Adjutant and Inspector-General of the State of Georgia for the Year1890. Atlanta: W. J. Campbell, State Printer, 1890.

Report of the Adjutant and Inspector-General of the State of Georgia for the Year 1891. Atlanta: Franklin Printing House, 1892.

Report of the Adjutant and Inspector-General of the State of Georgia for the Year 1892. Atlanta: Franklin Printing House, 1892.

Report of the Adjutant and Inspector-General of the State of Georgia for the Year 1893. Atlanta: Franklin Printing, 1893.

Report of the Adjutant-General of the State of Georgia for the Year 1894. Atlanta: Franklin Printing, 1894.

Report of the Adjutant-General of the State of Georgia for the Year 1895. Atlanta: Franklin Printing, 1896.

Report of the Adjutant General of the State of Georgia for the Year 1896. Atlanta: Franklin Printing, 1897.

Report of the Adjutant General of the State of Georgia from January 1, 1899, to October 17, 1900. Atlanta: Franklin Printing, 1900.

Report of the Adjutant-General of the State of Georgia from December 1st, 1900, to September 30th, 1901. Atlanta: Geo. W. Harrison, State Printer, 1901.

Report of the Adjutant-General of the State of Georgia from December 1st, 1901, to September 30th, 1902. Atlanta: Geo. W. Harrison, State Printer, 1902.

Satterlee, C. B. *Report of Inspection of the Georgia Volunteers and Georgia Volunteers, Colored, from September 25th, 1891, to April 5th, 1892*. Atlanta: Franklin Publishing House, 1893.

Texas

Biennial Report of the Adjutant General of the State of Texas for the Years 1903 and 1904. Austin: Von Boeckmann, Schutze, State Printers, 1904.

Gammel, Hans Peter Mareus Neilsen. *The Laws of Texas, 1827–1897*. 10 vols. Austin: Gammel Book, 1898.

Report of the Adjutant General of the State of Texas, Austin, December 31, 1880. Galveston: New Book and Job Office, 1881.

Report of the Adjutant-General of the State of Texas, Austin, February 28, 1882. Galveston: A. H. Belo, 1882.

Report of the Adjutant-General of the State of Texas, December 31, 1882. Austin: E. W. Swindells, State Printer, 1883.

Report of the Adjutant-General of the State of Texas, September, 1884. Austin: E. W. Swindells, State Printer, 1884.

Report of the Adjutant General of the State of Texas, December, 1886. Austin: Triplett & Hutchings, State Printers, 1886.

Report of the Adjutant-General of the State of Texas, December 1888. Austin: State Printing Office, 1889.

Report of the Adjutant General of the State of Texas for 1889–1890. Austin: Henry Hutchings, State Printer, 1890.

Report of the Adjutant General of the State of Texas for 1890–1891. Austin: Henry Hutchings, State Printer, 1892.

Report of the Adjutant General of the State of Texas for 1892. Austin: Ben C. Jones, State Printers, 1893.

Report of the Adjutant General of the State of Texas for 1893–1894. Austin: Ben C. Jones, State Printers, 1895.

Report of the Adjutant General of the State of Texas for 1895–1896. Austin: Ben C. Jones, State Printer, 1897.

Report of the Adjutant General of the State of Texas for 1899–1900. Austin: Von Boeckmann, Schutze, 1900.

Report of the Adjutant General of the State of Texas for 1901–1902. Austin: Von Boeckmann, Schutze, 1902.

Report of the Adjutant General of the State of Texas for 1902–1903. Austin, n.d.

Report of the Adjutant General of the State of Texas for Two Years Ending December 31, 1906. Austin, n.d.

Revised Statutes of Texas. Galveston: A. H. Belo, 1879.

Rules and Regulations for the Government and Discipline of the Texas Volunteer Guard.
Austin, 1895.

Virginia

Acts and Joint Resolutions Passed by the General Assembly of the State of Virginia at Its Session of 1870–71. Richmond: C. A. Schaffter, Superintendent of Public Printing, 1871.

Annual Report of the Adjutant General of the Commonwealth of Virginia for the Year 1873. Richmond: R. F. Walker, Superintendent of Public Printing, 1873.

Annual Report of the Adjutant General of the Commonwealth of Virginia for the Year 1876. Richmond: R. F. Walker, Superintendent of Public Printing, 1876.

Annual Report of the Adjutant-General of the State of Virginia for the Year Ending November 1, 1879. Richmond: R. L. Frayser, Superintendent of Public Printing, 1879.

Annual Report of the Adjutant-General of the State of Virginia for the Year 1879–80. Richmond: R. F. Walker, Superintendent of Public Printing, 1880.

Report of the Adjutant-General of the State of Virginia for the Years 1884 and 1885. Richmond: Rush U. Derr, Superintendent of Public Printing, 1885.

Report of the Adjutant-General of the State of Virginia for the Year 1886. Richmond: A. R. Micou, Superintendent of Public Printing, 1887.

Report of the Adjutant-General of the State of Virginia for the Year 1887. Richmond: A. R. Micou, Superintendent of Public Printing, 1887.

Report of the Adjutant-General of the State of Virginia for the Year 1888. Richmond: J. H. O'Bannon, Superintendent of Public Printing, 1888.

Report of the Adjutant-General of the State of Virginia for the Year 1894. Richmond: J. H. O'Bannon, Superintendent of Public Printing, 1894.

Report of the Adjutant-General of the State of Virginia for the Year 1896. Richmond: J. H. O'Bannon, Superintendent of Public Printing, 1896.

BOOKS

Adams, Cyrus Field. *The Republican Party and the Afro-American.* N.p., 1908.
American Medical Directory. Chicago: American Medical Association, 1921.
Appletons' Annual Cyclopædia and Register of Important Events of the Year 1879. 19 vols. New York: D. Appleton, 1885.
Bacote, Samuel William, ed. *Who's Who among Colored Baptists of the United States.* Kansas City, MO: Franklin Hudson, 1913.
Brock, Robert A., and Virgil A. Lewis. *Virginia and Virginians.* 2 vols. Richmond: H. H. Hardesty, 1888.
Butt, Israel LaFayette. *History of African Methodism in Virginia; or, Four Decades in the Old Dominion.* Hampton, VA: Hampton Institute Press, 1908.
Caldwell, Arthur Bunyan. *History of the American Negro, Georgia Edition.* 2 vols. Atlanta: A. B. Caldwell, 1920.
———. *History of the American Negro, Virginia Edition.* Atlanta: A. B. Caldwell, 1921.
Candler, Allen D., and Clement A. Evans, eds. *Georgia: Comprising Sketches of Counties, Towns, Events, Institutions, and Persons, Arranged in Cyclopedic Form.* 3 vols. Atlanta: State Historical Association, 1906.

Carter, Edward R. *Biographical Sketches of Our Pulpit*. 1888. Reprint, Chicago:
     Afro-Am, 1969.

———. *The Black Side: A Partial History of the Business, Religious, and Educational
     Side of the Negro in Atlanta, Ga*. Atlanta, 1894.

Coston, William Hilary. *The Spanish-American War Volunteer: Ninth United States
     Volunteer Infantry Roster, and Muster, Biographies, Cuban Sketches*. Middletown, PA,
     1899.

Cullum, George W. *Biographical Register of the Officers and Graduates of the US Military
     Academy at West Point, N.Y.* 3 vols. Cambridge, MA: Riverside, 1891.

Culp, D. W., ed. *Twentieth Century Negro Literature; or, A Cyclopedia of Thought on the
     Vital Topics Relating to the American Negro*. Atlanta: J. L. Nichols, 1902.

Cuney-Hare, Maud. *Norris Wright Cuney: A Tribune of the Black People*. New York:
     Crisis, 1913. Reprint, New York: Simon & Schuster Macmillan, 1995.

Du Bois, William Edward Burghardt. *The Souls of Black Folk*. Chicago: A. C. McClurg,
     1903.

———. *Black Reconstruction in America: An Essay toward a History of the Part Which
     Black Folk Played in the Attempt to Reconstruct Democracy in America, 1860–1880*.
     New York: Russell & Russell, 1935.

Evans, Clement A., ed. *Confederate Military History*. 13 vols. Atlanta: Confederate
     Publishing, 1899.

Fifield, James Clark. *The American Bar: Contemporary Lawyers of the United States
     and Canada*. Minneapolis: James C. Fifield, 1918.

Flipper, Henry Ossian. *The Colored Cadet at West Point: Autobiography of Lieut.
     Henry Ossian Flipper, USA*. New York: Homer Lee, 1878.

Floyd, Silas Xavier. *Life of Charles T. Walker, D.D., "The Black Spurgeon."* Nashville:
     National Baptist Publishing Board, 1902.

Gibbs, Mifflin Wistar. *Shadow and Light: An Autobiography*. N.p., 1902. Reprint,
     New York: Arno, 1968.

Hall, Josie B. *Hall's Moral and Mental Capsule for the Economic and Domestic Life of
     the Negro, as a Solution of the Race Problem*. Dallas: Rev. R. S. Jenkins, 1905.

Harden, William. *A History of Savannah and South Georgia*. 2 vols. Chicago: Lewis,
     1913.

Harris, Harrison L., M.D. *Masonic Text-Book: A Concise Historical Sketch of Masonry
     and the Organization of Masonic Grand Lodges, and Especially of Masonry among
     Colored Men in America*. Petersburg, VA: Masonic Visitor, 1902.

Harris, Nathaniel E., ed. *A Supplement to the Code of Georgia containing the Public Acts
     Passed by the General Assembly since 1873 and the Constitution of 1877*. Macon, GA:
     J. W. Burke, 1878.

Harris, Theodore D., ed. *The Western Memoirs of Henry O. Flipper, 1878–1916*. El Paso:
     Texas Western College Press, 1963.

Heitman, Francis Bernard. *Historical Register of the United States Army from Its Or-
     ganization, September 29, 1789, to September 29, 1889*. Washington, DC: National
     Tribune, 1890.

Herbert, Sidney. *A Complete Roster of the Volunteer Military Organizations of the State of
     Georgia*. Atlanta: Jas. P. Harrison, 1878.

Hopkins, John L., Clifford Anderson, and Joseph Rucker Lamar, eds. *The Code of the State of Georgia Adopted December 15, 1895.* Vol. 1. Atlanta: Foote & Davies, 1896.

Inaugural Souvenir, 1901. Washington, DC: Press of W. F. Roberts, 1901.

Johnson, William H. *History of the Colored Volunteer Infantry of Virginia, 1871–99.* Richmond: Virginia Historical Society, 1923.

Journal of the Common Council from January 14, 1873, to January 13, 1874. Detroit: Daily Post Book & Job Printing, 1874.

Kell, John McIntosh. *Recollections of a Naval Life, including the Cruises of the Confederate States Steamships "Sumter" and "Alabama."* Washington, DC: Neal, 1900.

Kenney, John A. *The Negro in Medicine.* Tuskegee, AL: Tuskegee Institute Press, 1912.

King, Edward. *The Great South.* Hartford, CT: American Publishing, 1875. Reprint, New York: Arno and the *New York Times,* 1969.

Kletzing, Henry F., and W. H. Crogman. *Progress of a Race; or, The Remarkable Advancement of the Afro-American from the Bondage of Slavery, Ignorance and Poverty to the Freedom of Citizenship, Intelligence, Affluence, Honor and Trust.* Atlanta: J. L. Nichols, 1897.

Knight, Lucian Lamar. *A Standard History of Georgia and Georgians.* 2 vols. Chicago: Lewis, 1917.

Lamar, Lucius Q. C., comp. *A Compilation of the Laws of the State of Georgia, Passed by the Legislature since the Year 1810 to the Year 1819, Inclusive.* Augusta, GA: T. S. Hannon, 1821.

Lamb, Daniel Smith, comp. *A Historical, Biographical, and Statistical Souvenir.* Washington, DC: R. Beresford, 1900.

Langston, John Mercer. *From the Virginia Plantation to the National Capitol; or, The First and Only Negro Representative in Congress from the Old Dominion.* Hartford, CT: American Publishing, 1894.

Lefanu, Alicia. *Henry the Fourth of France.* 4 vols. London: A. K. Newman, 1826.

Lester, George N., Christopher Rowell, and Walter B. Hill, eds. *The Code of the State of Georgia.* 4th ed. Atlanta: J. P. Harrison, 1882.

Lester, Paul. *The Great Galveston Disaster.* Philadelphia: H. W. Kelley, 1900.

Loyless, Thomas W., comp. *Georgia's Public Men, 1902–1904.* Atlanta: Byrd Printing, n.d.

Martin, Thomas H. *Atlanta and Its Builders: A Comprehensive History of the Gate City of the South.* 2 vols. Atlanta: Century, 1902.

Mather, Frank Lincoln. *Who's Who of the Colored Race.* Vol. 1. Chicago, 1915.

McDonough, Walter R., comp. *1905 Chicago Medical Directory.* Chicago: Chicago Medical Society, 1905.

Memoirs of Georgia: Containing Historical Accounts of the State's Civil, Military, Industrial, and Professional Interests, and Personal Sketches of Many of Its People. 2 vols. Atlanta: Southern Historical Association, 1895.

Morrison, Leonard Allison Morrison. *A History of the Kimball Family in America from 1634 to 1897.* Boston: Damrell & Upham, 1897.

Morton, Richard Lee. *The Negro in Virginia Politics, 1865–1902.* Charlottesville: University Press of Virginia, 1919.

The National Cyclopaedia of American Biography. 13 vols. New York: James T. White, 1892.

Northrop, Henry Davenport, Joseph R. Penn, and Irvine Garland. *The College of Life or Practical Self-Educator: A Manual of Self-Improvement for the Colored Race.* N.p., 1896.

Pollock, Edward. *Historical & Industrial Guide to Petersburg, Virginia.* Petersburg: T. S. Beckwith, 1884.

Proceedings of the Equal Rights and Educational Association of Georgia. Augusta: Loyal Georgian, 1866.

Quinn, Silvanus Jackson. *The History of the City of Fredericksburg, Virginia.* Richmond: Hermitage, 1908.

Ramsdell, Charles William. *Reconstruction in Texas.* New York: Columbia University Press, 1910.

Reed, Hugh T. *Upton's Infantry Tactics, Abridged and Revised, embracing the Schools of the Squad and Company, Skirmishers, Inspection, Etc.* Baltimore: A. W. Reed, 1882.

Reed, Wallace Putnam. *History of Atlanta Georgia, with Illustrations and Biographical Sketches of Some of Its Prominent Men and Pioneers.* Syracuse, NY: D. Mason, 1889.

Reuter, Edward Byron. *The Mulatto in the United States, including a Study of the Role of Mixed-Blood Races throughout the World.* Boston: Gorham, 1918.

Richings, G. F. *Evidences of Progress among Colored People.* Philadelphia: George S. Ferguson, 1904.

Stern, Joseph Lane. *Roster Commissioned Officers Virginia Volunteers, 1871–1920.* Richmond: Davis Bottom, Superintendent of Public Printing, 1921.

Still, William. *The Underground Railroad.* Philadelphia: Porter & Coates, 1872.

"Thirtieth Annual Report of the Superintendent of the Public School of the City of Richmond, Va., for the Scholastic Year Ending July 31, 1899," in *School Reports, City of Richmond, 1899–1903* (Richmond: Ware & Duke, Printers, 1900).

Thomas, Dean S. *The Confederate Field Manual with Photographic Supplement.* Richmond: Ritchie & Dunnavant, 1862. Reprint, Arendtsville, PA, 1984.

Twenty-Two Years' Work of the Hampton Normal and Agricultural Institute. Hampton, VA: Normal School Press, 1891.

Tyler, Lyon G., ed. *Men of Mark in Virginia.* 5 vols. Washington, DC: Men of Mark, 1907.

Van Epps, Howard, ed. *Supplement to the Code of the State of Georgia.* Vol. 4. Nashville: Marshall & Bruce, 1901.

[Virginia Military Institute]. *Register of Former Cadets.* Centennial ed. Roanoke: Roanoke Printing, 1939.

Washington, Booker T., Fannie Barrier Williams, and Norman Barton Wood. *A New Negro for a New Century: An Accurate and Up-to-Date Record of the upward Struggles of the Negro Race.* Chicago: American Publishing House, 1900.

Walker, Richard R. *A Brief Historical Sketch of Negro Education in Georgia.* Savannah: Robinson Printing House, 1894.

Whitted, Rev. J. A. *A History of the Negro Baptists of North Carolina.* Raleigh: Edwards & Broughton Printing, 1908.

Williams, Henry Smith, ed. *The Historians' History of the World.* 25 vols. London: Hooper & Jackson, 1908.

Year Book of the Augusta Georgia Chamber of Commerce. Augusta: Augusta Chronicle Job Printing, 1908.

ARTICLES

"Alumni of Crozer Theological Seminary." *Bulletin of the Crozer Theological Seminary* 1, no. 1 (October 1908): 70–90.

"Autrey." *Confederate Veteran* 16, no. 3 (March 1908): 239.

Browning, James B. "The Beginnings of Insurance Enterprises among Negroes." *Journal of Negro History* 22, no. 4 (October 1937): 422–24.

"Capt. George Monroe Autrey." *Confederate Veteran* 16, no. 3 (March 1908): 357.

"The Capture of the US Steamer 'Water Witch' in Ossabaw Sound, Ga., June 2–3, 1864." *Georgia Historical Quarterly* 3, no. 1 (March 1919): 11–27.

Corey, C. H. "Samuel H. Dismond, M.D." *Baptist Home Mission Monthly* 20, no. 6 (June 1898): 202–3.

"Deaths." *Journal of the American Medical Association* 75, no. 24 (December 11, 1920): 1661–62.

"Georgia's Patriotism and Gratitude." *Confederate Veteran* 14, no. 10 (October 1906): 442–43.

"John Holbrook Estill." *Confederate Veteran* 16, no. 5 (May 1908): xxxv.

"Lincoln Graduates in the Medical Profession." *Lincoln (PA) University Herald* 21, no. 2 (February 1917): 1–2.

"The Manhood of the Negro." *Baptist Home Mission Monthly* 20, no. 9 (September 1898): 336.

"Mayor J. Thompson Baird." *Confederate Veteran* 13, no. 7 (July 1905): 373.

"The New York Life in Georgia." *Insurance Times* 37 (November 1904): 463.

"Representatives Elect." *Journal of United Labor* 6, no. 9 (September 10, 1885): 1075–76.

Tyler, Lyon G., ed. "The Lee Family of York, Virginia." *William and Mary Quarterly* 24, no. 1 (July 1915): 46–54.

CITY DIRECTORIES

Abrams, Alexander, comp. *Directory of the City of Savannah for 1870.* Savannah: J. H. Estill, Publisher and Printer, 1870.

Chataigne, John Henry, comp. *Chataigne's Directory of Richmond, Va.* Richmond: J. H. Chataigne, 1882.

———, comp. *Chataigne's Directory of Richmond, Va., 1884–85.* Richmond: J. H. Chataigne, 1884.

———, comp. *Chataigne's Directory, 1895–96.* Richmond: J. H. Chataigne, 1896.

Goette, Henry Alphonsus, comp. *Goette's Savannah City Directory for 1904.* Savannah: H. A. Goette, 1903.

Haddock, Thomas M., comp. *Haddock's Savannah, Ga., Directory and General Advertiser.* Savannah: J. H. Estill, 1871.

Howard, Walter, comp. *Howard's Directory of Augusta, Summerville, and Turpin Hill, Georgia, and Hamburg, S.C., 1892–93.* Augusta: Chronicle Job Printing, 1892.

Maloney, T. J., comp. *Maloney's 1899 Augusta City Directory*. Augusta: Maloney Directory, 1899.

Morrison, Charles D., and Joseph V. Fourmy, comps. *Morrison and Fourmy's General Directory of the City of Austin for 1881–82*. Austin, TX: E. W. Swindells, 1881.

Polk, Ralph Lane, comp. *Atlanta City Directory for 1889*. Atlanta: R. L. Polk, 1889.

———, comp. *R. L. Polk's Augusta City Directory 1888*. Atlanta: R. L. Polk, 1888.

———, comp. *Augusta City Directory, 1889*. Augusta: R. L. Polk, 1889.

———, comp. *Augusta City Directory, 1891*. Augusta: R. L. Polk, 1891.

Rogers, George H., comp. *Rogers' City Directory of Savannah*. Savannah: George H. Rogers, 1877.

Sholes, Arthur Eugene, comp. *Sholes' Directory of the City of Atlanta for 1877*. Atlanta: A. E. Sholes, 1877.

———, comp. *Scholes' Directory of the City of Augusta, 1877*. Augusta: A. E. Scholes, 1877.

———, comp. *Scholes' Directory of the City of Augusta, 1883*. Augusta: A. E. Scholes, 1883.

———, comp. *Scholes' Directory of the City of Augusta, 1886*. Augusta: A. E. Scholes, 1886.

———, comp. *Sholes' Directory of the City of Savannah, 1886*. Savannah: A. E. Sholes, 1886.

———, comp. *Sholes' Georgia State Gazetteer and Business Directory for 1879 and 1880*. Atlanta: A. E. Sholes, 1879.

NEWSPAPERS

Alexandria (VA) Gazette
Atlanta Constitution
Augusta (GA) Chronicle
Austin (TX) Daily Statesman
Baltimore Sun
Bradstreet's (New York City)
Brenham (TX) Weekly Banner
Colored American (Washington, DC)
Colored Tribune (Savannah)
Daily State Journal (Richmond)
Dallas Daily Herald
Dallas Morning News
Der Deutsche Correspondent (Baltimore)
Fort Worth Gazette
Frank Leslie's Illustrated Newspaper (New York)
Galveston Daily News
Houston Post
Iola (KS) Register
Jeffersonian Republic (Stroudsburg, PA)
Macon (GA) Gazette
Macon (GA) Telegraph

Milan (TN) Exchange
National Tribune (Washington, DC)
Neu Braunfelser Zeitung (New Braunfels, TX)
New Journal and Guide (Norfolk, VA)
New Orleans Commercial Bulletin
New York Age
New York Standard
New York Times
Norfolk Virginian
Ohio State Journal (Columbus)
Panola Weekly Star (Sardis, MS)
Petersburg (VA) Daily Progress
Petersburg (VA) Progress-Index Appeal
Petersburg (VA) Lancet
Richmond Daily Dispatch
Richmond Daily Times
Richmond Dispatch
Richmond Planet
Richmond Times
St. Landry Democrat (Opelousas, LA)
St. Paul (MN) Daily Globe
Salt Lake Herald
San Antonio Daily Express
San Antonio Daily Light
Savannah Daily News Herald
Savannah Daily Morning News
Savannah Morning News
Savannah Morning Telegraph
Savannah Tribune
Savannah Weekly Echo
Seguin (TX) Record
Shenandoah Herald (Woodstock, VA)
Thomasville (GA) Times-Enterprise
United States Army and Navy Journal and Gazette of the Regular and Volunteer Forces
Washington (DC) Evening Critic
Washington (DC) Evening Star
Washington (DC) Evening Times

Secondary Sources

BOOKS

Alexander, Ann Field. *Race Man: The Rise and Fall of the "Fighting Editor" John Mitchell Jr.* Charlottesville: University of Virginia Press, 2002.
Anthony, E. Rotundo. *American Manhood: Transformations in Masculinity from the Revolution to the Modern Era.* New York: HarperCollins, 1993.

Ayers, Edward L. *Vengeance and Justice: Crime and Punishment in the 19th Century American South*. New York: Oxford University Press, 1984.

Barr, Alwyn. *A History of Negroes in Texas, 1528–1995*. 2nd ed. Norman: University of Oklahoma Press, 1996.

Barr, Alwyn, and Robert A. Calvert, eds. *Black Leaders: Texans for their Times*. Austin: Texas State Historical Association, 1981.

Bayor, Ronald H. *Race and the Shaping of Twentieth-Century Atlanta*. Chapel Hill: University of North Carolina Press, 1996.

Bederman, Gail. *Manliness and Civilization: A Cultural History of Gender and Race in the United States, 1880–1917*. Chicago: University of Chicago Press, 1995.

Berg-Sobré, Judith. *San Antonio on Parade: Six Historic Festivals*. College Station: Texas A&M University Press, 2003.

Bixel, Patricia Bellis, and Elizabeth Hayes Turner. *Galveston and the 1900 Storm*. Austin: University of Texas Press, 2000.

Blackett, R. J. M. *Beating against the Barriers: Biographical Essays in Nineteenth-Century Afro-American History*. Baton Rouge: Louisiana State University Press, 1986.

Blair, William Alan. *Cities of the Dead: Contesting the Memory of the Civil War in the South, 1865 –1914*. Chapel Hill: University of North Carolina Press, 2004.

Blassingame, John W., ed. *The Frederick Douglass Papers, Series One: Speeches, Debates, and Interviews, 1855–1863*. Vol. 3. New Haven, CT: Yale University Press, 1985.

Blum, Edward J. *Reforging the White Republic: Race, Religion, and American Nationalism, 1865–1898*. Baton Rouge: Louisiana State University Press, 2005.

Bruce, Robert V. *1877: Year of Violence*. Indianapolis: Bobbs Merrill, 1959.

Brundage, William Fitzhugh. *Lynching in the New South: Georgia and Virginia, 1880–1930*. Urbana: University of Illinois Press, 1993.

———. *The Southern Past: A Clash of Race and Memory*. Cambridge, MA: Harvard University Press, 2008.

Buckner, Timothy R., and Peter Caster. *Fathers, Preachers, Rebels, Men: Black Masculinity in US History and Literature, 1820–1945*. Columbus: Ohio State University Press, 2011.

Burkett, Randall K., Nancy Hall Burkett, and Henry Louis Gates Jr., eds. *Black Biography, 1790–1950: A Cumulative Index*. 3 vols. Alexandria, VA: Chadwyck-Healey, 1991.

Campbell, Randolph B. *Grass-Roots Reconstruction in Texas, 1865–1880*. Baton Rouge: Louisiana State University Press, 1998.

Carnes, Mark C. *Secret Ritual and Manhood in Victorian America*. New Haven, CT: Yale University Press, 1989.

Carrigan, William D. *The Making of a Lynching Culture: Violence and Vigilantism in Central Texas, 1836 –1916*. Urbana: University of Illinois Press, 2006.

Cashin, Edward J., and Glenn Eskew. *Paternalism in a Southern City: Race, Religion, and Gender in Augusta, Georgia*. Athens: University of Georgia Press, 2001.

Coleman, Kenneth, ed. *History of Georgia*. 2nd ed. Athens: University of Georgia Press, 1991.

Connor, Marline Kim. *What Is Cool?: Understanding Black Manhood in America*. New York: Crown, 1995.

Conway, Alan. *Reconstruction of Georgia*. Minneapolis: University of Minnesota Press, 1966.

Cooper, Jerry. *The Rise of the National Guard: The Evolution of the American Militia, 1865–1920*. Lincoln: University of Nebraska Press, 1997.

Corley, Florence Fleming. *Confederate City: Augusta, Georgia, 1860–1865*. Columbia: University of South Carolina Press, 1960.

Crow, Jeffrey J., Paul D. Escott, and Charles L. Flynn Jr., eds. *Race, Class, and Politics in Southern History: Essays in Honor of Robert F. Durden*. Baton Rouge: Louisiana State University Press, 1989.

Cunningham, Roger D. *The Black Citizen-Soldiers of Kansas, 1864–1901*. Columbia: University of Missouri Press, 2008.

Dabney, Virginius. *Richmond, Virginia: The Story of a City*. Rev. ed. Charlottesville: University Press of Virginia, 1990.

Delaney, Norman C. *John McIntosh Kell of the Raider Alabama*. Tuscaloosa: University of Alabama Press, 2003.

Directory of Deceased American Physicians, 1804–1929. 2 vols. Chicago: American Medical Association, 1993.

Dittmer, John. *Black Georgia in the Progressive Era, 1900–1920*. Urbana: University of Illinois Press, 1977.

Dobak, William A., and Thomas D. Phillips. *The Black Regulars, 1866–1898*. Norman: University of Oklahoma Press, 2001.

Dorsey, Allison. *To Build Our Lives Together: Community Formation in Black Atlanta, 1875–1906*. Athens: University of Georgia Press, 2004.

Doyle, Don H. *New Men, New Cities, New South: Atlanta, Nashville, Charleston, Mobile, 1860–1910*. Chapel Hill: University of North Carolina Press, 1990.

Drago, Edmund L. *Black Politicians and Reconstruction in Georgia: A Splendid Failure*. Baton Rouge: Louisiana State University Press, 1982.

Dyer, Thomas G. *Secret Yankees: The Union Circle in Confederate Atlanta*. Baltimore: Johns Hopkins University Press, 2001.

Fitchett, Elijah Horace. *The Free Negro in Charleston, South Carolina*. Chicago: University of Chicago, 1950.

Fitzgerald, Ruth Coder. *A Different Story: A Black History of Fredericksburg, Stafford, and Spotsylvania, Virginia*. N.p.: Unicorn, 1979.

Foner, Eric. *Freedom's Lawmakers: A Directory of Black Officeholders during Reconstruction*. New York: Oxford University Press, 1993.

———. *Reconstruction: America's Unfinished Revolution, 1863–1877*. New York: Harper & Row, 1988.

Foner, Jack D. *Blacks and the Military in American History*. New York: Praeger, 1974.

Fowler, Arlen L. *The Black Infantry in the West, 1869–1891*. Westport, CT: Greenwood, 1971.

Franklin, John Hope, and Alfred A. Moss Jr. *From Slavery to Freedom: A History of African Americans*. 8th ed. New York: Alfred A. Knopf, 2000.

Friend, Craig Thompson, ed. *Southern Masculinity: Perspectives on Manhood in the South since Reconstruction*. Athens: University of Georgia Press, 2009.

Friend, Craig Thompson, and Lorri Glover, eds. *Southern Manhood: Perspectives on Masculinity in the Old South.* Athens: University of Georgia Press, 2004.

Gaines, Kevin Kelly. *Uplifting the Race: Black Middle-Class Ideology and Leadership in the United States since 1890.* Chapel Hill: University of North Carolina Press, 1996.

Gatewood, Willard B., Jr. *Aristocrats of Color: The Black Elite, 1880–1920.* Bloomington: Indiana University Press, 1990.

———. *Black Americans and the White Man's Burden, 1898–1903.* Urbana: University of Illinois Press, 1975.

———. *"Smoked Yankees" and the Struggle for Empire: Letters from Negro Soldiers.* Fayetteville: University of Arkansas Press, 1987.

Glasrud, Bruce, ed. *Brothers to the Buffalo Soldiers: Perspectives on the African American Militia and Volunteers, 1865–1917.* Columbia: University of Missouri Press, 2011.

Goings, Kenneth W., and Raymond A. Mohl, eds. *The New African American Urban History.* Thousand Oaks, CA: Sage, 1996.

Goldstone, Lawrence. *Inherently Unequal: The Betrayal of Equal Rights by the Supreme Court, 1865–1903.* New York: Walker, 2011.

Gordon, Martin K. *The Black Militia in the District of Columbia, 1867–1898.* Washington DC: Columbia Historical Society, 1972.

Grant, Donald Lee. *The Way It Was in the South: The Black Experience in Georgia.* Secaucus, NJ: Carol, 1993.

Harlan, Louis R., and Raymond W. Smock, eds. *The Booker T. Washington Papers, 1911–1912.* Urbana: University of Illinois Press, 1972.

Hewett, Janet B., ed. *Texas Confederate Soldiers, 1861–1865.* 2 vols. Wilmington, NC: Broadfoot, 1997.

Hoffman, Steven J. *Race, Class, and Power in the Building of Richmond, 1870–1920.* Jefferson, NC: McFarland, 2004.

Hofstadter, Richard, and Michael Wallace, eds. *American Violence: A Documentary History.* New York: Knopf, 1970.

Hoganson, Kristin L. *Fighting for American Manhood: How Gender Politics Provoked the Spanish-American and Philippine-American Wars.* New Haven, CT: Yale University Press, 1998.

Hoskins, Charles Lwanga. *The Trouble They Seen: Profiles in the Life of Col. John H. Deveaux, 1848–1900.* Savannah: C. L. Hoskins, 1989.

———. *W. W. Law and His People: A Timeline and Biographies.* Savannah: Gullah, 2013.

———. *Yet with a Steady Beat: Biographies of Early Black Savannah.* Savannah: C. L. Hoskins, 2001.

Jackson, Luther Porter Jackson. *Negro Office-holders in Virginia, 1865–1895.* Norfolk, VA: Guide Quality, 1945.

Jacobson, Matthew Frye. *Whiteness of a Different Color: European Immigrants and the Alchemy of Race.* Cambridge, MA: Harvard University Press, 1998.

Jenkins, Earnestine, and Darlene Clark Hine, eds. *A Question of Manhood: A Reader in U.S. Black Men's History and Masculinity.* 2 vols. Bloomington: Indiana University Press, 2001.

Johnson, Charles. *African American Soldiers in the National Guard.* Westport, CT: Greenwood, 1992.

Johnson, Curt, and Richard C. Anderson Jr. *Artillery Hell: The Employment of Artillery at Antietam.* College Station: Texas A&M University Press, 1995.

Johnson, Kevin R., ed. *Mixed Race in America and the Law: A Reader.* New York: New York University Press, 2013.

Johnson, Michael K. *Black Masculinity and the Frontier Myth in American Literature.* Norman: University of Oklahoma Press, 2002.

Kantrowitz, Stephen. *More Than Freedom: Fighting for Black Citizenship in a White Republic, 1829–1899.* New York: Penguin, 2012.

Kennedy, Henry J., ed. *History of the Savannah Volunteer Guards, 1802–1992.* Greenville, SC: Southern Historical, 1998.

Kenner, Charles L. *Buffalo Soldiers and Officers of the Ninth Cavalry, 1867–1898: Black & White Together.* Norman: University of Oklahoma Press, 1999.

Kimmel, Michael S. *The History of Men: Essays in the History of American and British Masculinities.* Albany: State University of New York Press, 2005.

———. *Manhood in America: A Cultural History.* 3rd ed. Oxford: Oxford University Press, 2012.

Kinevan, Marcos E. *Frontier Cavalryman: Lieutenant John Bigelow with the Buffalo Soldiers in Texas.* El Paso: Texas Western, 1998.

Kousser, J. Morgan. *The Shaping of Southern Politics, Suffrage Restriction, and the Establishment of the One-Party South, 1880–1910.* New Haven, CT: Yale University Press, 1974.

Lewis, David L. *W. E. B. Du Bois: Biography of a Race, 1868–1919.* New York: H. Holt, 1993.

Link, William A. *Atlanta, Cradle of the New South: Race and Remembering in the Civil War's Aftermath.* Chapel Hill: University of North Carolina Press, 2013.

Linn, Brian McAlister. *The Philippine War, 1899–1902.* Lawrence: University Press of Kansas, 2000.

Listman, John W., Jr., Robert K. Wright Jr., and Bruce D. Hardcastle, eds. *The Tradition Continues: A History of the Virginia National Guard, 1607–1985.* Richmond: Taylor, 1987.

Litwack, Leon F. *Been in the Storm So Long: The Aftermath of Slavery.* New York: Alfred A. Knopf, 1979.

———. *Trouble in Mind: Black Southerners in the Age of Jim Crow.* New York: Alfred A. Knopf, 1998.

Lowe, Richard. *Republicans and Reconstruction in Virginia, 1856–70.* Charlottesville: University Press of Virginia, 1991.

Mahon, John K. *History of the Militia and the National Guard.* New York: Macmillan, 1983.

Mangan, J. A., and James Walvin, eds. *Manliness and Morality: Middle-Class Masculinity in Britain and America, 1800–1940.* Manchester, UK: Manchester University Press, 1987.

Markovitz, Jonathon. *Legacies of Lynching: Racial Violence and Memory.* Minneapolis: University of Minnesota Press, 2004.

Mason, Kenneth. *African Americans and Race Relations in San Antonio, Texas, 1867–1937*. New York: Garland, 1998.

McChristian, Douglas C. *Uniforms, Arms, and Equipment: The US Army on the Western Frontier, 1880–1892*. 2 vols. Norman: University of Oklahoma Press, 2007.

McComb, David G. *Galveston: A History*. Austin: University of Texas Press, 1986.

McConnell, Stuart. *Glorious Contentment: The Grand Army of the Republic, 1865–1900*. Chapel Hill: University of North Carolina Press, 1992.

Meier, August. *Negro Thought in America, 1880–1915*. Ann Arbor: University of Michigan Press, 1964.

Miller, Char, and Heywood T. Sanders, eds. *Urban Texas: Politics and Development*. College Station: Texas A&M University Press, 2000.

Mixon, Gregory. *The Atlanta Riot: Race, Class, and Violence in a New South City*. Gainesville: University Press of Florida, 2005.

———. *Show Thyself a Man: Georgia State Troops, Colored, 1865–1900*. Gainesville: University Press of Florida, 2016.

Moneyhon, Carl. *Edmund J. Davis: Civil War General, Republican Leader, Reconstruction Governor*. Fort Worth: Texas Christian University Press, 2010.

Montgomery, William E. *Under Their Own Vine and Fig Tree: The African-American Church in the South, 1865–1900*. Baton Rouge: Louisiana State University Press, 1995.

Muller, William G. *The Twenty-Fourth Infantry: Past and Present*. Fort Collins, CO: Old Army, 1972.

Muraskin, William A. *Middle-Class Blacks in a White Society: Prince Hall Freemasonry in America*. Berkeley: University of California Press, 1975.

Nankivell, John H. *The History of the Twenty-Fifth Regiment, United States Infantry, 1869–1926*. 1927. Reprint. Fort Collins, CO: Old Army, 1972.

Nevels, Cynthia Skove. *Lynching to Belong: Claiming Whiteness through Violence*. College Station: Texas A&M University Press, 2007.

Nieman, Donald G., ed. *African Americans and Southern Politics from Redemption to Disfranchisement*. 12 vols. New York: Garland, 1994.

Norrell, Robert J. *Up from History: The Life of Booker T. Washington*. Cambridge, MA: Belknap Press of Harvard University Press, 2009.

Nystrom, Justin A. *New Orleans after the Civil War: Race, Politics, and a New Birth of Freedom*. Baltimore: John Hopkins University Press, 2010.

Ochs, Stephen J. *A Black Patriot and a White Priest: André Cailloux and Claude Paschal Maistre in Civil War New Orleans*. Baton Rouge: Louisiana State University Press, 2000.

Ownby, Ted, and Nancy Bercaw, eds. *New Encyclopedia of Southern Culture*. 13 vols. Chapel Hill: University of North Carolina Press, 2005.

Perdue, Robert E. *The Negro in Savannah, 1865–1900*. New York: Exhibition, 1973.

Perdue, Theda. *Race and the Atlanta Cotton States Exposition of 1895*. Athens: University of Georgia Press, 2010.

Perman, Michael. *Emancipation and Reconstruction, 1862–1879*. Arlington Heights, IL: Harlan Davidson, 1987.

———. *The Road to Redemption: Southern Politics, 1869–1879*. Chapel Hill: University of North Carolina Press, 1984.

———. *Struggle for Mastery: Disfranchisement in the South, 1888–1908*. Chapel Hill: University of North Carolina Press, 2001.

Pinar, William. *The Gender of Racial Politics and Violence in America: Lynching, Prison Rape, and the Crisis of Masculinity*. New York: Peter Lang, 2001.

Pitre, Merline. *Through Many Dangers, Toils, and Snares: The Black Leadership in Texas, 1868–1900*. Austin: Eakin, 1985.

Provenzo, Eugene F., Jr. *W. E. B. Du Bois's Exhibit of American Negroes: "African Americans" at the Beginning of the Twentieth Century*. Lanham, MD: Rowman & Littlefield, 2013.

Rabinowitz, Howard N. *Race Relations in the Urban South, 1865–1890*. New York: Oxford University Press, 1978.

Rable, George C. *But There Was No Peace: The Role of Violence in the Politics of Reconstruction*. Athens: University of Georgia Press, 1984.

Rachleff, Peter J. *Black Labor in Richmond, 1865–1890*. Urbana: University of Illinois Press, 1989.

Rice, Lawrence D. *The Negro in Texas, 1874–1900*. Baton Rouge: Louisiana State University Press, 1971.

Richardson, Riché. *Black Masculinity and the US South: From Uncle Tom to Gangsta*. Athens: University of Georgia Press, 2007.

Robinson, Charles M., III. *The Fall of a Black Army Officer: Racism and the Myth of Henry O. Flipper*. Norman: University of Oklahoma Press, 2008.

Roediger, David R. *Working towards Whiteness: How America's Immigrants became White—The Strange Journey from Ellis Island to the Suburbs*. New York: Basic Books, 2005.

Rosen, Hannah. *Terror in the Heart of Freedom: Citizenship, Sexual Violence, and the Meaning of Race in the Post-Emancipation South*. Chapel Hill: University of North Carolina Press, 2009.

Russell, James M. *Atlanta, 1847–1890: City Building in the Old South and the New*. Baton Rouge: Louisiana State University Press, 1988.

Saxton, Alexander. *The Rise and Fall of the White Republic: Class Politics and Mass Culture in Nineteenth-Century America*. London: Verso, 1990.

Segal, Lynne. *Slow Motion: Changing Masculinities, Changing Men*. New Brunswick, NJ: Rutgers University Press, 1990.

Shadgett, Olive Hall. *The Republican Party in Georgia from Reconstruction through 1900*. Athens: University of Georgia Press, 1964.

Shaffer, Donald Robert. *After the Glory: The Struggles of Black Civil War Veterans*. Lawrence: University Press of Kansas, 2004.

Shaw, Barton C. *The Wool-Hat Boys: Georgia's Populist Party*. Baton Rouge: Louisiana State University Press, 1984.

Silber, Nina. *The Romance of Reunion: Northerners and the South, 1865–1900*. Chapel Hill: University of North Carolina Press, 1993.

Singletary, Otis A. *Negro Militia and Reconstruction*. Austin: University of Texas Press, 1957.

Staples, Robert. *Black Masculinity: The Black Male's Role in American Society*. San Francisco: Black Scholar, 1982.

Suggs, Henry Lewis, ed. *The Black Press in the South, 1865–1979*. Westport, CT: Greenwood, 1983.

Sumler-Edmond, Janice. L. *The Secret Trust of Aspasia Cruvellier Mirault: The Life and Trials of a Free Woman of Color in Antebellum Georgia*. Fayetteville: University of Arkansas Press, 2008.

Summers, Martin. *Manliness and Its Discontents: The Black Middle Class and the Transformation of Masculinity, 1900–1930*. Chapel Hill: University of North Carolina Press, 2004.

Terrell, Lloyd Preston, and Marguerite S. C. Terrell. *Blacks in Augusta: A Chronology, 1741–1977*. Augusta, GA: Terrell, 1977.

Thomas, James G., Jr., and Ann J. Abadie, eds. *New Encyclopedia of Southern Culture*. 24 vols. Chapel Hill: University of North Carolina Press, 2013.

Trapp, Dan L. *Victorio and the Mimbres Apaches*. Norman: University of Oklahoma Press, 1974.

Turner, Elizabeth Hayes. *Women, Culture, and Community: Religion and Reform in Galveston, 1880–1920*. New York: Oxford University Press, 1997.

Tyler, Ronnie C., ed. *The New Handbook of Texas*. 6 vols. Austin: Texas State Historical Association, 1996.

Varon, Elizabeth R. *Southern Lady, Yankee Spy: The True Story of Elizabeth Van Lew, a Union Agent in the Heart of the Confederacy*. New York: Oxford University Press, 2003.

Waldstreich, David. *In the Midst of Perpetual Fetes: The Making of American Nationalism, 1776–1820*. Chapel Hill: University of North Carolina Press, 1997.

Walker, Corey D. B. *A Noble Fight: African American Freemasonry and the Struggle for Democracy in America*. Urbana: University of Illinois Press, 2008.

Walter, John. *Rifles of the World*. 3rd ed. Iola, WI: Krause, 2006.

Weibe, Robert H. *The Search for Order, 1877–1920*. New York: Hill and Wang, 1967.

Weinert, Willie Mae. *An Authentic History of Guadalupe County*. Seguin, TX: Seguin Enterprise, 1951.

White, Virgil D., comp. *Index to Pension Applications for Indian Wars Service between 1817 and 1898*. Waynesboro, PA: National Historical Publishing, 1997.

Whites, LeeAnn. *The Civil War as a Crisis in Gender: Augusta, Georgia, 1860–1890*. Athens: University of Georgia Press, 1995.

———. *Gender Matters: Civil War, Reconstruction, and the Making of the New South*. New York: Palgrave Macmillan, 2005.

Williamson, Joel. *Rage for Order: Black/White Relations in the American South since Emancipation*. New York: Oxford University Press, 1986.

Wingfield, Marshall. *A History of Caroline County, Virginia*. Baltimore: Genealogical Publishing, 2009.

Wolters, Raymond. *Du Bois and His Rivals*. Columbia: University of Missouri Press, 2002.

Woodward, C. Vann. *The Strange Career of Jim Crow*. 3rd ed. New York: Oxford University Press, 1974.

Wright, Richard Robert, Jr., comp. *Encyclopaedia of the African Methodist Episcopal Church*. 2nd ed. Philadelphia: Book Concern of the A.M.E. Church, 1947.

Wyatt-Brown, Bertram. *The Shaping of Southern Culture: Honor, Grace, and War, 1760s–1880s.* Chapel Hill: University of North Carolina Press, 2001.

Wynes, Charles Eldridge. *Race Relations in Virginia, 1870–1902.* Charlottesville: University Press of Virginia, 1961.

Young, Earle B. *Galveston and the Great West.* College Station: Texas A&M University Press, 1997.

Zamir, Shamoon. *Dark Voices: W. E. B. Du Bois and American Thought, 1888–1903.* Chicago: University of Chicago Press, 1995.

ARTICLES

Alexander, Ann Field. "No Officers, No Fight!: The Sixth Virginia Volunteers in the Spanish–American War." *Virginia Cavalcade* 47, no. 4 (Autumn 1998): 178–91.

Amron, Andrew D. "Reinforcing Manliness: Black State Militias, the Spanish-American War, and the Image of the African American Soldier, 1891–1900." *Journal of African American History* 97, no. 4 (Fall 2012): 401–26.

Bacote, Clarence A. "Negro Officeholders in Georgia under President McKinley." *Journal of Negro History* 44, no. 3 (July 1959): 217–39.

Barr, Alwyn. "The Black Militia of the New South: Texas as a Case Study." *Journal of Negro History* 63, no. 3 (December 1978): 153–60.

———. "The Texas 'Black Uprising' Scare of 1883." *Phylon* 41, no. 2 (2nd Qtr. 1980): 179–86.

Cheek, William Cheek, "A Negro Runs for Congress: John Mercer Langston and the Virginia Campaign of 1888." *Journal of Negro History* 52, no. 1 (January 1967): 14–34.

Cunningham, Roger Dryden. "Breaking the Color Line: The Virginia Militia at the National Drill, 1887." *Virginia Cavalcade* 49, no. 4 (2000): 178–87.

———. "'A Lot of Fine, Sturdy Black Warriors': Texas's African-American 'Immunes' in the Spanish-American War." *Southwestern Historical Quarterly* 108, no. 3 (January 2005): 345–67.

———. "They Are as Proud of Their Uniforms as Any Who Serve Virginia: African American Participation in the Virginia Volunteers, 1872–99." *Virginia Magazine of History and Biography* 110, no. 3 (2002): 293–338.

Denman, Clarence P. "The Office of the Adjutant General in Texas, 1835–1888." *Southwestern Historical Quarterly* 28, no. 3 (January 1925): 302–22.

Diamond, B. I., and J. O. Baylen. "The Demise of the Georgia Guard Colored, 1868–1914." *Phylon* 45, no. 4 (4th Qtr. 1984): 311–13.

Dinnella-Borrego, Luis-Alejandro. "From the Ashes of the Old Dominion: Accommodation, Immediacy, and Progressive Pragmatism in John Mercer Langston's Virginia." *Virginia Magazine of History and Biography* 117, no. 3 (2009): 215–49.

Farley, M. Foster. "John Elliott Ward, Mayor of Savannah 1853–1854." *Georgia Historical Quarterly* 53, no. 1 (March 1969): 69–77.

Fletcher, Marvin. "The Black Volunteers in the Spanish-American War." *Military Affairs* 38, no. 2 (April 1974): 48–53.

———. "The Negro Volunteer in Reconstruction, 1865–66." *Military Affairs* 32, no. 3 (December 1968): 124–31.

Gatewood, Willard B., Jr. "Alabama's 'Negro Soldier Experiment,' 1898–1899." *Journal of Negro History* 57, no. 4 (October 1972): 333–51.

———. "North Carolina's Negro Regiment in the Spanish-American War." *North Carolina Historical Review* 48, no.4 (October 1971): 370–87.

———. "Virginia's Negro Regiment in the Spanish-American War: The Sixth Virginia Volunteers." *Virginia Magazine of History and Biography* 80, no. 2 (April 1972): 193–209.

Gordon, Martin K. "The Black Militia in the District of Columbia, 1867–1898." *Records of the Columbia Historical Society* 71–72 (1971): 411–20.

Harris, Robert L., Jr. "Charleston's Free Afro-American Elite: The Brown Fellowship Society and the Humane Brotherhood." *South Carolina Historical Magazine* 82, no. 4 (October 1981): 289–310.

"Henry Rutherford Butler, M.D., 1862–1931." *Journal of the National Medical Association* 51, no. 2 (September 1959): 406–8.

Jones, Trina. "Shades of Brown: The Law of Skin Color." *Duke Law School Public Law and Legal Theory Working Paper Series* no. 7 (October 2000): 1487–1557.

"Joseph Simeon Flipper." *Journal of Negro History* 30, no. 1 (January 1945): 109–11.

Lawrence, Alexander A. "The Night Lieutenant Pelot Was Killed aboard the 'Water Witch.'" *Georgia Review* 4, no. 3 (Fall 1950): 174–76.

Mahon, John K. "Bibliographic Essay on Research into the History of the Militia and National Guard." *Military Affairs* 48, no. 2 (April 1984): 74–77.

Matthews, John M. "Black Newspapermen and the Black Community in Georgia, 1890–1930." *Georgia Historical Quarterly* 68, no. 3 (Fall 1984): 356–81.

McDaniel, Ruth Currie. "Black Power in Georgia: William A. Pledger and the Take-over of the Republican Party." *Georgia Historical Quarterly* 62, no. 3 (Fall 1978): 225–39.

Mixon, Gregory. "The Making of a Black Political Boss: Henry A. Rucker, 1897–1904." *Georgia Historical Quarterly* 89, no. 4 (Winter 2005): 485–504.

Muskat, Beth Taylor. "The Last March: The Demise of the Black Militia in Alabama." *Alabama Review* 63, no. 1 (January 1990): 18–34.

Nackman, Mark E. "The Making of the Texas Citizen Soldier, 1835–1860." *Southwestern Historical Quarterly* 78, no. 3 (January 1975): 231–53.

Nelson, Christian G. "Rebirth, Growth, and Expansion of the Texas Militia, 1868–1898." *Texas Military History* 2, no. 1 (February 1962): 1–16.

———. "Organization and Training of the Texas Militia, 1870–1897." *Texas Military History* 2, no. 2 (May 1962): 81–149.

———. "Texas Militia in the Spanish-American War." *Texas Military History* 2, no. 3 (August 1962): 193–234.

Newton, Isham G. "The Negro and the National Guard." *Phylon* 23, no. 1 (1st Qtr. 1962): 18–28.

O'Brien, Mike. "Manhood and the Militia Myth: Masculinity, Class, and Militarism in Ontario, 1902–1914" *Labor / Le Travail* 42 (Fall 1998): 115–41.

Pitre, Merline. "A Note on the Historiography of Blacks in the Reconstruction of Texas." *Journal of Negro History* 66, no. 4 (Winter 1981–82): 340–48.

Reese, James. "The Evolution of an Early Texas Union: The Screwman's Benevolent Association of Galveston, 1866–1891." *Southwestern Historical Quarterly* 75, no. 2 (October 1971): 158–85.

Salvatore, Nick. "Railroad Workers and the Great Strike of 1877: The View from a Small Midwest City." *Labor History* 21, no. 4 (1980): 522–45.

Saunders, Robert. "Southern Populists and the Negro, 1893–1895." *Journal of Negro History* 54, no. 3 (July 1969): 240–61.

Singletary, Otis A. "The Negro Militia during Radical Reconstruction." *Military Affairs* 19, no. 4 (Winter 1955): 177–86.

———. "The Texas Militia during Reconstruction." *Southwestern Historical Quarterly* 60, no. 1 (July 1956): 23–35.

Stillman, Richard, II. "Negroes in the Armed Forces." *Phylon* 30, no. 2 (2nd Qtr. 1969): 139–59.

Trotter, Joe W. "African American Fraternal Associations in American History: An Introduction." *Social Science History* 28, no. 3 (Fall 2004): 355–66.

White, Shane. "'It Was a Proud Day': African Americans, Festivals, and Parades in the North, 1741–1834." *Journal of American History* 81, no. 1 (June 1994): 13–50.

THESES AND DISSERTATIONS

Adams, Olin Burton. "The Negro and the Agrarian Movement in Georgia, 1874–1908." Master's thesis, Florida State University, 1973.

Bacote, Clarence Albert. "The Negro in Georgia Politics, 1880–1908." Master's thesis, University of Chicago, 1955.

Black, Lowell Dwight. "The Negro Volunteer Militia Units of the Ohio National Guard, 1870–1954: The Struggle for Military Recognition and Equality in the State of Ohio." PhD diss., Ohio State University, 1976.

Blair, John Patrick. "African American Citizen Soldiers in Galveston and San Antonio, Texas, 1880–1906." Master's thesis, Texas A&M University, 2007.

Colby, Ira Christopher. "The Freedman's Bureau in Texas and Its Impact on the Emerging Social Welfare System and Black-White Social Relations, 1865–1885." PhD diss., University of Pennsylvania, 1984.

Davis, John Charles. "US Army Rifle and Carbine Adoption between 1865–1900." Master's thesis, US Army Command and General Staff College, 2007.

Findley, James Lee, Jr. "Lynching and the Texas Anti-Lynch Law of 1897." Master's thesis, Baylor University, 1974.

Foley, Ehren K. "'To Make Him Feel His Manhood': Black Male Identity and the Politics of Gender in the Post-Emancipation South." PhD diss., University of South Carolina, 2012.

Hinze, Virginia Neal. "Norris Wright Cuney." Master's thesis, Rice University, 1965.

James, Jeremy Wayne. "Alone in the Profession of Arms: America's First Three African American West Point Graduates." Master's thesis, Texas A&M University, 2007.

Ketzmann, Stephen P. "A House Built upon the Sand: Race, Class, Gender, and the Galveston Hurricane of 1900." PhD diss., University of Wisconsin, 1995.

Marshall, Mary Magdelene. "'Tell Them, We're Rising!': Black Intellectuals and Lucy Craft Laney in Post–Civil War Augusta, Georgia." PhD diss., Drew University, 1998.

Milner, Elmer Ray. "An Agonizing Evolution: A History of the Texas National Guard, 1900–1945." PhD diss., North Texas State University, 1979.

Nelson, Christian Gotthard. "History of the Texas Militia from Reconstruction to the end of the Spanish-American War." Master's thesis, Trinity University, 1961.

Olson, Bruce A. "The Houston Light Guards: Elite Cohesion and Social Order in the New South." PhD diss., University of Houston, 1989.

Purcell, Allan R. "The History of the Texas Militia." PhD diss., University of Texas at Austin, 1981.

Smith, Frances. "Black Militia in Savannah, Georgia, 1872–1905." Master's thesis, Georgia Southern College, 1981.

Taylor, Allen Clayton. "A History of the Screwmen's Benevolent Association from 1866–1924." Master's thesis, University of Texas, 1968.

Ward, Judson C. "Georgia under the Bourbon Democrats." PhD diss., University of North Carolina at Chapel Hill, 1947.

Wingo, Horace Calvin. "Race Relations in Georgia, 1872–1908." PhD diss., University of Georgia, 1969.

Online Sources

Angell, Stephen Ward. "Henry McNeal Turner (1834–1915)." *New Georgia Encyclopedia,* September 3, 2002. http://www.georgiaencyclopedia.org/articles/history-archaeology/henry-mcneal-turner-1834-1915.

Bartlett, Sarah. "Brown Fellowship Society (1790–1945)." BlackPast, September 14, 2010. http://www.blackpast.org/aah/brown-fellowship-society-1790-1945.

Biographical Directory of the United States Congress, 1774–Present. https://bioguide.congress.gov.

"Candler, Allen Daniel (1834–1910)." *Biographical Directory of the United States Congress.* http://bio-guide.congress.gov/scripts/biodisplay.pl?index=c000109.

"Capt. Henry N. Walton." AncestryUSA, Public Family Trees. http://mv.ancestry institution.com/viewer/1414b6c6-0c2e-4559-aeb7-1989d2ebc 9e9/21235291/1072208705 (subscription site).

Cater, Casey P. "William J. Northen (1835–1913)." *New Georgia Encyclopedia,* March 12, 2005. http://www.georgiaencyclopedia.org/articles/ government-politics /william-j-northen-1835-1913.

"Gen. Phill Glenn Byrd." Find-a-Grave, January 4, 2011. http://www.findagrave.com /cgi-bin/fg.cgi?page=gr&GSln=byrd&GSfn=phill&GSmn=glenn&GSbyrel =all&GSdyrel=all&GSob=n&GRid=63731800&df=all.

Georgia County Outline Map. Carl Vinson Institute of Government, University of Georgia, April 5, 2008. https://en.wikipedia.org/wiki/File:Georgia-counties -map.gif.

Groce, W. Todd. "John B. Gordon (1832–1904)." *New Georgia Encyclopedia,* December 10, 2004. http://www.georgiaencyclopedia.org/articles/government-politics/john -b-gordon-1832-1904.

Hulett, Keith. "James M. Smith (1823–1890)." *New Georgia Encyclopedia*, August 4, 2006. http://www.georgiaencyclopedia.org/articles/government-politics /james-m-smith-1823-1890.

"John Rutter Brooke, Major General, United States Army." Arlington National Cemetery, United States Army Personnel, May 29, 2000. http://arlingtoncemetery.net /jrbrooke.htm.

Keene, Jennifer. "Uncovering the Unknown Soldier: Black Militias, 1865–1917." Review of *Brothers to the Buffalo Soldiers: Perspectives on the African American Militia and Volunteers, 1865–1917*, edited by Bruce Glasrud. H-Net, http://www.h-net.org /reviews.showrev.pp?id=33096.

Luckett, Robert E. "Allen D. Candler (1834–1910)." *New Georgia Encyclopedia*, May 4, 2006. http://www.georgiaencyclopedia.org/articles/government-politics /allen-d-candler-1834-1910.

———. "Henry McDaniel (1836–1926)." *New Georgia Encyclopedia*, September 30, 2006.http://www.georgiaencyclopedia.org/articles/government-politics/henry -mcdaniel-1836-1926.

Miller, Aragom Storm. "Salter, Charles P." *Handbook of Texas Online*, July 31, 2014. http://www.tshaonline. org./handbook/online/articles/fsa93.

Myers, Barton. "Alfred H. Colquitt (1824–1894)." *New Georgia Encyclopedia*, March 3, 2006. http://www.georgiaencyclopedia.org/articles/government-politics/alfred -h-colquitt-1824-1894.

"Our History." National Baptist Convention, USA. http://www.nationalbaptist.com/ about-nbc/our-history.

"Pleasant Alexander Stovall." Find-a-Grave, May 28, 2012http://www.findagrave.com/ cgi-bin/fg.cgi?page=gr&GRid=90895208.

"Rev. Henry Haywood Mitchell, Sr." AncestryUSA, Public Family Trees. http://trees. ancestryinstitution.com/tree/1851768/person/598116253 (subscription site).

Texas—County Outline Map. Perry-Castañeda Library Map Collection, University of Texas at Austin. https://maps.lib.utexas.edu/maps/texas/texas-county _outline-2010.pdf.

Virginia Counties and Independent Cities Map. Wikimedia Commons, May 15, 2010. https://commons.wikimedia.org/wiki/File:Virginia_counties_and_independent _cities_map.gif.

Virginia Deaths and Burials Index, 1853–1917. AncestryInstitution. http://search .ancestryinstitution.com/search/db.aspx?dbid=2558 (subscription site).

Virginia Military Institute. "Charles Jeffries Anderson." Historical Roster Database. http://archivesweb.vmi.edu/rosters/record.php?ID=3190.

———. "Clifford Wallace Anderson." Historical Roster Database. http://www9.vmi .edu/archivesroster/ArchiveRoster.asp?page=details&ID=3191&rform=search; internet.

———. "James McDonald." Historical Roster Database. http://archivesweb.vmi.edu /rosters/record.php?ID=12042.

———. "William Harvie Richardson." Historical Roster Database. http://archive sweb.vmi.edu/rosters/record.php?ID=116649.

————. "Woodford Haywood Mabry." Historical Roster Database. http://archive sweb.vmi.edu/rosters/record.php?ID=1965.

"Woodford H. Mabry." Texas Military Forces Museum. http://www.texasmilitary forcesmuseum.org/hallofhonor/mabry.htm.

Woods, Michael. "Harris, Alfred W. (1853–1920)." *Encyclopedia of Virginia*. http://www.encyclopediavirginia.org/Harris_Alfred_W_1853-1920#contrib.

INDEX

NOTE: Photos are indicated with *italic* type, *n* denotes note reference.

Newton, Wash, 188
Nicholas, Charles B., 112, 116
Norcross, Jonathan, 135

O'Connor, Daniel, 39
Obear, William, 197–98, 241n39
Olmstead, Charles Hart, 97–100, 247n23

Palmer, William H., 153–54, 168–69
Parades, 165–72
Parker, Julius A., 77
Paul, Robert Austin, 81, 113–16, *114*, 171, 178–79, 253n83
Peek, George Meredith, 113, 252n74
Pelot, Thomas, 113
Peninsula Guards (Hampton, VA), 114
Petersburg (VA) Blues, 155
Petersburg (VA) Grays, 116
Petersburg (VA) Guard, 115–16, 155, 157
Pleasant, Louis M., 134, 141, 173, 258n54
Pledger, William Anderson, 21–23, 135–37, *136*, 227n28, 271n16
Police: incidents with, 37, 89–90, 168–71
Pooler, Robert W., 131–32
Prince Hall Masons, 4, 135, 138, 141–42, 144, 152–53, 205
Prize drill competitions, 175–81
Pruden, William Brewster, 144, 213
Putnam Blues (Eatonton, GA), 46

Queen City Rifles (Fort Worth, TX), 58

R. E. Lee Battery (Petersburg, VA), 116
Racial flexibility: discussion of, 2–4, 10, 14, 32, 60, 73, 117
Ray, Jacob, 108, 122
Redfield, Nelson C., 146
Reid, Warwick, 50, 235n72
Richardson, William Harvie, 51, 81, 109, 236n73
Richmond (GA) Guards, 45
Richmond (TX) Regulars, 58–59
Richmond (VA) Howitzers, 116, 171
Richmond (VA) Penitentiary: escape, 111–12; fire, 116–117
Richmond (VA) Zouaves, 50, 148, 166, 173

Richmond Hussars (Augusta, GA), 92
Roberts Rifles (Corpus Christi, TX), 128, 177, 226n21
Rockwell, William S., 26
Rome (GA) Star Guards, 46, 69, 239n9, 266n54
Roosevelt, Theodore, 5, 16, 199
Royall, William H., 24, 141–42
Rucker, Henry Allen, 138, 258n45
Ruffin, Emmitt F., 194–95, 272n18

Salter Rifles (Calvert, TX), 107
Salter, Charles Partin, 107, 250n58
Sandersville (GA) trial, 44, 96
Savannah (GA) Chatham Light Infantry, 35–36
Savannah (GA) Colored Volunteers, 35–36
Savannah (GA) Hussars, 16, 36, 89, 93, 102, 142, 166, 176
Savannah (GA) Light Infantry, 24, 26, 36, 141–42, 194, 241n32
Savannah (GA) Volunteer Guards, 38, 72, 90, 162–63, 166
Savannah (GA) Zouaves, 41
Savannah (GA): city military alarm, 93–96;
Schwarz, John, 93–94, 246n14
Scott, A. J., 198
Scott, W. T., 156
Screven, John, 38–39, 88, 90, 231n14
Seaboard Elliott Grays (Portsmouth, VA), 52
Seguin (TX) Guards, 109
Sessums, John, 76, 125, 242n48,
Sheppard, F. Marion, 46
Sheridan Guards (Houston, TX), 58, 76, 124–26, 238n92, 242n48
Sieker, Lamartine P., 76, 78, 242n50
Simmons, John C., 26, 93, 101–102, 142, 193, 249n37
Simmons, Wesley, 44
Sixth Virginia Volunteers, Volunteer Regiment, 18, 152, 157, 195–96, 271n11
Smith, James Milton, 11, 31, 35, 37–38, 43–45, 62, 65, 224n2,
Smith, Tony A., 58–59, 76
Sneed, A. C., 22, 239n14, 239n18,
Sneed, Nat D., 43, 65
Spencer, M. B., 22